THE
CHINA LOBBY
IN AMERICAN
POLITICS

*the text of this book is printed
on 100% recycled paper*

THE
CHINA LOBBY
IN AMERICAN
POLITICS

ROSS Y. KOEN

*Edited
with an
Introduction by*
Richard C. Kagan

*A Publication
of the Committee
of Concerned Asian Scholars*

HARPER & ROW, PUBLISHERS
NEW YORK, EVANSTON, SAN FRANCISCO, LONDON

THE CHINA LOBBY IN AMERICAN POLITICS

LIBRARY OF CONGRESS CATALOG CARD NUMBER: 73–5472

STANDARD BOOK NUMBER: 06-138885-8

DESIGNED BY ANN SCRIMGEOUR

And now abideth faith, hope, charity, these three . . .
I CORINTHIANS 13:13

To Mary . . .
who taught me the greatest of these

CONTENTS

INTRODUCTION
Richard C. Kagan

Ross Y. Koen's book was first printed in 1960, but its distribution was enjoined owing to pressures from the China lobby: over 4000 copies were destroyed by the publisher; less than eight hundred circulated. Many of these were stolen from libraries by right wing groups which literally replaced them with *The Red China Lobby*.[1] Others were placed under lock and key in rare book rooms in university libraries throughout the country.

This Introduction will neither attempt to summarize the contents of the book nor to bring the history of the China lobby up to date.[2] The book speaks admirably for itself on the composition of the lobby, the issues it exploited and the pernicious consequences it had on scholars and scholarly organizations of the Far East, on State Department personnel, and on American foreign policy. Since 1960, when the book was finished, the China lobby has been represented by the Committee of One Million. Its strength institutionally has waned. Final proof of its decline in strength since the 1950s is its failure to marshall a significant protest campaign against the seating of the Peoples' Republic of China in the United Nations or against President Nixon's visit to China.

The purpose of this introduction is to indicate the ways in which the China lobby has been a catalyst for defining anticommunism, pushing American political thought to the right, and forcing the scholar of Asian affairs into apolitical-objective scholarship. It suggests a way to approach an analysis of the China lobby within the political context of the 1950s and 1960s.

The China lobby consisted of an inner core of well-financed Nationalist Chinese officials and an outer fringe of right-wing American political elites. Both groups worked toward common goals together in the forties and fifties to support Chiang Kai-shek and his *raison d'être* of mainland recovery, and to discredit the opposition to him. While many of the individuals and organizations were officially reg-

1. Forest Davis and Robert A. Hunter with a foreward by Admiral W. Radford (USN ret.). New York: Fleet Publishing Corporation, 1963.
2. For a more current study, see: Stanley David Bachrack, "The Committee of One Million and United States China Policy. 1953–1963: Access and Foreign Policy" (Ph.D. thesis, University of California, Los Angeles, 1973).

istered as foreign agents of the Republic of China, the lobby, as Koen defines it, was composed of a broader network of people both foreign and domestic whose interests coalesced in a common purpose—the overthrow of communism in Asia.

A warning to the reader: whereas the term "lobby" in America usually conveys an image of a private group which attempts to influence policy, in the Republic of China one cannot distinguish between private and government groups. After decades of internecine struggle, assassinations, and purges, the Chinese government on Taiwan is run by a small clique of the Kuomintang (KMT) Party under the Generalissimo-President Chiang Kai-shek and his son, Ching-kuo. Chapter two provides specific testimony on the direct participation of Chiang in the workings of the lobby. Consequently, one unresolved issue always remains in this study: where does the lobby leave off and the KMT and Chiang's government begin?

The clearest and most relevant example of the Nationalist Chinese government's ties with the lobby concerns the censorship of Koen's book. When an advance copy of the book reached officials in the Chinese Embassy, it was considered as detrimental to good relations between the United States and the Republic of China. Working through the State Department, the Central Intelligence Agency, and the Federal Bureau of Narcotics, the KMT prevented the book from being published. *The Red China Lobby* describes in detail the reason most often given for withdrawing Koen's book. Its authors claim that Koen's statement on page xxi referring to the links between the lobby, the KMT, and the opium trade are completely false. They cite a letter from the head of the Federal Bureau of Narcotics as evidence. This Bureau along with the FBI has always claimed that the drug traffic was controlled by Red China. A recent book, *The Politics of Heroin in Southeast Asia*[3] effectively dispells this myth by pointing to the involvement of former soldiers of the Nationalist Chinese army in the opium trade in Southeast Asia. Other recently published research links the KMT, Air America, and a host of official Chinese Nationalists, South Vietnamese, and Laotians who are inextricably involved in the opium trade.[4] It is axiomatic, however, that until we know much more about the operations of the KMT and its allies in

3. Alfred W. McCoy, with Cathleen B. Read and Leonard P. Adams II, *The Politics of Heroin in South East Asia.* New York: Harper and Row, Publishers, 1972.
4. Frank Browning and Banning Garrett, "The New Opium War," Ramparts IX, 10 (May 1971): 32–39.

continental Asia, we will never know the complete story of the finances, involvements, and politics of the China lobby.

The successes of the lobby in the 1950s derived in part from the receptivity of American politicians to its point of view and its activities. After World War II, when America emerged as the predominant economic power in the world, American leaders recognized the opportunity to extend their economic and political control, and they equated national security with a world order which would accommodate the interests of the United States. In Asia, the dollar drove the British pound and the Russian ruble out of our Pacific "lake." Dutch, British, French, Russian, and Japanese systems of colonialism were replaced by a United States neocolonialism. In some cases the new governments were self-supporting (Japan) while in less stable areas client regimes were set up with American military backing (South Korea, South Vietnam, Laos, Thailand, and of course the Republic of China). The concerns of American political elites in the 1950s were thus no longer with domestic economic politics, but with the creation of a Pax-Americana.

Both the China lobby and American political leaders were united in their fervent policies of anticommunism abroad, and their tactics of pursuing anti-Communist crusades in the United States. The deep contradictions between the two groups emerged in the late sixties: whereas the lobby was organized by the Republic of China to promote Nationalist China's hegemony on the mainland and over Asia, American government officials used the lobby to discredit its opposition at home and promote U.S. hegemony in Asia. The recent abandonment of the lobby's foreign policy by former lobby supporter President Richard M. Nixon highlights this contradiction.

The lobby aided and abetted the elevation of anticommunism to a national cause by associating support of Chiang Kai-shek's regime with loyalty to the United States. To be critical of the Nationalist government was tantamount to giving "aid and comfort to the enemy"—an accusation of treason as defined in the U.S. Constitution. Anticommunism as foreign policy was infused with a fairly specific set of criteria, based on the Nationalist Chinese regime as the hope for a model against communism.

It entailed the superimposition of nationhood on political or military leaders who claimed control over residual patches of territory in the aftermath of a revolutionary anti-imperialist war. Regimes like those of Syngman Rhee, Chiang Kai-shek, Ngo Dinh Diem survived only through United States intervention. This was effected by military and police aid in order to secure and stabilize the area, economic support by ties with investment capital and the underwriting of "reforms" designed to promote the military and economic elites.[5]

But just supporting anti-Communist regimes would not suffice. Failure to prevent the "fall of territory to the Communists" would revive the lobby's charge of selling out China and other areas of Asia to the Communists. Any party in power in America knew that it would commit political suicide if it lost again to communism in Asia. This fear of domestic repercussions was one of the reasons we entered the Vietnam conflict, and it is also advanced as one of the reasons for not leaving without having accomplished our goal: an anti-Communist Saigon regime.

The lobby's success in interjecting the loyalty issue into considerations of foreign policy effectively denied the right to open dissent. Inside the government this was done by smearing all critics of a pro-Chiang policy with the taint of Communist sympathies. China lobby leaders furnished congressional investigative committees with reams of unsubstantiated charges which were printed by the government printing office at the taxpayers' expense and were then transmitted through the lobby's magazines and propaganda channels as authentic evidence of the disloyalty of the individuals involved. Their targets included journalists, foreign service officers, educators, and anyone whom the lobby considered threatened the sanctity of its objectives. By its standards, Dean Acheson, General George Marshall, John K. Fairbank, Will Durant, and Ross Y. Koen all were guilty.

The consequences of this activity matured in the 1960s. The tactics of the China lobby had placed all foreign service officers and government consultants on Asia in "psychic preventive detention" —the chilling phrase comes from one of the outspoken victims— O. Edmund Clubb. The dismissal of actual dissenters from the State Department and the intimidation of potential ones made the risks of informed criticism of basic policies too great for most officials. Critics and advisors wisely and justifiably sought employment in agencies that were beyond the reach of congressional investigative commit-

5. For a study of the way land reform was used in Japan, Taiwan, and Vietnam to support the economic and military elites, see Alfred McCoy, "Land Reform as Counter-Revolution: U.S. Foreign Policy and the Tenant Farmers of Asia." *Bulletin of Concerned Asian Scholars* III, 1 (Winter-Spring 1971): 15–49.

tees, namely, the Central Intelligence Agency, the National Security Agency, Rand, the president's staff, and so forth. Unfortunately in this milieu confidentiality, the honorable epithet for secrecy, obviated individual responsibility and eliminated individual and public accountability. From these agencies, cloaked in the shroud of presidential privilege, and masked with the mystiques of national security and technical competence, there later emerged private armies prosecuting executive wars, academic and military operatives waging counterinsurgency campaigns in self-serving collusion with rightwing groups in Asia.

The lobby's barrage of propaganda, its supporting role in the interminable investigations lasting many years, and its use of the public media for exposure not only destroyed individuals' lives through suicide (E. Herbert Norman), unemployment (Jack Service), and forced emigration (John Paton Davies, Jr.) but, even more dangerous to society though less visible, it reinforced and internalized the Cold War ethic among Asia scholars and political elites. The Asia experts became more conservative than the population. Issues like the recognition of Red China and the Vietnam teach-ins were not raised by the members of the Asian studies profession, but by politicians or scholars from other fields. The leadership of the first Vietnam teach-in at the University of Michigan notably lacked any representatives from Asian studies. The national leadership of the Vietnam teach-in, with the exception of Professor Mary Wright of Yale, failed to attract Asia scholars. Unlike the professional associations for historians, anthropologists, philosophers, and scientists, the Association for Asian Studies has still not gone on record against the Vietnam War.

However, it would be wrong to focus only on the lack of public responsibility in the field of Asian studies. Its response was in many ways conditioned by the changing nature of American politics. The 1950s and 1960s witnessed the rise of pluralism as the official ideology of the political elites. Pluralism has traditionally been defined as the operation of group politics which eschews violence, irrationality, emotionalism, disharmony, and disorder. It was assumed that multiple membership in different groups would lessen the possibility of taking an extreme position or chauvinistically pursuing the goals of just one group. The pluralist position stressed the role of rational, responsible, and effective political leadership which would insure stability and avert the spectre of the politicization of the masses. This venture into conservative political theory has reinforced a predeliction for working with or for government leaders, and has evinced suspicion of and antagonism to any political movement from the bottom.

Because of their stand against mass movements, the pluralists justified the mass apathy of the fifties, which had been conditioned by the stringent anticommunism of the Cold War. The pluralists wrongly identified hysterical anticommunism with extremist populist groups like McCarthyism and not with the behind-the-scenes activities of elite groups like the China lobby. As Michael Paul Rogin has pointed out,[6] McCarthyism itself was an elitist phenomenon, not an outgrowth of mass political involvement. Although pluralists claim to be involved in group politics, in fact, they are engaged in politics of the elites. They feel that they can in secret and with immunity from congressional or public scrutiny, make wise decisions in the public interest and that above all group conflicts and interests there is a public interest which only they comprehend.

The confluence of the purges in the 1950s with the growing acceptance of pluralism gave Asia scholars two alternatives: either to drop out or to seek protection within the elite structure. The CIA's reputation of protecting its employees from the McCarthyite witch hunts attracted many of them. Think tanks like Rand, and Hudson Institute, and research centers funded by foundations which had close government connections also sheltered scholars from campus incursions on academic freedom and enlisted their support for government operations. The China lobby's attack on the Institute of Pacific Relations (see chapter six) resulted in the dismemberment of that organization. The Institute of Pacific Relations could find no further foundation support for its activities and was forced to fold. Other organizations in the field of Asian studies found that they could garner foundation and government support only if they limited their international activities and if they became apolitical-objective in their scholarship. The definition of "apolitical-objective" was determined in a conservative manner by pluralist politics.

The consequences for scholarship are that the political limits imposed by the Cold War have become transformed into the political

6. Michael Paul Rogin, *The Intellectuals and McCarthy: The Radical Specter.* Cambridge, Mass.: Massachusetts Institute of Technology Press, 1967.

limits of apolitical-objective scholarship. The acquisition of unassail-
able professional expertise in a chosen area is seen as the qualification for criticizing and influencing the decision making in United
States foreign policy. But this "qualification" is undermined if the
scholar seeks a constituency outside of normal government and foundation channels. Safe and responsible criticism is not only based on
academic abilities but also on one's use of proper political channels.

Rejection of this relationship between scholarship and politics is
fundamental to the Committee of Concerned Asian Scholars (CCAS)
which was founded in 1968 in opposition to the silence of their own
profession and in recognition of the public irresponsibility of intellectuals and Asia scholars especially, to speak out publicly against the
Vietnam War and the imperialism of the United States which waged
that war. In an effort to bring these issues to the profession, the
CCAS in 1969 organized a panel on the effects of McCarranism on
the field of Asian studies. The panelists were O. Edmund Clubb,
Richard C. Kagan, Ross Y. Koen, Owen Lattimore, and Howard
Zinn; Robert J. Lifton served as Chairman.[7] The centrality of the
issue for the profession was evidenced by an attendance of two
thousand members at a four-hour presentation. Out of this panel
came many of the ideas in this introduction and the commitment to
publish this book.[8]

The China lobby has remained beyond exposure because the liberal elite was intimidated by it and retreated into pluralistic rationali-
zations as a defense against it; because the right wing supported the
lobby and its attack upon public debate; and because the left so
disdained the Republic of China that it dismissed it as an object of
investigation or as an enemy to discredit. The publication of Ross
Koen's book inaugurates the long overdue exposure of the lobby.
It opens up to further scrutiny the relations of the lobby and the
KMT with the CIA, the Navy, the Federal Bureau of Narcotics, the
Military Advisory and Assistance Group in Taiwan, the Air Force,
the international drug trade, and the right wings of the Democratic
and Republican parties.   •

Future research should not only concentrate on the lobby's role

7. The papers presented by Clubb, Kagan, and Koen were published in the *Bulletin
   of Concerned Asian Scholars* 4, May 1969.
8. I am also greatly indebted to my wife who helped shape this introduction, and to
   the members of the Center for Chinese Studies, the University of Michigan, who
   supplied critical analysis and secretarial aid.

in American politics but also on its relation to the Nationalist government, and its effects on the Chinese communities at home and abroad. How deeply is the lobby involved with the politics of the overseas Chinese community, the Nationalist's consulate system, and the issue of determining citizenship? Is the lobby used as a lever of control over Chinese in American communities? Does it have connections with the FBI that can be used to harass and deport troublesome citizens in American Chinatowns? How strong and direct are its alleged links with covert operations among overseas Chinese in Southeast Asia? Now that Americans freely discuss the operations of the Republic of China in the United States in the light of a solid core of information, these issues can and should be further examined.

Finally, the history of the China lobby and its legacy should sensitize us to the possibility of other lobbies which operate secretly in our government: a racist law and order lobby in the Justice Department, a benign neglect lobby in HEW, and a Saigon lobby in State. But our expectation of the government's tactics must not be frozen to experiences derived from the 1950s. Despite the fact that the Nationalist Chinese government has recently hired former Republican senator from California, George Murphy, and his public relations firm for $115,000 a year plus $20,000 a month for operating expenses,[9] the technique of legislative and public exposure for disloyalty has today been replaced by the easier charge of "conspiracy." The government, mirroring its own penchant for secrecy and its own conspiratorial elitist organization, now attacks its critics through closed grand juries, and for "intent" rather than for overt acts or writings. Preventive detention of the dissenter supplements the earlier "psychic preventive detention" of the critic. Furthermore, the focus of attention is again changing: this time from foreign policy to domestic policy. Our techniques of making the world safe for American-styled democracy are being used at home to make America safe for its pluralistic elites. The military, the CIA, the nature of our client regimes, the force of our imperialism are coming home to roost.

9. Sacramento *Bee*, July 21, 1971, p. 1.

A NOTE ON THE EDITING

Since this book is a historical document and in order to give the reader the most complete possible acquaintance with the original, no substantial editing has been done. Slight changes in the text were made on the following pages (numbers in parentheses refer to original edition): (ix) xxi, (24) 21, (31) 29, (33) 30, (42) 38, (47) 42, (50) 45, (54) 49, (59) 52–53, (62) 55, (76) 67, (87) 76–77, (137) 120, (155) 135, (201) 173, (203) 175, (219) 189, (229) 198, (231) 200, (241) 209 (282) 240.

AUTHOR'S PREFACE

United States policy toward China is more deeply involved in domestic politics than any other aspect of American foreign affairs. It was the one area specifically excluded by Senator Vandenberg in 1947 from the scope of bipartisan agreement. Partly as a result of this exclusion from bipartisan consideration, contention over China policy has virtually become a permanent feature of Republican-Democratic party battles and, at least since 1953, of somewhat less intensive battles between the conservative and moderate wings of the Republican party.

Today, both political parties in the United States have a vested interest in past positions on China policy which makes a new approach exceedingly difficult. Frederic W. Collins, the Washington correspondent of the Providence *Journal,* has stated the problem succinctly.

. . . Asia gave the Republicans, as the political challengers of the Administration, their ideal opportunity, which they enthusiastically exploited. The Administration naturally reacted defensively. Positions hardened on both sides. Today, the Republicans have a vested political interest in past positions, which is a handicap, to say the least, in adapting to new realities.

Ultimately, the dissension in Congress over American policy in China led to open questioning of the extent to which the protagonists in the controversy were influenced by the activities of lobbyists and pressure groups. The efforts of the Communists and forces opposed to Chiang Kai-shek have been the subject of many studies and have received widespread publicity. The pro-Chiang forces, on the other hand, have received comparatively little attention. Those forces, which came to be known as the China lobby, did, however, arouse concern in Congress and among certain elements of the press during the height of the controversy over China policy. Senator Wayne Morse charged in 1951 that the China lobby was "conducting a violent campaign against American policies in China, chiefly by charging that the State Department, and especially its Far Eastern Division, is a nest of Reds controlled by Communists and fellow travelers." A year earlier, Marquis Childs of the Washington *Post* had summarized the feeling of many government officials:

No one who knows anything about the way things work here doubts that a powerful China lobby has brought extraordinary influence to bear on Congress and the Executive. It would be hard to find any parallel in diplomatic history for the agents and diplomatic representatives of a foreign power exerting such pressures—Nationalist China has used the techniques of direct intervention on a scale rarely, if ever, seen.

The purpose of this study is to examine the nature of these techniques of intervention and to isolate and analyze the "campaign against American policies in China," allegedly conducted by the China lobby. The term "China lobby" as used here, however, is not narrowly confined to the Chinese agents of the Kuomintang, but refers—as it did in popular usage—to a multitude of diverse interests and groups which, in many cases, had little affinity for one another. These groups include Chinese, paid American agents, business organizations, missionaries, politicians, and many other categories. The term is employed here merely as a convenient expression to include all these elements.*

This examination will concern, in Part I, the attitudes which past experience with China had instilled into the American people and the manner in which these attitudes affected their disposition to accept an extreme explanation of postwar events in the Far East. Part II will examine the nature of the China lobby and identify the individuals and groups who were associated with its point of view; inquire into the specific incidents which were exploited by pro-Chiang propaganda;† and examine the extent to which the essential arguments, "evidence" and methods of the China lobby were accepted by those in a position to influence policy. Part III will examine the effects of that acceptance on such groups as the private Far Eastern experts, scholarly organizations, and State Department personnel. Finally, Part IV will examine the results of this acceptance in terms of policy.

Quite obviously, this is not the whole of the story of the China lobby. Few of the intricate financial dealings, the political contributions and payoffs, or the more intimate personal relations between the various participants have been detailed here. The reason is the

---

* The term "China lobby" is discussed on pages 29–30.
† The term "propaganda" as used in this study carries no value judgment or connotation. It will be used interchangeably with such expressions as "educational campaign," "information program," "point of view," "publicity effort," and so on, with no implication as to the truth or falsehood of the ideas expressed.

simple one that the details are either not available or cannot be sufficiently substantiated. During his investigation, the author encountered many individuals with intimate personal knowledge of these events who were quite willing to discuss them but who were unwilling to be quoted or cited as sources of information. In other instances, the sources could be revealed but the nature of the information was such that more positive proof than that which was available would have been needed in order to include it in this book.

There is, for example, evidence that some Chinese have engaged in the illegal smuggling of narcotics into the United States with the full knowledge and connivance of members of the Chinese Nationalist Government. The evidence indicates that several prominent Americans have participated in and profited from these transactions. It indicates further that the narcotics business has been a factor in some activities and permutations of the China lobby. Such matters can only be fully investigated and exposed, however, by legally established and sanctioned processes. A private scholar or investigator may aid these processes, but his studies can neither set them in motion nor substitute for them.

More important, the details of activities such as these, although often sensational and provocative, are only incidental to the broader processes by which official positions are reached on important questions of public policy. It is with these broader processes that *The China Lobby in American Politics* is primarily concerned. This study may help to balance the record; but its purpose extends far beyond that. It is an attempt, in a specific sphere, to probe the extent to which the thought processes, the self-images, and the struggle for power and profits, *within* the United States are more important, as sources of American policies toward other states, than are the nature and aims of the states toward which those policies are directed. If it serves to stimulate further thinking on that subject, then the study will have been well worth while.

The author owes a debt of gratitude to a far greater number of people than he can possibly list in this brief space. The greatest debt he unquestionably owes to his wife, Mary, whose faith, encouragement, and patience never failed to sustain him, and to whose technical skill the manuscript was consigned at many stages. He also owes much to Harry and Vivian Kantor whose encouragement and good sense meant far more than they could know. To the library staff of the University of Florida he is indebted for long and devoted effort. For many hours spent in reading and discussing the manuscript, he is particularly grateful to Professor Frederick H. Hartmann of the University of Florida; also to Professors Manning J. Dauer, William G. Carleton, Oscar Svarlien, and William E. Barringer of the University of Florida, to Reece McGee of the University of Texas, and to Gilbert Abcarian of Humboldt State College, California, all of whom read portions of the manuscript and made many helpful suggestions. The author alone is responsible, of course, for all errors and omissions of material fact and for any errors of interpretation or failure to draw correct conclusions.

I should like to thank the following for permission to quote previously published work: Caxton Printers, Ltd., *The China Monthly, Congressional Quarterly,* Devin-Adair Company, Harper and Brothers, Henry Holt and Company, Henry Regnery Company, Houghton Mifflin Company, Liveright Publishing Corporation, The Macmillan Company, Prentice-Hall, Princeton University Press, *The Public Opinion Quarterly, The Reporter,* Stanford University Press, University of Chicago Press, The Viking Press, Yale University Press, and *The Yale Review.*

ARCATA, CALIFORNIA
June 5, 1959

THE
CHINA LOBBY
IN AMERICAN
POLITICS

1 THE BACKGROUND
OF AMERICAN POLICY

1 THE AMERICAN PERSPECTIVE ON THE FAR EAST

The disillusionment and frustration exhibited by Americans in their attitudes toward China in the past ten years have usually been attributed to the fact of the Communist victory over the forces of the Kuomintang. As one student of American policy expressed it, "The real root of the bitterness in discussion of American policy toward China is the great and tragic fact that between the middle of 1945 and the middle of 1949 China was won by Communists who openly proclaimed their loyalty to Stalin."[1]

Unquestionably, the mere fact of the Communist victory in 1949, in spite of American support of a less radical solution to China's civil war, was sufficient provocation for a serious review of American policy. The mere fact of the Communist victory does not explain, however, why the review of previous policy and the formulation of a new approach should have taken place in the atmosphere of dissension and recrimination by which it was actually marked. Rather, the agitation which accompanied the American reappraisal and adjustment—if an adjustment can be claimed—to the new facts of life in China was an outgrowth of far more complex and deep-seated illusions than those directly related to the defeat of Chiang Kai-shek. To a large extent, the fear and frustration which have marked the reaction of the American people to the Communist conquest of China are a result of the fact that the views Americans held regarding the aims of foreign policy and the role of the United States in international affairs, although largely invalid, were nevertheless believed with such intensity that the believers remained vulnerable to arguments based on those views even after the policies which resulted from them failed to produce the desired result. Some elaboration of this point is necessary.

The traditional views of the American people regarding the objectives of their foreign policy have reflected three basic interacting aims. These aims were, first, the preservation of the security of the United States and the protection of the lives and property of Americans in foreign countries; second, the encouragement, within certain limited conditions, of the development of liberal democracy—at

3

least in form—in other areas of the world; and third, the absolute minimum involvement of the United States in international affairs as far as that is consistent with the first. As long as Americans have felt that these aims were being simultaneously realized, they have traditionally given little thought or attention to foreign policy. As a result, they have been only dimly aware—if indeed, they can be said to have been aware at all—that the simultaneous realization of these three basic aims depended on the continuing validity of at least three fundamental assumptions. First, it depended on the assumption that the achievement of liberal democracy was synonymous with the establishment of democratic forms; that liberal democracy, as defined and understood in the United States, was desired by and could be adapted to the needs of virtually any people; and that in the struggle to achieve democratic forms, only American encouragement and advice were needed. Second, realization of American aims depended on the assumption that active intervention to protect American security was made generally unnecessary by the existence of an effective balance of power which could prevent the formation of dangerous hostile alliances. Third, realization of American aims depended on the assumption that the United States economy was largely self-sufficient both as to resources and markets and that therefore "American property" (both markets and resources) was not of such vital concern to any decisive segment of the American people as to require large-scale active protection by the United States.

Until the end of the nineteenth century, these assumptions, on the whole, were probably quite valid. At least in those societies of which the American people had direct knowledge, the establishment of the forms of representative government which Americans interpreted as democratic seemed to be progressing with ineluctable force. Furthermore, the geographical position of the United States and the state of transportation and communications technology being what they were, the United States was relatively safe from any threat to its security. At the same time, the increasing demands of the growing population of the United States for goods and services seemed to present an insatiable challenge to its productive facilities, and little thought was given to the limits of available natural resources.

Since the beginning of the present century, these traditional assumptions concerning the position and role of the United States in world affairs have become progressively invalid. American policies for most of the last half-century have consisted primarily in attempts to achieve the three basic aims of the American people in spite of the increasing invalidity of the assumptions upon which those aims were based. American intervention in 1917 and again in 1941 was directed primarily toward preserving the conditions under which American security and the extension of democratic forms could be protected with a minimum of sustained American involvement. Refusal to join the League of Nations was based, in the final analysis, on a belief that World War I had achieved that goal. While many —perhaps most—Americans were convinced by 1941 that United States membership in a world organization dedicated to the principle of collective security was essential, they still thought of it primarily as a necessary evil—as the only way to maintain the conditions under which minimum American participation in international politics would continue to be possible.

These attitudes concerning the proper role of the United States in world affairs were complicated where the Far East was concerned by two additional factors. First, experience with Europe through two world wars and a closer acquaintance with the European multistate system had conditioned Americans to the necessity of collective action in that area. In contrast, they had no experience with collective action in Asia, and both their experience in the war with Japan and their lack of sympathy with European colonial policies gave Americans the impression that the United States had a legitimate interest in Asia which was unique among non-Asian states. Americans did not regard Russia as an Asian power. Second, prior American experience in Asia had resulted in a settled conviction that active intervention in the interests of American security and liberal democracy was even less essential in that area than in Europe. In fact, Americans believed that the only real requirement for the achievement of American aims in Asia was to secure the withdrawal of the European colonial powers. They believed that progress toward the achievement of these aims had been only temporarily disrupted by Japanese aggression which had forced the United States to intervene. Now, however, according to this view, it would be necessary only to defeat and possibly reform this aggressor in order that the conditions necessary for the realization of American basic aims, including that of noninvolvement, be restored. It was essentially this belief which made so attractive the postwar argument that a little military aid to Chiang Kai-shek was all that was necessary to maintain him in power and therefore ensure the American orientation of China in its newly won greatpower status.

In consequence of the first factor, both collective security and balance-of-power policies were applied in Europe but both, in practice, tended to be collective procedures. In Asia, however, a unilateralist approach was consistently emphasized. American insistence that general MacArthur have the sole responsibility for the occupation of Japan demonstrates the extent to which this was true at the end of the war. Unilateralist tendencies were also shown by the insistence with which the United States tried to determine which states and ruling groups could safely be trusted to form the anti-Soviet balance of power in the Far East. Even where security arrangements in the Pacific were collective in form (as in the SEATO organization), the United States controlled the selection of membership. The fact that this also meant that any blame for poor results necessarily would be assessed against the American policy per se was not always appreciated.

The leadership for collective procedures in Europe came from both the Administration and Congress, and from both Democrats and Republicans. The role assumed by the United States in the establishment of the United Nations, the willingness to undertake a joint occupation of Germany, and American efforts to negotiate multilateral peace treaties for the European states indicate the orientation of American policy. By 1947, however, the emerging ideological conflict and the clash of American and Soviet power had substantially modified American enthusiasm for collective security.

The decision to move openly to establish a power bloc in opposition to the Soviet Union was implemented, initially, by the Greek-Turkish Aid program and by the Truman Doctrine in the spring of 1947. This policy represented a shift away from collective security and toward a balance-of-power approach. The emphasis on collective—rather than unilateral—action and responsibility, however, was constantly maintained. Aid to Greece and Turkey was followed in rapid succession by the Marshall Plan, NATO, and efforts looking toward the unification of European defenses, and the rearmament of Germany. From this point forward, American policy in Europe was clearly oriented toward active leadership of like-minded powers. So long as it resulted in neither a war nor a dangerous Soviet victory, that policy was unlikely to encounter serious resistance at home. And, in fact, that collective policy was, in most essential respects, apparently successful for several years.

In Asia, meanwhile, the United States encountered a wholly different set of problems. The very defeat of Japan and the turmoil in China made the role of the United States vastly more important there than ever before. Those problems, moreover, were reflected against a background of American experience very different from American experience in Europe.

Americans believed that they had been deeply involved in Asian political affairs for a century or more. Trade and missionary activities on a private level, and the Open Door policy—well known to every school child—on the official governmental level, tended to reinforce this belief. The fact that this involvement was primarily on a verbal and moral level was seldom taken into account. The very nature of the American involvement often obscured the difference between private and official policy. The United States had indeed come close to seeing itself as the protector of the Chinese from foreign exploitation, and American trade and commerce in no way interfered with this image. The growth of trade with China even reinforced the feeling of benevolent affection. One of the major transcontinental railroads, the Northern Pacific, had the Chinese yin-yang symbol as its official emblem. Both it and the Great Northern were built with the expectation that their incomes would be augmented with revenues from trade with the Far East.[2]

Christian missions from the United States later became an important source of American contact with Chinese and other Asian peoples. Through schools and hospitals, missionaries from American churches introduced the education, science, and medicine of the Occident to China. The education carried on by the Protestant churches of the United States to acquaint their members, who were supporting the work, with the activities of the missionaries gave millions of Americans information about China. The accounts of the missionaries were usually sympathetic and concerned the peoples, cultures, and problems of the area. They, too, reinforced the picture Americans had of China.

The two major factors, hunger for markets and opportunities to invest capital profitably, and a long-cultivated interest in the welfare and salvation of the Chinese people, motivated the Open Door policy. The policy itself was an attempt to control the actions of foreign powers who were tempted by the potential riches and internal weakness of China. It was directed at Japan, Russia, and the European states interested in Chinese trade and territory.[3] Basically, the Open Door policy was a declaration by the United States that it was the policy of the government to protect American lives, property, and *other legitimate interests,* and

"to seek a solution which may bring about permanent safety and peace to China, preserve Chinese territorial and administrative entity, protect all rights guaranteed to friendly powers by treaty and international law, and safeguard for the world the principles of equal and impartial trade with all parts of the Chinese Empire"[4]

This statement was to be the basis of American policy for the first forty years of the twentieth century. Out of the manner in which it was implemented and applied, however, sprang many of the illusions concerning China which afflicted the American people after the Japanese surrender. After an extensive study of American diplomatic history, George Kennan came to the conclusion that the manner of initiation of the Open Door policy had these results:

. . . A myth was established which was destined to flourish in American thinking for at least a half-century. Neither the obvious lack of practical results, nor the disillusionment of Hay and the other persons involved, nor our unwillingness to bolster the policy in any forceful way, nor our subsequent departure from it ourselves—none of these things succeeded in shaking in any way the established opinion of the American public that here, in this episode of the Open Door notes, a tremendous blow had been struck for the triumph of American principles in international society—an American blow for an American idea.[5]

This illusion concerning the effectiveness of a verbal expression of policy continued for the next half-century in spite of the numerous occasions on which it failed to protect China from serious external pressures. Examples of these failures are (1) Russian encroachment on Manchuria after 1900,[6] (2) the transfer from Russia to Japan of railroad and port facilities in South Manchuria following the Russo-Japanese War,[7] (3) expansion of Japanese interests in China following World War I,[8] (4) the Soviet invasion of Manchuria and intimidation of the Nanking Government in 1929, and (5) the Japanese invasion of China between 1931 and 1941.[9]

Failure of the United States Government and the American people to recognize the ineffectiveness of the Open Door policy also led to a misunderstanding of the reason for the partial success which the policy seemed to achieve. According to Vinacke:

So far as success was met in making effective the principles (and that success was only partial even before 1931) it was because first Russian and then Japanese policy was restrained by the interests and actions of other states than the United States. In effect, up to 1931, there was at least a semblance of a balance of power in the Far East which operated to prevent any one state from following its own self-determined lines of interest in China.[10]

Having thus failed to understand the effects of their own policies on events in China since 1900, the American people were totally unprepared in 1945 to support the kind of intervention in China's internal affairs which might have maintained in power a government with a Western orientation. But when it developed that their refusal to intervene was accompanied by the creation of a government unfavorable to the United States, Americans were equally unprepared to accept that result. They were accustomed to believing that words and ideals were sufficient to control events in China. This is not to imply that the implementation of any particular policy by the United States would necessarily have resulted in a China oriented toward the West. Nor does the argument assume that the United States could have pursued sufficiently active policies in both Europe and the Far East at the same time. From the standpoint of pure logic unrestricted by facts, however, Americans were not precluded from assuming that both of these things were possible.[11]

An understanding of this result will be furthered by a brief examination of the wartime phase of American policy toward China. This phase of American policy was dominated from the beginning by two policies which were adopted as basic strategy in the early months of the war. Both of these measures were tentatively formulated in the year preceding the Japanese attack on Pearl Harbor and became a permanent part of American global strategy by the summer of 1942.[12] The first of these decisions can be stated quite simply as the "Europe first" policy; the second was the decision "to make China a Great Power."[13] These decisions reflected both American concern with the threat of Hitler's Germany and the assumption noted above that Americans generally regarded the Japanese threat as one which required less sustained American intervention than the European situation.

The decision to make Europe the area of primary concentration was made officially final and conclusive at the "Arcadia" Conference of December 24, 1941, to January 14, 1942. Discussions at this meeting of the American President and British Prime Minister were largely devoted to problems of the Pacific where the situation was immediately critical. But "even in the face of the Japanese advance there was no deviation from the principle already accepted by both [American and European allies] before Pearl Harbor—only the European theater was decisive."[14] It is significant in this respect that comprehensive plans for United States participation in the war in Europe had already been drawn up in a series called the "Rainbow" plans.[15] Similar preparations for strategic action by the United States in relation to China, however, "had not progressed beyond the staff study phase."[16]

In spite of this lack of preparation, it should be noted that there remained in the United States a deep-seated cleavage over the basic policy decision to defeat Hitler first. Many Americans continued throughout the war to urge that first attention should be given to Japan. This feeling was particularly apparent among certain Republicans. One Midwestern foreign affairs leader in Congress is reported to have remarked some years later, "We considered that the Republican war."[17] That attitude did not apply to all Republicans, but the Asiatic orientation among many of that party was well known. It was reinforced to an important degree by the activities of General Douglas MacArthur in whose eyes his own theater had taken on "truly millennial importance."[18] MacArthur's attitude is indicated by a report given to Navy Secretary Forrestal in 1944. The report was made by Bert Andrews of the New York *Herald Tribune* after an interview with MacArthur on Leyte and included the following:

> The Chinese situation is disastrous. It is the bitter fruit of our decision to concentrate our full strength against Germany. . . . We made the same old mistake of intervening in European quarrels which we can't hope to solve because they are insoluble. . . . Europe is a dying system. It is worn out and run down, and will become an economic and industrial hegemony of Soviet Russia. . . . The lands touching the Pacific with their billions of inhabitants will determine the course of history for the next ten thousand years. . . . If Chiang Kai-shek is overthrown [by Japan], China will be thrown into utter confusion.[19]

Largely as a result of this Pacific orientation in the United States, three major efforts were made in 1943 to demonstrate the seriousness of the American intention to make China a great power. In January a treaty was signed relinquishing our extraterritorial rights in China; in October, China was introduced as one of the signatories of the Four-Nation Declaration of the Moscow Conference, and on December 17th Congress passed an act repealing the Chinese Exclusion Laws.[20]

In spite of these concessions, however, the two basic policies noted above resulted in a paradox which was never resolved. It was never possible to ensure beyond reasonable doubt the defeat of Hitler first and at the same time raise the power and prestige of China to a "great power" level if that objective required that the Chinese be supplied with all they demanded in men, matériel, and political considerations.[21] Certain political concessions, such as those mentioned above, were helpful from the prestige standpoint. But they would not, in themselves, make China a great power. The accomplishment of that objective required substantial improvement in China's military vigor, but military support on such a level was precisely what the United States could not provide.

The confusion which resulted in American minds from the "great power" status accorded China on the one hand and her actual military weakness on the other was further increased by the competition in the United States between two distinct views concerning the nature of the Kuomintang regime in China. The competition between these two views began to take on serious proportions by the middle of 1943. One of these views—the one generally accepted in the United States up to this time—presented the Chinese as a gallant people fighting against overwhelming odds to preserve their independence and to establish democracy. While some recognition was given to the lack of internal unity and the military weakness of the Chinese Government, these factors were generally attributed to the long war with Japan, China's desperate need for war matériel, and the inability or unwillingness of the United States to supply those needs. Generalissimo Chiang Kai-shek was portrayed as a most far-seeing and enlightened Christian leader who would be a valuable anti-Communist ally. His wife, Madame Chiang, became a familiar figure who appealed to the sympathies of millions of Americans. According to this view, then, the United States should do everything in its power to strengthen Chiang's position and increase China's prestige in the Far East.[22]

The opposing view portrayed the generalissimo as an autocratic war lord who ruled China through a corrupt and feudal-minded Kuomintang party. According to this view, the Chinese Government had failed to gain and hold the mass support of the Chinese people. It had failed to carry out the agricultural and other economic reforms necessary to sustain China's effort against Japan. In fact, the proponents of this interpretation of events in China insisted that Chiang and his Kuomintang party were not really interested in the prosecution of the Pacific war. The Kuomintang, according to this view, was willing to leave that task to the United States while devoting its efforts to preparations for what Chiang considered the inevitable postwar struggle for control inside China.[23]

In contrast with the latter attitude toward the Chiang Government, the American people were confronted throughout the war years with a growing volume of literature which portrayed the Chinese Communist regime as the least corrupt, and as the most benevolent and democratic, of the forces with the potential power to take control in China. Most of those who wrote about the Chinese Communists had been in the areas of China under their control and were quite impressed with what they had seen. In such books as *Thunder Out of China, Report from Red China,* and *Red Star Over China,*[24] Americans were told that the Communists had achieved a broad measure of land reform, thrown off the feudal system, and freed the masses from the crushing burden of rent, taxes, and usurious interest charges. They were asked to believe that basic conditions as to food and clothing were better in Communist China than in Kuomintang China. Finally, Americans were told that this group which had brought social, political, and economic reforms to the areas of China under its control could retain its identity only by armed resistance against the determined efforts of the Kuomintang to destroy it.[25] At the same time, they were given to understand that the Chinese Communists were not dependent on Moscow for support. They were given the impression in some cases, in fact, that the Moscow and Yenan Communists were probably different brands with little direct contact.

The essential product of all these contradictions among the American people was a series of illusions which left them unprepared, both psychologically and on the basis of previous experience, when their onetime friend, ally, and dependent resorted after 1945 to the dubious technique of civil conflict as a means of resolving its differences. But regardless of the contradictions involved, Americans were accustomed to thinking of the Chinese as friends who needed and willingly accepted American Christianity, medical aid, and political ideas. They expected that the Chinese would, in the very nature of things, maintain a pro-American orientation. They considered that such would be a natural reaction, proper to a people who were thought to be basically democratic. Moreover, to discharge their accumulated obligations toward the American people—to whom they "owed" their freedom—the Chinese were naturally expected to continue to be America's most reliable allies in Asia.

Because Chiang Kai-shek had come to symbolize the apparent acceptance of American political and religious ideals, the people of the United States saw in him the personification of their China image. The real depths of the desire of the Chinese people for sweeping changes in their old way of life were grossly underestimated in the United States. Americans considered the Chinese revolution to be virtually completed, whereas, in actuality, it had barely begun. They were thus impelled to overestimate the effectiveness of Chiang's actual position and policies and to ignore the weakness of his leadership. These illusions concerning the nature of American policy in China and the internal Chinese situation were destined to produce a condition of shock among many Americans when the struggle inside China began to favor a group oriented toward the Soviet Union.

In this setting, the growing success of the Chinese Communists over the Kuomintang Government of Chiang Kai-shek was increasingly portrayed in the United States to be the result of a betrayal and sellout of China perpetrated by Far Eastern experts, Foreign Service officers, and State Department officials. According to this account, United States policy was sabotaged through the treasonous activities of Americans. By 1949 large sections of the public, the press, and the membership of Congress had come to believe the charge that Chiang Kai-shek and his Kuomintang regime were sold "down the Amur" by the Government of the United States.[26] The development of closer relations between Peking and Moscow following the Communist victory, and the increasing awareness of the extent to which the Soviets had aided the Chinese Reds in their war with Chiang, made the charges appear even more to be justified.

The concern with which the acceptance of this view of China's fall to the Communists was met in official quarters in the United States in indicated by the fact that efforts were made to refute it as Chiang's collapse became imminent. On August 5, 1949, the Department of State issued an eleven-hundred-page document attempting to explain and defend its past policies in China. That document is usually referred to as the China "White Paper."[27]

The charge that Americans were responsible for Chiang's loss received only brief direct mention by Secretary Acheson in his letter transmitting the White Paper to the President, but it was the subject of and the motivation for the entire document.[28] The "Letter of Transmittal" is an attempt to give a general answer to the charges and accusations, while the remainder of the document purports to provide a detailed and carefully documented reply. That it failed in this effort is adequately attested to by the fact that the controversy was not thereby ended. In fact, the controversy was soon to be sharply increased.

In October of 1949, the Chinese Communists formally established a government of all China, and Chiang Kai-shek was forced to flee with his army to the island of Formosa. Americans now had to face the fact that China was in the hands of an unfriendly government. Their "friend" had gone Communist. By this date, however, Americans had come to consider all movements in the world which bore Communist labels to be mere extensions of Moscow. That attitude toward the Chinese was strenghtened by the fact that Moscow's cold-war slogans were being increasingly echoed from Peking. Moreover, the Chinese Reds began what appeared to be a consistent campaign of harassment of the Western powers. To Americans, these tactics merely reflected the degree to which Soviet control had been imposed upon China.

No amount of wishful thinking or apologies could long hide the fact that Americans had been deprived of their two chief interests in China. The vast market potential would now be developed only by the Soviets or by the Chinese themselves. The foreign-mission field which had absorbed the energies of so many American Christians would now be severely curtailed or eliminated entirely. Moreover, the image of a grateful China acknowledging the benevolent guidance of their American "elder brothers" became impossible to sustain.

But more difficult realities were yet to come. For within the space of a single year, Americans were dying before Chinese guns in a war which was widely believed to have been precipitated by Moscow. From friends the Chinese had become actual enemies. It was, moreover, a war which Americans had not wanted to fight. They considered themselves to be engaged in a "police action" in which they had a moral responsibility to provide the leadership for the "free world." But in the exercise of that moral duty the United States found itself confronted on the battlefield of Korea with a new and powerful China. Within less than a year American casualties had mounted to a total of more than sixty-five thousand.[29] Thus, both the participation of China and the extent of the casualties seemed more in keeping with the traditional concept of war than with a mere "police action."

The Administration in Washington, however, continued to characterize activities in Korea as a police action and ultimately made it clear that a total military victory in Korea was not necessarily its aim. On the contrary, such political goals as greater cooperation between the United States and its allies, the stabilizing of the Far East on the basis of a recognized *modus operandi* between the United States and China, and the salvaging of United States power and prestige for use in other areas, assumed greater importance to the Administration than "winning" the war in Korea. Americans, however, were not accustomed to engaging in war for any purpose other than to "win." Thus they became confused and angry at finding themselves in such a "mess."[30]

As prospects for a peaceful and secure future "after the war" steadily deteriorated, Americans more and more directed their anger at both Washington and the Chinese Communists. Anger with Washington was based on an increasing willingness to believe that the policies which the United States had followed in China in the preceding years were the result of "stupidity at the top—treason just below." Americans were simply unable to believe that the Chinese could have made such a momentous decision as to substitute one form of government for another without the active participation and positive concurrence of Washington. With this attitude as a point of departure, it was a simple step to the conviction that the policies followed by the United States had been deliberately designed to turn China over to the Communists. In this atmosphere, there was little inclination among Americans to examine seriously the alternative policies which the United States might have pursued or to inquire sincerely and dispassionately into the possible consequences of each alternative.

Any attempt to generalize on either of these subjects is necessarily somewhat arbitrary. Nevertheless, it is possible to enumerate some five general policies which were logically available to the United States in China. In each case, several points of view concerning the feasibility of a particular policy is possible.

Of the five policy alternatives, two were the obvious extremes. In the succinct terminology of Secretary Acheson: (1) "it [the United States] could have pulled out lock, stock and barrel; (2) it could have intervened militarily on a major scale to assist the Nationalists to destroy the Communists."[31]

The first alternative, Acheson believed would ". . . have represented an abandonment of our international responsibilities and of our traditional policy of friendship for China before we had made a determined effort to be of assistance."[32] An American historian has rather accurately assessed the common attitude toward such a policy as one which ". . . would hardly have been adopted."[33]

Whether such a policy could have been adopted is, of course, a moot question. Whether it represented a logical course of action depends on the point of departure. To a thoroughgoing isolationist who believed the United States should not become involved in Europe's quarrels in Asia any more than in Europe's quarrels in Europe, it would have been quite logical to withdraw from China at the end of the war. A believer in hemispheric isolation could consistently argue that China and Russia, or the Kuomintang and Communists in China, should settle their own disputes. Likewise, one fully committed to self-determination could argue against American intervention if he were also convinced that the Chinese rather than Russia would determine the outcome.

On the other hand, it was precisely because the American people had rejected these approaches to foreign policy that they had become involved in World War II. In addition, they were fully convinced that the appearance of communism anywhere was merely a reflection of Soviet aggression. Abandonment of China to its fate was therefore a practical rather than a logical impossibility.

The other extreme was equally impracticable. In Acheson's opinion, "[T]he Communists probably could have been dislodged only by American arms." But he thought it obvious "that the American people would not have sanctioned such a colossal commitment of our armies in 1945 or later."[34] The historian quoted above believed it would have been equally impracticable from the Chinese side. According to him, the adoption of the second choice,

. . . would in effect have made [the government of China] an American puppet and China a part of an American empire in the thinly disguised form of the kind of protectorate which Great Britain once had over the native states of India. . . . Steps which some Americans and Chinese suggested would have tended in this direction. To have followed this course would have involved the United States more deeply in China than ever before. It would have aroused against the United States the intense nationalism which had been one of the characteristics of recent China.[35]

The other three choices of policy available to the United States were considerably more moderate than those discussed above. A third possible approach would have been to demand that the Nationalist Government first consolidate its position in a part of China which it might have been capable of holding. Aid from the United States would have had to be conditioned on compliance with this demand. Conceivably, Chiang might have been able to hold that part of China south of the Yellow River, or at most that part south of the Great Wall. The rest of the country, including Manchuria, would have been left to local governments or to the Communists. Success for this policy could not, of course, have been guaranteed. Indeed, if Secretary Acheson is correct in his estimate that the Nationalists were "weakened, demoralized, and unpopular," and had "dissipated their popular support and prestige in the areas liberated from the Japanese by the conduct of their civil and military officials," its success would have been very unlikely.[36] In any case, the Department of State seems to have been quite unwilling to take the responsibility such a policy would have entailed. The result might well have been that the Korean War would have been fought in China.

A fourth alternative for the United States would have been to attempt a *rapprochement* with the Communists in the hope of preventing their complete committal to Russia and in the hope that they would establish at least semifriendly relations with the United States. This policy had many advocates both at home and abroad. Latourette suggests that "the outcome of a somewhat similar course followed by Great Britain indicates that it would have failed."[37] Such a view, however, ignores the fact that Chinese reaction to British policy was conditioned to a considerable extent by their attitude toward the United States. It also fails to consider the difference in the attitude of the Chinese people toward Britain and America. Opponents of this policy, on the other hand, can point to close ideological ties between Moscow and Yenan as evidence that such a policy would not have been successful. All these arguments, however, are mere conjecture. What is important in this context is that any government in the United States which had attempted such a policy would have been deliberately risking its life in a very uncertain venture.

The fifth possible policy was to continue to support the idea of a united and powerful China as a bulwark against Japan and to hope that the "new China" would remain pro-American and open to American business. It required that the United States carefully refrain from any effort to coerce the Chinese into giving up their

responsibility for running their own government. Financial assistance, civilian technical aid, and military support and advice could
have been given to the extent that they were considered consistent
with the independence of China and the capabilities and freedom of
action of the United States. A logical extension of this effort would
have been an endeavor to avoid a civil war in China by working for
a compromise between the Communists and the Kuomintang. This
was, in the main, the policy which was followed by the United States.
Ultimately, when Chiang appeared to have lost the support of the
Chinese people, this policy required that the United States cease all
support for his cause except a bare minimum of economic assistance.

The policy conformed in every major respect to the traditional
views of the American people regarding the objectives of their
foreign policy. Had a Chinese government which was not anti-
American been maintained, no threat to American security would
have resulted. In fact, the belief that China now represents a threat
to the security of the United States is the result of an alteration of
American assumptions rather than a result of American policy. Furthermore, in the sense that the policy followed did not commit the
United States beyond its capabilities, it did preserve American
security. It was also an attempt to encourage the establishment of
democratic forms, and it required a minimum of direct American
involvement. The attitudes which developed toward this policy after
the Communist conquest of China—to the extent that such attitudes
were rational—were based on distinct assumptions regarding the
requirements of American security. The attitude adopted toward
this policy by the Chinese, as will be seen later, was based on a novel
assumption concerning the needs of American defense.

Three general estimates of American China policy are distinguish-
able. The first may be identified as that of the State Department, its
spokesmen, and its defenders; the second that of the anti-Chiang
critics;[38] and the third that of the pro-Chiang critics. For the most
part, the State Department and its defenders accepted the views of
Secretary of State Dean Acheson as he stated them in his letter to
the President accompanying the White Paper of 1949:

> The unfortunate but inescapable fact is that the ominous result of the civil
> war in China was beyond the control of the government of the United
> States. Nothing that this country did or could have done within the reason-
> able limits of its capabilities could have changed that result; nothing that was
> left undone by this country has contributed to it. It was the product of

internal Chinese forces, forces which this country tried to influence but could not. A decision was arrived at within China, if only a decision by default.[39]

The critics of United States policy were necessarily more diverse in their views than were the defenders, and generalizations concerning them are subject to many qualifications and exceptions. This is no less true of the anti-Chiang than of the pro-Chiang critics. In general, however, the anti-Chiang critics of American policy were inclined to accept the view that the outcome in China was the result of a decision made in China. But they also believed that United States policy had influenced that decision. One such view was expressed by Owen Lattimore:

My . . . view is that the policy we attempted to carry out in China was the right policy, and that it might have succeeded if we had at the same time favored and promoted a more rapid rate of change in the rest of Asia—if policy in China had been part of a uniform and rapid evolutionary process of change in colonial Asia.[40]

Other anti-Chiang critics felt that American actions *inside* China had affected more directly the result. According to this view, only full-scale military aid from the United States would have enabled Chiang to retain his dominant position in China. But since they also believed that direct American military action to maintain Chiang in power would destroy China's independence, they were unwilling to adopt such a policy even if it were "within the reasonable limits of [American] capabilities." These critics hoped, on the other hand, that Chiang's influence (which they believed would be pro-America) could be preserved in a coalition government. This objective led them to support American efforts to effect a compromise between the Kuomintang and Communist forces.

The primary fear of those holding this point of view was that an overeager American desire to extend aid would only deter Chiang from undertaking the necessary political and economic reforms and would encourage him not to make the concessions necessary for a compromise with the Communists. To this group, American aid should have been used as a weapon to preserve Chiang's influence in moderate form, not to maintain him in undisputed power. The chief weakness in American policy, they felt, was that the United States had become, in fact, too closely identified with the Kuomintang regime; that it had been too eager to grant Chiang's requests

for material support; and that this policy had resulted in unneces-
sarily alienating and antagonizing the Chinese Communists in the
face of overwhelming evidence that they could not be prevented
from securing political power. In the view of the anti-Chiang critics,
this weakness was intensified, perhaps even caused, by the constant
pressure placed on the Executive by the pro-Chiang opponents of
American policy to give more aid to the Nationalist Government.

The third general evaluation of American China policy—that of
the pro-Chiang critics—assumed that a China independent of Russia
was essential to the security of the United States. It also assumed that
a Communist China, or a China in which the Communists held
significant power, meant a Russian-controlled China. Having begun
with these assumptions, no excuse for failure to prevent the Communists from gaining political control in China could be accepted. The
proponents of this point of view were not dissuaded by the possibility that United States intervention against the Communists might
itself lead to the loss of Chinese independence. Communist conquest
meant—to them—the loss of Chinese independence in any case, and
it also meant the eventual Communist conquest of the United States.
The counterargument that a Communist victory in China did not
necessarily mean the loss of Chinese independence nor the isolation
and eventual conquest of the United States was a dangerous illusion
from this point of view. The very fact that such a result was possible
made it imperative that the United States use any means available to
prevent the Communist victory. In addition, the replacement of the
Nationalist with a Communist Government in China was viewed as
a military impossibility which could therefore be explained only as
the result of an inexcusable breach of faith by the American officials
who were responsible for policy in China while this debacle was
taking place.

This view of American policy in China is well illustrated by the
title of an article which appeared in *The China Monthly* at the end
of 1947. The article, entitled "The United States Sells China Down
the Amur," argued that China's difficulties were the result of American betrayal of the government of Chiang Kai-shek in the face of
Soviet aggression.[41] The argument was summarized in more succinct
fashion by Alfred Kohlberg in the same publication a few months
later.

According to the greatest living American, the question constantly asked
him is, "How did we get in such a mess 2½ years after our unconditional

victories over every foreign enemy? Was it because of stupidity or treason?" To which his answer is, "Both, stupidity at the top—treason just below."[42]

This point of view was made to order for the Chinese Nationalist Government. It could argue conclusively that the mere fact that the Chinese Communists had won the initial round could not, on the basis of these assumptions, be considered final. So long as there was a substantial body of Chinese resistance in being, it was argued, the United States had nothing to lose by supporting that resistance with all available means. And finally, since Chiang's government represented the only active opposition to the Chinese Communists, it could serve as a rallying point for all those Americans who held this attitude.

All three of the views outlined above had been clearly formulated and publicly espoused prior to the final catastrophe in America's relations with China. The primary question was which one would be given the most sympathetic hearing by the American people—on which explanation would the United States Government ultimately rely as the basis for its policy toward the Chinese People's Republic. Certainly the tendency to accept the most extreme explanation increased in direct ratio to the rise in emotional tension which resulted from the apparent increase in the danger to the United States from international communism. That tendency was heightened by the fact that the extreme view was consistently propagandized by the organized inner "core" of the China lobby, and that the propaganda, as the foregoing discussion shows, fell on fertile ground.

Recognition of the relationship of predisposition to the effectiveness of propaganda is a constantly recurring theme in the literature on the subject of public opinion and propaganda. The theme is implicit throughout Lippmann's work on public opinion.[43] Leonard Doob has stated explicitly the importance of existing attitudes to the successful completion of a propaganda campaign:

> In short, the process of the "formation of attitudes" through suggestion is also dependent upon pre-existing attitudes within the mental field; the "newness" of the attitude exists only to the extent that an integration differs from its parts.
> . . . It is clear that suggestion results from the manipulation of stimulus-situations in such a way that, through the consequent arousal of pre-existing, related attitudes there occurs within the mental field a new integration which would not have occurred under different stimulus-situations.[44]

A more recent student of propaganda has enlisted the aid of the psychologists to "demonstrate the great impact of value-related items like interest and already existing attitudes on the acquisition of information by people."[45] More specifically, Powell points out:

Hyman and Sheatsley [psychologists], also report that people seek information "congenial with their prior attitudes." . . . The inference is that persons with a certain attitude were more likely to expose themselves to information conforming to the attitude.[46]

The same observation was made several years earlier on the basis of somewhat less specific "laboratory" evidence. In a study devoted exclusively to propaganda, Edward L. Bernays remarked:

There has to be fertile ground for the leader and the idea to fall on. But the leader also has to have some vital seed to sow. To use another figure, a mutual need has to exist before either can become positively effective. Propaganda is of no use to the politician unless he has something to say which the public, consciously or unconsciously, wants to hear.[47]

In Bernay's opinion, the truth of propaganda affects considerably the tendency of the public to accept it. More recent students of the subject question that thesis and suggest that previously existing attitudes are a more important factor in the acceptance of propaganda than truth. One such doubter is the latest author quoted above:

Whether the truth will or will not be publicly accepted is no categorical matter. We suggest that truth will win under some, but not all conditions; that falsehood will be the victor under some but not all circumstances. For truth to prevail it must be a brand of truth consonant with the individual's predispositions and it must be susceptible of demonstration. The lie will have the advantage if it accords with the target audience's psychological system and if it cannot readily be disproved.[48]

The above generalizations concerning the relationship between propaganda and previously existing attitudes indicate why the China lobby was so successful in securing acceptance of its explanation of America's role in the Far East. That explanation was disseminated in an atmosphere of ignorance, confusion, and illusion. In fact, given the Communist victory, two factors were present which were virtually predestined to produce dissension among Americans over their China policy. The first factor was the absence of an informed understanding of events in China; the second was the failure to understand the conditions and limits under which the United States might have influenced those events.

The China lobby did not create these conditions. On the other hand, neither did the conditions preclude the possibility that the

American people would arrive at a rational understanding of what had occurred in China. The explanation ultimately accepted was the product of the mutual needs of the American public and the China lobby. In other words, there was a predisposition among the American people to accept an extreme explanation of events in China. But that extreme explanation had to be provided; the rationale had to be constructed, and the campaign to secure its acceptance had to be organized and financed. The China lobby performed these functions. The identity of the Chinese who served that cause, the manner in which they conducted their operation, and the identity and effectiveness of the Americans whom they drew to their support will be examined in the following section.

II THE CHINA LOBBY AND THE SPREAD OF ITS INFLUENCE

2 THE CHINA LOBBY IDENTIFIED

Official concern over the activities of Chinese propagandists in the United States can be traced back at least to 1941. By July of that year, according to Army historians, a myth concerning China had developed in Washington.[1] General Bruce Magruder confirmed the fact and indicated the nature of that myth shortly after his arrival in China in 1942. He informed the War Department that "Chinese and Sinophile propagandists had painted a grossly misleading picture of China's war effort, which if accepted at face value would gravely impair future American planning."[2]

Numerous additional references to propaganda and the use of pressure tactics on behalf of Chiang Kai-shek and General Claire Chennault indicate the extent of the awareness of Chinese pressures in Washington.[3] At least two Republican congressmen were concerned about the existence of such pressures as early as 1947. During the debate on President Truman's Greek-Turkish Aid proposal, Congressmen Howard Buffett of Nebraska and George Bender of Ohio expressed grave concern at the manner in which "the present Fascist Chinese government" is putting pressure on the Department of State and attempting *"to blackmail America."*[4]

Less than two years later, on January 29, 1949, the New York State Communist party seized on the issue and reported to its members that "a strong Chinese lobby is at work in Washington . . . trying to influence our Government authorities to continue support of the antidemocratic and unpopular Kuomintang elements."[5] Subsequent to this action by the Communist party, numerous articles discussing the China lobby appeared in American newspapers and periodicals. In August of 1949, *U.S. News & World Report* published information on the subject which prompted Representative Michael Mansfield to suggest that "the Lobby Investigating Committee . . . investigate the activities of the lobby now brazenly being conducted in the country in behalf of the National Government of China and certain personalities connected with it."[6] Mansfield's suggestion was not followed by Congress, but periodic manifestations of interest in the China lobby continued.*

---

* Several years later, Senator Harry Cain remarked on the Senate floor, "The fact is, as nearly as I can trace it, that the earliest demands for an investigation of the

This interest on the part of members of Congress reached a climax in 1951 during the hearings on the relief of General MacArthur from his command in Korea. On several occasions during these hearings, Senators Wayne Morse and Brian McMahon attempted to broaden the inquiry to include the activities of the China lobby.[7] Their questions led the *Congressional Quarterly* to publish a special issue presenting a "case study" of what the author described as "probably the most variously interpreted term now in the news."[8] The major reason for the confusion in interpreting the term emerged a few months later in what was to prove the most ambitious study of the China lobby undertaken up to that time. In an introduction to a two-issue series of articles in *The Reporter* magazine, Max Ascoli provided a description of the China lobby:

> The fall of China invigorated . . . a partnership between Chinese and American factions eagerly involved in the internal politics of each other's country. The Chinese partners are the agents of a government that can rule China again only if the United States destroys Mao's forces in an all-out war. The American partners are an ill-assorted lot—honest men deeply concerned with the plight of the Chinese people and of Chiang Kai-shek; fanatics possessed by the nightmare of a Communist conspiracy centering on some of America's highest leaders; and politicians who will stop at nothing in their hunt for power.
>
> This partnership of Chinese-American fear, ambition, and greed is the China Lobby—a nondescript tentacular affair that manages to use the craft of professional operators and the good will of well-intentioned amateurs.[9]

The view of the China lobby which thus emerges from the welter of charges and countercharges concerning its activities is one of considerable complexity. The one common denominator among the individuals and groups associated with the term "China lobby" appears to have been the desire to secure the backing and support of the United States for the government of Chiang Kai-shek. In its 1951 study of the China lobby, the *Congressional Quarterly* found "a wide assortment of interests—commercial, military, political, ideo-

China lobby originated with the Communist Party of the United States of America." From this, he concluded that others who had made charges concerning a China lobby "have been 'suckered' by the Communists from start to finish, or they have deliberately participated in a Communist maneuver." This argument is not supported by the facts presented above. See the *Congressional Record*, 82nd Cong, 2nd Sess., Vol. 98, Pt. 5 (June 6, 1952), p. 6759.

logical, religious—coming into the picture on one side or the other."[10]

The use of the term "lobby" in such a context is confusing, to say the least. The technical and legal definitions of the term normally apply to more closely knit and more highly organized groups than is apparently the case with the pro-Chiang forces in the United States.[11] Nevertheless, certain of the individuals, both Chinese and Americans, did act overtly as lobbyists. Certain of the groups also employed *paid* lobbyists to further their cause among members of Congress.

Thus, the individuals and organizations which emerge from the published information as associated with the China lobby can be divided into two distinct categories: (I) an inner "core" which consistently supported and pursued the interests of Chiang Kai-shek and the Kuomintang party, and (II) a kaleidoscopic array of affiliates who were increasingly allied to the Chiang regime in their sympathies. These two categories may be refined further to indicate more precisely their composition. Category I consisted of individuals and groups, both Chinese and American, whose personal interests were immediately dependent upon a continuation of American aid to Chiang. In some cases this dependence resulted from the fact that the individual's or organization's official position was contingent upon Chiang's remaining at the head of a recognized government. In other cases it rested upon purely financial considerations. For example, a paid agent would lose his income if Chiang lost his control of the recognized Chinese Government; or a business which depended on a contract or formal agreement with the government might be lost without Chiang in control. Category II, on the other hand, consisted of individuals and groups who supported Chiang Kai-shek for reasons of politics, ideology, or a particular set of assumptions regarding the requirements of American security.[12] Included in this group are those who merely used the China issue as an aid in their battle against the Roosevelt and Truman Administrations or the Democratic party, those for whom the dominant consideration was their fear of communism, and those who saw that the continuation of their religious efforts in China was dependent on the defeat of the Communist party.

The formation of the "inner core" of the China lobby began in the summer of 1940 when T. V. Soong, brother-in-law of Chiang Kai-shek, arrived in Washington. Soong held no official title, but his mission was clear—to secure American help for the Chinese Government which had held out alone for three years against the armed might of Japan. Soong, who shortly afterward became Chinese Foreign Minister, achieved only a modicum of success between then and V-J Day in securing financial aid for China. Department of State records show that $645 million in loans and $825.7 million in Lend-Lease aid went to China between 1940 and the war's end.[13] Of this amount, $500 million was in the form of a Treasury loan approved by Congress on February 7, 1942.[14] The United States retained no control over the disposition of these funds and was never able to secure information as to how they were spent.[15]

Following the passage of the Lend-Lease Act of 1941, Soong set up his own agency, called China Defense Supplies, Inc. It was patterned loosely after the British Purchasing Commission. Into this agency he brought William S. Youngman, Jr., who had been a general counsel for the Federal Power Commission. A number of other influential Americans, among them Whiting Willauer who had been a co-worker of Youngman's, and a few Chinese staffed China Defense Supplies. The Chinese were the "technical experts," the Americans the "advisers." In addition, Soong had developed close contacts with such high Administration officials as Harry Hopkins and Lauchlin Currie, administrative assistants to the President; Henry Morgenthau, Secretary of the Treasury; and journalists such as Henry Luce, Roy Howard, and Joseph Alsop.[16] Soong is reported to have once told a State Department official: "There is practically nothing that goes on in your government of which I do not learn within three days."[17]

Soong left the United States late in 1943. For a time he sought to smooth relations between Chiang and General Joseph Stilwell but achieved only slight and temporary success. For his efforts, Chiang deprived him for some months of all authority and placed him under house arrest.[18] In 1944, however, he was made Chinese Foreign Minister, a post which he held until 1947.[19] This position did not prevent his spending considerable time in the United States during the three years he held it. Moreover, Soong's absence from the United States was partially compensated for by the presence of his brother-in-law, H. H. Kung. Kung had been Minister of Finance in Chiang's government for the seven years prior to his resignation in 1944, at which time he was in the United States for medical treatment and "to handle economic and financial matters."[20]

During the period after Soong's departure from Washington there was far less need for persuasive Chinese in that city. In the White House was a President firmly convinced that China could be made a great power. Moreover, he had begun to send high-ranking American civilians to Chungking at regular intervals. Vice President Wallace, Wendell Willkie, and Donald M. Nelson all took turns at helping to convince Chiang that his interests were being served. In addition, some of the Americans whom Soong had courted in Washington were placed in strategic posts. Whiting Willauer moved from China Defense Supplies to a Foreign Economic Administration post which gave him supervision over both Lend-Lease to China and purchases from China. Joseph Alsop went to China on a Lend-Lease mission and stayed on as an assistant to General Chennault.[21]

During the last year of World War II and the succeeding two years, China's cause in the United States appeared to fare relatively well. True, there was strong criticism of the Kuomintang regime in substantial areas of the American press. But there were also powerful voices raised in defense of Chiang and his efforts, and substantial American aid was being extended to the Nationalist cause. Belief in Chiang's ultimate victory over the Communists increased as Kalgan and Yenan fell to his forces and American transport planes carried thousands of Nationalist troops into Manchuria. As late as September of 1947, Chiang told a Kuomintang conference that he had sufficient supplies for two more years of war against the Communists.[22]

Meanwhile, however, the Chinese did not neglect the staffing of their American offices. In 1944 a genial Chinese by the name of Chen Chih-mai arrived in the United States to take charge of propaganda.[23] Chen later became Minister Counselor of the Chinese Embassy and a key figure in the revived Chinese lobby. Among the propaganda organs maintained by the Chinese in the United States were a political party, two Chinese-language newspapers, a central news agency, and other outlets. All were supported, either directly or indirectly, by the Nationalist Government of China. The Kuomintang political party had itself long been registered as a foreign agent in the United States, under the name of the American Headquarters of the Kuomintang. The party was maintaining a main office in San Francisco with branch offices located in New York, San Antonio, Chicago, and Portland, Oregon. According to the 1951 report filed by the organization with the Department of Justice, there were approximately 3,825 party members in the United States.[24] The purpose of the party, according to this report, was "to secure and maintain interest of Chinese residents of the U.S. to aid and further the aims of the Central Executive Committee of the Kuomintang."[25] Income was derived principally from property rental, membership dues, and loans. Both income and expenditures amounted to about $18,000 during 1950, an increase of about $15,000 over the 1943–1944 period. Income for 1950 was augmented by a contribution, the source and amount of which are not revealed.

The Kuomintang party maintained two Chinese-language newspapers in the United States as its agents. They were not self-supporting and were partially subsidized by the party. Both papers stated that their purpose was to serve as outlets for the Chinese Nationalist point of view. One of the papers, *The Young China,* showed contributions from the Kuomintang during 1946 and 1947 of $4,830, and income from subscriptions and advertising from March, 1947, to February, 1948, of $71,473. The second paper, the *Chinese Nationalist Daily,* stated that its purpose was to serve as the "official organ" of the Kuomintang and answer all criticism of the Chinese Nationalist Government by newspaper editorials and articles, and "for other functions."[26] Its contributions from the Nationalist party amounted to $10,530 from 1944 to April, 1948.

Another agent of the Chinese Nationalist Government was its official information office, the Chinese News Service. From its headquarters in New York City, the News Service controlled offices in San Francisco, Chicago, and Washington. The functions of the agency included "dissemination of news and information through press releases, including *This Week in Free China,* and a fortnightly reference survey, *American Press Opinion.*"[27] Its operations in the United States were under the direct supervision of the Ministry of Information, Executive Yuan, Nationalist Government of China. Between 1945 and 1951, the Chinese News Service listed total expenditures of $1,114,355. A peak figure of $279,681 was listed for 1946.[28]

Two other agencies which operated directly or indirectly under the Chinese Nationalist Government are of sufficient importance to mention. The first, operated directly under the Chinese Government as the "foreign principal," was the Central News Agency. This was a news-gathering agency wholly owned by the Chinese Nationalist Government. It sold no service in the United States and produced no revenue. Prior to 1949, it was financed by appropriations from the Minister of Finance of Nationalist China and received $31,000 per month to operate its Washington and New York offices.[29] Operating indirectly under the Nationalist Government was a photo sales agency which listed the Chinese News Agency as its foreign principal. The agency, known as Paul Guillumette, Inc., operated on a contract basis for the Chinese News Service in the sale of photographs and films on China to American newspapers and other publications. The report filed by this agency indicated that the sales commissions were split between the photo agency and the News Service on a 50 per cent basis.[30]

During the period covered by these registrations, other Chinese arrived in the United States and took up the cause of securing more aid for Chiang. By mid-1948, H. H. Kung and his two sons, Louis and David, had taken up what is apparently permanent residence in the United States. During the same summer, the vice president of the Legislative Yuan (a Chinese governmental body), Chen Li-fu, made an extended visit to the United States. Chen Li-fu and his brother Chen Kuo-fu were the leaders of what was called the "CC Clique" in China.[31] The purpose of Chen Li-fu's visit to the United States was reported to be to attend a moral rearmament conference and to study American democratic institutions.[32] He had, however, formerly been Minister of Education in China, and the evidence would indicate that his chief reason for a trip to the United States was his interest in Chinese who were students in American schools. The Nationalist Government also employed a Dr. Mong Shou-ch'un as an inspector of educational facilities in the United States. Dr. Mong, however, had been carried on the Department of Justice foreign-agent list since 1945. In his supplementary report of May, 1951, he listed as his foreign principals Dr. Chen Li-fu and General Ho Ying-ch'in,[33] also a member of the CC Clique.[34] In this connection, it is perhaps of some significance that Article 14 of the "Rules and Regulations for Chinese Students Abroad" requires:

All the thoughts and deeds of the self-supporting students residing abroad must absolutely be subject to the direction and control of the Superintendent of Students and the Embassy. If their words are found to be contrary to the *San Min Chu I* [the three political principles of the Kuomintang] or their actions are irregular, they shall be . . . summarily recalled to China.[35]

Chen, however, was also interested in other things. He is reported to have presented a letter of introduction from Chiang Kai-shek to Governor Thomas E. Dewey who was then making his second race for the Presidency.[36] After his return to Shanghai, the following was published in the newspaper *Sin Wen Tien Ti:*

It seems absolutely certain that Governor Dewey will be elected President of the United States . . . According to Vice-President Chen Li-fu, should Dewey be elected, extraordinary measures will be taken toward giving military aid to China.[37]

It is clear from the above that prior to the 1948 elections the activities of the Chinese were largely confined to the ordinary diplomatic methods for securing financial and military aid from the United States. The legitimacy of the use to which American financial aid was sometimes put, however, has frequently been questioned. One incident which illustrates this point occurred in connection with the shipment of gold reserves to China early in the war. The gold was shipped as part of the $500 million Treasury loan made to Chungking in 1942.[38] Most of this money was apparently sold on the Chinese black market. A "Memorandum to President Roosevelt from Secretary of the Treasury Morgenthau," dated December 18, 1943, indicates the purpose of the aid and the result achieved:

The Chinese Government issued and sold dollar securities for yuan, setting aside $200 million of the aid granted by this country for the redemption of the securities. (These securities were sold at exorbitant profit to buyers . . .). I believe that the program made no significant contribution to the control of inflation.
. . . China could use these funds [that is, those still available] in selling gold or dollar assets for yuan, although in my opinion such schemes in the past have had little effect except to give additional profits to insiders, speculators and hoarders. . . .[39]

The identity of the "insiders, speculators and hoarders" who profited from this bonanza of American aid funds is still a matter of considerable speculation. Reports that T. V. Soong, H. H. Kung, and their families invested heavily and profited accordingly have circulated freely in the United States.[40] In addition, there have been repeated charges that some of these profits came back to the United States to be used in securing more aid for China.[41]

Dewey's defeat in the 1948 election presented the Chinese Nationalists with a serious problem. This was especially true when, almost immediately following the elections, the Truman Administration began a serious reappraisal of the entire program of aid to Chiang's government.[42] These developments were certainly partly responsible for the return of Madame Chiang Kai-shek to Washington on December 1, 1948.[43] They were also responsible for the revision and expansion of the China lobby which took place in the succeeding few months. From this time on, the personnel of the China lobby and the categories to which they belonged can be much more readily identified.

Madame Chiang apparently was responsible for the initial reorganization and expansion of Chiang's lobbying apparatus in the United States.[44] Most of her work was done in the Riverdale section of the Bronx, New York City. There, in the home of her brother-in-law, H. H. Kung, Madame Chiang held "weekly strategy meetings" with various groups of Chinese who could operate effectively in the arena of American politics.[45] The Chinese were either past or present holders of official positions in the Nationalist Government or possessed large private fortunes. In many cases one Chinese offered both advantages. According to one writer, the men who attended these sessions fell into two main groups. One, to which H. H. Kung and Madame Chiang's brother, T. V. Soong, belonged, "operated in and from New York and included men of means rather than government officials; the other, which worked in Washington, was composed of Chiang's most trusted chiefs of mission."[46] Chiang's mission included K. H. Yu, Chinese delegate to the International Bank; General Peter T. K. Pee, military attaché of the Chinese Embassy; General P. T. Mow, head of the procurement office of the Chinese Air Force; W. K. Li (Lee), Chinese representative on the Far Eastern Commission; and Chen Chih-mai, minister-counselor of the embassy.[47]

Chiang Kai-shek himself stepped down from the Presidency of China on January 21, 1949, and his position was taken by the Vice President, Li Tsung-jen. Li was hampered from the beginning by the necessity of retaining officials whose primary loyalty remained with Chiang. Dr. Sun Fo, who had become Prime Minister, headed a faction which moved many of the government offices to Canton and refused to cooperate with the Acting President.[48] On February 20th Ambassador John Leighton Stuart reported to Washington that Chiang "is already being influenced . . . by arguments of his indispensability from a small group of die-hard supporters whose motives are not entirely disinterested." "Meanwhile," he reported, "the Generalissimo is interfering in military affairs."[49] On April 4th the American consul general at Shanghai reported that "the Generalissimo, though outwardly cooperating [with the new government], is maintaining in effect independent political and military authority."[50]

With this situation existing in China, Madame Chiang, the embassy staff, and other chiefs of mission continued to report directly to Chiang Kai-shek. In mid-1949, the reports were placed on a more formal basis under arrangements which made it possible to bypass the embassy. Chiang was notified of the new system in a cable from his chiefs of mission, dated June 22nd:

. . . A summary report will be made once a week. If there is anything urgent, it will be wired as the occasion arises. The subject matter will be mainly reports and analysis of international current events. Hereafter such reports will be encoded and decoded by the Air Force office. It is intended not to sign them by name but to put the word "official" at the end. If you have any instructions about this matter please wire as the occasion arises.*

Later cables, some of which will be quoted below, show that in reality the reports deal almost exclusively with political develop-

---

* This is an excerpt from the first of a series of cables sent from Chiang's representatives in the United States to Chiang Kai-shek. The cables were made public as a result of the defection of one of the group, Gen. P. T. Mow, from the Nationalist cause. One version of the cables was ultimately inserted in the *Congressional Record,* 82nd Cong., 2nd Sess., Vol. 95, Pt. 5 (June 6, 1952) (pp. 6854–6871 in the Daily Record), by Senator Harry P. Cain. This was done in the course of a long speech in which Senator Cain attempted to show that "the China Lobby" was mostly the figment of an overworked imagination and the Communist conspiracy. According to information given to this author by a member of the Washington law firm of Roberts and McInnis, the original decoded version of the cables was turned over to that firm by General Mow. The cables were then translated by Chinese experts in the Library of Congress. In cooperation with Drew Pearson and Senator Wayne Morse, the contents of part of the cables were published. Senator Morse then inserted part of that version into the *Congressional Record, ibid.* (April 10, 1952), pp. 4021–4023. Following Morse's speech, Chen and Pee, two of Chiang's loyal employees, wrote to Morse seeking to cast doubt on the authenticity and source of the cables. Morse inserted that letter, together with a reply from Mow's attorney, William A. Roberts, into the *Record, ibid.* (April 16, 1952), p. 4073. In their letter to Morse, the Chinese had offered to allow him to examine the entire sequence of cables which they maintained had been sent by Mow alone—not to Chiang, but to his secretary, H. T. Chou. In consequence of this offer, Cain secured an English translation of the cable file and inserted it into the *Record.* Comparison of the translation made by Library of Congress personnel and the translation supplied to Senator Cain shows substantial differences in some cases. The differences, however, are more in the bluntness of the language than in the meaning. Furthermore, either version shows clearly that the cables were sent to Chiang, that they were not sent by Mow alone, and that they represent a clear effort to bypass the embassy. Why Chen and Pee should have misrepresented the content and source of the cables in their letter to Morse and then proved their misrepresentation by turning over the cables to Cain remains a mystery. (Hereinafter, these cables will be cited as "Cable, Chinese agents to Chiang, date.")

ments in the United States and their effects on American attitudes and policies toward the Chiang regime. The immediate reason for arranging direct reports to bypass the embassy arose because of the position of Kan Chieh-hou in the United States and his relations with Ambassador Koo, who had been appointed by Chiang Kai-shek. Kan was Li's personal representative in the United States. In the middle of 1949, he was seeking American aid to bolster the Acting President in his two-front battle with the Kuomintang on the one hand and with the Chinese Communists on the other. Chiang's loyal representatives apparently were not sure that Koo could be trusted in the struggle between Chiang and Li, and therefore sought an alternative means of communication. This doubt is indicated in a paragraph from the first report made by the group:

2. Kan Chieh-hou, accompanied by Ambassador Koo, went to see Marshall and Acting Secretary Webb. On the 22nd [he] visited President Truman, and had a meeting with Senator McCarran, but has not called in reporters. All quarters feel that his position is not clear.[51]

The possibility that Li might constitute a danger to Chiang's relationships in the United States was the subject of a message of November 28, 1949, a portion of which read:

It is said by Representative Judd that the Department of State may express to Kan Chieh-hou that if Li can get rid of the old corrupt forces and is in control of both military and political power, America will give him assistance. The idea is to deal a blow to the Chinese President.[52]

Because of this schism in Chinese governmental circles and the chain of circumstances which resulted in publication of the cables between Chiang and his agents in the United States, much information concerning the operations of the China lobby which would otherwise be very difficult to document is available. It should be kept in mind, however, that many of the agents of foreign governments are not required to make reports and their activities are therefore relatively safe from public scrutiny. One writer, remarking on the Attorney General's account of the administration of the Foreign Agents Registration Act, has noted some of the difficulties:[53]

The Department of Justice reports on the activities of only registered agents of foreign principals; we can only guess what the unregistered agents do. There are those who are either exempt by the law as duly accredited diplomatic and consular officers; foreign government officials; private businessmen in bona fide trades; fund raisers for foreign charitable causes; and persons active in religious, scholastic, academic, scientific or artistic purposes. There may be also some agents not entitled to exemption who fail to register for reasons of their own. There is no control of propaganda activities emanating from abroad through direct dissemination of information by mail and via the radio.[54]

Among other Chinese members of the post-1948 China lobby in Category I, but who appear to have been exempt from registration as foreign agents, were two sons of H. H. Kung. The older son, David, was reported to be the family financier after the retirement of his father. To that end, he was made joint managing director of the Central Trust Company in China early in World War II. In 1952 he was reported to be the largest stockholder in the Yangtze Trading Corporation, a Chinese company doing business in the United States.[55] The younger, and more active Kung son, Louis, is generally known as "the Major." For a number of years he was officially attached to the Chinese Military Staff Committee at the United Nations. He was also at one time a "technical adviser" to the Chinese Air Force in Washington. Under this diplomatic protection, "Major" Kung is reported to have been an important "courier" and "paymaster" for other Chinese agents.[56]

Many of the individual Chinese who served the cause of Chiang Kai-shek and the Kuomintang in the period prior to the election of 1948 obviously continued to function in the later period. The same is true of a number of business firms and other organizations. Thus, most of the registered information and education agencies of the Chinese Government continued their activities. Other organizations, on the other hand, did not come into existence until after the beginning of 1949. Three business firms which were registered either directly or indirectly fall into the former category. All three were corporations which were wholly owned by the Nationalist Government of China.

The first, the Universal Trading Corporation, was engaged in efforts to promote trade between the United States and Nationalist China. The second, the Chinese Oil Corporation, was interested in the procurement and export of petroleum products.[57] The third firm, the Bank of China, was never registered directly. The New York City branch of that bank, however, employed a public-relations firm as its agent in 1950, and in that manner came to be listed under the foreign-agent registrations. There were, in the United States, several branches of the Bank of China. They served an important function in all Chinese Government operations in the United States and other foreign countries. The seizure of the bank's home office in Shanghai by the Communists constituted a real threat to the continued operation of the Nationalist Government. It was that threat which led to the employment of a publicity agent by the New York Branch. As a Chinese business firm, however, it was not necessary for the bank itself to register as a foreign agent.[58]

The exemption of Chinese businesses and governmental agencies from the registration requirements of the Foreign Agents Registration Act did not apply to their American agents—either as individuals or as organized groups. Consequently, between 1942 and 1951 a total of eighteen agents for Nationalist China were registered in the United States. Of this total, ten were active in 1951.[59] Most of these agents were organizations employing staffs of varying sizes. A few were individual registrants.

Among the most important of the individuals was William J. Goodwin, a former member of the old Christian Front. Goodwin ran for Congress in 1936 with the support of Father Charles E. Coughlin's Social Justice movement, and for mayor of New York on the American Rock party ticket in 1941. In 1944 he became treasurer of the American Democratic National Committee which opposed Roosevelt's fourth-term candidacy. He also claimed credit for helping bring about the Republican congressional election victory of 1946.[60] On April 9, 1948, Goodwin registered under the Foreign Agents Registration Act as an agent for the National Resources Commission of China. His contract called for a salary of $30,000 for one year plus expenses. Expenses for the year, which terminated March 31, 1949, amounted to $22,857.[61] The following July, Goodwin again registered as an agent of the Government of the Republic of China through the Chinese News Service at a salary of $25,000 plus expenses of $9,776. In registering for the National Resources Commission of China, Goodwin stated that he had

. . . arranged meetings between Chinese Government representatives and businessmen, bankers, newspaper men, legislators and other leading citizens with a view to increasing their interest in the need for developing China as a future market for American business and also with a view to getting help from the U.S. for the Chinese Nationalist Government to establish stability. . . .[62]

In his job with the Chinese News Service, Goodwin's activities were directed

. . . toward presenting to the American public the viewpoint of Nationalist China, including a rebuttal of Communist propaganda which gained credence through constant repetition wittingly or unwittingly by newspapers and some government representatives [sic]. To this end I arranged meetings between Chinese Government representatives and newspapermen and members of Congress. Also I published letters—gave out interviews—and made a few speeches.[63]

The relationship between Chiang's official agents and Goodwin is clearly shown by comments in two cables sent in July and August of 1949. In July, Chiang was told:

Goodwin wants to go on in a positive manner with the work already begun. Key men in both the Republican and Democratic parties intend to support nonrecognition of the Chinese Communists, and also want to study further aid plans.*

Ten days later Goodwin's work again came in for comment:

At present the Democratic leaders fully realize the possible errors by the administration in their [policy] toward the Chinese Communists. The work of Miller and Goodwin has been to promote this realization, paying particular attention to [party] leaders, and at the same time seeking to avoid a party split and [the issuance of] unconsidered and extreme statements.†

Also registered as individual agents of the Chinese were Lester Knox Little, who filed in 1950 as a special adviser to C. K. Yen, Minister of Finance in the Nationalist Government, and John William Fleming, an export adviser and economic analyst for the Chinese Petroleum Corporation. Little was Nationalist Inspector General of Chinese Customs from July, 1943, until he became Yen's adviser. During the period of his employment for Yen, for which he received $1,000 per month, Little also served on the Economic Cooperation Administration's Advisory Committee on Underdeveloped Areas and as Chief of Customs Mission for the Allied Military Government in Japan.[64]

Among the business firms which served as agents of the Chinese

---

* Cable, Chinese agents to Chiang, June 22, 1949. An interesting variation of the Chinese-supplied translation of this cable is provided in a translation made by Library of Congress personnel. In the latter translation, it was Goodwin who was receiving the support of the leaders of both parties.

† Cable, Chinese agents to Chiang, August 1, 1949. (Bracketed interlineations in original translation from Chinese Embassy.) The Miller mentioned in this report was probably J. Paul Marshall, a Washington, D.C., attorney who was registered under the Federal Regulation of Lobbying Act as an employee of Goodwin, evidently an error in translation.

Nationalist Government, two were of special significance to the inner core of the China lobby. Foremost among the registered firms was an American public-relations company called Allied Syndicates, Inc., which registered in 1950 as an agent of the New York City branch of the Bank of China. According to its registration statement, the activities of Allied Syndicates for the Bank of China covered the "entire gamut of the public relations field."[65] For these activities, the firm received the sum of $50,000 in fees and $10,000 for expenses, plus reimbursement for a $17,500 fee paid to the Washington law firm of Sullivan, Bernard and Shea. The law firm was called in by Allied Syndicates at the request of the Bank of China "to provide legal counsel on certain problems."[66] The public-relations firm reported in its registration statement that one of its principal methods of "combating Communist propaganda" was "through 'conversations' with representatives of all forms of information media as well as civic organization executives." In addition, "American government officials were polled as to views on American policy and intervention in China, American public opinion in relation to China was analyzed and information on the Chinese situation was gathered through the public press and radio."[67] Included in the expenses paid out of the $10,000 allotment from the Bank of China were $3,703 in bills from the Mayflower, Statler, and Carlton hotels of Washington, D.C.; $1,308 for travel by American Airlines, and $554 for long-distance telephone calls.[68]

The job for which Allied Syndicates was hired by the Bank of China was described for one reporter by the founder and head of the firm, David B. Charnay. According to this report, Charnay described his efforts as a "straight publicity job."[69] The purpose "was to prevent the recognition of the Chinese Communist government and the consequent freezing, for that government's benefit, of the Bank of China's assets in this country." The methods used included "getting editors and reporters interested in the mistreatment of Americans by the Chinese Communists, particularly in the cases of captured Marines and Consul Angus Ward." Mr. Charnay also "set up the broadcast of Mme. Chiang Kai-shek's dramatic farewell to America in 1950 and was one of those who recommended Chiang's offer of Nationalist troops for Korea."[70]

The second business firm was never registered as an agent of the Chinese Government. It was apparently exempt from registration under the provisions of the law.[71] The firm, usually known as CIC, was established under the name of Commerce International (China), Inc. It was the principal operating subsidiary of a parent organization, Commerce International Corporation. CIC was apparently the successor to T. V. Soong's old China Defense Supplies, Inc., and served as the designated contractor for the Board of Supplies, Executive Yuan, Republic of China. Information on the origin and purpose of CIC is rather sketchy, but it appears that the China branch existed primarily for the purpose of serving in this contractual capacity with Chiang's military forces. Business relations between CIC and General C. J. Chou (Chiang's chief of staff and Air Force head) were established at least as early as 1949, after which CIC continued to be a major supplier of munitions, planes, and gasoline for the Formosa Government. Its continuing interest in maintaining American recognition of that government lay in the fact that CIC was making a substantial profit from these supplies. The methods used by CIC will become clearer shortly.[72]

The foregoing account of the personnel and organizations employed by the Chinese in the United States for lobbying purposes shows how their activities were directed toward two major goals. The first, of primary interest in the earlier period, was to secure increasing financial aid. But in many cases the interest of particular Chinese—and the Americans they employed—was directed more toward self-enrichment than toward improving the economic condition of China. The second goal, of increasing importance after the victory of the Communists on the mainland, was to prevent United States recognition of the Communist Government, and the consequent passing of Chinese assets in the United States to the control of that government. Even then, the first goal continued to be of importance, partly as a means of maintaining the position of Chiang and his party, partly as a means of preventing American recognition of the Mao regime. The defection of one of Chiang's most trusted chiefs of mission provides an excellent illustration of one instance in which funds from American sources were siphoned off into private accounts while at the same time they were being used to attract more funds.

On August 21, 1951, the Chinese Nationalist Government on Formosa accused their Air Force representative in Washington of having failed to account for almost twenty million dollars in Chinese funds and ordered him and his aide to return to Formosa.[73] At the office in the United States. The order to close the office had actually been issued on May 1st or earlier, but it was not announced by Taipei until August 21st.[74] The Chinese representatives concerned were Lieutenant General P. T. Mow and his executive assistant, Colonel Hsiang Wei-hsian.

Announcement of the Chinese Nationalist order was made by a government spokesman, Shen Chang-huan, stating these charges against General Mow:

Lack of a clear statement of funds used for buying military equipment; dereliction of duties, impeding the Air Force's fighting power; espousing the cause of "disloyal" staff members; refusal to hand over public funds, and undermining the government's prestige by spreading rumors.[75]

Colonel Hsiang immediately declared that the charges were false and began to make a series of countercharges against the Formosa regime. He charged specifically that his and General Mow's dismissal was "the result of reports sent to the Chinese Government by General Mow, as head of the Air Force office here in Washington, that certain Chinese officials on Formosa were misusing or seeking to misuse official funds."[76]

The situation thus created soon turned out to be a comedy of errors in which any attempt to separate fact from fancy only leads to greater confusion. Lack of an extradition treaty between the United States and Formosa allowed the American authorities to refuse a Chinese request that the two officials be extradited. General Mow, however, apparently fearing that he would be sent back for liquidation, went to Mexico. Colonel Hsiang and the Washington law firm of Roberts and McInnis were left to handle the situation in the United States. Ultimately, the Nationalist Government brought suit against Mow and Hsiang and a United States District Court ordered, in the absence of Mow, all funds and records, including seven million dollars in unspent money, turned over to the agents of Chiang Kai-shek.[77]

In the meantime, however, a sordid story of graft, corruption and attempted bribery had been released by the two accused Chinese. The most complete account of these stories, together with the available corroborative materials, appeared in a series of articles written for the Washington *Post* by Alfred Friendly. Seven of these articles have been inserted in the *Congressional Record* by Senator Wayne Morse of Oregon.[78]

According to Friendly, four departments of the United States Government investigated various aspects of the "morass of fraud and intrigue" which lay behind the recall of the two officers.[79] The investigations were primarily concerned with the operations of Commerce International (China), Inc. The efforts of General Mow and Colonel Hsiang to frustrate this company's plans were alleged to be the primary cause of their repudiation by the Formosa regime and Chiang Kai-shek.[80]

In the latter part of 1950, according to Friendly, Colonel Hsiang took evidence of CIC's (Commerce International China) operations to the staff of the Senate Preparedness Subcommittee. Under the direction of the subcommittee staff, he cooperated in developing the case and allowed himself to be used as a decoy to obtain further information. This inquiry was supervised by Donald C. Cook, vice chairman of the Securities and Exchange Commission, who acted as voluntary counsel for the subcommittee.[81] The inquiry disclosed that in its operations in the United States, Chiang Kai-shek's official contractor, CIC, had been involved in:

1. Forgery.
2. Fraudulent execution of Civil Aeronautics Administration Aircraft inspection reports.
3. Smuggling airplane parts out of the country without an export license.
4. Repeated misrepresentation of the facts to the American and British Governments to obtain export licenses.
5. Promiscuous slander of a large number of high Army and Air Force officers, and high civilian officials—including two departmental undersecretaries—with utterly false stories that some were accepting CIC bribes, and that others accorded it special extra legal favors.[82]

This author later examined affidavits and photostatic copies of letters written by Cook to Colonel Hsiang.[83] These documents implied that Colonel Hsiang was working to secure further evidence for the subcommittee staff. A request for further details on the investigation in September, 1953, however, was completely unsuccessful. Not only did the agency to which the records of the investigation had been entrusted deny that any such investigation had ever been made, but even Cook's position on the Securities and Exchange Commission was disputed. Presentation of positive evidence to the contrary changed neither the story nor the fixed expressions on the faces of the employees questioned. It might be added that an appointment arranged for the author through Senator Spessard Holland's office the previous day had given the agency warning of the subject of the interview.

In spite of repeated protests from General Mow, CIC continued to be a major supplier of munitions, planes, and gasoline for the Formosa Government. The purpose in using CIC for these purchases emerges clearly from the account given by Friendly. First, the company itself was reportedly making large profits. Second, there is a strong implication that General Chou was receiving a "kickback" for placing the orders through CIC. Third, and most important for the purposes of this inquiry, a group of retired American military and naval personnel appeared to be profiting handsomely.

The American military personnel became involved through the activities of a retired American admiral, Charles M. (Savvy) Cooke, Jr., former chief of staff to Fleet Admiral Ernest J. King. Admiral Cooke's last active service was as commander of the Seventh Fleet. During 1949 he wrote several articles for the Hearst press supporting the Nationalist cause. Late that year he went to Formosa as a correspondent for the International News Service. After his arrival in Formosa, Admiral Cooke found a way to act as an adviser to the generalissimo without being employed directly. Early in 1950, CIC arranged through Generalissimo and Madame Chiang Kai-shek to organize a group called the American Technical and Military Advisory Group to the Chinese Government. For this service, CIC received a fee of $750,000 a year. The company then employed Admiral Cooke to head the Military Advisory Group. Under his direction, a force of sixteen (one report places the number at thirty) additional retired American military personnel and a few civilians was assembled.[84]

The real importance of this group and its relations with CIC lay in its ability to affect the procurement of military supplies. The men employed and paid by CIC were the technical consultants to the Nationalists' armed forces. In that capacity they were in a position to channel contracts for supplies directly to CIC and permit them to bypass official Chinese procurement offices abroad. In addition, because they were retired American officers with experience in the Far East, they were also in a position to apply pressure in Washington to grant more money to Chiang with which to pay the exorbitant prices charged by their employer. The available records do not show whether Admiral Cooke or any of his group owned stock in CIC. Nor do they show whether the Americans were paid on a straight salary basis or on the basis of a commission on orders placed through CIC.

On October 19, 1951, Admiral Cooke made a special trip from Formosa to testify before the Senate subcommittee investigating the Institute of Pacific Relations. The burden of his testimony was a severe indictment of the United States Government for its failure to aid Chiang Kai-shek and to urge an immediate and substantial increase in that aid. The purpose of this subcommittee was "to investigate the administration of the Internal Security Act and other internal security laws." Since Admiral Cooke had no information on this subject, it appears that his sole purpose in testifying—and the committee's sole purpose in calling him—was to urge more American aid.[85] The service rendered to the Chinese by Admiral Cooke and William J. Goodwin illustrates the China lobby's need of Americans in carrying out its program.

But regardless of the efficiency with which the inner core was organized or the amount of money at its command, the goals which it pursued would have been impossible of attainment without large-scale indigenous support. Some such support was spontaneously available to the Chinese; the long history of American interest in China inevitably dictated that this should be so. On the other hand, the reaction of the American people to the corruption and inefficiency of the Nationalist Government during and after World War II tended to divert much of that support away from Chiang and dissipate it in other directions. No doubt it was partly their realization of this tendency which prompted the Chinese to hire public-relations specialists to promote their cause.

As has already been noted, Goodwin's responsibility was to present the viewpoint of Nationalist China to the American people and refute what he termed "Communist propaganda."[86] Goodwin also pushed these efforts among members of Congress. In an interview with Edward A. Harris of the St. Louis *Post-Dispatch* in 1950, Goodwin estimated that he had entertained about a hundred members of Congress a year. He thought he had converted about fifty of them to the cause of Nationalist China.[87] He also claims that he "laid the groundwork" for Senator Joseph R. McCarthy's charges of Communist infiltration in the State Department.[88] But whether or not Goodwin and other public-relations consultants hired by the Chinese were actually responsible for the policy of disseminating their propaganda through Americans, ample evidence of Chinese concern with the problem exists. Chiang's agents discussed the subject in their cables to him on several occasions.

Following the publication by the Department of State of the "White Paper" on China, the message of August 9th reported, "At present, these [sic] friendly to us feel that we must seize the opportunity to counterattack." The embassy then laid down the following program of action:

(a) Since the white paper is now receiving everyone's devoted attention, we must take this opportunity to immediately begin our itemized refutations, using the reputable and responsible people available to Your Excellency to publish the important documents not included in the white paper, such as the pressure on us during General Stilwell's time; the suggestions proposed by Currie and Lattimore while they were in China; General Marshall's request that we not occupy Chi-ih Feng and To Lun, and the consistent pressure put on us to make concessions to the Chinese Communists; and the promises made by the United States at the Cairo Conference and its subsequent violations; etc. [We should] bring up one point each week in order to keep the unbroken attention of the Americans. If we miss this opportunity, then the timely effect [of such a program will be lost].[89]

The effort to be made by the Chinese was clarified further in a telegram marked "secret" which bears the date of January 12, 1950. In that message, the author, who is not specifically identified, declared:

. . . there is no hope that the White House, Department of State, and the Democratic Party will consider further assistance to China in order to save the precarious situation. The only way for the Chinese Nationalists is to arouse popular opinion in an effort to make the authorities change their attitude. . . . The important people of the American Government waver during the negotiations. It looks as if they were cheating.

Acheson and Connally are utilizing an evil and detestable design. . . . They are probably trying to confuse the issues to achieve their objective.

According to my view, the present situation has reached a showdown. Sino-American diplomatic relations cannot be pursued in the customary way. We have to adopt unusual measure [sic]. I propose therefore that the entire documentation regarding our present negotiations be published at once in Washington so that the American people will know about our reasonable demands, and that there is absolutely no design to involve America in war. This will also show the mean negotiating measures and the breach of faith of the American authorities. This will produce a general understanding of the situation. Creation of American public opinion has not been based on reason but on documents. The above points have been carefully considered and discussed. We believe it is the only way to save the present situation.[90]

The nature of the documentation which the Chinese Embassy wanted to use for its propaganda in the United States had been made clear in a telegram of August 15, 1949:

As regards the policy set forth in the white paper, I feel we should immediately issue a supplementary document which would meet any refutations and criticisms [which might arise] point by point. . . . Every week one document can be *drawn up in rough draft* and released in Taipei after due consideration. I fear that the texts [of the documents concerned] sent to the United States by reporters in China were not necessarily complete and the manner of release was also restricted. . . . Prior to release we can arrange with [various] authors to select [suitable] reviews.

This telegram has been discussed with, and has the approval of, Ambassador Koo.[91]

The subjects which were suggested to Chiang as being suitable for propaganda purposes in the United States were precisely those which made up the lobby's propaganda line. All of these subjects involved placing the blame for Chiang's loss of power in China on the United States. As would be expected, however, many of the Americans who came to the support of Chiang and the Kuomintang did so on their own initiative or were persuaded to do so in ways which are not apparent or subject to verification. In some cases these Americans carried on their activities individually without associating with any organized group. In other instances they either joined existing groups or helped to form new organizations through which they could operate more effectively. A number of American publishers of books and periodicals also took up the cause of more firm and substantial support for Chiang Kai-shek and his government. Those American groups and individuals who thus affiliated with the China lobby can be divided for convenience into (1) private interests, and (2) individuals who held official or semiofficial positions.

An organization which was of foremost importance in the first classification operated throughout the war and postwar years as The China Monthly, Inc. The organization apparently existed for the sole purpose of publishing a periodical entitled *The China Monthly: The Truth About China.* The first issue appeared near the end of 1939. With the exception of a few issues which were missed, the magazine continued publication until 1951. Little information concerning the financial sources of *The China Monthly* is available. The semiannual statement of ownership, which is required by law, listed The China Monthly, Inc., as owner and publisher.[92] The editor, until his death in 1944, was the Right Reverend Monsignor G. Barry O'Toole. After that date the editorial responsibilities were assumed by Father Mark Tsai. Monsignor O'Toole was formerly rector of the Catholic University of Peking, but in 1944 he was listed as a professor of philosophy at the Catholic University of America, Washington, D.C.[93] In 1954 Father Tsai was regent at the Institute of Far Eastern Studies, Seton Hall University.[94] He later became head of a girls' school in Taiwan where he remained until his death.

The influence of *The China Monthly* was far greater than its relatively small circulation might indicate. It was probably unique among English-language American periodicals not under the direct control of the Chinese Nationalist Government in the consistency with which it denounced United States policy in China. In this regard, *The China Monthly* gave every appearance of being the official mouthpiece of the Chungking Government on matters which could not diplomatically be published in the official propaganda organs of that government. There is, however, no documented proof that this was true. On the other hand, the magazine was consistently at the forefront in every phase of pro-Chiang propaganda in the United States. In 1948 the editor claimed the distinction of having initiated the movement to brand as traitors Americans who were unsympathetic to Chiang:

The China Monthly was the first to distinguish between a loyal and disloyal citizen. While certain radio commentators and newspapers were as long as four years ago bitterly attacking the National Government of China and according high praise to the Chinese Communists, it was the first to point out that they were not speaking for America and that they did not have the best interests of America at heart. It unhesitatingly called them either misled-followers of Communistic ideologies or traitors to their country.[95]

Articles from *The China Monthly* frequently found their way into the *Congressional Record;*[96] it has been cited as a source of China lobby propaganda in congressional hearings,[97] and information which first appeared in that publication was often quoted again and again in other publications. No other publication in the United States seems to have forecast as accurately or as consistently the "line" which was later to be followed by Chiang's supporters in Congress as did *The China Monthly.* Finally, the magazine frequently served as the major organ for the dissemination of the views and attitudes of a number of Americans who were most prominently associated with the cause promoted by the China lobby.

One of the most bitter critics of United States policy in China who made frequent contributions to *The China Monthly* was a wealthy New York importer by the name of Alfred Kohlberg. Kohlberg's interest in China dates from his establishment of a textile manufacturing and exporting business in that country in the early 1920's.[98] His self-education in the aims and techniques of international Communism began, according to his own testimony, in 1944.[99] Shortly afterward, Kohlberg launched what was to prove a long-sustained attack on the Institute of Pacific Relations for what he alleged were pro-Communist activities.[100] Subsequently, from 1945 to 1950, Kohlberg employed the medium of *The China Monthly* for the publication of a dozen or more articles attacking American policy in China and those who supported it.[101] In addition, Kohlberg wrote hundreds of letters to members of Congress, Secretaries of State, the President, and newspaper and magazine editors. He traveled to China, Japan, and Washington, appeared five times before congressional committees, and subsidized at least two magazines.[102]

One of the magazines subsidized by Kohlberg, *Plain Talk*, can be classified among the business firms affiliated with the China lobby. While it is doubtful that it was a financially profitable venture, the origin of *Plain Talk* appears to have been closely associated with Kohlberg's desire to have a readily available vehicle for the dissemination of criticisms of American policy. The editor during its four-year span of life was Isaac Don Levine, the managing editor, Ralph De Toledano. Both have been well-known bitter critics of the Truman Administration.[103] Also, as will be seen later, many of the authors who wrote for *Plain Talk* were associated in other ways with the efforts made in the United States in behalf of Chiang and the Chinese Nationalists.

A number of other books and periodicals helped to create a more favorable climate of opinion toward the Chinese Nationalist Government in the United States. Foremost among the periodicals were *Collier's* and the *Saturday Evening Post* (after 1947); *Human Events*, a "weekly newsletter reporting from Washington on politics, business, labor and taxes";[104] *American Mercury; Reader's Digest; U.S. News & World Report; The New Leader; Life.* Other magazines carried numerous articles in the same vein, but those named have been most consistent in their support of Chiang. Certain newspapers were also consistent in their criticism of American policy and in their defense of the Chinese Government. Outstanding in this respect were the

New York *Journal-American*, which was often quoted in *The China Monthly;* the Washington *Times-Herald;* the *Examiner,* both Los Angeles and San Francisco; the Oakland *Tribune,* and the Manchester, N.H., *Union Leader.*[105] Among the book publishers, Henry Regnery and Devin-Adair have published a large percentage of the manuscripts most critical of the United States and most laudatory of the Nationalist Government of China.[106]

In addition to the publishing enterprises, a number of opinion-molding organizations took up the cause of the Chinese Nationalists. Among these organizations were several which were organized for the specific purpose of coordinating the existing support and creating additional support for more American aid to China. In other cases, already existing organizations took up the cause. In many instances the same individuals comprised, simultaneously, the major working force in several of the groups.

The most active of the organizations which were established for the specific purpose of promoting aid to China was the American China Policy Association. Established in early 1946 and operating under the leadership of Alfred Kohlberg, the ACPA soon surpassed all other organizations in the volume and directness of its attacks on United States policy in China. The association was apparently organized at the initiative of the late J. B. Powell, a former American correspondent in China, and Helen Loomis, a former missionary-teacher in China.[107] Kohlberg evidently joined the group soon after its founding and was made vice president and shortly thereafter chairman of the board.[108] Powell served as president of the association until his death in 1947. He was succeeded for one year by former Congresswoman Clare Boothe Luce, wife of the owner and publisher of *Time, Life,* and *Fortune* magazines. Following the tenure of Mrs. Luce, the office of president was filled by William Loeb, owner and publisher of the aforementioned Manchester, N.H., *Union Leader.* According to Kohlberg, the association was dedicated solely to the furthering of American interests:

. . . By resolution the American China Policy Association, Inc., limited its members to persons of American citizenship and provided that only Americans could be brought as guests to its Board meetings, so that America's interest, only, should be presented for consideration.[109]

From its creation until 1953, the American China Policy Association published a tremendous volume of literature in the form of letters, pamphlets, brochures, reprints of Communist directives, and statements of purpose, press releases, and book reviews. Most of these were prepared and published in the office of Alfred Kohlberg at 1 West Thirty-seventh Street, New York City, and carry that address on their headings. In fact, it is probably safe to say that the ACPA would hardly have made an impression outside its own membership had it not been for Kohlberg. Most of the literature issued by the organization was signed by him, although a few pieces were signed by Helen Loomis, the secretary-treasurer, and by William Loeb after he became president. Typical of the approach and attitude of the association is a press release of July 27, 1947, which accompanied the release of a letter to General Albert C. Wedemeyer on the eve of his departure for China on a mission for President Truman. Although not directly stated, many of the criticisms leveled at American policy by the ACPA are implied in the press release:

The statement to Lt. General Albert C. Wedemeyer, Ambassador to China, of which a photoplate reproduction is enclosed, was authorized by the Executive Committee of the American China Policy Association on July 17 and was mailed to General Wedemeyer the following day.

It is released for next Sunday so that the original will reach General Wedemeyer before the release date.

The statement of this Association urges General Wedemeyer to return to the traditional American policies supported by the United States in the Far East since 1899. It urges full implementation of the Open Door Policy and complete return to the policy enunciated by President Roosevelt in the note of Secretary Hull to Ambassador Nomura, November 26, 1941. It also urges that the pledges of President Roosevelt at Cairo be honored and that both our Government and the Soviet Union respect the pledges agreed to at Yalta and later spelled out in the Sino-Soviet agreements of August 14, 1945, which promised "to extend economic aid and military supplies only to the National Government."

The Association's statement proposes this line of policy as the only means of avoiding the continuance of Communist inspired rebellion in China which would inevitably drift into World War III.[110]

In addition to Kohlberg, the most active members of ACPA, in terms of writing and speaking on the China issue were Freda Utley, Irene Kuhn, Clare Boothe Luce, Max Eastman, Representative Walter H. Judd, Geraldine Fitch, the Reverend William R. Johnson, Isaac Don Levine, and Margaret Proctor Smith.[111] Others on the fifty-eight-member Board of Directors who contributed their time on behalf of the organization were Dr. Maurice William, a vice-president, Major General David P. Barrows, William Henry Cham-

berlain, George Creel, and Roscoe Pound. The Executive Committee was composed of a smaller number of the most active members.[112]

Two other organizations, established for the express purpose of
exerting pressure for greater American aid to China, operated—
somewhat intermittently—between 1949 and 1952. The first to be
organized was the China Emergency Committee in early March of
1949. It became inactive later in the same year. The committee was
registered under the Lobby Registration Act and included on its
National Advisory Council, Representative Walter H. Judd, Representative B. Carroll Reece of Tennessee, a fromer chairman of the
Republican National Committee, and Irene Kuhn of the American
China Policy Association. Chairman of the group and largely instrumental in its founding was Frederick C. McKee, a Pittsburgh indus-
trialist and philanthropist who has long been active in politics.[113]
McKee's active participation in groups interested in foreign-policy
questions dates back at least to 1938, at which time he served on the
executive committee of the American Committee for Non-Participa-
tion in Japanese Aggression. Since then, he has served on numerous
committees, including the American Association for the United Nations and Free World, Inc.[114]

Following the demise of the China Emergency Committee,
McKee helped to organize and became chairman pro tem of the
Committee to Defend America by Aiding Anti-Communist China.
Vice chairmen for the organization were Gen. William J. Donovan,
head of the wartime OSS; Charles Edison, former Governor of New
Jersey and former Secretary of the Navy; and Herbert Welch, New
York Episcopal Bishop. James G. Blaine, former director of United
China Relief, Inc., served as treasurer.[115]

Former Ambassador to Poland, Arthur Bliss Lane, David Dubinsky, James A. Farley, Jay Lovestone, Clare Boothe Luce, and Dr.
George A. Fitch were also on the Board of Directors of the Com-
mitte to Defend America. Dubinsky was president of the International Ladies Garment Workers Union, second vice president of the
AFL, and vice president of AFL's Free Trade Union Committee. The
president of the Free trade Union Committee was Matthew Woll
who was also on the executive committee of the American Jewish
League against Communism—of which Kohlberg was president.[116]
Lovestone was a New York labor leader and one time general
secretary of the Communist party of the United States. Dr. Fitch,

YMCA secretary and former deputy director of UNRRA in China, was also the husband of Geraldine Fitch who was on the Executive Committee of the American China Policy Association. Some measure of the degree of coordination between the Committee to Defend America and the American China Policy Association is indicated by the presence of ten persons of the ACPA's fifty-eight-member Board of Directors on the Committee to Defend America's fifty-one-member board.

An additional measure of the coordination between many of the groups which espoused the Chinese Nationalist cause is indicated by the extent to which pro-Chiang articles written by members of these two groups found their way into the publications of other organizations which took up that cause. For example, both Freda Utley and Edna Lonigan of the ACPA wrote issues of the *Economic Council Letter* published by the National Economic Council, Inc. Merwin K. Hart, president of NEC, frequently quoted Alfred Kohlberg and the publications of ACPA.

The Committee for Constitutional Government also served as an outlet for literature supporting the Chinese Nationalists and attacking United States policy in Asia. This group was organized in 1937 for the purpose of fighting Roosevelt's Supreme Court proposals. Since that time its literature has covered many national policy topics, mostly, however, domestic issues. It has what is perhaps the largest mailing list of any similar organization—reported to be around 350,-000 in 1950.[117] CCG literature sent out on special issues has run into millions of copies. Alfred Kohlberg was carried on the list of advisory members printed on its letterhead in 1951. Among the publications on China sent out by CCG in 1950–1953 were articles by Freda Utley, William R. Johnson, Robert B. Dresser, and John T. Flynn. At least two of the articles by Miss Utley were reprints of articles which first appeared in Kohlberg's magazine, *Plain Talk.* Another was a reprint of a *Human Events* article. These mailings from the Committee for Constitutional Government were sometimes in the form of special issues, sometimes in the regular publication, *Spotlight for the Nation.*

Another organization, which was closely associated with the Committee for Constitutional Government, distributed much of John T. Flynn's material, including reprints of his radio broadcasts. Called "America's Future, Inc.," pieces sent out by this organization were also included in CCG mailings and carried CCG advertising.

One of the primary targets of all these organizations has been the membership of Congress. Just how many have had their attitudes toward China substantially influenced by this propaganda would be difficult, if not impossible, to determine. The American China Policy Association has reported, however, that Senator Owen Brewster used Freda Utley's book *The China Story* as the basis of his "grilling of Acheson" during the MacArthur hearings.[118] Also, Louis Budenz has testified at some length concerning his relationship with Kohlberg, McCarthy, J. B. Mathews, contributing editor of *American Mercury,* and Robert Morris (who has frequently been used by the Republicans as counsel for committee investigations).[119] It has also been reported on numerous occasions that Kohlberg furnished much of the material for Senator McCarthy's attack on the State Department and the IPR.[120] These incidents will be examined in detail in later chapters. For the present, it is sufficient to note that the most ardent congressional supporters of aid to Generalissimo Chiang Kai-shek and his Nationalist forces have been Senators Owen Brewster (R., Maine), Styles Bridges (R., N.H.) who received a $1,000 campaign contribution from Kohlberg in 1948;[121] James O. Eastland (D., Miss.), Harry P. Cain (R., Wash.), Homer Ferguson (R., Mich.), Bourke B. Hickenlooper (R., Iowa), William F. Knowland (R., Calif.), Pat McCarran (D., Nev.), Joseph R. McCarthy (R., Wis.), H. Alexander Smith (R., N.J.), and Representatives O. K. Armstrong (R., Mo.), Walter H. Judd (R., Minn.), Joseph W. Martin, Jr. (R., Mass.), Lawrence H. Smith (R., Wis.), and John M. Vorys (R., Ohio).

The foregoing identification of the major sources of pro-Chinese Nationalist propaganda in the United States shows clearly that it was not the result of accidental or haphazard "shooting in the dark," but, rather, was a well-orchestrated dovetailing of the interests of the China lobby inner core with the political and social interests of domestic groups in America. The following chapters detail how the basic fear of communism, abroad and at home, enabled Chiang's agents and their American friends to exploit issues and events to marshall support for Chiang Kai-shek and attack those critical of his regime.

3 MAJOR ISSUES EXPLOITED BY THE CHINA LOBBY

The increasing victories of the Chinese Communists after 1947 presented the Kuomintang party with a problem of overriding importance. That problem was the absolute necessity that the Kuomintang retain some part of China under its control if it hoped to survive. Given this necessity, the primary foreign relations task of Chiang and his government was to regain the sympathy and support of the United States. In that undertaking, skillful utilization of the fears and illusions of Americans represented the difference between extinction and survival for the government of Chiang Kai-shek.

The intermediate goals were clear. First, it would be necessary to convince Americans that a strong and friendly China under Chiang Kai-shek was essential to their own security. Second, it would be necessary to instill among the American people a conviction that their representatives had failed to support Chiang to the desirable and necessary extent.

In pursuing these objectives, the Chinese who remained loyal to Chiang found a very useful tool in the American tendency to believe, when their hopes were not fulfilled, that they had been betrayed. In the postwar era, this American tendency found expression, for the most part, in fears of Communist infiltration. Consequently, certain events which occurred during the period in which Chiang's power was deteriorating were so exploited by the China lobby that they seemed to confirm those fears. The events which were thus exploited ranged from basic wartime policy decisions on strategy to the conviction of a former American official for perjury. Six such events will be discussed in this chapter. They will be taken up in the order of their occurrence for the sake of clarity. It should be borne in mind, however, that the greatest effect of the exploitation of these events occurred after the fall of China, which in many cases was several years after the occurrence of the events themselves.

These six events were: (1) the Yalta Agreement of 1945, (2) the Amerasia Affair, which broke in June of 1945, (3) the resignation of Ambassador Patrick J. Hurley in November of 1945, (4) the failure of the Marshall Mission in 1946 and 1947, (5) the "spy ring" revelations of the ex-Communists and the conviction of Alger Hiss, and (6) the war in Korea.

The Chinese and their American spokesmen continued after World War II to stress the importance of China to the security of the United States. Even after the defeat of Japan they continued to argue that the "Europe first" decision had been a fundamental mistake in policy. Meanwhile, however, new issues offering effective opportunities for exploitation arose. The first major incident involved a wartime policy agreement, made with Russia at the Yalta Conference in 1945.

The fundamental approach of the China lobby to the agreements made by President Roosevelt and Prime Minister Stalin at Yalta is epitomized in the phrase "the Yalta betrayal." A monograph which appeared under that title in 1953 fairly well sums up the gist of the argument in the concluding remarks on China:

> Consequently, our concessions of [Chinese] territory which did not even belong to us, besides being immoral and illegal, were based on ignorance and stupidity. There are those who believe that they were based on treacherous submission to the idols of the Communist world revolution.[1]

The author had already made it quite clear that he fully agreed with the latter group.

A great host of other writers have expressed the same sentiments even more bluntly. The attack on the Yalta Agreement was launched from Chinese sources shortly after the news of the conference was made public but many months before the text of the agreement was released. Significantly, the attack was based on the exclusion of Chiang Kai-shek from the conference and the assumption that therefore Roosevelt and Churchill had completely succumbed to all Stalin's demands.[2]

From this time until 1953, the attack on the concessions which were made to Stalin at Yalta was vigorously pressed. The opposition to that portion of the agreements which applied to China was relatively mild during the first two years. Nevertheless, some of the criticisms were forecasts of what was to come. A review of the buildup toward the climax, which came in 1951, is in order.

On May 15, 1946, a group of "65 leading Americans" released a statement which they called the "Manchurian Manifesto." Among those who signed the document were Admiral H. E. Yarnell, Congressman Walter H. Judd, Mrs. Clare Boothe Luce, Alfred Kohlberg, Henry R. Luce, and John B. Powell. The "Manifesto" charged:

> This agreement was not only made behind China's back, but at Yalta America was pledged to deliver the promised concessions in Manchuria and Mongolia to Soviet Russia, whether the Chinese Government agreed or not.

In addition, this statement argued that the Yalta Agreement was a direct violation of the pledge which President Roosevelt had previously made to Chiang at Cairo to restore to China all territories which Japan had taken by force, including Manchuria.[3] These charges were to be repeated, usually in almost the same words, over and over in the next few years.

Early in 1947, *The China Monthly* returned to the attack in an editorial which was entitled "The Sins of Yalta." The tone was still relatively mild as the editor declared, "Had not the late President Roosevelt and the former Prime Minister Winston Churchill themselves, without the knowledge, much less the consent of China, handed over Manchurian privileges and concessions to Stalin, Russia certainly would not now dare to exercise so exclusive a right over Dairen." He concluded that "Dairen is nothing but a sin of the Yalta Conference."[4]

The real attack on the agreements and results of Yalta was launched in the middle of 1947 by two of Chiang's staunchest American supporters. Kohlberg, in what he termed an attempt to find a reason for Roosevelt's action, declared that the President had "bought" Stalin's aid in the Pacific war out of pique with Chiang Kai-shek. Here is his explanation:

> . . . While their Nationalist brothers fought the Japanese, [in 1944] the [Chinese] Communists were increasing their attacks on the Government. This moment was chosen by President Roosevelt to demand that *the Government of China* as well as China's armies be put under the orders of General Stilwell. In case of refusal General Stilwell was authorized to threaten withdrawal of American forces and American lend-lease. . . . Chiang Kai-shek . . . refused, and Roosevelt had to back down and recall Stilwell. . . .
>
> President Roosevelt did not forget his rebuff and the following February at Yalta he offered Stalin, who had not requested it, control of the Manchurian railroads and possession of Port Arthur and Dairen. This was done in spite of the 1943 promises of Cairo. . . .[5]

This was to prove only the beginning of Kohlberg's attacks on the Administration's China policy. He was joined by many other Americans, as well as by their Chinese friends. One of the attacks, which supplemented that of Kohlberg, grew out of an article published in *Life* magazine by William C. Bullitt.[6] The article was made the subject of a lead editorial in *The China Monthly*.[7] The support which the Chinese were now getting from Americans emboldened them to add the charge of treason. Roosevelt and Churchill, declared the editorial, "were playing the part of traitors."[8] This statement by the editor of *The China Monthly* brought the line to be followed by the China lobby directly into the open. Thereafter, the terms "traitors" and "betrayal" became standard epithets with China lobby writers. A former American missionary to China, the Reverend William R. Johnson, carried the theme forward in the next issue of *The China Monthly*. Johnson repeated all the arguments noted above.

He then concluded this part of his argument with a question to which he gave his own answer:

How is it to be explained that in the brief period of 15 months between the issuance of the Cairo Declaration on December 1, 1943, and the Yalta agreement of February 11, 1945, America's China Policy was completely reversed from that of the restoration and defense of China's territorial integrity to the surrender to Russia in effect, of more than Japan had taken from China together with a pledge accepting for the United States the responsibility of forcing China to deliver all that was promised? . . . *First, the position to which America's China policy was secretly committed at Yalta was clearly foreshadowed in the Red Propaganda prior to the Yalta Conference: and second, there obviously had been and there still remains a coterie of the Communist front stealthily working within the State Department which participates in the briefing of Ambassadors and Presidents in Chinese Affairs. Thus they serve the purposes of our enemies rather than our own.* [9]

The betrayal theme was given added meaning in the article now under consideration. For Johnson: *"To force a coalition Government upon China is worse than folly. It is betrayal."*[10] This statement is indicative of the more extensive use which was to be made of the betrayal theme in the future. Any actions which were opposed by Chiang and his supporters were now to be classified as betrayal, appeasement of communism, and aid to the enemy. This had, of course, long been the approach of the Chinese toward any criticism of Chiang and the Chinese Government in the American press. It was only logical that it should be extended to official acts of the American Government.

The purpose of this characterization of American policy is amply demonstrated by an article published in June, 1948, written by Kohlberg, in which he listed "concessions" by the United States "since the infamous Yalta Conference." The reasons which he attributed to the "concessions" are more interesting in some cases than the concessions which he alleged.

First, Kohlberg argued that Manchuria was given to Russia "with a still secret clause giving them all Japanese military installations as reparations."

Second, he claimed that the northern half of Korea was given to Russia "so they could build a Korean Communist Government to take over."

Third, according to Kohlberg, the southern half of Sakhalin and the Kurile Islands were turned over to the Russians in order that they might "cut off American occupied Japan from the American Aleutian Islands."

Fourth, he alleged that one and one-half million dollars' worth of Lend-Lease materials were given to Russia so that she "could provide liberally for the Chinese and Korean Communist armies."[11]

Characterizations of the Yalta agreements similar to those made by Kohlberg continued to appear. Two pamphlets which were entirely devoted to presenting the viewpoint of the China lobby illustrate the techniques. The pamphlets were distributed by the Committee for Constitutional Government.[12] In the first case, the author asserted, "The notorious Yalta deal, which broke our promises to our Chinese Allies and delivered Manchuria to Bolshevism, reeked of duplicity."[13] The author of the second pamphlet used similar language:

As regards the present status of our China policy, its formulation and execution remains in the hands of those who shaped and have controlled it throughout this period of China's betrayal. . . .

This six years of effective American collaboration with the Kremlin and of studied blindness in the State Department to Moscow's growing encroachments upon China and the constantly increasing menace of millions of Soviet trained and equipped puppet forces, is only to be accounted for by accepting the facts of the guilty connivance of a top-ranking group of American saboteurs of our well-founded, long-held China Territorial Integrity Policy [sic].[14]

These reactions of pro-Chiang groups in the United States toward the agreements made at Yalta provided an almost irresistible explanation for America's postwar problems. Such an explanation, in the setting of American confusion regarding China, was simple, plausible, and almost impossible to disprove. China lobby interpretation of other events served to strengthen their explanation of Yalta, for the techniques used by the Chinese to secure "American support as an atonement for the betrayal at Yalta"[15] were not confined to attacks on the agreements made at that conference. Another incident, known as the Amerasia Affair, came to public attention a few months after the meeting at Yalta. An examination of the facts in this case is a necessary prerequisite to an understanding of the use made of it by the China lobby.

The first public knowledge of the Amerasia case came on the morning of June 7, 1945. During the preceding night, agents of the Federal Bureau of Investigation had arrested six suspects on a charge of "conspiracy to violate the Espionage Act."[16] The arrests were made as the result of several months' work on the part of the FBI and the Criminal Division of the Department of Justice.

The chain of events began in February of 1945, when an alert member of the Office of Strategic Services discovered a suspicious similarity between a restricted OSS document and an article which had just been published in a magazine called *Amerasia*.[17] The Federal Bureau of Investigation was called in to investigate the possibility that there was a leakage of information from certain government offices. After finding evidence of such leakage, the investigation was continued for approximately three months.[18]

Deeply involved in the leakage of information was the editor of *Amerasia,* Philip J. Jaffe. The magazine, described as "A Review of America and the Far East," was first published in March of 1937 by Amerasia, Inc.[19] Initially, Frederick V. Field owned 50 per cent of the stock and Jaffe 49 per cent of the stock of Amerasia, Inc.[20] On January 21, 1944, Amerasia, Inc., was legally dissolved, but publication of the magazine was continued on a fortnightly basis as a sole proprietorship under the editorial supervision of Kate L. Mitchell and Jaffe.[21] Field apparently severed all connection with *Amerasia* late in 1943 or early in 1944. The original purpose for publishing *Amerasia,* according to Field, was the lack of opportunity for the expression of opinion in the publications of the Institute of Pacific Relations. Field was then serving as executive secretary to the American Council of the IPR.[22]

. . . A number of us in our several years of work in the institute had developed certain ideas. We were interested in conclusions to be drawn from research as well as the research itself. One of the best ways to insure the institute itself, to insure it remained in the research field and avoided becoming political, was to establish an organization, and where we could blow our steam off outside the institute [sic].[23]

Both Jaffe and Miss Mitchell have been identified as Communists before congressional committees.[24] Miss Mitchell has denied the charges;[25] Jaffe refused before the Tydings Subcommittee to answer questions concerning his alleged Communist affiliations.[26] The magazine which they published was extremely anti-Chiang, highly critical of American policy in China, and to a considerable extent pro-Chinese Communist. Its circulation was small—somewhat under two thousand.

The FBI investigation produced clear evidence that Jaffe had established contacts in the Department of State, and perhaps other agencies of the government, through whom he was receiving "classified" information in the form of reports on the political, economic, and military situation in the Far East. Jaffe had apparently collected the reports for use in the publication of his magazine. The initial assumption of the FBI, however, was that there was a distinct possibility that they were being passed to foreign agents. Equipment found in the Amerasia offices gave rise to the belief that some of the documents were being reproduced for that purpose. It was largely these circumstances which led the FBI to undertake an investigation and a three-month surveillance of the suspects.

The arrest, on the night of June 6, 1945, of Jaffe and Miss Mitchell, two State Department employees, a naval officer, and a reporter, brought the case into the open. The State Department personnel were John Stewart Service, a Foreign Service officer who had returned from the Far East about two months prior to this date, and Emmanuel Larsen, who was at the time doing routine research in the Division of Far Eastern Affairs. The Naval officer, Lieutenant Andrew Roth, was serving as liaison officer between the Office of Naval Intelligence and the Department of State. Mark Gayn, a free-lance reporter, concluded the list.

The case was presented to a grand jury by the Department of Justice in August. Three of the defendants, Service, Gayn, and Miss Mitchell, waived immunity and agreed to testify before the grand jury. All three were closely cross-examined. As a result of the grand jury proceedings, Jaffe, Larsen, and Roth were indicted. The grand jury refused by a vote of fifteen to five to indict Gayn. Miss Mitchell was freed by a vote of eighteen to two; and Service was cleared by a unanimous vote.[27] Of the three suspects indicted, Roth's case was subsequently dropped for lack of evidence. The evidence against Jaffe and Larsen was considered by Justice Department officials to be "tainted" by the fact that it was secured through illegal search and seizure. Larsen discovered this fact through the careless remark of an FBI officer and filed a motion to quash the charges. At this point the Justice Department accepted a plea of guilty to lesser charges from Jaffe, and a fine of $2,500 was imposed by the court.[28] Larsen was subsequently induced to plead "no defense" to the same lesser charges and was fined $500.

The Amerasia case has been the subject of two congressional investigations and was given substantial consideration in the deliberations of the Loyalty Security Board in its hearings regarding John S. Service. The first investigation, conducted by the so-called Hobbs Committee of the House of Representatives, was devoted exclusively to the case.[29] The investigation was apparently conducted in an attempt to determine the validity of the frequently reiterated charge that the failure of the grand jury to indict all of the defendants, and of the court to mete out more severe penalties, was the result of a "cover-up" or "whitewash." The report of the committee stated:

After a most painstaking study we certify that there is no evidence, no hint, justifying adverse criticism of either grand jury, any prosecuting attorney, FBI, judicial, or other official.[30]

The conclusions of this committee concerning the character of the documents involved in the Amerasia case are also of interest:

Few, if any, of the identifiable classified documents involved in this case had any real importance in our national defense or our war efforts.[31]

The second investigation of the Amerasia Affair was conducted by a subcommittee of the Senate Foreign Relations Committee, and resulted in certain very definite conclusions. The subcommittee found that the original FBI investigation in 1945 had produced "no instance of anybody ever using one of these documents for anything except the purpose of publication in *Amerasia,* or elsewhere."[32] The subcommittee majority stated its findings as follows:

It has been charged widely, by Senator McCarthy as well as by others that the Amerasia case is the key to an espionage ring in the State Department. The evidence clearly establishes that this is not true. . . .

Our inquiry has been thorough and designed to develop every logical source through which information of relevance to the case might be obtained.

This case has now been considered (1) by the Hobbs committee of the House of Representatives in 1946; (2) by a special grand jury in New York in 1950; and (3) by this subcommittee. In each instance the conclusion is the same—indeed, the only conclusion which the facts will support—that no agency of our Government was derelict in any way in the handling of the Amerasia case.[33]

Initially, the Amerasia case aroused a storm of controversy in the American press. Many newspapers severely criticized the government for its arrest and prosecution of the defendants. Their remarks were largely based on the view that Jaffe had done nothing more than what most other conscientious newspapermen were doing—or at least trying to do—at the time. Many also felt that the action taken against Jaffe was motivated primarily by the State Department's anger over his indictment of American policy. One newspaper chain, Scripps Howard Newspapers, however, printed a series of articles presenting what The China Monthly called "the facts in the case."[34] They were highly critical of the government's handling of the case and suggested that it involved espionage—perhaps treason.[35]

Prior to the grand jury's decision in the case, the editor of The China Monthly took the position that the arrests proved certain observations previously made in his magazine:

During the past months when waves upon waves of systematic and merciless criticism were striking China and her war effort, our constant conviction was that these attacks could not possibly be coming from sound and genuinely American minds. . . .

The arrest of three newspaper men, two State Department officials and a Naval officer prove that our observations have not been wrong.[36]

The editorial concluded with a number of quotations from newspaper and periodical items which were critical of the government's action. The purpose of the quotations, according to the editor, was to show that those publications' "first loyalty is to their ideology and adopted fatherland," Communist Russia.[37] The papers from which the quotations were taken were PM, Nation, Shanghai Evening Post and Mercury, and the New York Herald Tribune.

In late 1946, one of the most repeatedly cited, paraphrased, and quoted reports concerning the Amerasia case appeared in Kohlberg's magazine Plain Talk.[38] According to the Tydings Subcommittee, this article consisted of "setting forth an extremely perverted account of the Amerasia case. . . ."[39] The author of the original version, Emmanuel S. Larsen (one of the convicted defendants), testified that much of the actual writing of the *published* version of the article was done by the editors of the magazine, Isaac Don Levine and Ralph De Toledano.[40] An examination of what Larsen insists was his draft of the article and the version which appeared in *Plain Talk* shows that there is little similarity between the two.[41] The Senate subcommittee quoted above considered this *Plain Talk* article to be one of the "three well-defined sources [which] have been largely responsible for the charge that disloyal individuals in our State Department have been responsible for the 'failure of America's China policy.' "[42]

Only occasional references to the Amerasia case were heard between 1946 and 1950. In the latter year the entire episode was disinterred by Senator McCarthy during his attack on the Department of State.[43] Many of McCarthy's charges which concerned the Amerasia Affair were taken directly from the *Plain Talk* article which had supposedly been written by Larsen. For example, six of the seven specific charges which McCarthy directed against John S. Service were taken almost verbatim from that source.[44]

Thus, in spite of the published results of the investigations of the Amerasia case, the myths concerning it continued to appear in China lobby sources. The official interest of the Chinese in the case was revealed shortly after McCarthy revived it in 1950. A cable to Chiang from his agents in Washington indicated that the author was aware of the generalissimo's intimate familiarity with the case. He suggested that any revelations which might be made in the current "reinvestigation" would "influence greatly the political set-up."[45] Nothing new was revealed in the reinvestigation, but American spokesmen for the China lobby continued to describe the episode as a case of espionage. The number of documents involved rose in their exaggerations from three or four hundred to three thousand. The participants in the affair were consistently portrayed as having been protected by the Executive branch of the government. The entire episode was treated by the China lobby as providing substantial additional evidence of the existence of a Communist conspiracy which helped to explain the "Yalta betrayal."

A typical example of the treatment given the case by American writers for the China lobby is contained in the following extract from a pamphlet distributed by the Committee for Constitutional Government late in 1950:

The clutch which Acheson had gained on the State Department by the time the war ended was revealed startlingly in the events which followed the AMERASIA Espionage Case in 1945.

This case was the first public disclosure of the presence of Soviet agents in the State Department. Briefly, the F.B.I. received evidence early in 1945 that someone in the Department was feeding confidential reports and papers to Philip J. Jaffe's pro-Communist magazine, AMERASIA. After months of investigation the F.B.I., on June 6, 1945, arrested the following individuals on charges of stealing or receiving such top secret Government documents: Kate L. Mitchell, Editor of AMERASIA; Philip J. Jaffe, Co-Editor of AMERASIA; Mark J. Gayn, Writer; John S. Service, State Department Foreign Service Officer; Emmanuel S. Larsen, State Department Research Expert on China Affairs: Andrew Roth, Liaison Officer between the Office of Naval Intelligence and the State Department.

F.B.I. search of the AMERASIA offices in New York revealed more than 100 files of top secret and highly confidential documents which had been stolen from the State, War and Navy Departments and from the O.S.S. and the O.W.I. during the war. Among the papers found was a detailed report showing the disposition of all the units in Chiang Kai-shek's army—information which would be of priceless value to the Chinese Communists.

It would be expected that such a sensational exposure would have shaken the State Department from stem to stern, and would have critically weakened the Russia-appeasement faction. No such thing happened. Some mysterious influence promptly went to work to hush up the whole shameful scandal.

Department of Justice representatives presented the case to the Washington Grand Jury in such a way that only Jaffe, Larsen and Roth were indicted. Gayn was cleared, notwithstanding the fact that 200 secret documents were found in his apartment. The F.B.I. evidence showed that Service had been in improper correspondence with Jaffe from China, and that Max Granich, a Russian agent, working under Vassili M. Zubelin, General Secretary of the Russian Embassy at Washington, had been assigned to act as go-between for Jaffe and Service. Nevertheless, his case was dropped. Later the indictment of Roth, who appears to have played an important role in Jaffe's activities, was nolled. Jaffe was allowed to plead guilty and was fined $2,500; Larsen was fined $500.

When an attempt was made by outraged Congressmen to institute a House investigation of this unsavory case, mysterious influences again intervened, and Administration leaders succeeded in smothering it.[46]

The next incident to be exploited by the China lobby in its campaign to convince Americans that China had been betrayed was the resignation of Patrick J. Hurley from his post as Ambassador to China. The essential facts surrounding Hurley's resignation are as follows:

By the middle of 1944, United States officials were becoming increasingly concerned over the lack of unity in China. On August

30, 1944, Ambassador Gauss stated his government's view on the situation in a discussion with Generalissimo Chiang Kai-shek. He expressed grave misgivings concerning the "internal problem which finds the armed forces of China facing one another instead of facing and making war upon Japan. . . ." He also expressed his hope "that a peaceful solution for this situation can be found among themselves by the Chinese."[47]

President Roosevelt had by mid-1944 decided to give only conditional support to Chiang Kai-shek. In order to survey new military possibilities in China, he appointed General Patrick Hurley as his personal representative in August, and dispatched him to China with the primary purpose of finding a way "to unify all the military forces in China for the purpose of defeating Japan."[48] Within two months after his arrival, on November 17, Hurley replaced Clarence Gauss as Ambassador to China. His experience in Chungking convinced him that the success of his mission "was dependent on the negotiations already under way for the unification of Chinese military forces. Accordingly, shortly after his arrival he undertook active measures of mediation between the Chinese National Government and the Chinese Communist Party."[49] Hurley's failure to achieve this goal by May of the following year prompted Secretary of War Henry L. Stimson to write Under Secretary of State Joseph Grew

. . . that unless there was some agreement between the Chinese government and the Chinese Communists, American military problems in China would become very complicated as the Soviet forces advanced to areas in contact with the Communists; and that such an agreement seemed a necessary preliminary to a Sino-Soviet accord.[50]

By the end of World War II, a Sino-Soviet agreement had been signed, but neither unity nor peace had been achieved in China. Not even a truce between Communists and Kuomintang had been arranged. General Hurley had failed in that undertaking on which he considered the success of his mission to be dependent. Nevertheless, he continued to entertain high hopes for success when he left Chungking for Washington on September 22, 1945. These hopes were short-lived, however, and, on November 26, 1945, an angry letter of resignation was released to the public by the ambassador.[51]

All the information available concerning the events surrounding Hurley's resignation have failed to make the causes for it entirely clear. He has referred to a number of incidents which he indicated led to his abrupt decision.[52] Herbert Feis, however, believes that these should be regarded as incidents only and not as the real causes for the resignation.[53] It is clear that Hurley felt insecure in his relationship with both the State Department and the President. He was no doubt mistrustful of the Foreign Service officers who, he thought, were trying to undermine and defeat his efforts, and he at least suspected that the Administration was not so firm in its support of the Kuomintang as he would have liked. Furthermore, he may have perceived—though none of his statements specifically refers to it—that the task of bringing the two factions in China together to form a free, unified, and democratic nation could not be fulfilled.[54]

There is no question but that Hurley's resignation was influenced by heavy pressure brought to bear on him by certain Chinese and American supporters of Chiang Kai-shek in the United States. He had been alternately threatening and offering to resign ever since his return to Washington from China in September. Only the day before his resignation was announced, together with a statement containing scathing criticism of American policy, however, Hurley had agreed to return to his post.[55] The fact that he did not return to China but, instead, released the news of his decision to the press along with a blast at the State Department and the Foreign Service is strongly indicative of outside pressure. Furthermore, Hurley has shown, in testimony before a Senate Committee, the nature of this pressure during the period immediately preceding these events:

About that time *someone* called my attention to the Daily Worker and the Chicago Sun and to certain speeches made by a man who was supposed to be a Communist Member of Congress named Delaney,[56] all of which indicated to me that my secret reports to the State Department were made available to the Communists.

And then Wang Shih-chieh, the Minister of Foreign Relations, had told me that my good friend, Jim Byrnes, had said to him that the war was over and they were going to give my place to a deserving Democrat.

Well, about that time a Dr. Qoa, who was at the United Nations, came down to *warn me again* that if I would go to China, the idea was to get me over there and find some pretext for public discharge.

Well, I didn't quite believe that, but the publication of my secret statements in the Daily Worker and in several other left-wing papers and publication of facts that could be obtained no place except from the State Department—I became convinced and I think now that I was wrong in including President Truman in it, and without going back after his generous offer, I resigned, sent him my resignation, and I understood that he was aggrieved because he had fully understood I was going back and the plane had been set up to take me.[57]

It is thus clear that persons who were concerned about United States attitudes vis-à-vis Chiang Kai-shek and the Kuomintang, including Chinese representatives, had been in touch with Hurley. They apparently did not wish him to return to China. Reflection on this incident and the events which have resulted from it suggests the conclusion that Hurley was partly motivated by reluctance to accept the responsibility for the failure of his own policy. The desire to turn that failure to the advantage of his party may also have played at least some part in his decision.

Whether or not that was Hurley's intention, his resignation set off a furious debate in Congress. The line-up in Senate discussion of the issue was largely on a party basis. The longest and most emotional appeal was made by the Senator from Nebraska, Kenneth S. Wherry.[58] His address was followed by the introduction of a resolution requesting the appointment of a special committee of five senators to investigate the "policies, operations, administration, and personnel of the Department of State."[59] The State Department, however, was not without support in this debate. The Chairman of the Senate Foreign Relations Committee, Senator Connally, made a long and detailed analysis of the Hurley charges in which he pointed out the inconsistencies and lack of specific evidence in the accusations.

Early in the following month a series of hearings was held by the Senate Foreign Relations Committee which heard testimony from the former ambassador and from Secretary of State Byrnes. No report of these hearings was ever issued, but a later writer on the subject has expressed the conclusion, after reading the hearings, that "it is hard to trace any coherent dividing line between what Hurley thought should be done about China and what the government was planning to do."[60]

Regardless of these difficulties in accounting for Hurley's actions, the *Plain Talk* version of the Larsen Article discussed above claimed to explain the incident. The article closed with the following "Editor's Note":

Ambassador Hurley was next to go. The road was clear for the pro-Soviet China bloc to take over the Far Eastern Division of the State Department [after Grew's ouster]. The policy which General Stilwell attempted to force down the throat of our ally Chiang Kai-shek as a means of defeating Japan was entrusted to General Marshall *after* Japan's defeat by America and *after* the rape of Manchuria by Soviet forces.[61]

There were from the outset serious difficulties in the attempt of the Chinese and their friends to make effective use of the Hurley resignation. The difficulty stems from the fact that one of the primary bases for the China lobby attack on American policy was the contention that the Department of State promoted Communist purposes by attempting to effect political and military unity between the Chinese Communists and the Kuomintang Government of China. This purpose was fully supported, however, by General Hurley. The fact that he did not consider it a pro-Communist purpose, is made abundantly clear by the following comment on his early efforts at reconciling the two factions.

> At the time I came here Chiang Kai-shek believed that the Communist party in China was an instrument of the Soviet Government in Russia. He is now convinced that the Russian Government does not recognize the Chinese Communist Party as Communist at all and that (1) Russia is not supporting the Communist Party in China, (2) Russia does not want dissensions or civil war in China, and (3) Russia desires more harmonious relations with China.
>
> These facts have gone far toward convincing Chiang Kai-shek that the Communist Party in China is not an agent of the Soviet Government. He now feels that he can reach a settlement with the Communist Party as a Chinese political party without foreign entanglements. When I first arrived, it was thought that civil war was inevitable. Chiang Kai-shek is now convinced that by agreement with the Communist Party of China he can (1) unite the military forces of China against Japan, and (2) avoid civil strife in China.[62]

General Hurley continued his efforts to bring about political and military unity between the Communist and Kuomintang factions until his departure from China on September 22, 1945. In fact, the greatest degree of success in this endeavor appeared to have been reached just about that time.[63] Hurley continued to hold the same view of Chinese Communist-Soviet relationships at least as late as December, 1945, more than two weeks after his resignation.

In response to a question from Senator Austin, during the hearings, Hurley replied that he did not believe the Chinese Communists were getting any aid from outside. He further told the Senate committee to

. . . please distinguish between them [the Chinese Communists] and the Union of Soviet Socialist Republics, because they are different, and all of this time Marshal Stalin and Commissar Molotov had been telling me, and throughout the entire period of the vicissitudes through which we passed so far as I know they have kept their word to me, that, as I stated yesterday, Russia—and this is my own analysis, it is not a quotation—does not recognize the Chinese armed Communist Party.[64]

This is a strange statement in view of the subsequent actions of the China-first groups in the United States. No other governmental official ever went quite so far to disclaim publicly any connection between the Chinese Communists and Moscow. In fact, even the supposedly Communist and pro-Communist writers acknowledged a closer connection between Yenan and Moscow than Hurley was willing to admit. The Foreign Service officers most frequently accused of a Communist bias had repeatedly warned that the Chinese Communists were ideologically attuned to Moscow and would turn in that direction for aid and support if the United States persisted in its support of the Kuomintang.

In spite of these facts, Hurley was never accused of having participated in a Communist maneuver, promoted a Communist purpose, or followed a pro-Communist line.[65] On the contrary, he was treated with the utmost courtesy and respect and frequently quoted on the pro-Communism of other governmental officials.

It was in regard to the latter point that Hurley supplied Chiang's backers with some of their most effective arguments. His angry resignation, his charge that he had been sabotaged by pro-Communists in the Foreign Service, and his unceasing support of Chiang Kai-shek provided an immunity for Hurley which he could hardly have enjoyed otherwise. If the China lobby wished to use Hurley's charges, however, they could hardly reject the man who had provided them. The solution to the dilemma thus created was simply to declare that Hurley was a "great American," ignore the role which he had played in trying to implement the coalition policy, but air at length his criticisms of American officials and policies.[66]

Usually the China lobby writers and spokesmen simply repeated the original charges which Hurley had made through direct quotations from Hurley's letter of resignation or his statements before congressional committees.[67] John T. Flynn's treatment is typical. He also managed to imply that the American Foreign Serrvice officers were connected significantly with the Institute of Pacific Relations:

The Institute of Pacific Relations carried its infamous project into China itself. Its staff members managed to turn up more often than not, as agents of the American State Department in China. . . . General Patrick Hurley, who was sent to China as the personal envoy of President Roosevelt, directed his efforts toward preventing the collapse of the Chinese government. This was in 1945, and he wrote President Truman, after Roosevelt's death, that it was no secret that the policy he was sent to promote in China "did not have the support of all the career men in the Department [sic]. The professional foreign service men sided with the Chinese Communists' [sic] armed party and the imperialist block of nations whose policy it was to keep China divided against herself. Our professional diplomats continuously advised the Communists that my efforts in preventing the collapse of the Nationalist [sic] government did not represent the policy of the United States. These same professionals openly advised the Communist armed party to decline unification of the Chinese Communist army with the Nationalist [sic] army unless the Chinese Communists were given control." Hurley then requested the withdrawal of these career men. The men named by Hurley for return to America were George Atcheson, Jr., Chargé d'Affaires of the American Embassy, John P. Davies, consul and later second secretary, Fulton Freeman and Arthur Ringwalt, secretaries, John Stewart Service, Raymond P. Ludden, Hungerford G. Howard and Philip D. Sprouse.[68]

The impressions created in this quotation provide an excellent example of the use made by the China lobby of Hurley's accusations. Several points need clarification. Not one of the officers mentioned in this account appears in the list of "staff members" of IPR from 1936–1951.[69] Neither do any of them appear in the lists of authors of the two major IPR publications.[70] The fact is that none of them was ever more closely associated with IPR than as a subscriber to its periodicals. Hurley had promoted the very policy which Flynn and other pro-Chiang writers were denouncing. Hurley was challenged on numerous occasions to produce proof of his charges that American representatives were advising the Chinese Communists to decline unification of their forces with those of the Nationalists; he was never able to do so.

The same technique was employed by Joseph P. Kamp in a pamphlet entitled *America Betrayed.* His remarks were then incorporated into another pamphlet written by Robert Dresser.[71] The practice of quoting, paraphrasing, and citing each other's work was widespread among the Americans who were affiliated with the China lobby. This practice was particularly noticeable in lobby treatment of General George Marshall's 1946–1947 mission to China which was the next incident to be exploited.

The difficulties encountered by the China lobby in its attempts to use the Marshall mission equaled in many respects those faced in using the Hurley resignation. The reason, however, was quite different. Exploitation of the Hurley resignation had been difficult because Hurley had attempted to *implement* the coalition policy. Exploitation of the Marshall mission, on the other hand, rested partly on *attacking* the coalition policy as a Communist maneuver. In addition, Marshall's great prestige made an attack on his mission to China even more formidable. Ultimately, the difficulties in Marshall's case were largely resolved by attributing his actions to naïveté and ignorance—to "honest though mistaken efforts"—and to pro-Communist advice from the Far Eastern Division of the Department of State.[72]

On the day of Hurley's resignation, President Truman announced the appointment of General George C. Marshall as his "Special Representative in China with the personal rank of Ambassador."[73] Marshall's directives were laid down in a policy statement of December 15, 1945.[74] The specific purpose of the mission was to bring about a truce in the civil war and to assist in arranging negotiations looking toward "political unity" and the integration of all armed forces into the Chinese National Army.

This task was not one formulated by the United States and imposed upon the Chinese. Rather, the Chinese Nationalist Government had long insisted that the Kuomintang-Communist struggle could not be settled by military means and had requested the United States to lend its aid in bringing about a truce and amalgamating the two armies. Such a task could be accomplished only through political negotiations.[75] Generalissimo Chiang had himself stated on numerous occasions that it should be clearly recognized "that the Chinese Communist problem is a purely political problem and should be solved by political means."[76] But in the final analysis Chiang was not convinced of the truth of his own words, and time after time, from October, 1945, to the end of Marshall's efforts, negotiations between the two parties were interrupted by armed clashes in the field. The initiative in these clashes did not lie wholly with either side.[77] But regardless of who was to blame for the clashes, or for refusing to make reasonable concessions toward a truce, or for breaking the terms of a truce, Marshall's orders were that Chiang was not to be abandoned.[78]

Until his return from a hurried trip to the United States in the latter part of April, 1946, Marshall "remained aloof from the political discussions because that was a Chinese affair."[79] His efforts were

directed rather to the arranging for and supervising of a truce between the warring factions. The breakdown of this truce resulted in
his becoming more directly involved in the political factors which
"consisted of an effort to find some way to break down the differences between the two sides in carrying out the policies adopted by
the political consultative conference [*sic*]."[80]

Following the failure of these negotiations either to bring about
a permanent truce or to indicate any progress in the political arena,
an embargo on the further shipment of arms and military supplies
to China was imposed in August. The reason for this embargo—the
object of much criticism in later years—was quite simple. Marshall
was in the unenviable position of attempting to supervise a truce
which was unenthusiastically accepted. Furthermore, the group
which he was committed to support was the more frequent violator
and was breaking the truce in a manner and under circumstances
which Marshall felt could lead only to inevitable disaster.[81] Marshall
"was being placed in the untenable position of mediating on the one
hand between the two Chinese groups while on the other the United
States Government was continuing to supply arms and ammunition
to one of the two groups, namely, the National Government."[82] In
spite of the embargo, however, the Nationalist armies of Chiang
Kai-shek continued to make gains during breakdowns of the truce
throughout 1946. By the end of the year "the Nationalist Government was at the peak of its military progress."[83]

From this point on, a definite deterioration in the Nationalist
Government's military position set in. Early in 1947, the year in
which this deterioration began, Marshall was recalled to the United
States and shortly thereafter appointed to the position of Secretary
of State. Throughout the period of his efforts in China no voice had
been raised in Congress either as to the policy he was attempting to
carry out or as to the method of its implementation. On the other
hand, there were numerous occasions on which members of
Congress, including some of those who were later to raise their
voices in biting criticism, spoke out in praise of Marshall's efforts
and inserted articles and editorials of praise into the *Congressional
Record.*[84] Both Congresswoman Clare Boothe Luce and Congressman Judd, to give but two examples, were lavish in their praise.
Furthermore, there has been no denial of the claims of Senators
Sparkman and McMahon that there was no real criticism of United
States policy in China during the many hearings held in executive

session by the Senate Foreign Relations Committee from 1946 through 1948.[85]

Considerable controversy concerning the cause of the decline in the Nationalist military position has since developed, particularly in regard to the aid supplied by the United States. The pro-Chiang group has argued that the failure of the United States to supply adequate arms and munitions resulted in such losses of both morale and firepower as to bring about the defeat of the Nationalist armies in the field. The Democratic administration in the United States has contended, on the other hand, that the Chinese Nationalists lost no battles because of a shortage of supplies, equipment, or ammunition; bur rather that inept leadership, corruption, and loss of confidence in the government were responsible for their defeat. An examination of the evidence now available indicates that, in order to accept the position of the pro-Chiang proponents, one must ignore entirely the arguments and evidence presented by the Administration in support of its case.[86] Contrary to the arguments of the pro-Chiang forces, there is little reason to believe, on the basis of all the evidence available, that anything short of all-out aid in money, material, *and men* would have saved China from Communist control.[87]

Three major elements appeared in China lobby efforts to use the Marshall mission to bolster its argument that China was betrayed by the United States. The first element consisted in the charge that the attempt to force the Chinese Government into a coalition with the Communists was itself betrayal.[88] The second element was an argument that the truces worked out between Communist and Kuoumintang armed forces under Marshall's supervision were advantageous primarily to the Communists. The third element consisted of a threefold proposition concerning the availability of ammunition to the Nationalist regime. This element received the major attention of China lobby spokesmen in the United States and, for that reason, will be used here to illustrate the techniques used in exploiting the Marshall mission.

The accusation that the United States, under the influence and direction of Marshall, failed to supply Chiang with adequate arms and ammunition was based on three separate but related aspects of American policy; namely, (1) that Marshall was promoting a Communist purpose in placing an embargo on arms shipments to the Kuomintang during the period in which he was attempting to mediate the civil war, (2) that such arms and ammunition as were provided were inadequate, were often unserviceable, and were sold to the Chinese Government at excessive prices, and (3) that the State Department under Marshall sabotaged the 1948 China Aid Act (which provided $125 million in military credits) at the very time that the Communists were being armed by the Russians with captured Japanese equipment.

The attack on the Marshall mission was launched late in 1947, almost a year after Marshall's return from China.[89] Six months later, Kohlberg joined the attack with more specific reference to the arms question:

> From V-J Day until March 4 of this year, Chiang received no arms or ammunition from us except small dumps left behind when our forces withdrew from China and one lot of rifle ammunition specially made for his old rifles (not American arms) left over in this country. On March 4 the surplus in the Pacific Islands . . . was made available to China, but prior to that secret instructions went to those islands that nothing was to be declared surplus unless *unserviceable.*
>
> . . . . With enough arms and ammunition, the armies of Chiang Kai-shek can recover all China and Manchuria in a matter of years.[90]

The following month *The China Monthly* carried a very curious article written by Vincent Torossian. In almost no respect did it conform to the usual line of that magazine. One can only speculate that the article was published because it confirmed the view of the editors that the situation in China was approaching a crisis and last resort measures might soon become necessary. The most curious passage, however, reads as though it had been written by an American Foreign Service officer:

> Last year its [the Nationalist Government] armies held the initiative in the fighting. Today its military forces are being cut up, surrounded or driven back on almost all fronts. Why? Certainly *not* because of lack of American assistance. At present the Nationalists *still* have more arms and better equipment than the Commies. . . . Even with large scale U.S. military aid . . . the National Government would be unable to win the war unless it were to make some radical changes in its composition, structure and policy. If it does make these changes, it can win without American help.[91]

Whatever the explanation for this divergence from the line otherwise followed by *The China Monthly,* corrective measures were soon applied. In October, the magazine ran an article, the author of which was identified as "Colonel W. Bruce Pirnie." A summary of the article will show that it laid down a line which was never deviated from afterward:

One American military expert has informed a Congressional group that the "State Department or its agencies has consistently hamstrung the Chinese National Government." This . . . policy . . . has brought the Nationalist armies to the point where they are so short of ammunition that they cannot undertake any sustained offensive, and . . . are doomed to ultimate defeat by the Communist rebels, who are abundantly supplied with the arms and ammunition of the defeated Japanese. For this, the blame is placed solely upon State Department practices.

. . . Someone [in the State Department] blocked the plan for supplying Nationalist armies with surrendered German equipment after a few rifles had reached China. Export licenses for commercially purchased munitions have consistently been refused. The 39 division program and the eight and a third group air program which we were obligated to complete were suspended.

We armed those Chinese divisions and later disarmed them by discontinuing the program of our own making. . . . All of this to force a coalition government in China of Nationalists and Communists. . . . All surplus property sold to China in the Pacific has to be demilitarized.

While Congressional pressure in late 1947 forced certain war supplies in the Pacific to be released to the Chinese, it is noteworthy that the State Department publicized this as "over 60,000 tons." . . . Less than 2,000 tons was immediately useful. [Actually, the analysis given in the article shows that 3,200 tons was immediately useful and that all except 4,682 tons was almost immediately useful if properly employed, although it may not have been the most critically needed type.]

. . . If the will of Congress in the matter of rapid military supplies is carried through . . . it is reasonable to predict electrifying results by way of victories for the Nationalist Government over the Communist enemy . . .

Americans with . . . inside knowledge stand . . . convinced that . . . [except] for the activities . . . mentioned . . . the National Government of China could successfully have solved its internal problem . . . with little or no help from the United States.

Sadly enough now . . . many of our military men . . . are unwilling to hazard a guess as how much may be required [sic]. . . .

We should consequently make sure that this job of aiding China's war effort be given to men who have the interest and will to carry it through. Those who for one moment hinder it should be branded publicly as betrayers of United States security.[92]

The final suggestion of the author may not have been a command, but from that time forward it was customary for all discussions of China's military supply problem by pro-Chiang writers to follow it. A series of such articles in *The China Monthly* during 1949 and 1950 constantly repeated exactly the same charges and never failed to brand "those responsible" as traitors to United States security. The final article in this series came shortly before the outbreak of the Korean War and was written by Kohlberg.[93]

Each of the books and pamphlets published following the United Nations intervention in Korea covered the same ground in regard to arms and ammunition for China. Freda Utley devoted an entire chapter to what she called "Too Little, Too Late—The Facts About 'Aid to China.' "[94] Her opening paragraph read:

The record of America's China policy since 1945, as briefly outlined, shatters the myth that China was lost to the Communists simply because of the shortcomings of the National Government. Examination of the figures of "military aid" to China leads to the conclusion that it was lack of ammunition, as well as too much American interference to the benefit of the Communists, which gave the victory to Stalin.[95]

The primary purpose of this chapter in Miss Utley's book was to show: (1) that Acheson's and Marshall's estimate that the United States had given "over $2 billion" in aid to China was greatly exaggerated, (2) that the aid given included very little ammunition, (3) that adequate ammunition was the most serious need for the Chinese Nationalists, and (4) that the Communists were armed and supplied by Russia from captured Japanese stocks.

Flynn argued the same points. Both Flynn and Miss Utley quote a Colonel L. B. Moody to support their arguments.[96] Robert B. Dresser employed quotations from other spokesmen to present the same arguments as Kohlberg, Miss Utley, and Flynn. His quotations from other writers and speakers on the points discussed above included Bullitt, General Chennault, General MacArthur, and Joseph P. Kamp.[97] In a subsequent pamphelt, published in 1951, in which he detailed all the same arguments, Dresser quoted his first effort.[98]

At the time the first major attacks on United States policy in regard to military aid to Chiang were being prepared, the Chinese and their friends were in desperate need of new material to aid in their campaign to convince Americans that Communist influence was affecting their government's policy in China. Time was rapidly running out for Chiang. Though an appropriation for aid had been pushed through Congress, it was both insufficient and too hedged about by restrictions to suit the Chinese. Unless a firm commitment for support of the generalissimo by the United States could be secured before his final loss of the mainland, the difficulties of securing aid would be greatly increased.

The concern of the Chiang lobby, however, arose from the fact that they had not yet been able to catch the attention and sympathy of the American people. The Yalta agreements, the Amerasia affair, the Hurley resignation, and the failure of the Marshall mission had all been exploited to the limit. But more concrete "proof" that these developments had occurred because of traitorous activities was necessary.

By the middle of 1948 the needs and desires of the Republican party and the China lobby began to coincide. The Republicans had controlled Congress for two years for the first time since 1930. They were confident of winning the Presidency in November but less sure that they could retain a majority in Congress. They needed a new approach to increase as much as possible their chances of winning control of both branches of government.

The Chinese in Washington were also looking forward to a Republican victory. They had promised Chiang that such a victory was virtually a certainty and would result in more aid for him. The problem was how to keep their needs before the American people and thus assure themselves that a Republican victory would also be their victory. It was in this context that the Republican-controlled House of Representatives provided the China lobby with its most convincing and directly applicable source of material to date.

In July, 1948, the House Committee on Un-American Activities began a series of hearings in which a number of ex-Communists gave testimony concerning Communist "espionage activities" in the United States prior to and during World War II. The most prominent of those to appear as witnesses were Louis Budenz, Elizabeth Bentley, and Whittaker Chambers.[99]

Two factors relating to the allegations that Communists had infiltrated the United States Government were important to the campaign to convince Americans that China was conquered by the forces of Mao Tse-tung because of American traitors. First was the fact that the charges, once made, could not be disproved. Second was the fact that the number of individuals who could ultimately be included was virtually limitless. As a consequence of the first factor, writers for the China lobby consistently employed the technique of associating a particular official who had been named by an ex-Communist with responsibility for American policy in China. This allegation was then followed by the statement that that official had been named as a Communist or tool of the Communists.

As a consequence of the second factor, new names of employees or former employees of the government were constantly added to the list of those with alleged Communist connections. A typical example is the fact that in 1951 three former Foreign Service officers who had served in China were named, for the first time by ex-Communists, as Communists or Communist sympathizers. All three had long been targets of the pro-Chiang groups in the United States. The three officials were John Carter Vincent,[100] John Stewart Service[101] and John P. Davies.[102]

Few of the early allegations of the ex-Communists concerned government personnel engaged in the formulation of United States policy for China. Among those mentioned in the 1948 hearings, however, Lauchlin Currie, Harry Dexter White, and Alger Hiss have been foremost among those charged with the responsibility for sabotaging American China policy. The nature of the charges made against Hiss, Currie, and White rendered them excellent targets for the China lobby. They were highly placed officials who had all, at some time, been associated, at least indirectly, with the formulation of American policy toward China. In none of these three cases were their functions so narrowly circumscribed as to make the belief that they had an important role in the "betrayal" of China implausible. Two additional elements were needed, however, if the accusations of the ex-Communists were to be of maximum use to the China lobby—first a conviction resulting from the charges, and second, an unmistakable tie to China. The charges against Hiss ultimately provided both of those elements.

The Hiss case was important because it represented the only successful prosecution of a prominent government official for pro-Communist activities. It gave all those elements in the United States who were anxious to prove heavy Communist infiltration and dominance of the wartime and postwar American Government a specific case to cite. In addition, Hiss attended the Yalta Conference in 1945. The fact that he was later convicted under circumstances which labeled him as a Communist agent was seized upon as convincing circumstantial proof that the conference had resulted in a betrayal of American interests. This contention rests, however, on the assumption, either implied or stated, that Hiss was in a position to influence policy at Yalta. The facts do not support such an assumption.

In the first place, the Secretary of State, the chairman of the Joint Chiefs of Staff, the President's personal adviser on military affairs, Admiral Leahy, and the President's close friend and political adviser, Hopkins, accompanied him to the conference. In the second place, a careful study of the available records of the Yalta Conference reveals that Hiss was little more than a "court stenographer."[103] The above conclusion is fully supported by a report of the New York *Times* which accompanied that newspaper's release of the text of a substantial portion of the record of the conference. The *Times* Story declared:

> Nowhere do the documents indicate that Hiss was a policy maker at Yalta. On the contrary, the records show him as a technician . . .[104]

Thus, even though it can now be shown clearly that Hiss did not play an influential role at Yalta, the fact of his presence at that conference was exploited to the full. By assuming his importance as a policy maker and relating the assumed importance to his subsequent conviction, a totally erroneous conclusion was fostered.

The campaign of the China lobby spokesmen to use the accusations of the ex-Communists to convince Americans that China was betrayed began even before the conviction of Hiss was a certainty. In his efforts to discredit the White Paper on China, Kohlberg described its editor, Philip Jessup, as "a close associate of alleged espionage agents such as Alger Hiss, Guenther Stein, Philip Jaffe, Anna Louise Strong, etc."[105] Jessup also, according to Kohlberg, omitted and concealed "the public missions of Owen Lattimore and Lauchlin Currie and the two secret wartime missions of Currie," and "the part that Harry Dexter White, charged with espionage before the Un-American Activities Committee, played in the allocation of wartime aid to China."[106]

This technique of associating government officials who had been accused of pro-Communist activities with the formulation of policy for China, and then alluding to the charges against them, was extensively employed by pro-Chiang authors. After the conviction of Hiss, however, the use of innuendo and indirect accusation was no longer necessary. The more direct method of attack employed after the court's decision is illustrated by the following passage written by Joseph P. Kamp and quoted in China lobby literature. Kamp argued that the revelations made by Chambers regarding Hiss

> . . . helped us to understand the amazing Yalta sell-out of China to Russia in 1945.
>
> For Alger Hiss was at Yalta as State Department advisor to President Roosevelt. At the Yalta Conference he sat behind the worn and exhausted Roosevelt, then only a few weeks from his grave, whispering advice into his

ear on the vital decisions which gave China, Poland and Eastern Europe to Stalin.[107]

Flynn accords similar treatment to the role played by Hiss at Yalta:

> But, strangest of all, this agreement [on China] was made at Yalta by Roosevelt in a secret meeting with Stalin. Even Secretary of State Stettinius, who was at Yalta, was not permitted to be present, and later, when he asked Roosevelt what had been done there, Roosevelt put him off. Only the Communist Alger Hiss was permitted to attend Roosevelt—Hiss, the secret Soviet espionage agent and then high-ranking political advisor of the State Department and member of the IPR.
> . . . But Hiss, of the IPR—a Communist agent in the State Department —knew.[108]

The pro-Chiang press in the United States repeated this charge in almost every conceivable form. Once the prosecution of Hiss was successfully concluded, there was almost no limit to the number of people who could be brought into the China story in the same manner as Currie and White provided they were named by the ex-Communists as having participated in Soviet efforts at espionage. A government official better suited for this role than Hiss would have been difficult to discover. Hiss had an almost unblemished reputation. He had risen from the lowest of the professional ranks in the civil service to the highest, and had moved from that position to the presidency of the Carnegie Endowment for International Peace. Hiss had emphatically maintained his innocence in sworn testimony before grand juries and congressional committees. Nevertheless, a majority of one jury and the entire membership of another had refused to accept his denial.

With this background, it is hardly surprising that individuals later accused by ex-Communists found the American public poorly prepared to accept their denials. This was particularly true if the accused individual had any kind of China background. When therefore, in the two years following the conviction of Hiss, ex-Communists named virtually every private and public American specialist on China who had expressed anti-Chiang sentiments as having been Communist sympathizers or agents, the China lobby found itself with almost limitless opportunities. The results of the seizure of these opportunities will be examined later.[109] First, however, one further event which proved useful to the China lobby must be reviewed.

Timing proved to be an important factor in the China lobby's efforts to exploit the Hiss case. Less than six months after the jury handed down its decision, the final event needed by the Chinese to stave off disaster occurred. A war in which the Chinese Communists were soon pitted against the United States—the ultimate issue— broke out in Korea.

A detailed examination of the extent to which the invasion of South Korea was made possible by the Communist conquest of China is quite beyond the scope of this study. The same limitations apply to an investigation of the degree to which non-Korean Communists precipitated that action. The important fact is that the outbreak of the Korean conflict made the final realization of two of the goals of the China lobby almost a certainty. In the first place, it virtually assured the Chinese of increased American aid to enable them to take more of the responsibility for the defense of Formosa. Second, so long as the United States was fighting in Korea, it was unlikely that the Communist Government of China would be recognized. This was particularly true after the Chinese entered the conflict. The second goal was, of course, a prerequisite for the continuation of the first.

The Chinese recognized immediately the relationship between Korea and the fulfillment of their goals. The first telegram to Chiang from the embassy in Washington after the invasion contemplated increased aid. More important, it suggested that Chiang should make no promises in response to any possible American request. The suggestion from the embassy was to ". . . wait until the situation is clarified and then answer."[110] Obviously the Chinese recognized that they were in the better bargaining position.

Chiang's agents in the United States were extremely anxious to have the Chinese Communists enter Korea. One of the earliest telegrams suggests that whether China sent troops would be an important factor in determining the advantage to be gained by the Formosa regime from the Korean conflict. By September, the Chinese on Formosa obviously had concrete information of Chinese Communist intentions. Nevertheless, the embassy group emphasized the point that the northward movement of Chinese troops toward Korea should not be brought to the attention of the American people. In addition, Chiang was advised to "satisfy American psychology" by telling the people of the mainland of China not to permit the Communists to utilize them in Korea.[111] In other words, this move was made solely for its effect in the United States.

A few days later the Formosa group was greatly encouraged by the prospect of American troops crossing the thirty-eighth parallel in Korea. Such a move, they believed, would bring the Communists in. If that should occur, cabled the embassy in Washington, "Then our position would become very important." Furthermore, Chiang was advised that in view of this situation he should not make commitments so readily. The American friends of the Chiang group advised: "We should insist that if America wants our cooperation and facilities they should be extended on the basis of reciprocity."[112] The Korean War, in addition to producing the stepped-up campaign of the Chinese, led to a great outpouring of "literature" on their behalf in the United States. All the old "Chiang first" voices joined to denounce as traitors any American who had ever suggested that perhaps the United States should seek an alternative to backing the Kuomintang regime of Chiang Kai-shek. This operation was planned and directed by the Chinese. They clearly recognized the necessity of spreading their propaganda through Americans who could not be associated directly with the government or the Republican party. The plan to use unofficial American sources was outlined to Chiang in cablegrams from his agents in the United States:

Republican members of the Senate Foreign Relations Commission issued a united declaration attacking post-war Far Eastern policy. The Republican is actively opposed to that part of far eastern policy which relates to our country [sic]. If the Korean war is not brought to a conclusion during this election period, this will be their principal issue. Our country should keep completely out of American internal politics. But the Democratic Party cannot avoid unreasonable attacks on our government and our President. Our neutral American friends advise us to be prepared to dispute such unreasonable attacks with actual facts so as to avoid misunderstanding on the part of the people. If we leave everything to be argued for us by the Republican Party this will not be very satisfactory. If we are to correct misinterpretations, we should make use of people outside the government. This method will be more effective. . . .

. . . We should have patience but we shouldn't overlook opportunities in our struggle in the United Nations and in our propaganda activities in America.[113]

Thus the Korean War served as a vehicle whereby the China lobby could reach the minds of the American public. The propaganda was designed first to convince Americans that it was an unnecessary war fought in the wrong place at the wrong time. From this premise it was but a short step to the idea that the United States had been unsuspectingly dragged into that war by traitors. The trail of those traitors led through China. The way back to safety and an end of fear and war also led through China—by way of Formosa. In the two years following the dispatch of the cable quoted above these ideas were fed to the American people in a constantly growing stream. The Reverend William R. Johnson contributed a pamphlet entitled *China, Key to the Orient—and to Asia*. Robert Dresser provided a summary of the views and arguments of the China lobby for the previous five years in *How We Blundered Into Korean War and Tragic Future Consequences*. He further elaborated his views a few months later in *What Caused the Nation's Crisis—Incompetency or Treachery?* These were followed by Freda Utley's *The China Story*, John T. Flynn's *While You Slept*, and *The Lattimore Story*, and Senator McCarthy's attack on General George Marshall,[114] to name only a few of the outstanding examples.

The abundance and formidable nature of this propaganda is beyond question. The impression which it made, the manner in which it was received, require further examination.

4 THE PATTERN OF ACCEPTANCE

The pattern by which the China lobby viewpoint came to be accepted in the United States proceeded along two separate but related paths. First, the earlier advocates of greater aid and support of Chiang became more vociferous and extreme in their advocacy. Second, groups which had previously been silent or neutral on the question of aid to China were won over to active support of the cause.

This pattern of acceptance can be traced through four points of reference. In the order of the extent to which they are revealing, these points of reference are (1) the tendency to support requests for aid to Chiang's Kuomintang regime in China and Formosa; (2) the use of the views of China lobby propagandists concerning incidents such as the Yalta agreements, the Amerasia Affair, and the Hurley resignation; (3) the specific use of, and references to, materials originating with China lobby sources; and (4) the adoption of the tactics and techniques of the China lobby in the criticism of American policy and those who made it.

This examination of the manner in which the lobby's viewpoint came to be accepted will be confined primarily to the political party leaders, members of Congress, and the press. The object will be to show the progressive acceptance of the China lobby "line" among these opinion-leading groups between 1947 and 1951. It will proceed from the period of relative quiescence concerning American policy in 1945 and 1946 to the period of increasingly critical attitudes in 1947. It will then show how pro-Chiang spokesmen were increasingly provided with congressional forums in 1948, and succeeded in securing an appropriation for military aid to China in that year; how the steadily deteriorating position of Chiang's forces in 1949 brought wider acceptance among Democrats and internationalist Republicans; and how these and other events combined to produce a favorable climate for the McCarthy charges against the Department of State in 1950. At this point, the extent to which two investigations, that of the McCarthy charges in 1950, and that concerning the MacArthur recall in 1951—together with the attitudes then prevalent in the American press—had set the stage for additional congressional investigations will be examined.

The outstanding fact concerning American attitudes toward China in 1945 and 1946 was that there was almost no criticism of American policy and virtually no support for increased aid to the Kuomintang Government. Only four members of Congress expressed any real concern for China during the entire two-year period. Two of these members, Representatives Clare Boothe Luce and Walter Judd, were among the initial members of the Board of Directors of the American China Policy Association. The other two, Senators Kenneth Wherry and Styles Bridges, were less concerned with China, per se, than they were with differences of viewpoint on policy in the Department of State and the possibility that those differences might stem from pro-Russian influences. The concern which they expressed during this early period was confined for the most part to a reaction to Ambassador Hurley's resignation. In the Senate "investigation" into Hurley's charges, Bridges and Wherry led the attack.[1] Otherwise, little opposition to the Administration's China policy was heard in the Senate.[2]

The most sustained criticism of American China policy in the House of Representatives came from Walter Judd, who as early as the middle of 1944 accused American Communists of major responsibility for "China's great present peril."[3] In the same speech, Judd insisted that "China's crisis is no longer a question of whether we shall aid China, but whether China can or will aid us."[4] This attack came at a crucial moment in the exchange of notes between Chiang and President Roosevelt which led to the relief of General Stilwell. Thereafter, Judd regularly inserted into the *Congressional Record* his own observations on China's need for more aid and "sympathetic" understanding, letters from constituents supporting his views, and magazine and newspaper articles urging aid for China.[5]

Clare Luce made similar efforts on behalf of China. Late in 1944, she described China as "the greatest country in the world in terms of what counts most—individual human souls . . . the oldest civilization in the world . . . too patient to know how to complain against her allies."[6] A year later she proclaimed that "to gain the most elementary economic stability, she [China] still needs much help from us, and this we owe her . . ."[7] After the formation of the American China Policy Association, the views of its members were inserted into the *Congressional Record* by Mrs. Luce.[8]

The Marshall mission to China ended in failure early in 1947. Marshall's great prestige was undoubtedly partly responsible for the reluctance to criticize American policy while that effort was being made.[9] Its end, therefore, marked the beginning of renewed efforts in behalf of Chiang. Ironically, it was Senator Vandenberg who set those efforts in motion—ironically because Vandenberg's major interest at this time lay in maintaining bipartisanship in foreign affairs. And disagreements over China were ultimately to prove to be the major issue in the breakdown of bipartisanship. On January 11, 1947, in a speech at Cleveland, Vandenberg urged the Administration to "shift its emphasis" away from the policy of supporting Communist participation in the Chinese Government.[10] A letter written a month later reveals, however, that Vandenberg's mind was still open where China was concerned:

> Frankly, I do not believe that the withdrawal of our troops from China "abandons the Chinese to the Communists." . . . But I have no illusions about China's future under any prospectus. It is the greatest speculation of the ages.[11]

Nevertheless, Vandenberg's expressed anxiety over American policy in China, coupled with expressions of the opinion that bipartisanship did not include China, encouraged further efforts to commit the United States to a program of additional aid to Chiang.[12] These efforts do not appear to have reached any serious proportions before Congress adjourned for the summer. Nevertheless, the Department of State made three changes which have been attributed to these pressures. John Carter Vincent was transferred from his post as head of the Far Eastern Division to that of Minister to Switzerland; the arms embargo on Nationalist China was lifted; and Secretary of State Marshall agreed to send General Wedemeyer to make another survey with recommendations on China.[13]

According to Wedemeyer, his mission to China was instigated by Congressman Judd.[14] Judd also is reported to have confirmed this view.[15] Any hope which the congressman may have entertained of using Wedemeyer's report to bolster his China-aid campaign was thwarted, however, by the fact that it was suppressed with a top-secret classification. But suppression of the report only served to arouse widespread suspicion that its contents supported a stepped-up program of aid. This suspicion was given added impetus by two events which occurred shortly after the report was submitted to the President. The first of these events was the publication of William C. Bullitt's famous "Report on China" in *Life* magazine.[16] The second was the appearance of several pro-Chiang witnesses, including Wedemeyer, before the Senate Appropriations Committee. Bullitt's article, which was described later as "the opening gun in the long-delayed great assault on the administration's conduct of relations with China,"[17] in addition to repeating the familiar argument that Soviet control of China would eventually mean the doom of the United States, declared that Roosevelt and Churchill "secretly, behind the back of China," sacrificed to Soviet imperialism the vital rights of China. Moreover, the author viewed the Yalta Agreement as the most unnecessary, disgraceful, and potentially disastrous document ever signed by a President of the United States. It was "disgraceful," declared Bullitt, "because all the weasel words in the world cannot convince any fairminded man that we kept our Cairo pledge to China."[18]

In very few cases can the source of information used in an attack on the China policy of the United States be so easily identified as in this article written by Bullitt for *Life*. No instance can be found in which Bullitt had protested American policy prior to his China assignment.[19] His "report" was written as a result of his having been sent to China as a reporter for the Luce publications, *Time* and *Life*, and it came directly from Chinese whom Bullitt interviewed during his trip. He was not reporting on events which had taken place in 1947 but was passing on to his American readers a story about past events which had been created in Nanking for Bullitt's American audience. He had no direct contact with, or official responsibility for, the events on which he was reporting. His article apparently, however, was quite satisfactory to *Life*. As one writer later remarked:

> Thereafter Henry Luce, moved undoubtedly by his long family ties with China as well as by his anticommunism, kept his publishing empire up in the vanguard of American supporters of Nationalist China. His influence in Republican party circles, especially in the Northeast, was considerable. Here, even for those in the GOP who knew nothing about China, was a loudly anti-communist issue which Republicans, happily uninvolved, could raise against Truman. . . .[20]

Bullitt's article and the attention given to China by the Luce publications kept the China issue at the forefront of congressional thought and led directly to the second event which focused attention on the suppressed Wedemeyer report. President Truman called a special session of Congress in November, 1947, to provide emergency aid for Europe in anticipation of consideration of the full

Marshall Plan program the following year. Judd had just returned from the Far East where he had talked with MacArthur, and was now determined to include China among the nations destined to receive American aid. He was joined in this effort by Representative John Vorys. Under this leadership, the House Foreign Affairs Committee reported out an interim aid measure which included China.[21] The House accepted this authorization with little criticism. The weakness of the pro-China bloc was soon demonstrated, however, by the omission of China from the appropriations bill which came from the House committee under the chairmanship of John Taber.

While these actions were being taken in the House, the Senate Foreign Relations Committee had agreed to omit China from its recommendations after Secretary Marshall had promised during the hearings that he was preparing to submit to Congress a $300 million economic-assistance program for China. That amount was about equal to the economic part of the aid recommended by Bullitt. The Senate Appropriations Committee under the chairmanship of Styles Bridges, however, was less willing to submit to State Department pressures. In the hearings held by his committee in December, 1947, Bridges summoned Wedemeyer, Judd, Bullitt, and Alfred Kohlberg as witnesses.[22] Under questioning by Bridges, Wedemeyer acknowledged that the report on his trip to China had been classified "top secret" and that he "would be embarrassed if the committee asked me to reveal the contents of my report, without the authority of the President or the Secretary of State."[23] He did agree, however, to "give you my observations as a normal observer in that area, and I would try to delineate in my mind between the information, that I received as the result of my special position, as a special envoy, and the information that I would have obtained had I been an ordinary observer. . . ."[24] Subsequent to this testimony, the American China Policy Association issued a special news release reporting Wedemeyer's remarks as follows:

"I personally think he" (Chiang Kai-shek) "is a fine character, and that you gentlemen on this Committee would admire him and respect him."

Chairman Bridges: "Do you think it urgent that we give military supplies and economic assistance to China at this time?"

General Wedemeyer: "Yes sir, I do."

Chairman Bridges: "Do you think . . . we have kept our promises to China over the years?"

General Wedemeyer: "No sir, I do not."[25]

Actually, Wedemeyer made important qualifications in his answer to the last question which were not included in the ACPA release.* Nevertheless, his answers were couched in terms which could be used to advantage by Chiang's supporters. The ACPA also issued a special bulletin setting forth the views presented by Kohlberg and noting that the statements were made "on the invitation of Chairman Styles Bridges."[26] The result of these hearings was the earmarking by the committee of $20 million for China. Senator Vandenberg succeeded in changing this on the Senate floor to $18 million so that it would fit a previously authorized "post-UNRRA" program.[27] Thus, acceptance of the pro-China view had reached the point where a renewal of economic assistance, though small, was possible.

Furthermore, as 1947 drew to a close there were indications that

* Wedemeyer's full answer to the question by Bridges was: "No, sir, I do not. I do not say that in a malicious way. There were conditions, Mr. Chairman, that may have precluded the fulfilment of many of our commitments. I could enumerate some of these difficulties, but I do know of a few instances wherein we have not fulfilled our commitments to China" (United States Senate, 80th Cong., 1st Sess., Committee on Appropriations, *Hearings*, December 17, 1947).

It is interesting to compare these remarks with certain statements contained in Wedemeyer's classified report. It should be kept in mind that the contrast between the answers quoted above in the text, and the statements below, is also typical of the ambiguities in the original report. That is to say, it contained recommendations both for the immediate extension of American aid and arguments against it:

"Although the Chinese people are unanimous in their desire for peace at almost any cost, there seems to be no possibility of its realization under existing circumstances. On one side is the Kuomintang, whose reactionary leadership, repression and corruption have caused a loss of popular faith in the Government" (DOS, *United States Relations with China, 1949,* p. 769).

"The spreading internecine struggle within China threatens world peace. Repeated American efforts to mediate have proved unavailing. It is apparent that positive steps are required to end hostilities immediately. The most logical approach to this very complex and ominous situation would be to refer the matter to the United Nations.

"The Communists have the tactical initiative. . . .

"China is suffering increasingly from disintegration. . . .

"A program of aid, if effectively employed, would bolster opposition to Communist expansion. . . .

"Due to excesses and oppressions by government police agencies basic freedoms of the people are being jeopardized. Maladministration and corruption cause a loss of confidence in the Government. *Until drastic political and economic reforms are undertaken United States aid can not accomplish its purpose"* (ibid., p. 773 [italics added]).

"Moral support of the National Government by the United States will, in bringing about military success for the National Government, be of importance in proportion to the degree of actual material assistance, *provided there are concurrent drastic political and economic reforms"* (ibid., p. 810 [italics added]).

conversion of the Republican party to the China lobby viewpoint had reached the point where large-scale military aid could be contemplated. In November, Governor Dewey, in a speech interpreted as the opening gun for the 1948 Republican presidential nomination, took up the battle for aid to China. "If China falls," the governor argued, "we may reasonably assume that all Asia is gone, and Western Europe and the Americas will stand alone—very much alone in a hostile world."[28] Dewey repeated the familiar argument that the Japanese attack on Pearl Harbor was precipitated by American defense of China and deplored "the history of our own broken pledges."[29]

In mid-February, 1948, Secretary Marshall submitted proposals to Congress for a China-aid program. He recommended that $570 million in economic assistance be provided over a fifteen-month period. He suggested that the experience gained during this time would provide guidance for possible future programs. No proposal for military aid was included, partly because it would have been inconsistent with the previous American policy of opposition to the continuation or extension of the civil war in China, partly because it was thought "the program was sufficient in size to free the major portion of the Chinese Government's own foreign exchange assets for the purchase of such military supplies, from foreign sources, as it might need."[30]

During the long debate on this measure in the Republican-controlled Eightieth Congress, the Senate reduced the period of time from fifteen months to twelve months. Further, it reduced and split the appropriations. Among the recommendations were $338 million for economic aid and $125 million as a special grant to be used at the discretion of the Chinese Government. The latter was in response to a House provision which earmarked $150 million for military aid, and it was contemplated by the committee that the special grant would be used for that purpose.

In the House, a provision was inserted which would have authorized the placing of United States military personnel with Chinese troops in the combat areas to give strategic advice. That provision was eliminated by the Senate with the concurrence of the Administration for the reason, as Senator Vandenberg stated, that

. . . . Your committee believes that as a matter of elementary prudence that this process must be completely clear of any implication that we are underwriting the military campaign of the Nationalist Government.[31]

The bill, as finally passed, authorized $338 million for economic aid and $125 million for military aid. When it came to the appropriation process, however, Congress granted only $275 million for economic aid and $125 million for military aid; a total appropriation substantially less than that requested by the Administration.

One incident which occurred during consideration of this measure in the Senate shows the deference then being extended to those supporting the pro-Chiang view. A separate China-aid bill had been sent to the Senate floor accompanied by a Foreign Relations Committee report which was bitterly critical of Chiang Kai-shek. The next day Senator Vandenberg withdrew the report and submitted a substitute which began as follows:[32]

> In the judgment of the committee, the Nationalist Government of China, led for 20 years through tremendous difficulties by the selfless patriotism of Generalissimo Chiang Kai-shek, represents our common contest against threats to international peace and security and against Communist agression, and deserves support within our resources. . . .[33]

In spite of these concessions, the form in which the China Aid Act of 1948 was passed by Congress gave conclusive evidence that Chiang's view of his value to the United States did not command sufficient support to open the doors of American arsenals. On re-reading the secret transcipts of the Foreign Relations Committee in 1951, Senator McMahon reported without contradiction that "the discussion showed a complete, unanimous agreement in the committee that the Chinese situation was just hopeless."[34]

A different view prevailed, however, in the House Foreign Affairs and Un-American Activities committees, and in the Senate Appropriations Committee. The Foreign Affairs Committee held hearings on the foreign-aid bill in March. Three witnesses who held strong pro-China views were called to support military aid. "Judge" N. F. Allman, a former United States consul at Shanghai, who at the time of his testimony was legal adviser to American firms doing business in China, recommended a "positive, realistic recovery plan" rather than "mere relief," and advocated both economic and military assistance.[35] Wedemeyer declared that economic aid would not suffice, and doubted the advisability of any amount of economic aid unless it could be protected by military aid.[36] Dr. William M. McGovern, a special investigator for the committee, reported that, "to suppress the Commies, the immediate need is military supplies and techniques."[37]

The House Commitee on Un-American Activities issued a "Report on the Communist Party of the United States as an Advocate of Overthrow of Government by Force and Violence" in May. One section of the report was devoted to China. In addition to a few references to Communist publications and American newspapers, the sources of information cited in the report to support the committee's views were William C. Bullitt, Freda Utley, Geraldine Fitch, Archbishop Paul Yu-pin, and George Sokolsky. The burden of the report was to discredit the opponents of China aid.[38]

Senator Bridges, as chairman of the Appropriations Committee, again relied on Alfred Kohlberg as one of those from whom he sought information on China. In May, Kohlberg made public a letter to Bridges in which he asked to be pardoned for "my delay in complying with your request for a report based on my recent trip to China."[39] The report dealt primarily with China's need for military aid and the effects of the "Wallace-Truman policy," In June, Kohlberg was invited by Bridges to present a statement before the committee, in which Bridges apparently concurred, setting forth his views of postwar American policy and the steps which should be taken in the future:

During these 2½ years President Truman, with the assistance of three different Secretaries of State, has so completely lost the peace in Europe, in the Near East, in Korea, in China, and almost everywhere in the Far East, that I find our people turning almost in resignation to the thought of a third world war as a corrective for these errors. Since my return from China and Japan in March, I have been frequently asked, "how did we get into our present mess?" "Is it because of stupidity or was it treason?"[40]

As step Number Two in his program for the future, Kohlberg proposed:

Unrestricted trade relations shall be permitted only with nations entering the alliance outlined in step three. Trade relations with Communist-controlled nations and areas shall be prohibited. Trade relations with other nations and areas shall be controlled so that no materials which may directly or indirectly promote the war potential of the communist areas may thereby reach such areas.[41]

The final and complete collapse of the Chinese Nationalist military forces began in September, 1948. Within four months, all of Manchuria and North China, including Peiping, was in Communist hands. About the time this collapse began, Senator Bridges recruited a former colleague, Senator D. Worth Clark of Idaho, to undertake a special mission to China and make a report on financial, economic, and military conditions. Since 1944, Clark had been practicing law in Washington in association with Thomas G. Corcoran and William Youngman, two of T. V. Soong's old China Defense Supplies employees. Clark is reported to have recalled later that "the idea popped up at a cocktail party at the Chinese Embassy."[42] Russell Smith, executive vice president of the Bank of America, a depository of substantial Chinese funds, accompanied Clark as financial and economic adviser. Edward B. Lockett, another old China hand, went along to write the report. Part of the expenses for the party were reportedly paid by the Nationalist Government.[43] The report recommended, "as the only program to rescue China from Communism, immediate and extensive direct military aid to the Nationalists, combat advisory aid, financial aid for the military operation, financial aid to stabilize the currency, and American supervision of expenditures."[44]

The deepening crisis which faced the Nationalists early in 1949 soon led to increasing pressure in Washington for acceptance of the view that the United States was largely responsible for that crisis. On February 7th, President Truman was presented with an urgent inquiry from fifty-one Republican representatives concerning future plans for support of non-Communist China.[45] This move was followed a few days later by the defection to the China bloc of the first influential Democratic member of the Senate. On February 25, 1949, Senator Pat McCarran of Nevada introduced a bill to provide $1½ billion in economic, financial, and military aid to the Nationalist Government of China. The money was to be provided on a loan basis with Chinese customs collections pledged as collateral.[46] Two weeks later, fifty senators, half Republicans and half Democrats, addressed an appeal to the chairman of the Foreign Relations Committee, Senator Tom Connally, for full hearings and debate on McCarran's proposal.[47] The signers of the appeal did not necessarily endorse the provisions of the bill. They were apparently motivated primarily by a concern for bipartisan harmony on European aid which was then being considered by the Senate. In any case, the appeal was largely nullified by the publication of a letter to Connally in which Acheson flatly opposed McCarran's proposal but indicated that he would welcome congressional action to extend the authority of the China Aid Act of 1948 to permit commitment of remaining unobligated portions of that appropriation.[48] About one half of the 1948 appropriation remained unspent at that time.

Acheson's proposal was accepted by Congress.[49] In the acceptance, however, the strength of the China bloc was shown by its successful insistence that the President be limited in the expenditure of the funds to *non-Communist* areas of China. This provision—and the debate on its phraseology—implied, at least, that the money might be spent to aid the Communists in the absence of such a limitation.[50] In the Senate, the battle for the limitation was led by Knowland.

Acheson's letter to Connally opposing the McCarran bill prompted Senator Bridges, on April 15th, to launch a full-scale attack on the State Department's conduct of relations with China. Bridges was joined in his attack by McCarran and Knowland, but their resolution, of April 21st, proposing a joint House-Senate investigation of China policy was buried in the Foreign Relations Committee.[51] Once again the pro-Chiang faction was thwarted in its effort to secure action on American China policy. But a new opportunity was presented on June 24, 1949, when the Department of State submitted the name of Walton Butterworth for confirmation in his position as Assistant Secretary of State for Far Eastern Affairs.[52] The lead in the debate opposing the confirmation of Butterworth's appointment came from Senator Brewster of Maine. He was joined by Bridges, Knowland, and Ferguson of Michigan. The basis of their opposition was well stated by Senator Bridges:

> . . . I do not know whether Mr. Butterworth formulated the policies [for China], or whether Mr. Butterworth took orders from those who did formulate the policies, but in either case he is a symbol of failure, he is a symbol of a policy which failed in one of the greatest areas of the earth.[53]

The most important support acquired by the China bloc in this contest, however, came from Senator Vandenberg. The basis of his opposition to Butterworth's appointment was somewhat different from that stated by Bridges but it was significant, nevertheless:

> [T]he Senior Senator from Michigan thought it was a very great mistake in public policy, in the appointment of a new Assistant Secretary in charge of far eastern affairs in general, and in China in particular, not to bring a fresh point of view to the assignment, rather than simply to continue the regime which, for one reason or another, is inevitably connected with a very tragic failure of our policies in the Far East.[54]

Butterworth's appointment was ultimately confirmed, but not until it had been passed over fourteen times in Senate discussion. Confirmation was voted on September 27, 1949, in a highly partisan roll call on which only five Republicans and no Democrat crossed party lines. Neither Senator McCarran nor Senator Vandenberg was present for the final vote.[55]

Meanwhile, a move to prevent the recognition of the Chinese Communist regime was initiated by Senator Knowland. On June 24th, the same day Bridges and Connally had clashed over Butterworth's appointment, a letter to President Truman was released over the signatures of sixteen Republicans and five Democrats requesting assurance that the United States would not recognize Communist China. In order to avoid embarrassing him, Vandenberg was not asked to sign the letter.[56]

Vandenberg's reluctance to be drawn into the conflict over China stemmed from his fear of alienating Marshall. At the same time, he had accepted to a substantial degree the pro-Chiang point of view. In letters believed to have been written in June and August of 1949, Vandenberg made his attitude clear:

> . . . I presume you have been reading about the flare-up in the Senate over our China policy. I *had* to get into it—couldn't stave it off any longer. But I hate to have any part of it because I dislike to say *anything,* which reflects on anything that George Marshall ever did. . . . I think he was somewhat misled by the boys on the Far East desk in the State Department. In any event, our China policy has been a tragic failure and, now that the chips are down, I can't help saying so.[57]

A few weeks later he elaborated on the subject:

> . . . Speaking of China, I am . . . [on] the front pages here today with my brief statement on the "White Paper." . . . Nothing that I said about China warranted any such attention. I simply wanted to nail down the fact (among others) that the China "crime" goes back to Teheran and Yalta where F.D.R. sold Chiang Kai-shek down the river in order to get Joe Stalin into the Jap war (just four days before the Japs surrendered). But it's very easy to criticize, looking backward, and I am not disposed to do much of it. . . .[58]

The adherence of McCarran, Vandenberg, Brewster, and Ferguson to the views of the openly committed members of the China bloc constituted an important addition to the strength of that group. It still lacked sufficient power, however, to tie the State Department's hands in the formulation of policy for the Far East. The release of the "White Paper," to which Vandenberg made reference in the letter quoted above, brought a new and bitter condemnation from Bridges, Knowland, Wherry, and McCarran which was a forecast of

things to come.[59] But two new policy decisions, destined to provide
the basis upon which the gathering forces could form a solid front
of opposition, faced the Department of State. The first question
concerned the recognition of the new Communist regime in China
and the substitution of its delegates for those of the Nationalists in
the United Nations. The second question was whether to defend
Formosa against a Communist attack from the mainland.

The question of recognition remained largely academic because
of the failure of the Chinese Reds to observe even the minimum
requirements of diplomatic courtesy.[60] The Administration apparently realized, however, that a decision to defend Formosa would
make any subsequent consideration of the recognition question just
as academic from the Chinese Communist point of view. That is, if
the United States were to embark on a military defense of Formosa,
the Chinese Communists would inevitably become increasingly an-
tagonistic and the difficulty of any future *rapprochement* would be
substantially intensified. These were apparently the "political" reasons behind President Truman's decision of December 22, 1949,
that no military defense of Formosa would be undertaken.[61] The
Nationalist Chinese and their friends, however, realized that recognition of the Red regime would mean the permanent abandonment
of Formosa by the United States. Their task, therefore, was to prevent recognition as long as possible and try in the meantime to
secure a decision to defend Formosa on grounds of the strategic
utility of the island to the defense of the United States. They recognized that once the decision to defend was implemented it would be
very difficult to reverse. Ultimately it was the Communists who
provided the basis for reversing the December decision. Their failure either to conduct themselves in such a manner that the United
States could extend recognition to the new government in Peking,
or to take Formosa at the time when they were expected to do so,
meant that the United States Government still had the same freedom
of choice when fighting broke out in Korea as it had had in December. Given that freedom of choice and those circumstances, the later
decision was made on *military* grounds.[62]

In the meantime, however, two conditions had combined to increase substantially the acceptance of the China lobby view. First, the
realization by all the pro-Chiang forces of the close connection between the recognition question and the defense of Formosa had
resulted in a tremendous press campaign opposing recognition of

the Peiping Government and stressing the importance of Formosa to the security of the United States. Early in January, 1950, this campaign received a substantial boost when Herbert Hoover made the headlines by advocating American naval defense of Formosa. He was promptly joined by Senator Taft. On the following day, a guidance paper, sent out by the State Department advising its officials to minimize the importance of Formosa, since its fall "is widely anticipated," leaked to the press through General MacArthur's command in Tokyo.[63] Knowland, who had arranged for Hoover's statement, immediately seized on the "leaked" guidance paper to underscore further the attack on the Administration.[64] Senator Alexander Smith, who had made a trip to Formosa the previous fall and returned opposing American recognition of the Communists and advocating occupation of the island if necessary to save it from Mao, joined Knowland in demanding that the guidance paper be made public.[65]

While these developments on the policy-making level were rapidly producing a deadlock as far as the Administration's freedom of maneuver was concerned, new difficulties were being created in another direction. The conviction of Alger Hiss, Acheson's sympathetic comment on it, and the publicity given to the Judith Coplon and Klaus Fuchs espionage cases had again raised the issue of Communists in government. Then, on February 9, 1950, at Wheeling, West Virginia, Senator Joseph R. McCarthy, of Wisconsin, created a nation-wide sensation with the following statement in a public address:

Ladies and gentlemen, while I cannot take the time to name all the men in the State Department who have been named as active members of the Communist Party and members of a spy ring, I have here in my hand a list of 205—a list of names that were made known to the Secretary of State as being members of the Communist Party and who nevertheless are still working and shaping policy in the State Department.[66]

McCarthy had struck a direct blow for one of the major theses of the China lobby. Since 1943 the Chinese Nationalists and their spokesmen in the United States had been insisting that American Far Eastern policy was being made by Communists for Communists. Various members of Congress and other public officials had, on occasion, repeated the charges and sought corroboration. Investigations by both Legislative and Executive agencies had produced evidence indicating that a problem of Communist infiltration did, in

fact, exist. In spite of the sensational headlines which these charges
and investigations had occasionally produced, however, no general
acceptance of the thesis that American policy was Communist-
controlled had been in evidence. Four committees of the Republican-controlled Eightieth Congress, for example, had examined the
evidence in the State Department security files. Since no report was
submitted by any of the committees, it can only be concluded that
they did not consider that evidence to be significant or indicative of
disloyalty in the department.[67] Now, however, from January of
1950 on, a rapidly increasing acceptance of the Communist-influence thesis became evident.

It can now be seen that this rapidly increasing tendency to accept
the Communist-influence explanation, which had been so assidu-
ously advanced by the China lobby, was a product of several con-
verging factors. In terms of the lobby itself, the Clark mission had
provided new ammunition and incentive. The Republican loss of the
presidential and congressional elections in 1948 had given sharp
warning that Democrats, as well as Republicans, must be converted
to the pro-Chiang view. Furthermore, the Democratic party split had
shown that Southern Democrats (Dixiecrats in 1948) were more
sensitive to the Communist issue than those in control of the national
party. Finally, Madame Chiang had returned to the United States to
direct personally the efforts of the Chinese, to employ paid lobbyists
to promote the cause, and to coordinate the activities of friendly
Americans.

All these events occurred in a climate which was increasingly
favorable to the kind of campaign being conducted by the China
lobby. Chiang and the Kuomintang had been driven from the mainland and had sought refuge on the island of Formosa. The Department of State had published its apologia for its previous China policy
and had thereby provided its critics with new weapons for the attack.
The conviction of Hiss, the increasingly hostile attitude of the Chinese Communist regime, and the growing truculence of the Soviet
Union's efforts to obtain United Nations membership for Mao Tse-
tung's government further conditioned American attitudes.

This was the setting in which McCarthy's attack on the Department of State was made. The fact that it was accorded a sufficient
measure of attention to result in a detailed investigation of his
charges by a committee of the United States Senate specially designated for the purpose is, in itself, indicative of the extent to which

China lobby propaganda had been accepted. The results of the investigation, however, indicated clearly that the viewpoint expressed by that propaganda had not yet been widely accepted among the Democrats on the Foreign Relations Committee. The subcommittee found that McCarthy's charges were a "fraud and a hoax perpetrated on the Senate of the United States and the American people."[68]

Nevertheless, throughout the hearings, the members of the Tydings Subcommittee were urged by witnesses and the minority counsel to accept the China lobby description of Owen Lattimore, the Department of State, and the Foreign Service officers who had served in China.[69] They were also urged to accept the China lobby version of the Amerasia Affair. The majority of the committee refused to accept this advice. It was primarily because of that refusal that the committee chairman, Senator Millard Tydings, was subjected to a campaign of vilification and slander which was to cost him his Senate seat in the elections of that year.

Another indication of the chagrin promoted among Chiang's American spokesmen by this rebuff in the Senate is provided by the bitterness with which Senator Tydings was attacked by China lobby writers. Ex-Communist Freda Utley, for example, followed her appearance before the committee with a direct attack on his fairness as chairman:

[Millard Tydings's] endeavors to extract "evidence" favorable to those accused by McCarthy, as contrasted with his reluctance to permit witnesses against them to testify, was evident throughout the proceedings of the Committee over which he presided.[70]

Despite the refusal of the Tydings investigation to accept the China lobby version of American actions in the Far East, new opportunities were in the offing. The outbreak of open warfare in Korea and the decision of the United States to intervene helped to create a more receptive attitude both among government officials and the public generally. A rash of literature reflecting this new willingness to listen was soon in evidence. A new and more attractive opportunity for the China lobby to place its case before the public came in a sensational congressional hearing in 1951.

The occasion for this hearing was the recall of General Douglas MacArthur from his post of command in the Far East. The investigation covered the entire range of United States relations with China from the Wallace mission in 1944 to MacArthur's recall in 1951.

The extent to which the China lobby line was adopted by the committees which conducted the hearings is abundantly evident in the transcript. Much of the questioning by committee members, especially the Republican members, was clearly designed to promote a pro-Chiang point of view rather than to elicit information. A detailed review of the record is not necessary, however, to determine the extent to which the members of the investigating committees adopted pro-Chiang propaganda as their own views. The degree to which that occurred can be readily determined from the minority report.*

The attitude expressed in the report on Secretary of State Acheson was that "under his guidance, the objective of American foreign policy has been primarily to conciliate certain of our associates in the United Nations rather than to advance the security of the United States." The minority was also of the opinion that "the Secretary of State was unable to defend successfully the postwar policies of the State Department in the Far East."[71] This was a considerably milder criticism of Acheson than that commonly made by the China lobby. It was, however, in the same vein and it was supplemented from the Senate floor by demands that he resign or be fired.[72]

With this attitude toward Acheson as a point of departure, the minority proceeded to adopt as its own every major feature of the China lobby point of view. In accepting the key element in this approach, that the Chiang Government fell because of the lack of American support, the minority report used the same phraseology and evidence as the China lobby.

In regard to military support of the Chinese Nationalists, the minority felt that after Vice Admiral Badger's testimony "it could only be concluded that the failure of the United States to deliver promptly sufficient arms and ammunition to the Republic of China was a major cause for its subsequent defeat by the Communists."[73]

* "Report of Certain Members of the Joint Armed Services and Foreign Relations Committee of the United States Senate," *Military Situation in the Far East*, Pt. 5, pp. 3563–3605. This report was signed by Republican Senators Styles Bridges, Alexander Wiley, H. Alexander Smith, Bourke B. Hickenlooper, William F. Knowland, Harry P. Cain, Owen Brewster, Ralph E. Flanders. In addition, Senators Saltonstall and Lodge submitted individual views in which they concurred with many of the views set forth in the minority report; *ibid.*, pp. 3559–3560, 3659–3662. Senator Wayne Morse specifically repudiated these conclusions. Senator Charles Tobey was the only Republican who did not submit a report. No Democrat signed the minority report or submitted a report of his own.

The minority merely notes that the testimony of General Barr, who was the commander of the United States military mission to China and therefore had direct contact with the ground forces, was in direct conflict with that of Admiral Badger.[74] This group of senators, however, preferred to accept the views of the admiral whose only direct contacts with the military situation were in the form of visits to selected areas under the control of the Nationalist regime.[75] The key argument is summed up as follows:

A policy of supporting the Republic of China should have been the firm and continuing policy of the United States. President Chiang Kai-shek was and is the outstanding anti-Communist leader in Asia. Our enemy in Asia and throughout the world has been identified as Russian Communism.

. . . We have not been convinced that Chiang lost China for any other reason than that he did not receive sufficient support, both moral and material, from the United States.[76]

In its appraisal of the responsibility for this lack of support for "our ally, Chiang Kai-shek," the Republican minority followed China lobby propaganda almost to the letter. Part of the blame, according to the report, lay in the fact that "the propaganda campaign against the Republic of China was vicious." Under this statement as a paragraph heading, the minority report said:

We have been greatly disturbed by the evidence which shows the terrific impact of the propaganda campaign against the Chinese Nationalist Government, originated by forces both within and without the United States. The constant attacks upon the leadership of Chiang Kai-shek and the repeated assault upon the alleged corruption and graft of his associates softened the fiber of Nationalist resistance, especially since many of these attacks originated within a nation which claimed to be aiding and supporting the Republic of China.

It is clear that the defection of a friend is more destructive of morale than the victory of an enemy.[77]

In regard to the Yalta Conference as an element in Chiang's failure, the minority relied heavily on General Hurley.

. . . General Hurley presented to the committee a complete exposition of the diplomacy during the period of the Yalta Conference. General Hurley maintained that Yalta was one of the greatest tragedies in the history of American diplomacy, since it appeased Russia and nullified the provisions of the Atlantic charter.[78]

In a paragraph entitled "Yalta is a great tragedy of American diplomacy," the senators argued that:

The turning point of American foreign policy in the Far East was the Yalta Agreement of February 1945. The Secretary of State has vigorously defended the agreements made at Yalta. . . .

The evidence of Gen. Patrick J. Hurley, Ambassador to China at this time, however, contradicts this "explanation" of Yalta. In the opinion of General Hurley:

"The surrender of the principles and objectives by the State Department at Yalta created the confusion, the crisis which confronts our Nation today" [*sic*].

The report then cited testimony of General MacArthur, Admiral Leahy, and General Leslie R. Groves to bolster its argument, and closed the section with the following comment:

From John Hay to Cordell Hull, America maintained the "open door" in China. At Yalta America slammed the "open door."[79]

Nowhere in the entire report is Harriman's documented refutation of Hurley's testimony mentioned.

Other features of the China lobby propaganda line which were adopted by the minority group are fairly adequately summarized in the paragraph headings used in the report. The most significant are: (1) "The victory won by our Armed Forces in the Pacific has been squandered by our diplomats." (2) "It has been impossible to determine who wrote the instructions for General Marshall on his mission to China." (3) "Some United States officials were so opposed to Chiang Kai-shek that they were automatically on the side of the 'Red Regime.'" (4) "It has not been the consistent policy of the United States to support the Republic of China." (5) "If the Republic of China had received effective military aid from the United States they might have defeated the Communists." (6) "The administration believed that the Chinese Communists would work in harmony with the Nationalists in a coalition government." (7) "The administration has been unduly preoccupied with the defense of America in Europe to the neglect of the defense of America in Asia." (8) "The administration has sole responsibility for the failure of our Far Eastern policy." (9) "The problem of Communist infiltration in our Government is still unresolved." (10) "The advice and information of our ablest and most experienced officials has been ignored."[80] The officials whose advice "has been ignored" were General MacArthur, Ambassador Hurley, General Wedemeyer, Admiral Leahy, and Admiral Badger.[81]

A few paragraphs from the "Conclusions" to the report show

clearly the extent to which the minority of these committees had accepted the viewpoint of the China lobby.

The administration's Far East policy has been a catastrophic failure

A candid survey of the position which the United States now occupies in the Orient leads to the conclusion that the administration's management of affairs in the Far East represents the most desolate failure in the history of our foreign policy. This management has been heedless in its neglect of our interests; the upshot has been catastrophe.

. . . Then (after World War II), with an appalling swiftness, the position of the United States was undermined, compromised and finally shattered. For this ruinous collapse, the administration in general and the State Department in particular has a direct and dreadful responsibility.

For years, the Russian Communists had plainly stated that international revolution was their aim. An international conspiratorial apparatus was under their control and in this apparatus the Chinese Communists had important places. Their hope of capturing the whole of China was freely acknowledged, their umbilical connection with Moscow well understood. The most intransigent enemy of the Chinese Communists was Chiang Kai-shek, and, for years before Pearl Harbor, he had carried on a war both against the invading Japanese and the Chinese Communists.

In 1943, at Cairo, the United States had made the most solemn undertaking that Korea should be set free and that territories previously wrested from the Chinese Republic should be restored. At the time of President Roosevelt's death on April 12th, 1945, these commitments were presumably still in force. The secret agreements at Yalta were then unknown, not a single Russian soldier was engaged in the Far East, and the forces of the United States were within striking distance of the very heart of Japan.

On August 8, 1945, the Russians entered Manchuria, and after a few days of skirmishing, the Japanese resistance on the Asiatic mainland was over. There followed the movement of the Chinese Communists into the vacuum which the Russians conveniently provided. Later in the year . . . a formal demand by President Truman was served upon the Chinese calling for a cessation of hostilities between the Nationalists and the Communists and insisting that a "national conference of representatives of major political elements in the country agree upon arrangements which would give those elements a fair and effective representation in the Chinese National Government." In this manner the fatal coalition policy was imposed upon our Ally.

President Truman has had four Secretaries of State:

. . . The third, George C. Marshall, undertook the imposition of the coalition policy while acting as the President's special representative in China. After his appointment as Secretary of State in January 1947, he continued for almost 6 months the embargo on arms shipments to the Chinese Nationalists. While declaring that "intervention by any foreign government in these matters would be inappropriate," the administration in a most practical sense did so interfere and indirectly aided the ultimate Communist triumph [in] China.

The fourth, Dean G. Acheson, is associated with a long series of vacilla-
tions and equivocations, the net result of which has been to encourage
Communist aggression. His statement that the policy was to "wait until the
dust settles" is an example of this. . . . Still another illustration of Secretary
Acheson's indirect encouragement of the Communists was his statement on
May 31, 1950, to Members of Congress in the Library auditorium that the
United States would not use the veto to prevent the seating of Communist
China in the United Nations.[82]

The recall of General MacArthur and the subsequent investigation of American Far Eastern policy resulted in a greatly increased
interest in that subject on the part of the American people and the
press. Ordinarily, such public interest and discussion of a major
foreign-policy issue could be expected to produce a salutary result.
A recent American historian has noted, however, that in this case:

The focal point of public discussion . . . was not the problem of construct-
ing a new policy or policies adapted to the changed situation in the Far East,
but responsibility for the failure of the policies which had been followed in
China. It was obviously essential to establish the reasons for failure and the
extent of failure of one method of solution as part of the process of definition
of methods which would have a greater possibility of success. . . .
But the focus on responsibility was quite different from this sort of examination of the reasons for success or failure. . . . Thus, appraisal by critics was
primarily directed toward embarrassing and weakening the administration
rather than toward establishing sound lines of future development.[83]

Under these circumstances, it is hardly surprising that the tendency of Congress to accept the China lobby explanation for events
in China should have been reflected in the nation's press. In fact,
certain segments of the press had long since shown a tendency to
accept this explanation even more readily than most members of
Congress. By 1951 this tendency had become almost universal.

The degree to which the press had adopted the attitudes of the
China lobby is perhaps best revealed by the drastic shift which took
place in the New York *Times* between 1944 and 1952. In the earlier
year, the *Times* advised the American people editorially to keep an
open mind about "the so-called Communist China," and warned that
they had no right to accept "the Chungking spokesman's" word as
gospel.[84] A few months later the same newspaper published a famous dispatch from Brooks Atkinson which stated that the removal
of General Stilwell represented inside China "the political triumph
of a moribund, anti-democratic regime that is more concerned with
maintaining its political supremacy than in driving the Japanese out

of China," and that "relieving General Stilwell and appointing a successor has the effect of making us acquiesce in an unenlightened, cold-hearted autocratic political regime."[85]

Less than a year later, the *Times* reacted to the Sino-Soviet Treaty which the United States had helped to promote by declaring, "A victory for peace as great as any scored on the battlefield has been won by Russian and Chinese statesmanship." The editorial concluded, "It is one of the virtues of the Russo-Chinese agreements that they are based on reality and mutual interest instead of abstract theory, and it is this element which makes them the great contribution toward peace that they so plainly are."[86]

Compare the above with the following editorial items from 1952. Speaking of a recent message by Chiang Kai-shek to the Chinese National Assembly on Formosa, in which he referred to certain powers in the Western world that had "kicked us while we were down, encouraged the enemy to knock us out and rejoiced at our defeat," the *Times* advised: "If the shoe fits, wear it. In our case the shoe fits." As to the 1949 White Paper, the editorial continued: "The new Administration will gain stature if it repudiates this diplomatic blunder. We do not believe any longer in the basic philosophy of the White Paper."[87]

Two additional items indicate the extent of the change in attitude experienced by the *Times*. The first was a "news" item reporting with obvious pleasure a front-page editorial in the New York *World-Telegram and Sun* urging General Eisenhower "to criticize the record of General George C. Marshall as special Ambassador to China and Secretary of State." According to the *Times*, the editorial stated:

"General Marshall's record as special Ambassador to China and Secretary of State is one of the dark pages in the history of American diplomacy. It is the key to the loss of China as an ally, key to the outbreak of war in Korea."[88]

The second item was a *Times* editorial rejoicing that Eisenhower had made foreign policy an issue. Said the editorial writer, "The major criticisms which General Eisenhower directed against the conduct of American foreign affairs by the Administration now in power seem to us to be fairly made and sufficiently documented." The editorial went on to decry the fact that "Mr. Stevenson's advice to the country has been not to waste time in 'tearful and interminable post-mortems.' "[89]

These items clearly indicate the extent of the shift of position which the *Times* had undergone. But they indicate also that the *Times* did more than merely report the controversy over China policy. It became a part of the controversy; it took sides on it and eventually, within the space of a few years, reversed its position entirely. If this change had occurred only in the New York *Times*, it would hardly have been of any real significance. The experience of the *Times*, however, was typical of newspapers and popular periodicals, both large and small, throughout the United States.

The cause of this reversal is not difficult to understand when it is remembered that the shift in attitude came after the conviction of Hiss, after the apparently permanent "loss" of China, and after the confusion, frustration, and pain produced by the war in Korea. Furthermore, the reversal took place in direct proportion to the extent that these attitudes were given wide publicity and a degree of official sanction by congressional acceptance. It is hardly surprising, therefore, that local media of communication throughout the country should show the same change in attitude as that reflected in the *Times*. The authors, editors, and reporters who keep the people "informed" are subject to the same pressures, frustrations, and fears as are the people for whom they write. It is only natural that they should have sought an explanation for the fact that their prior expectations regarding American-Chinese relations had not been realized.

Why they should have accepted the particular explanation they did, however, is a different question. The nature of the explanation accepted is indicated in the examples from the *Times* to have been largely pro-Chiang, and to have rested on the betrayal thesis. It is clear that these developments in the presentation of the story of American Far Eastern policy by the various media of communication did not take place without a concomitant evolution in other areas of American political life. The press, the news reporters and analysts, the scribes and journalists do not make history. But they record and report, and the manner of the recording and reporting may influence the direction in which the historical forces move. This is particularly true in those areas where the understanding which the reporting engenders—or fails to engender—is the warp of history. For, as a former Secretary of both State and War, has remarked, "History is often not what actually happened but what is recorded as such."[90]

The events related in the foregoing pages reveal the extent to which the China lobby line had come to be accepted by the end of

1951. Three additional specific congressional investigations are pertinent to this inquiry. They are (1) the investigation of the IPR by a subcommittee of the Senate Judiciary Committee, (2) the investigation of Philip C. Jessup by a subcommittee of the Senate Foreign Relations Committee in connection with his nomination as United States Representative to the United Nations, and (3) the investigation of tax-exempt foundations by a special committee of the House of Representatives. In order to avoid confusion and unnecessary repetition, the results of these investigations, which show a still further progressive acceptance of China lobby attitudes, will be considered in the chapters which follow. They are inextricably intertwined with the effects which that acceptance produced.

III SPECIFIC EFFECTS OF ACCEPTANCE OF CHINA LOBBY VIEWPOINT

5 EFFECTS OF ACCEPTANCE ON PRIVATE FAR EASTERN SPECIALISTS

Many Americans, for reasons which have already been indicated, were well acquainted by the beginning of World War II with various aspects of Chinese civilization. Very few, however, could qualify as "experts" in the sense that they were also trained observers, reporters, and interpreters of political phenomena. This scarcity of specialists, who both knew China and were trained to report and interpret its politics to Americans, contributed substantially to the effects which the acceptance of China lobby ideas ultimately produced. That is, the very fact that their numbers were so sharply limited increased their vulnerability.

The purpose of the next three chapters is to show the specific effects of the acceptance of China lobby attitudes on this small group of experts. The effects will be examined in terms of three separate categories of specialists: (1) the private specialists, (2) the scholarly organizations and foundations, and (3) the governmental (primarily State Department) specialists. Any such distinction is somewhat arbitrary, since the individual specialists, both private and governmental, made up the personnel of the scholarly organizations, and since private specialists were frequently called on for governmental assignments. The manner in which the effects became apparent was sufficiently different for each category to warrant separate consideration. At the same time, certain preliminary observations may be made about each one.

For one thing, the American experts tended to divide generally into two rather distinct schools. One group was primarily interested in the more traditional, seemingly more stable China of the Christian missions, the Kuomintang, the treaty ports, and the International Settlement. They were more familiar with and felt more comfortable among those elements of Chinese society which had been most exposed to Western influence. The other group placed greater emphasis on the revolutionary, rapidly changing China of mass poverty, illiteracy, and discontent. Where the first group concentrated primarily on the elements in Chinese society which had seized power and were desperately trying to retain it, the second focused its attention on those elements which were seeking new levels of power and

113

influence. Whereas the first group emphasized what had been accomplished by the Kuomintang in the way of bringing a new unity to China, resisting outside aggression, and promoting a stable and peaceful rate of change, their colleagues of the opposite school were more interested in the criticisms, demands, and aspirations of those who did not share the legitimate power. Consequently, the second group dwelt primarily on the failures, the weakness, and the underlying instability of the governing forces.

Neither of these groups denied the reality of the Chinese revolution, but they disagreed on the state of its development and future prospects. They also disagreed on the implications of the revolution for American policy. The essential difference lay in the judgments made by the two groups concerning the future of the Kuomintang and the Communists in China and the attitudes which the victor would adopt toward the United States after the civil conflict in China was decided.

The one group believed that Chiang Kai-shek could retain his control in China with only a minimum of help from the United States. They believed that he represented the forces in China which were "democratic" in the American sense and that these forces would ultimately win out. Their victory, according to this view, would result in a China which would be pro-American and anti-Soviet. This view naturally attracted a great many Americans who considered themselves anti-Communist "experts" on communism but whose knowledge of China was severely limited. The group as a whole believed that Communists everywhere were merely tools of Moscow and that all Communists, therefore, were in direct and irreconcilable conflict with the United States. They tended to resolve all questions of foreign policy into a single problem of communism versus anti-communism—into a problem which was essentially one of morality rather than one of power.[1] This factor undoubtedly accounted to a large extent for the fact that the "ex-Communists" almost invariably supported the pro-Chiang point of view.

The opposing school of China specialists was largely composed of those who either supported the basic policy of noninvolvement which the United States attempted toward China after 1945, or of those whose criticism of that policy was based on the fear that it was, nevertheless, tied too closely to the fortunes of Chiang. This group of specialists was not inclined to ask whether the revolutionary forces in China were pro-American. In fact, its members often recognized the anti-American tendencies of those forces and attempted to indicate the conditions under which those tendencies would be likely to increase or decrease. To them, the central question was not which group in China was pro-American, but rather which group was most likely to win. Since they felt that the answer to the latter question was in doubt—and probably could not be decided by the United States—their interest lay primarily in explaining the revolutionary forces to the American people and in exploring the processes by which the United States might gain the confidence and friendship of those forces. Since these specialists believed that the revolutionists —among whom the Communists were an important element— would probably control the future of China, they also believed that the United States must, for the sake of its own interests, avoid alienating those forces, and must make friends with them and help provide the leadership for them. They were equally convinced that Chiang Kai-shek and the Kuomintang, whatever their past accomplishments, could not provide that leadership.

General Claire Chennault and General Joseph Stilwell were to a considerable extent representative, among military men, of these two schools of "China experts."[2] The dichotomy which divided Chennault and Stilwell was largely the dichotomy which divided the two schools. Chennault believed in the existing power elites; Stilwell believed in the aspirants. It is not surprising, therefore, that throughout the controversy in the United States over China, the China lobby spokesmen tended to identify themselves with Chennault, their opponents with Stilwell.

Among the well-known military personnel who tended to agree with Chennault's point of view were MacArthur, Hurley, and Admiral Badger. Among Stilwell's supporters, on the other hand, were Marshall and Barr. General Wedemeyer cannot be counted among the members of either group, although in testimony before various committees of Congress after 1947, he tended to become more and more pro-Chiang,[3] and, as a consequence, he came to occupy an important place among the spokesmen of the pro-Chiang view.

Among the government civilian specialists, none appears to have adopted a view which would have placed him in the Chennault school after early 1945. Hurley was an exception if he is considered in a civilian rather than a military capacity. Several of the Japan specialists, however, such as Joseph Grew, Eugene Dooman, and Stanley Hornbeck, were considered friendly to the Chennault point of view. A long list of civilian, government China specialists, on the other hand, strongly supported the Stilwell view. The roles played by several of these specialists and what happened to them as a result will be considered later.[4]

Among the remaining, and by far the largest, group—the private civilian specialists—the overwhelming majority supported the Stilwell view that Chiang would lose if left to his own devices and that he should therefore be forced by the threat of abandonment to meet American conditions for further aid. In fact, between 1944 and 1949, this view was held by such an overwhelming preponderance of the private China specialists that hardly a voice which could be called "expert" was raised in opposition. The only counterinfluence to the views held by these specialists came from certain members of Congress, the Chinese, and a few individuals such as Bullitt, Kohlberg, Miss Utley, and a few former missionaries. None of these individuals could be classified as China specialists who both knew China and were trained to report and interpret its politics to Americans. A list of the private specialists who were skeptical of Chiang's future, on the other hand, included the names of virtually all those who were known at that time as scholars and reputable reporters in the field of Chinese affairs. It would include, to name only a few of those best known, such academicians as John Fairbank, Nathaniel Peffer, Owen Lattimore, Lawrence Rosinger, T. A. Bisson, Derk Bodde, Harold M. Vinacke, Charles P. Fitzgerald, Benjamin Schwartz, Kenneth S. Latourette, William C. Johnstone, W. W. Lockwood, and Dorothy Borg. It would also include such well-known journalists as Theodore White, Richard Lauterbach, Edgar Snow, Harrison Forman, Israel Epstein, and Brooks Atkinson.

After the Communist victory in China (that is, beginning late in 1949), a few of the academic specialists began openly to voice a pro-Chiang view and argued that those specialists who had previously expressed a lack of confidence in Chiang and a belief in the ultimate triumph of the Communists had contributed substantially, by those expressions, to the Communist victory.[5] A number of those who took this view also supported the charge that the specialists who had opposed close American collaboration with Chiang had either been pro-communist or had been dupes of the Communists. The most prominent of the academic specialists to adopt this view were David N. Rowe, William Mc Govern, Karl Wittfogel, Kenneth Colegrove, and George E. Taylor.[6] There is no reason to believe that these individuals adopted this view after Chiang's defeat. It must be kept in mind, however, that their attitudes were not publicized and remained largely unexpressed, so far as the public media were concerned, until after the Communist victory.

The silence of the China specialists who might have publicized the arguments for a more vigorous support of Chiang meant, in practice, that the public agencies—government, news media, and scholarly organizations—came to be very largely dominated in the 1944 to 1949 period by those who believed that the Chinese revolution had not been completed and that it was no longer controlled by Chiang. Moreover, because there were so few China specialists, all of them —both government and private—tended to maintain close ties and associations, both personal and institutional. They attended the same meetings, read and reviewed the same books, and relied on one another for information. They tended to belong to the same organizations and to call on one another for special assignments in the realm of research and study. This tendency of the China specialists toward close collaboration and association created an impression of unanimity which substantially increased the impact of these individual scholars' views on the American public.

Given these conditions, it was necessary that the spokesmen and agents for Chiang Kai-shek should seek to discredit the prevailing school of thought. Their task increased in direct proportion to the impact which that school made on the attitudes of the American people and on United States policy. The object of the pro-Chiang groups was to bring about a change in American policy. But so long as the dominant group of China specialists retained their reputations for objectivity, and so long as their support of the American "national interest" was not seriously questioned, the burden of proof for the argument that the policy advocated by the specialists favored the Communists rather than the United States rested on the challengers. It is fairly safe to say, in fact, that only the constant insistence that the writers and professional China specialists had been guilty of extensive "Communist connections" enabled the China lobby to make an effective case for its attack on United States policy. Consequently, the attack on the policy of the United States toward China was accompanied from the beginning by a direct, personal attack on that school of specialists who emphasized the "unfinished task" of the revolutionary forces in China and expressed a lack of faith in Chiang's future.

Whether deliberately or not from a tactical point of view, the effort to change United States policy toward China began with an attack on the private Far Eastern specialists with the least obvious governmental connections. In February, 1944, a former rector of the Catholic University of Peking denounced Nathaniel Peffer, who "owns the soft impeachment" of being "an expert on China."[7] Peffer, who had attempted to steer a middle course between the critics and idealizers of the Chinese Government, was accused of having rehashed "in meticulous detail all the standard lies devised by Red propaganda and all the misleading half-truths urged by unintelligent American criticism."[8] Others who were attacked in the same article as "Red Snipers . . . who are eager to potshot the Chungking government and chant the praises of Yenan," were Pearl Buck, T. A. Bisson, Vincent Sheean, Elsa Maxwell, and Agnes Smedley.

Accusations involving Communist sympathy and the use of Communist sources was thus adopted very early as the method for discrediting the China specialists in the United States who were not pro-Chiang. In the June, 1944, issue of *The China Monthly*, a new group of Americans came under attack. A "group of Harvard professors" who had protested China's supervision of her students in the United States and accused the Chinese Ministry of Education of exercising "thought control" were the primary targets. Columnists such as Hanson W. Baldwin, and George Sokolsky, as well as Demaree Bess and the *Saturday Evening Post*, and Theodore White and *Life* magazine, were included in the attack.[9] Baldwin, Sokolsky, and *Life* later changed their approach and sources of information and were restored to favor among the pro-Chiang groups. Not satisfied, however, these groups continued their attacks on the private specialists and added new names to the growing list of "enemies of China."

By early 1945, the accusers were taking pains to point out that all anti-Chiang attitudes were really only artfully concealed Communist propaganda.[10] The minister-counselor of the Chinese Embassy, Chen Chih-mai, took up the question in February of 1945, and pointed out that an analysis of American opinion on China prepared by the embassy staff showed that the China problem was "presented here entirely out of proportion to its actual dimensions."[11]

In the middle of July of 1945, the Chinese Government stepped in with an attempt at more direct methods for controlling criticism of its activities. The method was to refuse entry visas to American writers who had been unfriendly toward the Chiang regime. Darrell Berrigan of the New York *Post* and Harold Isaacs of *Newsweek* were the first victims. Others were added to the proscribed list later.[12]

Beginning about this time—the middle of 1945—a number of new books on China appeared in the United States. Most of them were written by authors who were unfriendly to the Kuomintang Government. They received very critical reviews in the pro-Chiang press. Every such book was given detailed attention with extensive efforts to refute both the arguments and the facts.[13] In addition, two Chinese, Lin Yutang and Hollington K. Tong, published what amounted to the official Chinese versions of China's recent history.[14] Both authors were official spokesmen for the Chinese Nationalist Government. As would be expected, their books were highly praised by the pro-Chiang press.

No advantage would be gained by a long and detailed account of the many efforts made by the Chinese and their spokesmen between 1945 and 1950 to discredit and destroy the reputations of the private China specialists in the United States. Many of the details of those efforts will emerge in the discussion of the attacks on the scholarly organizations and the State Department specialists in the two chapters which follow. It is sufficient to note here that the efforts did continue and that they were finally extended from the periodical piece to the bulkier realm of the monograph. One of the first of the latter was a pamphlet published by William R. Johnson in 1950.

Johnson, it will be recalled, had long been in the forefront of Chiang's supporters in the United States. One of the purposes of his first pamphlet was to expose those "who are determined that China go Communist." He placed many of the outstanding specialists in that category:

> . . . Among authors, lecturers and moulders of public opinion, whose utterances have similar import are (or were) Edgar Snow, T. A. Bisson, L. K. Rosinger, Gunther Stein, Agnes Smedley, Victor Yahkontoff, Anna Louise Strong, Vera Dean, John K. Fairbanks [*sic*], Harrison Forman, Theodore White, Analee Jacoby [*sic*] and a considerable percentage of our newspaper and magazine writers, commentators and playwrights, and, most amazing of all, some ministers and religious leaders.[15]

Published at about the same time or shortly thereafter were pamphlets by Robert Dresser,[16] Walter Judd,[17] General Chennault,[18] and John T. Flynn,[19] and books by General Chennault,[20] Hollington Tong,[21] Freda Utley, [22] and Flynn.[23] The last two books contained the most comprehensive efforts to destroy the reputations of the China specialists. The authors summarized all the arguments which had previously been made by such publications as *The China Monthly, Life, The New Leader, Reader's Digest, Plain Talk*, and the pamphlets noted above, as they set about the task of branding the China specialists as Communists or Communist sympathizers.

In accomplishing this task, Miss Utley and Flynn found it necessary to indict a long list of publications in the United States which had dealt with the subject of China. Few of the specialists and journalists who wrote about China from 1943 to 1948 escaped their denunciations.

Freda Utley, for example, stated the case quite clearly:

. . . Most newspapers, and nearly all other media of public information, so far as China was concerned, were firmly in the hands of a minority [*sic*] of writers, professors, and lecturers representing the pro-Chinese Communist views of the State Department.[24]

Flynn attempted a more analytical approach. "What is the explanation of the red stain in these American journals?" He then explained that they were not actually Communist organs. Neither were their editors Communists. The impression which he leaves, however, is unmistakable:

What more could they have done to promote the tragedy which today racks the whole Far East? . . . The simple truth is that the deadly success of their tragic errors was made possible by the fact that they were not Communists, that they were pouring out all this false—stupidly false—propaganda in old and respected American journals.

Flynn mentioned "certain national magazines," book reviews in the New York *Times* and New York *Herald Tribune* and "other journals," as the sources of this propaganda.[25] Previously, however, he had also named *Collier's, The Saturday Evening Post, Harper's, Atlantic Monthly, The Saturday Review*, the *Nation*, the *New Republic*, and a list of twenty-two "pro-Communist" books. Among these twenty-two books were all those which had previously been branded as pro-Communist by *The China Monthly*, the American China Policy Association, and other pro-Chiang organizations and publications. Flynn's list included *Solution in Asia* and *Situation in Asia* by Owen Lattimore; *Report from Red China* by Harrison Forman; *China's Crisis* by Lawrence K. Rosinger; *Thunder Out of China* by Theodore White and Annalee Jacoby; *The Challenge of Red China* by Guenther Stein; *The Stilwell Papers*, edited by White; *The United States and China*, by John K. Fairbank; *China Shakes the World* by Jack Belden, and *The Chinese Conquer China* by Anna Louise Strong.[26]

Freda Utley did not entirely agree with Flynn concerning the cause of the pro-communism among American writers and specialists on the Far East. She did, however, list the same publications, name the same writers, denounce the same articles and books.[27] In a somewhat ambivalent attitude, Miss Utley had some difficulty deciding just who among the China correspondents was least pro-Communist. At one point she was sure that Tillman Durdin was "politically one of the best informed correspondents" and "saw through Chou En-lai."[28] Then again, she thought Arch Steele "was undoubtedly the best informed, most intelligent and objective of all American correspondents in the Far East. . . . He alone among the correspondents in China . . . was to preserve his balance, and his unique capacity for distinguishing between appearance and reality."[29] Miss Utley was certain, however, that their views were blacked out by "the American friends of the Chinese Communists."[30]

At the time these attacks were being written and published, they were also being given official sanction through congressional action. During the height of the controversy over the recall of General MacArthur, in 1951, Senator Brewster delivered a long speech on the Senate floor which he entitled, "A Guidebook to Ten Years of Secrecy in Our China Policy."[31] One of Brewster's major arguments was that during the period 1945–1950 the reviews of books on China in the New York *Times* and the New York *Herald Tribune* had been written almost entirely by Communists and pro-Communists. Brewster's speech was then made a part of the record of the MacArthur Hearings.[32] The individuals thus characterized by Brewster constituted a substantial percentage of the private Far Eastern specialists in the United States.

Later congressional investigations proved to be even more effective media for disseminating the accusations of the China lobby against the private American China specialists and giving an aura of legitimacy to those charges. The effect was achieved largely through associating them with Owen Lattimore and the IPR. The result can best be understood through a review of Lattimore's experiences.[33]

Lattimore is well known among Far Eastern specialists as a writer and expert on the interior areas of China and Mongolia. He has lived and traveled extensively in that area and speaks the languages and dialects of the region fluently. His knowledge of the history, geography, culture, and nascent nationalism of China and inner Asia is extraordinary if not unique among Americans. One student has written of him:

His interest focused, in time, upon the little-known areas of inner Asia —upon Mongolia in particular—and he became the oustanding interpreter of this region, writing of it not only in scholarly papers but also in books and magazine articles intended for more general consumption. Because what he wrote was readable, it has sometimes been disparaged as unscholarly by his detractors; but among experts the world over, his *Inner Asian Frontiers of China*—to cite only what appears to be the most highly regarded among his several books—is generally considered scholarship of the highest order and an invaluable contribution to Western understanding of the Far East.[34]

In short, Lattimore was the perfect example of the type of individual who had to be discredited if the attitudes of the China lobby were to be successfully substituted for those of the China specialists who had previously held the attention of the American public. For as long as American scholars were free to disseminate their information, and as long as they retained the confidence of the American people, the China lobby's version of the value to the United States of Chiang and the Kuomintang would remain in serious question.

Lattimore first came under serious public attack in an article by Kohlberg published in October, 1945.[35] The article, entitled, "Owen Lattimore: 'Expert's Expert,' " followed the pattern already established in the attacks from Chinese sources on American China specialists. The source of a part of the attack is revealed in a reference to Lattimore's appointment as a political adviser to Chiang in 1941. In that reference, Kohlberg professes to quote Chinese— unidentified—as having "asked their American friends why, if President Roosevelt wanted to send an adviser, did he have to pick a Red?"[36]

This attack on Lattimore was in part—perhaps wholly at the beginning—merely a supplement to Kohlberg's campaign to secure control of the Institute of Pacific Relations.[37] It soon, however, became much more than that. In the course of a speech on the Hurley resignation on November 28, 1945, Senator Wherry made reference to a *modus vivendi* which Secretary of State Hull had considered proposing to Japan in 1941. Wherry's reference to the *modus vivendi* was rather ambiguous; his characterization of Lattimore, however, was quite clear.

But when that plan reached Chiang Kái-shek, in that momentous hour when the fate of America was hanging between peace and war, there stood at Chiang Kai-shek's elbow another one of the Communist fellow-travelers, Owen Lattimore, a notorious champion of Communist revolutionary tactics and philosophy. There he stood in that critical moment, as the agent of the United States Government, the State Department, not only did Chiang Kai-shek turn this plan down [*sic*], but Owen Lattimore wrote to the President's representative . . . a passionate appeal against the sending of that note to the Japanese. How does it come about that Communists or Communist sympathizers in this country and worshippers of Soviet Russia manage to find themselves so often at the very point where the switch must be turned one way or the other to determine the course of our Government.[38]

The campaign to discredit Lattimore, as well as other Far Eastern specialists, continued for another four years. Kohlberg carried on his efforts in *The China Monthly, Plain Talk,* and statements and news releases from the American China Policy Association. He was joined in this campaign by both Chinese and other Americans. An article, written by a Chinese residing in the United States early in 1949, reveals the character of the criticisms usually made.

An unusual confusion reigns among thinking people the country over as to the issue in conflict between giving military aid to China for an independent and free China, and doing nothing. . . . Owen Lattimore's recent articles in the Seattle *Times* brought nothing to light regarding the issue at stake. He endeavored to make the confusion permanent by the injection of the ideological concept. . . .

This blissfully innocent idea and the confusion underlying it will disappear quickly when we realize that Owen Lattimore's interpretation of the Chinese situation is based upon the falsification of history and gross distortion of truth. . . .

. . . To understand the strategic importance of China in power and geographic factors at this critical moment needs penetrating intelligence and broad wisdom. This is certainly beyond the capacity or will of Lattimore. . . .

But it is self-evident that China is a victim of imperialistic exploitation. This was made possible by the old China hands in the old days and the China "expert," such as Lattimore, nowadays. . . . American policy in China as described by Lattimore does not aim to treat the Chinese government as an ally but as a mere instrument of policy. This sounds like high-handed imperialistic power politics. . . .

No decent person would take advantage of the innocent public because they do not possess a true knowledge of the Chinese peasants. Yet Lattimore does. . . .

The failure of the U.S.A. to form a definite China policy with a view of world peace has been conditioned to a large extent by the confusion and ignorance of self-proclaimed China experts such as Lattimore. The American position in the efforts for world peace is being undermined by policies such as that advocated by Lattimore. . . .

Have we had enough of Lattimore's political line? He failed to recognize a peaceful and constructive force in the Kuomintang. Now, he is putting out a disguised reactionary policy in urging the U.S.A. and the Soviet Union to accept nationalism for China's future. . . .

It is not surprising that Lattimore cannot agree with Congressman Walter H. Judd and Mr. William C. Bullitt, for they want an independent and free China to fit into a world-wide peace. . . .

There is no fact to sustain Lattimore's statement that the victories of the Red Army in China are achieved by the popular support [*sic*]. What truth there is to it can be realistically balanced by saying that this country should not have sent millions of soldiers twice to Europe to defeat the popular supported winning armies of Germany [*sic*]. And thus it was all wrong that this country sent more than 90% of the lend-lease aid in arms and supplies to USSR and England, in addition to the opening of a second front to save the collapsing Soviet Union [*sic*]. . . . It is a proved fact that the Chinese

Communist Party has no popular support whatsoever from the Chinese people or particularly the Chinese peasants. . . .

Owen Lattimore will fail if he is still pursuing the destruction of democracy in China. He just does not have enough nerve to confess that he is promoting the interest of the Soviet Imperialism.[39]

For almost five years, therefore, Lattimore was under frequent and severe attack from pro-Chiang forces in the United States. The media for these attacks ranged from an article in *Columbia* (a publication of the knights of Columbus),* to the floor of the United States Senate. Most of the attacks were mere repetitions of those previously made. They were usually quotations or paraphrases, often unacknowledged, of statements by Kohlberg or Freda Utley. Finally, on March 30, 1950, Senator Joseph McCarthy presented to the Senate a complete résumé of all the attacks previously made on Lattimore by Kohlberg.[40] It was these charges which made bold headlines across the nation and focused attention on Lattimore as the central figure.

Subsequent to the presentation of McCarthy's charges against Lattimore, a long series of hearings was held by a subcommittee of the Senate Committee on Foreign Relations, popularly known as the Tydings Committee. Lattimore was a star witness at those hearings. McCarthy's accusations were supplemented by two former Communists, Budenz and Miss Utley. Budenz, for example, in a statement made to the subcommittee on April 20, 1950, named Lattimore for the first time as a member of a Communist cell in the Institute of Pacific Relations. This accusation was made approximately six weeks after McCarthy's first public charge. Lattimore's name came up in the course of a general statement:

[Testimony by Budenz] In this cell there was also Owen Lattimore. This I know from reports received in the Politburo, and given to me officially as managing editor of the Daily Worker. . . . In a specific meeting to which I refer, Mr. Lattimore was commended by Frederick Vanderbilt Field and Earl Browder for the fact that he had been responsible for the placing of a number of Communist writers in the organs of the Institute of Pacific Affairs. . . .

Senator Tydings. Was Mr. Lattimore present at the meeting where this occurred?

---

* James F. Kearney, S. J., "Disaster in China," *Columbia* (September, 1949), reprinted in *State Department Employee Loyalty Investigation*, Pt. 2, pp. 1660–1665. This article was quoted by Senator McCarthy in his charges against Lattimore (see *ibid.*, p. 1525), and by Louis Budenz in testimony before the Tydings Subcommittee. Kearney later advised the FBI that the information in the article was obtained from Kohlberg (see *ibid., Report*, p. 146).

Mr. Budenz. Oh, no, sir. He was not there.
Senator Green. Do you know Mr. Lattimore?
Mr. Budenz. Do you mean personally?
Senator Green. Yes.
Mr. Budenz. I do not.
Senator Green. Have you ever seen Mr. Lattimore?
Mr. Budenz. No, sir; I have not.[41]

In subsequent testimony the same day, Budenz was asked:

Mr. Morgan. The statement has been made, I believe in substance that Owen Lattimore is a Communist subject to Communist discipline. I will ask you if you have ever exercised discipline over him.
Mr. Budenz. I have participated in meetings of the Politburo which have exercised discipline over him, and to that extent was a participant in the discipline. Personally I have not exercised any such discipline.[42]

In addition to this point concerning Lattimore's affiliation with the party, Budenz accused Lattimore of having followed the Communist line during his editorship of *Pacific Affairs* (the journal of the international office of IPR which Lattimore had edited from 1934 to 1940).[43] He also asserted that Lattimore had directed the Wallace mission to China toward Communist objectives,[44] been "helpful" to the Communists in the Amerasia case,[45] and consistently followed the changing party line on China.[46] These were the same accusations which had been made against Lattimore by the pro-Chiang press for five years. During the course of his testimony, Budenz identified a number of other Far Eastern specialists and reporters on China as Communists. Among those so identified were Joseph Barnes, Harriet L. Moore, Haldore Hanson, Lawrence K. Rosinger, Edgar Snow, and T. A. Bisson.[47] These names had been selected by Budenz from among the contributors to *Pacific Affairs.* All had long been the targets of pro-Chiang groups in the United States.

Miss Utley largely confined her accusations before the subcommittee to Lattimore. She did, however, add to the list of "pro-Communist writers" the names of Theodore White, Richard Lauterbach, and Jack Belden.[48] As to Lattimore, Miss Utley told the subcommittee, "I am testifying here because I consider America is the hope of the world, and that people like Mr. Lattimore menace our security and freedom."[49] The main burden of her testimony is indicated by her promise to "show how closely Lattimore's writings have followed the Communist Party line since 1938. . . ."[50] She did not argue—and this is consistent with the China lobby viewpoint—that Lattimore was an espionage agent,[51] nor that she had direct knowledge that he "ever has been a member of the Communist party."[52]

On the other hand, she did not think his following the "switches in the Communist Party line" constituted anything "so very different" from being a member of the party.[53]

The majority of the subcommittee to which this testimony was presented rejected in its entirety the characterization of Lattimore urged upon it by Budenz and Miss Utley. In its conclusions on Lattimore, the *Report* of the investigation stated:

Far from being the "architect of our Far Eastern policy," we find that Mr. Lattimore has had no controlling or effective influence whatever on that policy. His views have but been among those of hundreds of others that have gone into the cauldron from which emerges the source material that the policy-makers of our State Department employed in making their judgments.

We find no evidence to support the charge that Owen Lattimore is the "top Russian spy" or, for that matter, any other sort of spy. Even the testimony of Louis F. Budenz, if given the fullest weight and import, could establish no more than that the Communists used Lattimore to project a propaganda line anent China. . . .

Owen Lattimore is a writer and a scholar who has been charged with a record of procommunism [*sic*] going back many years. There is no legal evidence before us whatever to support this charge and the weight of all other information indicates that it is not true.[54]

Senator Lodge, one of the two Republican members of the subcommittee, came to much the same conclusion in regard to Lattimore, although he would have liked more information on certain points.[55] Some of that additional information was soon forthcoming. In July, 1951, the Internal Security Subcommittee of the Senate Judiciary Committee, under the chairmanship of Senator McCarran, began an inquiry centered on the Institute of Pacific Relations but with Lattimore as a principal target. It was apparent from the beginning that the subcommittee, and especially its chairman, were bitterly hostile toward Lattimore. This hostility is difficult to understand or explain. One student of the subject has attempted to outline the possible reasons:

Perhaps it grew out of the fact that Lattimore had reacted to the charges against him with indignation and had struck back at his accusers lustily and irreverently. In *Ordeal by Slander,* published in 1950, he treated with blistering scorn the kind of so-called anti-communism that equates liberalism with disloyalty and ignores all the traditional American concepts of decency and fair play. By the time he was at last allowed to come before the McCarran Subcommittee and refute in public the accusations that had been made against him publicly, he came with a prepared statement that expressed a long-pent-up anger and a rankling sense of injustice. It was not a mild statement, not even, perhaps, a mannerly one. A softer answer might have been more politic. But it is doubtful, in view of the subcommittee's evident animus, that even the softest of answers could have turned away its wrath.[56]

Whether this is an adequate explanation must be judged against the fact that Senator McCarran had long before shown his complete acceptance of the pro-Chiang view of American relations with China. Senators Smith, Ferguson, and Jenner had displayed similar attitudes. In any case, the chairman made his position clear in a preliminary statement to the first public session at which Lattimore appeared:

The Daily Worker has devoted many columns to its condemnation of this committee, its members, and the manner in which it has operated. Every Communist in America has taken opportunity to cast invective and discouraging and disparaging remarks with reference to this committee and its membership. We were fully advised before we undertook this task that such would be the course and procedure. It is not at all out of line with the general procedure of the Communist Party and Communists generally in the world. . . .
A statement has been filed today by the witness [Lattimore]. . . . The witness must be responsible for the full gravity of his remarks produced in that statement. In that statement there is carried out the same policy as has been carried out against this committee. Intemperate and provocative expressions are there set out and elaborated upon.[57]

Following this statement, criticism of the committee was equated with Communist tactics if not with actual pro-communism.

Lattimore spent thirteen days testifying under close cross-examination before the subcommittee. The basic difference between Lattimore and the members of the subcommittee throughout the questioning concerned the interpretation of Lattimore's actions and written remarks during the previous fifteen to twenty years. The questions of the subcommittee members and counsel were based on the assumption that all Lattimore's acts and writing had been designed to further the cause of the Soviet Union. Most of his attention during those years had been concentrated on the Far East. The questioning therefore was based primarily on the assumption that his actions had had the effect of furthering Soviet interests in China. A further assumption underlying the committee's approach to Lattimore was that he had been a major influence in the shaping of American policy in China—at least after 1941. Lattimore's concern, on the other hand, was to refute such an interpretation of his work.

During the course of these hearings, numerous ex-Communists, refugees from the Soviet Union, and a few specialists on China gave to the subcommittee their opinions and interpretations of Lattimore's efforts. Some direct testimony, and numerous sworn statements from his American colleagues, were introduced into the subcommittee's record in defense of Lattimore. The bulk of the accusations against him, however, consisted of an elaboration of the charges which had emanated from China lobby sources for the previous six years. The evidence adduced to support the accusations was derived primarily from the employment of two methods. One method was to "analyze" Lattimore's published views over a period of years to determine the extent to which they had conformed to the subcommittee's version of the "Communist Party line."[58] The other method was to examine the activities of the IPR, and of Lattimore specifically, during the period in which Lattimore served as editor of *Pacific Affairs* or was otherwise "connected" with the organization to determine the extent to which those activities had "promoted Communist purposes."

In pursuance of the first method, numerous excerpts from Lattimore's writing were extracted and made a part of the hearings of the subcommittee. Most of these excerpts purported to show procommunist attitudes, although Lattimore was allowed to insert excerpts designed to show anti-Communist attitudes. Lattimore, however, failed to convince the committee. A number of excerpts from his publications, considered by the subcommittee to be pro-Communist, were reprinted in the report. None of the items having the opposite import were included or cited in the report.

The subcommittee relied more heavily on the second method to support its *major* charge against Lattimore. The report notes a number of instances in which witnesses testified that Lattimore was told about the Communist sympathies or affiliations of a number of persons who wrote for IPR publications. The subcommittee concluded from such testimony that Lattimore therefore "knew" that such persons were Communists.[59] Two former Soviet officials, who had since become refugees from Russia, testified concerning certain incidents which they interpreted as proving that Lattimore was a trusted member of the Communist apparatus. Again, Lattimore's explanation of these events and his part in them was not accepted by the subcommittee or cited in the report.[60] On the other hand, extensive citations to the derogatory accusations were included.[61]

As a result of these hearings, the Senate Internal Security Subcommittee concluded that "Lattimore was for some time, beginning in the middle 1930's, a conscious, articulate instrument of the Soviet Conspiracy."[62] The report further charged:

(a) Owen Lattimore testified falsely before the subcommittee with reference to at least five separate matters that were relevant to the inquiry and substantial in import;

(b) Owen Lattimore . . . [was] influential in bringing about a change in United States policy in 1945 favorable to the Chinese Communists;

(c) Owen Lattimore . . . knowingly and deliberately used the language of books and articles . . . in an attempt to influence the American public by means of pro-Communist or pro-Soviet content of such writings.[63]

At the close of the hearings, the subcommittee, with the concurrence of the Committee on the Judiciary and the full membership of the Senate, recommended "that the Department of Justice submit to a grand jury the question of whether perjury has been committed before the subcommittee by Owen Lattimore."[64] This recommendation resulted in the lodging of a formal charge against Lattimore by the Department of Justice. A grand jury, in turn, indicted Lattimore on five counts of perjury.[65] The litigation which resulted from this indictment was not finally disposed of until almost three years later. The court twice threw out the key counts of the indictment on the grounds that they were too vague and lacking in precision to sustain a charge of perjury. The Justice Department ultimately asked the court to dismiss the indictment.[66]

The result of this series of events for Lattimore was thus not as serious, from the legal standpoint, as it might have been. His escape from a possible fine and prison sentence, however, cannot obscure the fact that the initial purpose of the attack on Lattimore was largely achieved. The long months which he was forced to spend in preparation for his appearances before congressional committees and in preparing his defense against charges of perjury left little time for research and publication on the subject of China and the Far East. More serious, however, was the impairment of Lattimore's reputation (as a scholar and specialist on the Far East) by the wide publicity given to the accusations made against him and the fact that those accusations had been given the sanction of the United States Senate.

In addition, other Far Eastern specialists who had been associated with Lattimore became more vulnerable to attack because of his experience. The mere statement that an American specialist on China had been associated with him was henceforth sufficient to cast doubt on the integrity of that specialist. Furthermore, in the same congressional proceedings as those which had involved Lattimore, many other specialists had been accused by ex-Communists of participating in Communist activities. Being accused of pro-communism and disloyalty was not a new experience for those specialists. But as in the case of Lattimore, the handling of the accusations by the McCarran Subcommittee tended to give them greater credence and provided an official source for citation.

The report of the subcommittee—which purports to be a summary of the evidence taken in the hearings and a statement of the conclusions drawn from that evidence—contains a long list of "individuals who were the subjects of sworn testimony describing their affiliations with the Communist Party of the United States or another country."[67] This list includes, among those "identified as members of the Communist Party," such well-known authors on the Far East as Joseph F. Barnes, T. A. Bisson, Israel Epstein, John K. Fairbank, Philip Jaffe, Owen Lattimore, Harriet L. Moore, Lawrence K. Rosinger, Anna Louise Strong, and Maxwell S. Stewart. Among those "named in sworn testimony as having collaborated with agents of the Soviet Intelligence apparatus" were Barnes, Epstein, Lattimore, and Miss Strong, plus Jaffe and Andrew Roth from the Amerasia case.[68] The same individuals, along with some eighty others, were listed in the report under the heading "Summary of Communist Affiliations by Individuals with Their IPR Functions."[69] Among the most important of the Far Eastern writers added by this list were Dorothy Borg, William C. Johnstone, Edgar Snow, and Richard Watts.

In the section of the report entitled "Communist Party Connections," the subcommittee pointed out that "individuals listed should not be judged solely on the basis of any single item of evidence, or the statement of a single witness, but rather on the basis of the over-all pattern of behavior within the sphere of Communist activities."[70] In spite of this caveat, however, the general tone of the report, the multiple listing of names of Far Eastern specialists in a context which labeled them as Communist, and the constant repetition of expressions such as "cited as a Communist" after the names of these specialists, militated against an unprejudiced appraisal of the accusations.

Some measure of the extent to which the professional reputations of the China specialists were affected by acceptance of these allegations may be gained by noting the changes which took place in their book-reviewing activities after 1951. In the years 1945 through 1950, twenty-two reviews—out of a total of thirty dealing with political, economic, and social developments in China—were contributed to the New York *Times* by writers who had been the targets of the China lobby. The breakdown was as follows: Bisson—1,

Fairbank—4, Isaacs—1, Jacoby—6, Lattimore—1, Peffer—6, and Snow—3. During the same period, thirty of a total of thirty-five such titles were reviewed for the New York *Herald Tribune* by the same authors, plus four others who had been attacked by the China lobby. The breakdown of the *Herald Tribune* reviews was as follows: Barnes —1, Fairbank—2, Isaacs—4, E. Lattimore—5, O. Lattimore—12, Snow—1, Stein—1, and Watts—4. During the years 1952 through 1956, by contrast, no reviews appear to have been written for the *Times* or *Herald Tribune* by *any* of the above writers. This change gains added significance from the fact that two reviewers not considered anti-Chiang by the China lobby provided four items for the *Times* in the earlier period but contributed six items in the later period. A similar situation occurred with reference to the *Herald Tribune*.[71]

It is thus apparent that one of the specific effects of the acceptance of the China lobby point of view was the virtual destruction of the public and governmental reputations and influence of many of the foremost private China specialists in the United States. The effects of these developments also extended to the organizational framework within which these specialists functioned, and through which their specialized knowledge was largely channeled. An examination of the nature and extent of those additional effects is therefore pertinent.

6 EFFECTS OF ACCEPTANCE ON SCHOLARLY ORGANIZATIONS AND FOUNDATIONS

The very complexity of Chinese civilization and the intensity of the interests of Western peoples in China virtually dictated that specialists whose interests were oriented toward that area of the world should organize to promote research and the publication of the results of their studies. The growing importance of China to American security in the period preceding World War II also assured the increasing value of organizations of China specialists as sources of information and as media for locating and training additional specialists. The functions performed by such organizations have been indicated by the executive secretary of the Institute of Pacific Relations:

> It was our purpose to provide facts and diverse opinion so that the public could make up its own mind. Mr. Root, Mr. Hughes, many of our Secretaries of State have said that the Government has great difficulty in acting intelligently because of the lack of an informed public opinion. So far as the Pacific was concerned we conceived our role to get the facts, to provide a variety of opinions, analyses from all sorts of points of view so that the public, the Government, press, and business could make up its own mind.[1]

The need for scholars trained in the techniques of observing and reporting on the Far East was felt equally by government and by private institutions. Similarly, government specialists frequently found it necessary to seek information from private specialists, while private specialists often had need of the data gathered by government agencies. These mutual needs led the private specialists quite naturally to encourage the active participation of government experts in the affairs of the scholarly organizations. At the same time, the personnel needs of government agencies often led them to turn to the private scholarly organizations for aid.[2]

Thus, when American policy toward China came under attack, it was virtually inevitable that the effects should extend to the scholarly organizations which were concerned with the Far East. This was especially true since the very nature of the attack on the policy required an attack on those private specialists who had helped to formulate and publicize the assumptions which provided the basis

132

for the policy. These private specialists, however, also constituted the majority of the memership and staffs of the scholarly organizations.

The most immediate and direct effects of the acceptance of China lobby propaganda were unquestionably felt by the organization most intimately concerned with the Far East, the Institute of Pacific Relations. Ultimately, however, these effects were also felt by other organizations (such as the Foreign Policy Association and the Council on Foreign Relations) and by the foundations (such as Ford, Carnegie, and Rockefeller) which provided much of the money to finance the undertakings of the scholarly organizations. Before proceeding to an examination of these effects, a word about the Institute of Pacific Relations is in order.

The IPR was established in 1925 for the purpose of coordinating information and research on the Pacific area. It was composed of an international headquarters or secretariat, called the Pacific Council of the Institute of Pacific Relations, and various national councils, which served as the coordinating agencies in each country. The American Council of the IPR, like most of the other national councils, was composed of businessmen, scholars, teachers, journalists, government officials, community leaders, and other persons interested in contemporary Far Eastern problems. The headquarters for the institute (Secretariat of the Pacific Council), originally located in Hawaii, was eventually moved to share offices with the headquarters of the American Council in New York. Persons referred to below as "members of the IPR" were actually either members of the American Council or held official positions in the Secretariat of the Pacific Council.[3] In a few cases, they were in both positions.

In 1951 the executive secretary of the American Council described the organization as follows:

The Institute of Pacific Relations is an association composed of national councils in 10 countries. Each national council is autonomous and carries on its own work in its own distinctive way. Together they cooperate in an international IPR program of research, publications, and conferences. This program is directed by a Pacific Council in which each national council is represented, and administered by a small international secretariat working in New York under the direction of the Pacific Council. . . .

The work of the international Institute of Pacific Relations is financed principally by contributions from its national councils and by grants from foundations. In the 26 years from 1925 through 1950 total receipts amounted to $2,569,000, an average of about $100,000 a year. Of this total, 48 percent came from the Rockefeller Foundation and the Carnegie Corp., 40 percent came from the national councils, 9 percent from sales of publications, and 3 percent from miscellaneous sources. . . . United States sources, including foundations, supplied 77 percent of the organization's income. . . .

The American Institute of Pacific Relations derives its funds from membership subscriptions, gifts from individuals and corporations, and grants from foundations. From 1925 through 1950 its total net income was $2,-536,000, of which 50 percent came from foundations . . . , 33 percent from individual and corporate contributions, 12 percent from sales of publications, and 5 percent from miscellaneous sources.[4]

In order to understand the role of the IPR, it is necessary that several points be kept clearly in view. First, the Pacific Council was a *private international* organization. Second, the member councils, while ostensibly private, were in some cases, such as the wartime Japanese and Chinese councils under governmental pressure, and the Soviet Council was inevitably subject to the control of the party. Third, while the member councils could, if they chose to do so, adopt a purely nationalistic attitude in the conferences and in their publications (and in some cases they were forced to do so by their governments), the Pacific Council, because of the very nature of its purpose and organization, was required to maintain a strictly nonpartisan and nonnational approach. In fact, the officers of the Pacific Council were frequently in the position of having to suppress criticisms of the governments of member councils in its publications in order to avoid antagonizing the members and thereby destroying their own usefulness. Fourth, the fact that the Pacific and American councils were located together and the fact that their staffs were not always clearly differentiated placed a burden on the American Council to refrain from antagonizing other members which was not shared by the other councils. On balance, the remarkable thing about the IPR was that it was able to deal at all with controversial social, political, and economic matters which were of interest to the governments of member councils.

The initial attack on the IPR was apparently motivated by an incident—at first glance totally unrelated—which occurred in early 1943. At that time, Alfred Kohlberg was chairman of the Executive Committee of the Board of Directors of the American Bureau for Medical Aid to China,[5] which was one of the constituent societies of United China Relief. Numerous reports from staff members of ABMAC and UCR, in 1943, indicated the existence of considerable graft and incompetence in the Chinese Army medical services, which were receiving aid from ABMAC. In June of 1943, Kohlberg made a trip to China to check on the accuracy of these reports. Kohlberg himself has testified that the reports of graft and incompetency were confirmed by American Government officials in China and the field officers of United China Relief.[6] He insisted, however, that his own Chinese-conducted tour of five provinces revealed the charges to be "either completely untrue or greatly exaggerated."[7]

Shortly after his return from China, Kohlberg launched an effort to secure more of the funds from United China Relief for his own organization, ABMAC. This effort took the form of a direct personal attack on two of the principal operating officers of UCR; the chairman of the Program and Disbursements Committee, Edward C. Carter; and the Field Director in China, Dwight Edwards. At the direction of Charles A. Edison, president of UCR, Kohlberg's charges against Carter and Edwards were reviewed by a committee consisting of Paul G. Hoffman, Henry R. Luce, and James G. Blaine. After a long hearing, the committee dismissed the charges as unfounded, and exonerated both Carter and Edwards.[8]

The importance of this episode lies in the fact that Carter was also at that time secretary general of the Pacific Council of the IPR. Having lost his fight with United China Relief, Kohlberg resigned from the American Bureau for Medical Aid to China and severed all connections with UCR. A few months later he began what was to be a long-sustained attack on the Institute of Pacific Relations and on Carter personally.

According to Kohlberg's account, he began to realize early in 1944 "that the lies about the Chinese Government and Army were Communist propaganda; and that the main source for spreading them in this country was the Institute of Pacific Relations."[9] Subsequent to this realization Kohlberg prepared an "88-page study" on IPR publications which he submitted to the trustees and certain other personnel of the institute. This "study" purported to be an analysis of the major periodical publications of the Pacific Council (*Pacific Affairs*) and the American Council (*The Far Eastern Survey*).

Kohlberg reported that his study of the content of these publications from 1938 to 1944 showed:

1. No criticism of Japan in those 7 years, except of her rural land system;
2. No single criticism of Communist China; and

3.   No single criticism of the Soviet Union; whereas I found;
4.   Severe criticism of the Chinese Government, alternating with praise, closely following the alternations of the Soviet Union's foreign policy and of the Communist press.[10]

To illustrate his fourth point, Kohlberg stated that a study of the Communist press in the United States for the same years showed alternating periods of Soviet policy and Communist line on China as follows:

Prior to the Hitler-Stalin past [*sic*] of Aug. 23, 1939 .... Praise
Then until June 22, 1941 (Hitler invasion of Russia) .... Abuse
Then until summer of 1943 .... Praise
Since summer of 1943 .... Abuse[11]

In addition to the above contentions, Kohlberg posed a number of questions to the members and trustees of the IPR. Among the questions were, (1) whether there was a sinister purpose behind the Communist-inspired campaign of the IPR to discredit China, (2) whether or not the publication of untruthful statements regarding China and Chiang Kai-shek constituted treason, and (3) whether the publications of the American and Pacific councils of the IPR had closely followed the Communist line in alternate praise and abuse of the Chinese Government.[12]

The initial response of the officers and trustees of the Institute of Pacific Relations to Kohlberg's charges was to reply, "The Executive Committee and the responsible officers of the American Council find no reason to consider seriously the charge of bias."[13] The trustees apparently thought this would be the end of Kohlberg's attack. If so, they were quite mistaken. From 1945 to 1947, Kohlberg continued on the offensive in newspapers, magazines, and the courts.

On March 22, 1947, Kohlberg formally presented his charges to a meeting of trustees and members of the IPR, called specifically for that purpose. He had previously secured a mailing list of the membership, sent them a detailed statement of his accusations, and requested that they either come to the meeting or mail him their proxy votes. His intention was to establish a committee to investigate his charges. Kohlberg's resolution was decisively defeated by a vote of 66 to 1,163.[14]

Up to this point, Kohlberg's attack on the IPR (as in his attack on Lattimore), whatever motives may have prompted it, seemed to be primarily a unilateral effort. It was apparently directed, however, toward promoting a positive, pro-Chiang point of view in the publications of the institute. The failure of this attempt early in 1947 was followed by Kohlberg's resignation from the IPR and the beginning of his active participation in a new organization, the American China Policy Association.[15] Here he found an effective medium of expression and, even though his initial efforts had apparently failed, he expanded his attack on the IPR to the entire range of American policy toward China. That expansion was implicit in certain of the remarks contained in his letter of March 18, 1947, to the members of the IPR:

> In order to keep this letter within reasonable length, I have omitted going into the following:
> . . . (7) Members of our Board of Trustees and our staff managed to get control of the Far Eastern Division of the State Department, UNRRA and OWI, where they loaded all three with pro-Communists. Two of them, Owen Lattimore and John Carter Vincent, accompanied Henry Wallace to China in 1944. . . .
> (8) Four of the six persons arrested in the Amerasia case were connected with the IPR.[16]

Although Kohlberg omitted going into details of these questions in his letter, he did not neglect them in other media. Nor were they neglected by other pro-Chiang groups. At every opportunity, both points were made with great elaboration. Freda Utley, John T. Flynn, Walter Judd, the Reverend Johnson, and Robert Dresser based much of their writing on these two ideas in their attempt to prove the contention that China was conquered by the Communists because of treason in the United States. In this manner the attack on the Institute of Pacific Relations became an important element, along with the attack on the private Far Eastern specialists, in the China lobby's explanation of American responsibility for Chiang's loss of control in China.

As in so many other elements of China lobby propaganda, the attack on the IPR had few serious effects on the organization until certain other developments had helped to create a favorable climate of opinion. Once the loss of China to the Communists, the conviction of Hiss, and the intervention of the Chinese in the Korean War (to list only a few of the outstanding events) had created sufficient confusion and frustration among the American people, however, the extreme explanation offered by the China lobby was accepted and acted upon. In this case as in the others, the effects were made apparent through the official action of Congress. Kohlberg anticipated such a result in his letter of March 18, 1947, to the members of the IPR, in which he expressed the opinion, "Our trustees will not act and if we wait until Congressional investigation reaches us, it may be too late to save our institution and even our good reputation."[17]

The prelude to congressional action occurred early in 1950. At that time, three years after the defeat of Kohlberg's attempt to secure control of the IPR, his charges were incorporated in Senator McCarthy's attack on the United States Department of State. McCarthy's accusations, which included charges against the IPR as an organization, as well as a long list of people allegedly connected with it, almost exactly paralleled those previously made by Kohlberg.[18] Nevertheless, the Tydings Subcommittee, which investigated McCarthy's allegations, devoted little attention to the IPR as such. By contrast, the McCarran Subcommittee concentrated its whole attention on it.

The public phase of the investigation anticipated by Kohlberg began on July 25, 1951. The investigation was conducted by the Internal Security Subcommittee of the Committee on the Judiciary, under the chairmanship of Senator McCarran of Nevada. The public hearings were preceded by several months of closed hearings, and by study of the files of the IPR by the staff of the subcommittee.[19]

A review of these hearings, of the report issued by the subcommittee, and of the manner in which the information produced by the hearings was used in the report is necessary in order to show the extent to which the effect of the investigation on the IPR was in fact an effect produced by the acceptance of China lobby views. The extent to which the committee had accepted those views is clearly implied in its statement of the object or purpose of the investigation. In the words of the report, the members of the subcommittee were attempting to determine:

(a) Whether or to what extent the Institute of Pacific Relations was infiltrated and influenced or controlled by agents of the communist world conspiracy;

(b) Whether or to what extent these agents and their dupes worked through the Institute into the United States Government to the point where they exerted an influence on United States far eastern policy; and if so, whether and to what extent they still exert such influence;

(c) Whether or to what extent these agents and their dupes led or misled American public opinion, particularly with respect to far eastern policy.[20]

Obviously the last objective in itself, from a dispassionate point of view, would have required that the members of the committee either know or determine through the hearings exactly what the facts concerning Far Eastern policy were. Nevertheless, no United States Secretary of State, current or former, was called to testify. General Marshall was not called. Nor did any civilian or military official, or representative of the press, who had spent any appreciable amount of time in Communist-held areas of China, appear before the committee. On the other hand, the committee heard testimony from eight ex-Communists, three persons who claimed to have been former Soviet officials, and a number of the most extreme pro-Chiang critics of American China policy. Among the latter were Bullitt, Chennault, Admiral Cooke, Harold Stassen, and Wedemeyer.[21] Most of the other witnesses called before the committee were people who had been accused of Communist sympathies, affiliations, or activities. Throughout the course of the hearings, no expression of fact or opinion, or interpretation of fact, concerning events or policy in China, which did not coincide with the preconceptions of the committee members, was permitted to stand without strenuous efforts by the committee personnel to refute it.[22] On the other hand, testimony which agreed with the preconceptions of committee members and their counsel was not only allowed to stand unchallenged but was often encouraged by prompting, leading questions, and rephrasing of statements into more "acceptable" language.[23]

Evidence of the attitude with which the committee undertook its task of investigating the IPR and "the extent to which subversive forces may have influenced or sought to influence the formulation and execution of our far eastern policy" emerges from the opening statement made by the chairman.[24] In that statement McCarran attempted to set forth the views with which the committee had begun its task:

It is virtually impossible to define fully and accurately, in the abstract, the components of disloyalty or subversion. The inner currents of the human mind are at best difficult to gage [sic]. Motives are often so obscure that sometimes one does not fully comprehend his own impelling urges, and may completely misjudge the motives of an associate. Successful conspirators usually are consummate dissemblers; and thus the acts of such persons are often shrouded in the darkness of stealth, accompanied by acts of misdirection, or clouded by ambiguity of meaning.

. . . It is possible to verify the loyalty of an ex-Communist, in large part, by the very extent of his willingness to give full and frank testimony against the Communist Party.[25]

An approach to testimony which assumes the loyalty and truthful-ness of ex-Communists, and implies that anyone who criticized the Government of Chiang Kai-shek or urged greater American-Soviet cooperation was either a "consummate dissembler" or did not "fully comprehend his own impelling urges," is, for obvious reasons, open to objection on grounds of fair procedures and objective worth. And in fact the committee concentrated its attention in its report entirely on "evidence" which sought to condemn American policy in China; conversely it ignored all defense of that work and policy. The report which resulted was an extremely prejudiced presentation of the facts developed in the hearings.[*]

One of the many incidents which illustrates such prejudice, and in which the conclusions followed both the spirit and phraseology of pro-Chiang propaganda, concerned the Wallace mission to China.

The mission of Vice President Wallace to China brought more pressure on the Chinese Government by the United States and this pressure also coincided with the recommendations of the Chinese Communists.

With Wallace on the mission were John Carter Vincent, Owen Lattimore, and John N. Hazard. Louis Budenz, who lived this episode from the vantage point of editor of the Daily Worker, and who was a member of the National Committee of the Communist Party, testified that the Wallace mission was an aid to the Communists in that the Communists had two men with Wallace, Lattimore and Vincent, who were guiding the mission along Commu-nist lines.[26]

What the members of the subcommittee considered to be the "evidence" to support this characterization of the Wallace mission was cited in the report. The citations included Budenz's argument that the Communists approved Wallace's suggestion to President Roosevelt that General Stilwell be removed or have his political functions curtailed. No citations to the contrary evidence or to other interpretations of the Wallace mission or the Stilwell removal were included in the report.[27][†]

---

[*] The American Council of the IPR prepared a detailed reply to the McCarran Subcommittee after the *IPR Report* was issued. See *Commentary on the McCarran Report on the IPR* (New York: American Institute of Pacific Relations, 1953).

[†] On this point, Joseph Alsop presented a substantial argument (*IPR Hearings,* Pt. 5, pp. 1403–1489) designed to show that this characterization of the Wallace mission was false. Alsop argued, in fact, that the Communists wanted Stilwell retained in his post in China in order further to disrupt relations between the United States and Chiang. The subcommittee cited none of Alsop's evidence and testimony in the report. Alsop's purpose was to refute previous testimony given by Budenz. The subcommittee adopted, without qualification, the Budenz argu-ment.

Using these methods, and without citing the qualifying and contradictory evidence in its files, the subcommittee published certain conclusions which served effectively to condemn the IPR. These conclusions illustrate both the complete acceptance of China lobby views and the extent to which that acceptance had served to destroy the reputation of the IPR as a scholarly organization. The subcommittee's report, which was ultimately accepted for publication by the entire Senate, consisted of four major accusations against the IPR. Although not always clearly delineated because of duplication and overlapping in the report, the four major accusations were: (1) that the primary activity of the IPR resulted in promoting the interests of the Soviet Union; (2) that the IPR was not an objective, scholarly research organization but was, rather, a pressure group which misled the American people on the subject of the Chinese Communists and as to the purposes and aims of the Soviet Union; (3) that the IPR was extensively infiltrated with Communists; and (4) that the IPR was instrumental in changing American policy in China from support of Chiang to support of the Communists.

The first accusation—that the major activity of the IPR was to promote the interests of the Soviet Union[28]—was based primarily on the entirely correct finding that IPR officials—particularly Carter, Lattimore, Harriet Moore, and W. L. Holland—had made extensive and sustained efforts in the 1930's to enlist the support and cooperation of the Soviet Union in the work of the organization. These efforts had eventually resulted in the creation, in 1934, of a Soviet Council composed of representatives of several existing Soviet organizations.[29] Efforts to secure the *active participation* of the new Soviet Council then continued from 1934 to 1945.

In fact, officials of the IPR often exerted considerable effort to avoid antagonizing the Soviets. While this attitude was entirely understandable in view of their objectives and the climate of opinion of that period, it appeared highly suspicious in the prevailing mood of 1951. The subcommittee took the position that the IPR became, as one witness expressed it, a "cover-shop":[30]

. . . It is like a double-way track. On one line you get information from America through this institute. On the other hand, you send information which you would like to implant in American brains through the same channel of the institute.[31]*

---

* Considerable space is taken up in the report with the testimony of Barmine, Bogolepov, and a third ex-Soviet official, Poppe. Whatever the value of this

Using this characterization of the IPR as a point of departure, the subcommittee arrived at its second major accusation—that the IPR was not an objective, scholarly research organization, but was, on the contrary, a pressure group which misled the American people on the subject of the Chinese Communists and as to the purposes and aims of the Soviet Union.[32] This accusation was based partly on what appears on the surface to have been a serious misunderstanding of the relations between an organization and its members, and between a publication and those who contribute articles to it.* In discussing the "ostensible aims of the Institute of Pacific Relations," for example, the report quotes an "emphatic" comment by Holland that ". . . no IPR publication has advocated communism or urged acceptance of Communist policies or programs." The report then continues:

> It may be observed . . . that, if this statement is true, then the IPR failed in the purpose which Mr. Holland simultaneously attributed to it of providing "a forum in which issues of the day may be debated from all points of view." If pro-communism was excluded, then it is not the case that the IPR permitted all points of view.[33]

These comments indicate that the subcommittee failed to distinguish between an *IPR publication* advocating a point of view as a matter of policy (to which Holland's comment was a reference), and an *individual* advocating a point of view *in* an IPR publication.

This misunderstanding was of importance to two of the specific items in the subcommittee's general accusation that the IPR was not, in fact, an objective, scholarly organization. The first such item consisted of the charge that the IPR was "interlocked" with other organizations:

> The group of IPR activists who comprised the IPR family did not by any means limit their sphere of action to the IPR framework. They were zealous in journalism, the universities, and in government, and they were found in

---

testimony, the actual records from the IPR files (the memoranda of conversations and conferences and the correspondence between officials of the Soviet and Pacific councils), some of which were included in the records of the hearings, were far more to the point. They show that the officials of the Pacific Council had little success in securing the active cooperation of the Soviet Council in the affairs of IPR at any time; after 1939 there was practically no participation by the Soviets.

*   A reading of the rather long discussion of this question in the *Report* (pp. 63–70), raises some question as to whether there was actually a misunderstanding of this relation on the part of the authors, or whether the relation was purposely obscured.

especially heavy concentration in a number of organizations with interests and aims falling directly or indirectly within the sphere of interest of the IPR itself. The IPR was, indeed, one of a system or galaxy of organizations which were interrelated both by similarities of interest and by interlocking of active personnel. . . . The other organizations in the system all in one way or another influenced United States public opinion. It is impossible to understand the nature of the IPR and the IPR family, or their relation to public opinion, without having in mind the system of which they were one part.[34]

This paragraph was followed in the report by a section devoted to a review of certain organizations with which members of the "IPR family" were also "connected." The organizations reviewed were: (1) Committee for a Democratic Far Eastern Policy, (2) The China Aid Council, (3) the magazine *Amerasia*, (4) the magazine *China Today*, (5) the American-Russian Institute, and (6) the Allied Labor News, a syndicated news gathering agency.[35]* Various citations in the review purport to show interlocking of these organizations with the IPR.[36] The terminology used in the report to indicate the connections of individuals with the various organizations, including the IPR, is often difficult to evaluate. Nevertheless, examination of the cited evidence fails to substantiate the claim of the subcommittee that there was a significant "interlocking of active personnel."†

* It should be noted that the only organizations thus reviewed were those which the subcommittee contended were Communist controlled, although the report noted that IPR personnel were active in many other organizations which were apparently not so controlled.

† Exhibit 1334 (see note 36, above) is an excellent—and typical—illustration of this point. The table lists the names of forty-three individuals who supposedly comprise the interlocking relationship between IPR and the Committee for a Democratic Far Eastern Policy. One of the forty-three, Talitha Gerlach, was never associated with IPR in any way except that she wrote two letters to the headquarters office in 1943. She was never a member, contributor, or employee of IPR. The "connection" of the other forty-two with the two organizations is indicated as follows. One is listed as a "reference" for CDFEP. This relates to the fact that a 1946 circular distributed by CDFEP quoted from an article by this individual which had previously appeared in the *New Yorker*. He was a member of the IPR board of trustees. Four were individuals whose books had been recommended by CDFEP; they are not shown as either members or sponsors of the organization. The cited connections of these four with IPR were as follows: One had a book "promoted" in *Pacific Affairs* in 1944, more than a year before the formation of CDFEP; one had written an article for *Pacific Affairs* in 1940; one had been a research associate, and another a staff member of IPR. Fourteen individuals were listed as "consultants" for CDFEP. Their "connections" with IPR were: three were members (subscribers) only; six were "writers," of whom five had contributed a single item from two to ten years earlier; two were "authors" whose books had been "promoted" in IPR publications; one coauthored an IPR pam-

Another of the specific charges which the subcommittee made to substantiate its general accusation that the IPR was not an objective, scholarly organization was that an analysis of IPR publications showed that "the net effect of the IPR activities on United States public opinion has been pro-Communist and pro-Soviet, and has frequently been such as to serve international Communist, American Communist, Chinese Communist, and Soviet interests and to affect adversely the interests of the United States."[37] The report recognizes that "no statistical study could encompass or reflect a qualitative appraisal,"[38] but that problem had already been overcome by an earlier observation:

... The presence in the IPR literature of a considerable bulk of "neutral" [that is, not positively anti-Communist] writing, if along with it and on dynamically significant issues there is a body (even though relatively small in quantity) of tendentious writing weighted in a single main political direction, only gives added significance and effect to the latter. Non-Communist or "neutral" writing plus predominantly pro-Communist writing means, whatever the exact percentages, a net pro-Communist effect.[39]

With this and a considerable number of other comments of similar import as justification, the subcommittee presented a number of examples of what was characterized as pro-Communist writing. Many of the examples used as evidence in the hearings came, not from IPR publications, but from other publications for which in-

---

phlet more than ten years earlier; one had once been a staff writer and editor; and another had once been an editor for IPR. Eight individuals were listed as "writers" for CDFEP. Of these eight, one was listed as a "collaborator" of IPR, three were members (subscribers) only, and the remaining four, listed as "writers," had contributed one item each to IPR publications. Six individuals were listed as sponsors of CDFEP. (One of these six, rather than having sponsored the organization itself, had merely sponsored a dinner given under the auspices of the organization. He was an IPR trustee.) Of the other five, two were members of IPR only; the remaining three had contributed one item each to IPR publications before CDFEP was organized. One individual, who was listed as an editor for CDFEP, had been a member only of IPR five years prior to the organization of CDFEP. Seven individuals were listed as officers of CDFEP. Six of the seven were also listed as writers and members of IPR and two of the six had written for IPR publications during the period in which CDFEP was an active organization. One officer (F. V. Field) had been secretary of the American Council from 1936 to 1940. He resigned that position five years before CDFEP was organized, but had continued to serve on the IPR Board of Trustees until 1947 which was also the year in which he was listed as an officer of CDFEP. One person was listed as a member of the Executive Committee of CDFEP and was also shown as a writer and member of IPR. His last contribution to an IPR publication, however, was in 1938.

dividuals characterized by the report as "IPR activists" wrote. The presentation of these examples was followed by a statistical analysis which led the subcommittee to the following conclusions:

> To sum up, at least three-tenths of all the items that have appeared in the Far Eastern Survey in the period under study have come from pro-Communist sources. During the Field-Lattimore period (1934–40) almost half the material came from such sources.
>
> Pro-Communist contributions in *Pacific Affairs* have been proportionately less. They amount only to about one-sixth. However, during his term as editor, Lattimore managed to raise the share contributed by such sources to nearly one-fourth of the total.[40]*

It should be noted that the publications of the member councils generally avoided obvious attacks on the governments of other member councils. This rule was violated, if at all, only in reference to Japan after 1937. The McCarran Subcommittee took the point of view, however, that criticisms of the Soviet Government and Soviet policies should have been published by the IPR *because* these policies were Communist. But such criticism could come only from anti-Communist sources. Had the IPR included such material in its publications, it would have been in the position of also having to include criticisms of non-Communist governments and policies written by Communists. The subcommittee, however, was equally critical of that approach and, in fact, attempted to find examples of such criticisms, which it then used as a basis for condemning the IPR.

A third specific element in the subcommittee's general accusation that the IPR was not an objective, scholarly organization was based on an insistence that "activists" in the organization virtually dominated public-opinion media in matters concerning the Far East. Ac-

---

* Certain observations concerning the analysis which preceded this summary are necessary. (1) Its validity rests on the list of fifty-nine individuals who were considered pro-Communist by the subcommittee. That list included those who "were identified by one or more witnesses testifying under oath before the subcommittee, or by documentary evidence on record before the subcommittee, as having been affiliated with one or more Communist-controlled organizations cited as such on page 146 . . ." (Report, p. 100). (2) It is based on a characterization of the contributor rather than on an analysis of the contribution. (3) It deals only with the material in the two IPR publications *Far Eastern Survey* and *Pacific Affairs,* and omits the far greater bulk of material in pamphlets and books published by or sponsored by the IPR. (4) It ignores the fact that *Pacific Affairs* was the organ of an *international* body of which the Soviet Union was a member and which customarily invited contributions reflecting the point of view of any member council so long as it was not an attack on the government of another member council. .

cording to the subcommittee, "a considerable portion of the IPR activities operated not to discover, analyze, assemble and publish data . . . but to influence public opinion." The effort in this direction was not limited to "books, magazines, pamphlets, and so forth," but extended also to "promotion, public relations, lobbying, propaganda, etc."[41] The report also argued that "IPR authors frequently wrote also for general magazines and for ordinary commercial book publishers."[42] More important, however:

> They were heavily concentrated in one particular journalistic area which is of the highest significance in the determination of public opinion: namely, the book-review pages of those journals which have the greatest effect on the sales and distribution of books.[43]

The committee found this concentration peculiar and sinister in spite of its recognition that virtually all Far Eastern specialists in the United States were members of IPR:

> The IPR had, in short, a near monopoly on the presentation to the public of material dealing with the Far East. In university circles, this meant that teachers, scholars, or students who were or became interested in problems of the Pacific were in practice virtually compelled to become at least passive members of the IPR—that is, at least members in the minimum sense that meant subscribing to its publications—and that they were dependent in their field to a considerable extent on the work of the IPR.[44]

This concentration of Far Eastern specialists provided a basis for a third major accusation against the IPR. Again, it was an accusation which had been made for years by the China lobby. Stated in its most succinct form, this was the charge that the American and Pacific councils of the IPR were extensively infiltrated with Communists who constituted an "inner core" which determined the real nature of the organization. This accusation was in addition to the first charge dealt with above, which accused the top IPR officials—particularly Carter, Holland, Lattimore, and Harriet Moore—of promoting the interests of the Soviet Union. That charge was based on the relationship between those officials and the Soviet Council. In this case, however, the accusation was that the American and Pacific councils had themselves come to be dominated by Communists. It was based on a specific definition of a "Communist" which had long been advocated by the China lobby.[45]

Preliminary to the section entitled "Communist Influence in the Institute of Pacific Relations," the report examined this question of who is a Communist:

In dealing with Communist penetration and influence, one must be aware of the various grades, shades and variations of those operating within the Communist orbit and serving the interests of Joseph Stalin. It is not merely a simple matter of locating an openly avowed card-carrying member of the Communist Party. . . .

Obviously among the best sources of information as to the nature of the Communist conspiracy are those who have actually participated therein, who have sincerely broken with the movement, and who are seeking to expose its true nature in their effort to combat that movement and serve the interests of the United States. Among the witnesses in this group are [the "ex-Communists"]. . . . Testimony of these witnesses points to the need for distinguishing between rank and file Communists or Communist Party officials, who openly assert their beliefs in communism, and those who hold responsible positions elsewhere and who, while maintaining their fraternal relations with the party, may even repudiate the party openly. Individuals in the latter group may not be permitted to give any indication of association with Communists or the Communist apparatus . . . They may have been instructed not to display any Communist membership, and to avoid any public relations with Communists. . . . Thus Mr. Budenz declared most Communists do not carry party cards but are yet subject to Communist allegiance. . . . Mr. Budenz also called attention to what he termed "allies of the Communists" whom the Communists hail as liberals and progressives. . . . Actually, party credentials are seldom necessary for Communist operations. At times Communist operatives would be simply referred to, by official sources, as "our men" or "one of ours." . . .

It was in view of these complexities that committee counsel, in questioning witnesses, often insisted the word "Communists" be used to connote a person under Communist discipline or who has voluntarily and knowingly cooperated or collaborated with Communist Party members in furtherance of Communist Party objectives. In other words, in weighing the degree and significance of Communist infiltration and influence in any organization, it is necessary to proceed from this broad basis.

From the standpoint of our national security it should be noted that a well-intentioned but fuzzy-minded fellow traveler can be almost as dangerous as a knowing conspirator. From the standpoint of Joseph Stalin, he can be equally fruitful merely by serving as an unwitting instrument of Communist trickery.[46]

On "this broad basis," the subcommittee constructed a list of "54 persons connected in various ways with IPR [who] were identified by witnesses as participants in the Communist world conspiracy against democracy."[47] A footnote breaks this number down into forty-six as having been "cited as Communist Party members," and eleven of the forty-six plus eight others as having been "cited as collaborating with agents of the Soviet intelligence apparatus."[48] Thus the total of fifty-four. Another list, entitled "Summary of Communist Affiliations by Individuals with Their IPR Functions," con-

tained a total of eighty-eight names.[49] It included the fifty-four on
the first list plus thirty-four others. The additional thirty-four names
on this list were "IPR individuals," who "made one or more trips
to Communist territory"; or were "writers for official publications
of the Communist Party or the Communist International or of a
Communist government"; or "were the subject of action by either
an agency of the American Government or a foreign non-Communist government on grounds involving loyalty or national
security."[50]

This list lay at the heart of the subcommittee's characterization of
the IPR as an organization dominated by Communists. It contained
the name of virtually every individual accused by the subcommittee
of having had a pro-Communist influence on the IPR. Although
these individuals comprised only a very small percentage of those
who were employed by IPR or whose books and articles were published by IPR during the twenty years covered by the investigation,
they were considered by the subcommittee to have been the key
personnel.[51] Considering the importance attached to these eighty-
eight individuals by the subcommittee, a brief analysis of their relationship to the IPR and of the evidence concerning their identity as
Communists is pertinent.*

Of the eighty-eight individuals listed in the "Summary," twenty-
four had no real connection with the IPR. The breakdown is as
follows. Two who are listed as employees of IPR do not appear
actually ever to have been employed.† Four are listed as "supporter," which meant that they were never employees, officers, or
contributors, but may have been asked for some advice or service
by an IPR official at some time.‡ One was a member of the Japanese

---

* The list of eighty-eight names also contains such information as (1) the alleged
IPR connection, (2) the alleged Communist connection(s), (3) whether or not the
Communist allegation was denied, and (4) the affiliation of the individual with
alleged Communist organizations. In most cases citations are given to the evidence
in the record of the hearings on which the information is based. The analysis which
follows is based on a check of all cited references in the hearings and, where
indicated, a follow-up of other information developed in the course of the hearings and included in the printed record.

† The listing of Harriet Chi is not supported by the cited source; the cited source
for Katherine Terrill is not supported by Exhibit 801.

‡ The evidence for the supporter classification is extremely meager. In the order of
their appearance on the list, however, Solomon Adler, who was a representative
of the Treasury Department in China, was mentioned by Holland, in a letter to
Chi Ch'ao-ting, as one of three persons by whom Chi might send back a reply to
Holland's letter during World War II when mail was slow and uncertain. This is
the only evidence of Adler's support for the IPR; there is no indication that he

Council, but was never connected with the Pacific or American Council.[52] One was a secretary of the American Council for a brief period in 1933, but appears to have had no connection except that of ordinary member after that date.[53] Six were members only, which means that they subscribed to one or more IPR periodicals. Ten were either invited to an IPR conference or at some time attended an IPR conference but are not shown to have had any other connection. Those who did attend in this category, apparently were observers only.*

Twenty-nine individuals on the list of eighty-eight were classified as "writers." Nineteen of these were "identified as members of the Communist Party" by witnesses before the subcommittee or were "named in sworn testimony as having collaborated with agents of the Soviet Intelligence apparatus." Of these nineteen, twelve were either reported to be dead or "out of the country or otherwise unavailable for subpena" [sic]. Four were never called to testify; three appeared before the subcommittee and refused to say whether they were ever Communists. The other ten of the twenty-nine "writers" were not "identified" by witnesses as Communists. Twenty-four of the twenty-nine, however, had written fewer than five items each for IPR publications during the twenty years covered by the investigation.[54] All were independent authors whose articles had been accepted for publication by the IPR. Most of the twenty-nine had published only one item under IPR auspices.

Six of the individuals on the list under consideration were trustees of the IPR for varying periods of time.† One of these six, Mortimer Graves, was not "identified" as a Communist by any witness. Three of the remaining five denied under oath the accusations against

---

delivered a letter to Holland or was ever asked to do so. Lawrence Duggan's support for the IPR is supposedly shown by the fact that he was consulted on the "possibility of establishing IPR groups in certain Latin-American countries." Nothing ever came of this proposal. The evidence for the other two "supporters," Lamont and Miss Gerlach, is equally meager.

* Harry Dexter White illustrates the use made of this category. His only connection with IPR was apparently the fact that he was proposed as one of the government officials who might be invited to attend IPR conferences. He was apparently invited twice; he attended on neither occasion. So far as the record shows, he was never a member, trustee, or officer of the IPR, and none of his writing was ever published by IPR.

† In those instances in which individuals appear in more than one category, for example, writer and member, or writer and employee, or trustee and employee, the most significant relationship is used for this analysis. In terms of affecting the policies and activities of the IPR, the significant categories appear to be first, employees, and second, trustees.

them; one refused to answer the pertinent question; the other was Hiss. It should also be noted that one of these trustees, John Carter Vincent, was appointed on a complimentary basis for one year, during which time he attended no meetings. Two others, Hiss and John K. Fairbank, became trustees in 1947.

The remaining twenty-nine individuals were employed by IPR for varying lengths of time during the period covered. Sixteen of these twenty-nine were not "identified" by any witness as Communists. Five of the remaining thirteen denied under oath the charges which were made against them and were never prosecuted for perjury. Of the remaining eight, three were unavailable for subpoena and five refused to answer questions concerning their Communist affiliations.

Thus, of the thirty-five individuals on the list who had significant connections with the IPR (six trustees and twenty-nine employees), seventeen were not identified as Communists. An additional eight denied the accusation under oath and were not prosecuted for the denial. This leaves a total of ten who were "identified" as Communists and either refused to deny the accusation or were not called before the subcommittee. Of these ten, Hiss and Len De Caux were trustees on a board which usually numbered about fifty. Three of the eight employees left the employ of the IPR prior to 1941, one was not employed after 1942, and another left in 1944.[55] One of the remaining three was not employed until 1948, and one (Field) resigned his position as an employee in 1940, but continued to serve as a trustee until 1947. The single remaining member of the list, Helen Schneider, was "identified" as a Communist (by Budenz) and refused to deny the accusation. She was employed as business manager of *Pacific Affairs* from April of 1946 to April of 1949.[56]

Having prepared the ground with its list of "Communist affiliations by individuals with their IPR functions," the subcommittee issued its fourth and final major accusation against the IPR. The charge was that the IPR was instrumental in changing American policy in China from support of the "recognized government" to support of the Communists. Three general periods were covered in the report. The first period was introduced with the general charge:

A group of persons associated with the Institute of Pacific Relations attempted, between 1941 and 1945, to change United States policy so as to accommodate Communist ends and to set the stage for a major United States policy change, favorable to Soviet interests, in 1945.[57]

The subcommittee argued:

All during this period, 1941–45, it was the publicly expressed and clearly defined official policy of the United States to aid the Government of Nationalist China. . . . It was also United States policy to keep the armies of that Government fighting the common enemy, Japan. But, during this period there developed a distinct undermining of this policy.

Through three different approaches, efforts were made to bring pressure on the Nationalist Government, by the United States Government, to cause a change in the policies of the Chinese sovereign state.

They were: (1) The efforts of Foreign Service officers in the field, 1943–44; (2) the Henry A. Wallace mission; and (3) the directive to General Marshall and its implementation.[58]

These charges were further supplemented in the report by the following contentions: (1) Currie sent Lattimore to advise Chiang in 1941;[59] (2) IPR personnel worked to prevent a truce between the United States and Japan in 1941;[60] (3) the IPR maintained close relations and a continuing liaison with the White House through Currie;[61] (4) reports of the Foreign Service officers in the field closely paralleled IPR policies;[62] (5) the Wallace mission to China in 1944 carried out the policies of the IPR and the Communists;[63] (6) the IPR was active in United States postwar planning;[64] and (7) the IPR brought Soviet agent Vladimir Rogoff to confer with IPR policy planners in the United States Government.[65]

The second period covered in the report was introduced with the statement:

Owen Lattimore and John Carter Vincent of the Institute of Pacific Relations were influential in bringing about a change in United States policy in 1945 favorable to the Chinese Communists.[66]

It was further argued that:

During the period 1945–49, persons associated with the Institute of Pacific Relations were instrumental in keeping United States policy on a course favorable to Communist objectives in China.[67]

These arguments were supplemented with information purporting to show various attitudes toward Chiang Kai-shek. The subtitles in this section read: (A) IPR Against Aid to Chiang; (B) General Marshall Intervenes in China;[68] (C) American Assistance to Chinese Government Stopped in 1946; (D) United States Policy Discourages Aid to Chiang; (E) John Carter Vincent Against Chiang; and (F) Other IPR Leaders Against Chiang.[69]

The third period dealt with in the report was the last year prior to the outbreak of war in Korea. The section is subtitled "How Persons Associated with the IPR Were Influential in 1949 Shaping and Moving United States Policy in the Direction of Communist Objectives."[70] The main subjects covered are (1) the issuance of the White Paper on China in August of 1949, (2) the three-day conference for a review of China policy held by the Department of State in October of 1949, and (3) the State Department's struggle with the question of recognition of the new Communist regime in China in late 1949 and early 1950. In regard to each of these subjects, the report insisted that the Department of State had followed a pro-Communist policy prepared by the IPR and carried out by IPR personnel in the Department.

The condemnation of the Institute of Pacific Relations by the McCarran Subcommittee could hardly have been more thorough. It condemned the organization for having attempted to extend its international character by cooperating with the Soviet Council. It condemned it for having allegedly failed to maintain its objective, scholarly character as a research organization. It condemned it as a Communist-dominated organization. Finally it condemned it for having influenced United States policy in what the subcommittee termed a pro-Communist direction. Even before the issuance of the report, the effects of the investigation were felt beyond the confines of Congress.

Early in 1952, John T. Flynn delivered a series of lectures, over "more than 220 stations," which he entitled "Why Korea? Story of Blackest Intrigue and Betrayal in America's History."[71] Flynn opened his first broadcast on the subject with these remarks:

I want to tell you a story of intrigue—revolutionary intrigue in this country—perhaps the strangest episode of its kind in the history of this nation. It's the kind of thing that happened in France before the French Revolution and that was common in Russia. But nothing like this ever happened in America before.

As you know, we are bogged down in Asia—trapped in Asia—a hundred thousand Americans killed or wounded. Countless billions of dollars are pouring out in an impossible war where no man can see the end. How did this happen? It did not happen by accident. It happened according to plan and I now want to tell you the incredible story of this plan.

... This happened because Russia armed and supported the Chinese Reds and because the United States refused to support and disarmed the Chinese Nationalist Government. Thus we gave China to communism. . . . Now the question is: Why did we abandon the Chinese Nationalist Government?

The charge has been made that this was the result of the combined action of a group of men in the American State Department teamed up with a group of pro-Communist organizations which dominated American policy and resulted in our disaster in Asia. Who were these men and women responsible for this appalling disaster, and why did they do it? I propose in this and the next four broadcasts to try to tell you this almost unbelievable story. We know the truth now because a Senate Committee of five Democrats and four Republicans, known as the McCarran Committee, have been investigating this question for nearly a year and the facts are now all available.

. . . The American people knew little of China and still less about the strange instruments of Communist propaganda. This made a perfect set-up for the friends of Red China in America. Strange as it may seem, their task was simple. Their chief aim was to penetrate those bureaus in the American government which decided our policy toward China. There were many organizations formed by these pro-Red Chinese lovers, but there was one organization which was the master organization. . . . It was called the Institute of Pacific Relations—the IPR—and this became the center of this movement. The master organization was called the Pacific Council of the IPR. There was another called the American Council of the IPR and it was these two which did the job.[72]

What followed in Flynn's broadcasts was a very accurate summary of the report which the McCarran Subcommittee issued some four months later. A year later, Flynn published a book which he entitled *The Lattimore Story,* with the subtitle "The full story of the most incredible conspiracy of our time."[73] In an earlier book, Flynn had credited the United States Government with the primary responsibility for the policies followed in China.[74] In *The Lattimore Story* he adopted the more orthodox view—the view of the McCarran Subcommittee—of a conspiracy headed by Owen Lattimore and the IPR.

A footnote on the subject of the IPR in a recent work on American foreign policy, by a reputable American political scientist, gives some indication of the effect which the acceptance of China lobby views by the McCarran Subcommittee has had:

Of importance . . . is the question of direct Communist influence in the IPR, which was commonly regarded in those years as the authoritative organization for research and publication on the Far East. No brief summary here can do justice to the massive weight of evidence accumulated by the McCarran Committee during its long investigation in 1951 and 1952. By the standards reasonably applicable to congressional probes, this one was conscientious and productive. Its 5,000 pages of testimony, with extensive and orderly documentation, deserve more respectful attention than they have received from most liberal critics, many of whom have not even bothered to read the committee's 200-page report. Unfortunately, there is room here only to state a personal conclusion: that a Communist solution for Asia was favored by a large enough proportion of the active participants in the American IPR to affect substantially the content of its publications and the character of its public relations work and contacts with government.[75]

The real story of the effects suffered by the IPR as a result of the acceptance of China lobby views is told in the annual reports issued by the American Council since 1951.[76] Foundation grants fell from $30,000 in 1951 to $15,000 in 1952. No further grants from foundations have been reported.* Total income of the American Council dropped from $77,000 in 1951 to $18,600 in 1956. During the same period, membership contributions fell from $35,000 to $13,-000 and total members from 933 to 341.[77]

The finances of IPR were seriously affected also by the revocation of the organization's tax exemption status in 1955. The action was taken by T. Coleman Andrews, then Commissioner of Internal Revenue, at the specific request of Senator James Eastland who had succeeded McCarran as chairman of the Judiciary Committee and chairman of the Subcommittee on Internal Security. This action, which denies tax exemption on contributions to the IPR, was initiated by Andrews himself rather than in the Division of Tax-exempt Organizations where such matters are usually handled.[78] The ruling is still (June, 1959) in effect, and the international IPR office has filed suit in New York Federal Court after having waited for over three years for a reply from the Internal Revenue Service on its appeal for a reconsideration of the 1955 ruling. The case is not expected to come to trial until early 1960. In March of 1959, IPR requested a summary judgment in its favor because the Government had failed to produce any concrete instances in which the IPR had attempted to "influence Government policy and Government officials." The request was denied, and the judge ruled that the McCarran Report would be admissible as evidence and, therefore, there was substantial disagreement on matters of fact which would have to be settled

---

* The exact relationship between IPR's troubles with Congress and the loss of foundation support is difficult to judge because the foundations were already beginning (before the McCarran investigation) to end their practice of giving *general support* grants to private organizations other than universities. There is no doubt, however, that the climate of opinion which resulted from the acceptance of China lobby views affected many influential foundation trustees and thus made the foundation officers much more cautious about recommending grants to organizations which had become "controversial." Equally significant is the fact that all large corporate donations to the IPR ceased after 1951.

in a trial. According to a recent communication from IPR officials, Internal Revenue personnel have admitted that "*except* for the McCarran committee allegations, they cannot produce any concrete evidence to substantiate their charge that the IPR attempted to influence Government policy and Government officials."

The cumulative effect of these events on the IPR have been such that, in 1957, the Executive Committee of the American Council gave serious consideration to going out of existence.[79] An effort was actually made early in the year to persuade a new organization in New York—the Asia Society—to take over American IPR functions. The new organization was founded under the leadership of John D. Rockefeller, 3rd, whose family fortune had once provided substantial support for the IPR.

The full measure of the tragedy which today has fallen on the Institute of Pacific Relations may be gleaned from the purpose of the new Asia Society and the reaction of its leaders to the proposal that it assume the functions of the American Council. The Asia Society "has begun its operations by concentrating mainly on social and cultural activities (particularly dinners and receptions for visiting South Asian dignitaries and the organization of exhibits of South Asian art) but expects to expand its work into the educational field."[80] The response to the proposal that the Society take over the functions of the American IPR, however, was more than merely negative. According to the Executive Secretary of the American Council:

It is enough to say that no such plan for taking over the work of the American IPR seemed feasible at the time or in the near future and that the Society does not at present plan to conduct scholarly research or publish a journal similar to the *Far Eastern Survey*. Nor did it seem to the Society's leaders that it would be able to serve as the American national unit of the International IPR.[81]

The effects felt by the IPR as a result of the acceptance of China lobby views soon extended to a vast array of other organizations. This extension of effects resulted initially from two conditions. First, many of the Far Eastern specialists who were accused in the process of the condemnation of the IPR were also affiliated with other organizations. Second, the tendency to characterize organizations on the basis of a judgment of a small minority of the membership resulted in the constant addition of new organizations to the subversive lists.

The condemnation visited on the IPR by the McCarran Subcommittee transferred most easily and directly to the foundations which provided much of its financial support, the Carnegie Corporation and the Rockefeller Foundation. Other organizations devoted to research, publication, and the financing of research, however, soon fell under the same shadow. The extent to which the acceptance of the kind of ideas held by the China lobby affected these other organizations is best illustrated by the report of a special committee of the House of Representatives which was issued on December 16, 1954.[82] That committee, known as the "Reece Committee," was authorized in 1953 to

. . .conduct a full and complete investigation and study of educational and philanthropic foundations and other comparable organizations . . . and especially to determine which such foundations and organizations are using their resources for un-American and subversive activities; for political purposes; propaganda, or attempts to influence legislation.[83]

The committee decided at the outset "to confine our inquiry chiefly to the activities of the foundations in what are known as the 'social sciences.' "[84] Its concept of the kind of activities in which a foundation should engage is indicated early in the report:

. . . Their [the trustees'] financial power gives them enormous leverage in influencing public opinion. They should thus be very chary of promoting ideas, concepts and opinion-forming material which run contrary to what the public currently wishes, approves and likes.[85]

The Reece Committee's report quoted extensively from the testimony of Kenneth Colegrove and David N. Rowe, both of whom had been heavily relied upon by the McCarran Subcommittee for criticism of the IPR. The report also quoted extensively from testimony given by Alfred Kohlberg before a House Committee which was similar to and preceded the Reece Committee.[86]

The IPR was automatically designated an organ of the Communist party in the Reece report through reference to the report of the McCarran Subcommittee just as it had previously been listed by the House Committee on Un-American Activities in its *Guide to Subversive Organizations* simply by citing the McCarran Committee report. For example, one of the conclusions reached by the Reece Committee reads:

With several tragically outstanding exceptions, such as *The Institute of Pacific Relations,* foundations have not directly supported organizations which, in turn, operated to support Communism. However, some of the larger foundations have directly supported "subversion" in the true meaning of that term, namely, the process of undermining some of our vitally protective concepts and principles. They have actively supported attacks upon our social and governmental system and financed the promotion of socialism and collectivist ideas.[87]

The committee's report shows conclusively that its major concern was with (1) "leftist tendencies" in the social sciences, and (2) what the committee termed "internationalism" and "globalism." As to the first concern, the report was quite specific:

Moreover, the Communists do not always work directly. In their desire to undermine our society they operate more frequently than not by indirection, supporting causes which merely tend to the left but cannot be identified as actually Communist.

The main concern of this Committee is not with Communism. We agree with Professor Rowe in his estimate that the greater danger lies in the undermining effect of collectivist or socialist movements. Externally, Communism is the greater danger; internally, socialism offers far greater menace.[88]

The second major concern of the committee, internationalism, was elaborated at some length:

Some of the major foundations have had a significant impact upon our foreign policy and have done much to condition the thinking of our people along "internationalist" lines. What is this "internationalism" which meets with such hearty foundation support? Professor Colegrove in his testimony described it well. He said:

"In my opinion, a great many of the staffs of the foundations have gone way beyond Wendell Wilkie with reference to internationalism and globalism. . . . There is undoubtedly too much money put into studies which support globalism and internationalism. You might say that the other side has not been as fully developed as it should be."

Professor Colegrove pointed out that "the other side" had been well represented in Congress but that the foundations had seen fit to support only the one point of view or approach. He felt that there is a definite tendency to "sacrifice the national interest of our country in dealing with foreign affairs." He said:

". . . But there is too frequently a tendency of Americans not to think in international conferences on foreign policy about the national interest of the United States. We are thinking always of what is the interest of the whole world.[89]

The committee found that this kind of thinking was responsible for having led the foundations and scholarly organizations along dangerous paths of research and publication:

However well-meaning the advocates of complete internationalism may be, they often play into the hands of the Communists. Communists recognize that a breakdown of nationalism is a prerequisite to the introduction of Communism.[90]

The extent of the damage to American security which the committee attributed to the foundations holding such attitudes had been previously indicated:

Alertness on the part of the Rockefeller and Carnegie trustees, and expenditure of the time necessary to see to the use made of the public's money by I.P.R. might have saved China from the Communists and prevented the war in Korea.[91]

On the basis of these fears, the Reece Committee examined and found wanting a large number of the most important foundations and scholarly organizations in the United States. In addition to the Carnegie and Rockefeller foundations, the committee accused seven other foundations specifically of having been penetrated and used by the Communists. They were the Marshall Field Foundation; the Garland Fund; the John Simon Guggenheim Foundation; the Heckscher Foundation; the Robert Marshall Foundation; the Rosenwald Fund; and the Phelps Stokes Fund.[92] It was also severely critical of the several agencies of the Ford Foundation.[93]

Among the large coordinating agencies of the scholarly organizations which were condemned by the committee were the American Council of Learned Societies, the Social Science Research Council, and the American Council on Education. These were in addition, of course, to the IPR. The criticism was based on the allegation that these agencies were intermediary organizations between the foundations and the specific operating organizations, and the allegation that the intermediary organizations had been themselves infiltrated and had promoted Communist causes.[94]

No point would be served in attempting to list all of the specific operating scholarly organizations which came under the committee's scrutiny and condemnation. It would include virtually every such organization in the United States—and some, such as the Royal Institute of International Affairs, not in the United States—which concentrates primarily in the field of the social sciences. Specific examples of those most severely attacked—primarily from the standpoint of their "internationalism"—were the International Relations Clubs supported by the Carnegie Endowment, the Foreign Policy

Association, the Council on Foreign Relations, the Social Science Research Council, and the American Friends Service Committee.[95]

One final question should perhaps be dealt with. That question is, so what? Does the fact that most of the foundations and organizations dealing with international affairs and the social sciences were investigated and condemned by the Reece Committee actually have any deleterious effect on those organizations? An observation from the report of the minority for the same committee provides a sufficient answer:

> It must be remembered that even though the Congress soundly rejects and repudiates the majority report, as it should, [but which Congress did not do] the report will stand forever in all its spuriousness as a "majority report" of facts and sober conclusions of a majority of the members of a duly constituted committee of the House of Representatives of the United States and will be quoted by every fear peddler in the Nation as incontrovertible fact.[96]

The experience of the Institute of Pacific Relations gives adequate testimony to the fact that the minority was not speaking solely in the realm of supposition.

7 EFFECTS OF ACCEPTANCE ON STATE DEPARTMENT FAR EASTERN SPECIALISTS

The effects which the acceptance of China lobby views produced on the private specialists and scholarly organizations provide an indication of the fate which was in store for the State Department's Far Eastern specialists. The goal of the China lobby in its attacks on the private specialists and scholarly organizations was merely to disprove their arguments and discredit them as specialists. The goal of the attacks on the Department of State, however, was to secure the dismissal of its China specialists and the repudiation of their policies. This chapter will examine the extent to which acceptance of the lobby's views led to the fulfillment of that aim.

Attacks on the State Department's China policy began early in the postwar period and set a pattern which was maintained long afterward. On December 10, 1945, Representative Dondero delivered a long speech on the floor of the House of Representatives in which he attacked the State Department and revived the Amerasia Affair.[1] The attack was made shortly after the resignation of General Hurley as Ambassador to China and reflected the same pro-Chiang Chinese influence.

John S. Service, the Foreign Service officer involved in the Amerasia Affair, was one of the specific targets of Dondero's attack. In the course of his remarks concerning Service, Dondero drew on articles which had previously been published in the Washington *Times-Herald* and the San Francisco *Examiner.* The two articles, in turn, were based on "information" attributed to Bishop Paul Yupin. The bishop was at that time on the staff of *The China Monthly* and had returned from China only a short time before. He had previously served as "unofficial adviser to the Chinese delegation" at the San Francisco Conference on the United Nations and was in the United States on a diplomatic passport at the time of Dondero's speech.[2]

This speech was by no means the first attack to be made on the Department of State for the policy followed in China. Nor was it the first attack from pro-Chiang sources. It did mark the beginning, however, of a long series of attacks on the State Department which made the Hurley resignation the point of departure, clearly reflected Chinese influence, and exploited such incidents as the Amerasia case and the Yalta decisions. Other events, such as the Wallace mission of 1944, the ex-Communist revelations, and the Marshall mission, were later used in these attacks.

The appointment of Marshall as President Truman's special representative to China immediately following Hurley's resignation tended to limit the attacks during most of the following year. In October of 1946, however, the first issue of *Plain Talk* was published by Kohlberg. The revised version of the article entitled "The State Department Espionage Case," the original version of which was written by Emmanuel Larsen, was the outstanding feature of the issue.[3] The material in the article included one idea which was destined to become one of the most persistent and groundless myths in the repertory of the China lobby. It concerned the departure of Joseph Grew from his position in the Department of State.

According to the article in *Plain Talk,* Grew and Acheson were engaged in a battle for control of the State Department in which first one and then the other appeared to gain the upper hand. During the summer of 1945, in which the Amerasia case was before the courts, Grew left the government service and Acheson took over his position as Under Secretary of State. The *Plain Talk* article implied that the replacement of Grew with Acheson was a victory for the "pro-Soviet" elements. It purported to quote Jaffe as having remarked to Larsen, "Well, we've suffered a lot, but, anyhow, we got Grew out."[4]

This story soon became a permanent feature of China lobby attacks on the Department of State. In later versions, the name of Eugene Dooman was added to that of Grew, and it was claimed that both Grew and Dooman were forced out of their positions in order to make way for the group which wished to deliver China to the Communists. Years later, John T. Flynn was still arguing that, "the first victory . . . was the ousting of Grew and Dooman, and the installation of Acheson."[5]

Actually, the departure of Grew and Dooman from government service was the result of routine replacement of men who had already served past the age of normal retirement. Both men had long service in the Japanese section of the Foreign Service and in other positions in the Department of State, mostly in connection with

Japanese affairs. They were considered by many people at the time to be in favor of a "soft peace" toward Japan. Consequently, a considerable campaign had been carried on in the press—including the Communist press—of the United States against the policies which Grew and Dooman supposedly favored. They were frequently termed "pro-Japanese," and there were insistent demands from many sources that they be removed from policy-making positions. Dooman retired on August 31, 1945, after thirty-three years of service. Nowhere in the record of his later testimony before the McCarran Subcommittee is there any intimation that he was removed, kicked out, or forced to retire.[6]* Secretary Acheson has positively asserted that Vincent, who had been accused of forcing him out, had nothing to do with Dooman's retirement.[7]

There is even more positive evidence as to the facts of Grew's retirement. In reply to an inquiry from John S. Service several years later, Grew wrote as follows:

I was not forced to resign as Under Secretary of State. Myths about this have arisen. For some time I had wished to retire. The war was then over. I had completed 41 years of service. I had passed the usual age limit, and I was at that time in ill health and was facing a possible major operation. It was, therefore, entirely on my own initiative that I insisted on retiring, even though Secretary Byrnes strongly urged me to continue in service. Those are the facts . . .[8]†

In spite of this clear denial by Grew and the failure of Dooman to confirm the charges that he was forced out, pro-Chiang spokes-

---

* It is noteworthy that all examples of the press campaign against Grew and Dooman which were included as evidence before the McCarran Subcommittee were taken from the Communist press. This, in spite of the fact that practically the entire press of the United States carried items of a similar nature from the major wire services and the New York *Times* News Service.

† Freda Utley's account of this incident indicates the extent to which the *Plain Talk* version was accepted among pro-Chiang groups:
  "If it had not received active support from some of President Roosevelt's closest advisers, perhaps the Davies-Service group would never have been able to drown out the voices of such experienced State Department representatives as Joseph Grew, the former United States Ambassador to Japan, who was head of the Far Eastern Division of the State Department until he was forced to resign in 1945 as a result of his attempt to bring the Amerasia conspirators to judgment. He was supplanted by John Carter Vincent, and from that moment, the IPR-State Department-pro-Chinese Communist axis became almost all-powerful." (*The China Story*, p. 116).
  The errors in this paragraph are worthy of note: (1) Grew was not head of the Far Eastern Division, (2) he was not forced to resign, (3) he took no initiative in the Amerasia case, and (4) he was not supplanted by John Carter Vincent, since Vincent held none of the positions formerly held by Grew.

men continued to repeat the story. On July 18, 1950, shortly after the outbreak of war in Korea, Representative Judd revived and enlarged the accusation:

I urge our government to call back into emergency service statesmen like Grew, Hornbeck, Dooman, Berle, and others—men who are real experts on Asia or on communism, *men whom the left wing boys pushed out of the department.* You will recall that Alger Hiss was a key man in the Far Eastern Office from 1939 to 1944 when the pattern of building up the Chinese Communists and building down the Chinese Government was established.[9]

Shortly after the original publication of this story in *Plain Talk* in 1946, a new attack on the Department of State was launched from the same source. The occasion for the attack was the delivery of a statement on American foreign policy by John Carter Vincent at a Far East luncheon of the American Foreign Trade Council on November 11, 1946. Vincent, then Director of the Office of Far Eastern Affairs, was quoted as saying:

"Last but far from least we have China. . . .
"I believe it is unsound to invest private or public capital in countries where there is widespread corruption in business and official circles; where a government is wasting its substance on excessive armament, where the fact or threat of civil war exists, where tendencies toward government monopolization exclude American business, or where undemocratic concepts of government are controlling."[10]*

This statement by Vincent, made in the presence of the Chinese Ambassador to the United States, evoked a strong reaction from pro-Chiang sources. The New York *World-Telegram*—which invariably espoused the cause of the Chinese Nationalists—responded with strongly worded editorials protesting Vincent's remarks.[11] On December 4, 1946, the American China Policy Association released the text of a letter to Secretary of State Byrnes denouncing Vincent and demanding a disavowal of his statement and the issuance of an official apology to the Chinese ambassador. The letter insisted that "Mr. Vincent's sympathies with the Yenan rebellion in China, and the precision with which his statements conform to the policies laid down in the Communist press, are self-evident."[12] *The China*

---

* It is worth noting that, in the text of the speech, ten paragraphs intervened between the first sentence in the above quotation and the paragraph which follows. The main paragraph actually occurred after Vincent had completed the section on China and had begun a summary of his remarks which related to the Far East as a whole. The title of the address was "American Business with the Far East."

Monthly joined in the attack on Vincent and quoted the *World-Telegram*'s attack on the Department of State:[13]

"Responsibility for ["our retreat in China"] must be charged up to intrigues in the State Department and to a yielding by the administration to the propaganda of the Communists and fellow travelers in this country."[14]

These attacks on the State Department continued on a gradually increasing scale throughout 1947 and 1948. The major charges during this period concerned the Yalta decisions, the "suppressed" Wedemeyer report, and the lack of sufficient military aid to the Nationalist Government. The presidential election campaign of 1948, however, provided the China lobby with more lucrative sources of ammunition than had ever previously been available. At the height of the election campaign, Kohlberg published an article in which he raised a wholly new series of charges against the Department of State. The inspiration for the attack was the publication of the *Stilwell Papers,* edited by Theodore White.[15] As Kohlberg viewed it:

The real importance of this book to one studying the new American Dead End scholarship of the Harvard-Marxist school lies in the omissions and misrepresentations of White, a product of Harvard and of the Institute of Pacific Relations. The crux of the whole Stilwell story lies in his connection with the plot developed in May 1943, when he returned to Washington. A small group including Alger Hiss, Owen Lattimore, Lauchlin Currie, Edgar Snow and later John Carter Vincent, planned to slowly choke to death and destroy the government of the Republic of China and build up the Chinese Communists for post-war success.

Into this plot were brought Henry Wallace (then Vice-President) and Dean Acheson, Ass't-Secretary of State, though both were probably confused tools and unaware of the sinister forces they were aiding. . . .

The mile-stones in the success of this plot were:

1. Henry Wallace's mission to China in 1944 and his still-secret report to President Roosevelt, laying down the plan to build up the Communists.

2. The demands of Chiang Kai-shek after Henry's return in 1944 with the ultimatum of September 19th which Chiang rejected, resulting in the recall of Stilwell and the humble pie eaten by Roosevelt just prior to the election.

3. The plotting behind General Hurley's back and his eventual resignation when Secretary Byrnes supported the plotters.

4. The Marshall mission to China to gain a truce during which the Russians could equip the greatly inferior Communist forces.[16]

This characterization of the story behind the Stilwell affair is typical of the manner in which every major effort of the Department of

State—and some minor ones—were to be treated by pro-Chiang spokesmen. Kohlberg, in this case, was careful in his treatment of Acheson. He was equally careful in his identification of Stilwell with the "plot," saying, "Although probably not one of the plotters General Stilwell for personal reasons abetted it to a considerable extent by his actions and certainly did nothing to oppose it."[17] General Marshall was also excluded from the plot, although not by specific mention. The policy of refraining from personal attacks on Marshall was then in line with Chinese strategy.[18]

The reason for associating Stilwell and the Wallace mission with the policies of the Department of State is easily understood. At the time Kohlberg's article was published, Wallace was running for President on the Progressive party ticket which was supported by the Communists. This support rendered Wallace vulnerable to attack on charges of pro-communism. But Wallace had been accompanied on his 1944 mission to China by John Carter Vincent and Owen Lattimore. While in China they had conferred with John P. Davies, Jr. (one of the primary targets of General Hurley's charges) and John S. Service, who was attached to General Stilwell's staff. Thus, through a series of associations, three well-known China specialists in the State Department were "connected" with Lattimore and Wallace in a manner which could be made to appear suspicious five years after the fact. Kohlberg's charges that Wallace returned to the United States and laid down the plan to "build up the Communists" became a favorite theme of Chiang's propagandists.

Two years later, the Reverend William R. Johnson summarized the arguments which were made by pro-Chiang spokesmen following Kohlberg's initial effort. According to Johnson, the report which Vice President Wallace submitted to President Roosevelt after his return from China in 1944 was "reportedly written by Owen Lattimore" and "advocated a change in the United States China policy; [sic] that would shift American support from the Central Government to the Chinese Communists." He then went on to say that in the State Department's White Paper, which he characterized as a "brazen effort to falsify history," the "very existence of the Wallace Report was denied."[19] Some comment on this account is in order.

In the first place, there is voluminous sworn testimony before the McCarran Subcommittee that Lattimore had nothing to do with writing the Vice President's report. That testimony was given by Wallace and by those who accompanied him on the mission.[20] Johnson, of course, covered himself by the use of the term "reportedly."

Second, Johnson's statement that Wallace's report advocated a change in United States policy which would "shift American support from the Central Government to the Chinese Communists" is not supported by the document itself. Considering the circumstances of the time, the conditions then current in China, and the purposes of the Vice President's visit, no such interpretation is possible.[21]

The third misleading statement in Johnson's comment on the Wallace report concerned its treatment in the White Paper. All the evidence indicates that the Department of State was completely sincere in denying the existence of the report. Wallace gave his account of the trip directly to the President. He apparently never discussed it with any of his companions. Vincent, at least, supposed that any report which Wallace might make would be oral. No copy of the statement was transmitted to the Department and therefore, of course, did not appear in its files.[22]

Kohlberg's opening of the new line of attack on the Department of State, which brought Wallace and Stilwell into direct contact with the betrayal thesis, coincided with the first public hearings, in the fall of 1948, involving Hiss. Henceforth, the China lobby writers were to concentrate heavily on what they termed a "Vincent, Davies, Service clique" inside the Department, carrying out a "Wallace, Lattimore, Hiss conspiracy." This development also coincided with the reviving of the China lobby "inner core" under the direct supervision of Madame Chiang.[23] During the remainder of 1948 and the first eight months of 1949, these new accusations, and charges that the United States failed to provide Chiang with adequate ammunition, were the dominant notes in the propaganda emanating from pro-Chiang sources. Then, on August 5, 1949, the State Department itself provided a vast new source of material for the attack by issuing the White Paper on *United States Relations with China*.

From the time the White Paper was issued, it became an important element in the attack on the Department of State. The Chinese had been fully aware of the impending release of the document. They were also cognizant of its contents and kept Chiang informed of day-to-day developments concerning its release. The first available telegram on the subject from the Chinese Embassy in Washington to the generalissimo shows the extent to which Chinese agents kept Chiang informed of every thought and action of the American Government:

. . . Whether or not the White Paper will be released is still under consideration by the highest government authorities. This morning General Marshall met with Secretary of State Acheson to discuss this problem. General Marshall expressed to Acheson that he was still gravely concerned with our future policy toward China. His position is of extreme importance.[24]

The Chinese view of the White Paper was summarized in December by Kohlberg, who admitted:

Last July, I visited Generalissimo Chiang Kai-shek in Formosa and had two lengthy discussions with him. One of the matters we discussed was the forthcoming State Department White Paper on China.[25]

Having thus revealed that the source of his information was Chiang and that the ideas and interests he would discuss were Chiang's, Kohlberg continued:

Careful study of the White Paper reveals that its purpose could not be to discredit the Nationalist Government—it charges incompetence, corruption, bad strategy and poor propaganda, but not bad faith. Nor could its purpose be to excuse State Department failure; throughout it reveals State Department plotting to betray the National Government and nowhere even excuses nonimplementation of the recommendations of the Wedemeyer Report of 1947, which outlined a method for stopping the Communists at a reasonable cost.

The real purpose of the White Paper seems, in spite of the omission of many important documents, to be to reveal to the Chancellories of the world the story of the American betrayal of the Republic of China. What could be of greater aid to the Soviet Union than this?[26]

The treatment of American policy in the article under discussion covered the entire range of China lobby propaganda. Although it was primarily directed at the White Paper, the argument began with a section entitled "Three-Fourths of Our Taxes Because of China." This discussion was followed by sections on the "Open Door Policy, America's New Policy, Who Is Responsible? The Henry A. Wallace Report, Stilwell's Recall, Jap Arms to the Communists, No Arms for China, and Bad Chinese Strategy Was American." After these points were disposed of, Kohlberg turned to Wedemeyer's report and opinions and concluded with a long section on "What the White Paper Conceals." The last was actually a statement of what Kohlberg thought should have been included in the document in view of his interpretation of its purpose. It also opened what was to prove a long-sustained attack on former Ambassador-at-Large Philip C. Jessup, under whose direction the White Paper was prepared.

In the article under discussion Kohlberg pointed out how Jessup's role in the compilation of the White Paper might be used to provide the intellectual link between the White Paper, China experts in general, and the Institute of Pacific Relations:

Professor Jessup . . . had a long background of co-operation with the extreme-left wing groups in study of and propaganda on the Far East. A close associate of such exposed pro-Communists as Edward C. Carter, Owen Lattimore, Frederick V. Field, Harriet Lucy Moore . . . Professor Jessup has produced in the White Paper a weird and unprecedented document.[27]

The combining of the attack on the intellectuals with the attack on the Department of State was given added status in somewhat more abstract terms in an article published two months later by a Chinese author, Chia-you Chen:

The self-proclaimed China experts have usurped the power of American public opinion and have become a special class in American politics. Their prime concern is to maintain their position as the leading force in American public opinion. Let us make no mistake about it that that special class of self-proclaimed China experts rely on distortion and falsehood. They are intellectually incapable of comprehending the principle of democracy. Their background and their academic standing makes it clear that they lack interest in mankind. They came to power by hypocritical talk and by disguising themselves as idealists.

Chen then linked the "experts" with the White Paper, anti-Chiang sentiments, and pro-communism:

The condemnation of Chiang Kai-shek's administration as corrupt, inefficient and reactionary was another master design of the International Communist Movement to discredit in order to destroy. It is a general practice for the self-proclaimed China experts to deal only with superficial phenomena. They must carry their lies to fantastic extremes in order to confuse the general public and thus make the public the victim of their propaganda machine. Their condemnation of Chiang Kai-shek was a phase of China that could not be substantiated by facts. It is no surprise that the *White Paper* was decisively biased against the Chinese people and the Chinese government by the subversive heresies of these self-proclaimed China experts.[28]

The combining of all these lines of attack immediately following publication of the White Paper proved to be a fortuitous development for the China lobby. For release of the document was followed very shortly by a serious effort on the part of the Department of State to reappraise its policy toward China. The experts, as it turned out, were to play a significant role in that effort at reappraisal.

Beginning early in 1950, however, there followed in rapid succession the abandonment of Formosa, the stalemate between Congress and the Administration over aid to Chiang, and the Communist attack in Korea. It was the latter which provided the signal for a sharp intensification of the attack on the Department of State.

The direct connection which was to be posited between Korea and the "betrayal" of China was made poignantly clear by Representative Judd in a speech to the House of Representatives on July 18, 1950, which was reprinted and released in pamphlet form by the National Industrial Conference Board, Inc.:

I [reported] . . . in November 1947 . . . a long conversation I had with a great Korean patriot, Mr. Kim Koo. . . .

I said to him, "What should America do now? We have delayed two years hoping we could get agreement with the Russians that would reunite Korea, but cooperation with them hasn't worked here any better than anywhere else. Should we delay longer, waiting for the UN Commission . . . ? Should we go ahead in South Korea anyway, hold elections, set up a defense force, and try to get the country on its feet and withdraw our forces? Or what?"

He studied a minute and then said, "It doesn't make any difference what you do now. There isn't any way to get Korea so that she can be independent and secure and self-sustaining, until you solve the Communist problem across the border in Manchuria."

I asked various other questions, to all of which he replied in substance, "There is no way you can solve the problem so that we can be independent and secure until you help China remove the Communist menace in Manchuria."[29]

In the months which followed, a long series of books and pamphlets was issued, repeating and restating in myriad forms all the charges and accusations which had previously been raised against the Department of State. Now, however, the Korean War gave them greater meaning and interest. The specific accusations, for the most part, were directed at the China specialists who had served the government. The ultimate targets were Secretary of State Acheson and all those who might in the future toy with the idea of recognizing Communist China or permitting her to become a member of the United Nations.

The Department of State had unwittingly contributed immensely to this effort by issuing the White Paper. That document made available to spokesmen of the pro-Chiang point of view much of the raw materials on which decisions regarding policy in China had been based. Some of those materials had already been made available to the Kuomintang and its agents through leaks of information from the State Department itself, members of Congress, and the Justice Department and FBI.[30] The Administration could hardly hope to gain, however, by releasing vast additional numbers of documents to be taken from context by its enemies and interpreted to their advantage. That this was the effect is nevertheless clearly shown in a pamphlet by William R. Johnson, *China, Key to the Orient,* dated August 21, 1950, and distributed by the American China Policy Association. The pamphlet was based largely on material from the White Paper. A "summary index" stated:

"[The pamphlet] shows how General Marshall prevented the Chinese Nationalist Armies from seizing the Chihfong Gateway to Manchuria and the Tolum Gateway to Outer Mongolia, thereby throwing these passes open to the passage of Russian and Chinese troops and constant communication between the then relatively weak Chinese Communists and Moscow. (Page 13) It shows how the State Department followed the recommendations of the Henry Wallace Report, fitting into the Kremlin design. (Page 8) The sharp difference between General Marshall and General Wedemeyer, who favored support of the Chinese Nationalists . . . is described. (Page 15) How the Chinese Nationalists, according to the Legislative Reference Service, received only a fraction of the financial support the State Department claims they received, is told. (Page 17) The manner in which the State Department took the recommendations of known supporters of Russian designs, rejecting opposed advice, is documented. (Page 17) How the operation of State Department policy in China led inevitably to Pearl Harbor [*sic!* Korea?] is fully traced. (Page 15–16) The support of Formosa as a possible means of eventually recovering what has been lost is urged. (Page 29)"[31]

Johnson's conclusions concerning those responsible for the conditions described followed in detail those previously indicated. In his opinion, the White Paper, "when fully understood," showed that the Soviet Union controlled the Chinese Communists and "manipulated United States officials and American China policy so as to take control of China." He assured his readers that the White Paper could only be understood in terms of what it "omits" and in what it "mutilates and falsifies."[32] More specifically, he argued:

There are those who brief presidents, vice-presidents, presidential representatives, ambassadors and Congressmen relative to the Far East; who are determined that China go Communist. [*sic*] Among these, as their records and their published writings show are Dean Acheson, Owen Lattimore, Alger Hiss, John Carter Vincent, Laughlin Currie, John Service, and many others.[33]

A pamphlet distributed by the Committee for Constitutional Government in October summarized all the charges previously made against the Department of State. Compiled almost entirely from previously published sources, the author quoted Judd, Bullitt, Chennault, the New York *Journal-American,* the Providence *Journal,* Fulton Lewis, Jr., Joseph Kamp, and Senator McCarthy.[34]

During the ensuing year, two books were published—one by Freda Utley, the other by John T. Flynn—which continued to agitate and repeat the charges against the Department of State and demand that the China specialists be fired. Much of the documentation for these journalistic efforts came directly from the White Paper. Senator McCarthy also continually repeated his charges. His favorite sources for quotations to indicate what he considered disloyalty on the part of the China specialists were—in addition to Kohlberg—Hurley, Flynn, Miss Utley, Chennault, MacArthur, Bullitt, and Wedemeyer.[35] Again, the White Paper was immensely useful.

Study of the books and pamphlets which disseminated pro-Chiang propaganda after June of 1950 shows that their primary purpose was to prevent United States recognition of Communist China and secure American opposition to United Nations membership for the Red regime. This purpose was revealed particularly in the recommendations which the authors made on American China policy and in their suggestions for reader action. Johnson, for example, entitled the closing section of his pamphlet, "China's Recovery of Independence Is a Prerequisite of Lasting Peace."[36] By "recovery of independence," Johnson left no doubt that he meant restoration of mainland China to the control of Chiang Kai-shek and the Kuomintang. He warned his readers repeatedly that the Department of State would continue to seek the recognition of Red China.

The covers of these pamphlets and books also revealed the purpose. One of Dresser's efforts contained on its cover the following warning from the Committee for Constitutional Government which distributed it:

The U.N., abetted by some in our State Department, may still attempt to admit the Chinese Communist government as a member, and to place Formosa under its control . . . You may wish to protest to President Truman and to your representatives in Congress against such recognition and urge that General MacArthur's viewpoint be upheld and Formosa kept permanently out of the control of a potentially hostile government.[37]

Johnson's pamphlet suggested:

Only immediate widespread and continuous public protest to the President, the Secretary of State and to Congressmen gives any substantial hope that our Government will be induced to make full and legitimate use of the Veto against any such sell-out of the Chinese Republic, or of Korea by the creation of a buffer state at her expense. There should also be vigorous insistence that, when the a-bomb is used, it be used only against the Soviet Union.[38]

Dresser proved, shortly thereafter, to be even more deeply concerned for the future of Formosa:

The present discussions in the United Nations regarding Communist China indicate a possibility that she may be admitted to the United Nations in place of Nationalist China, and that the fate of Formosa may be placed in the hands of the United Nations. The danger to our security involved in these decisions is terrifying. If Formosa should be turned over to Communist China, or if Chiang's hands should be tied, our chance of stopping the Communist tide in Asia would be lost—an issue which is by all odds the most important facing the American people today.[39]

The spokesmen for Chiang Kai-shek agreed on the cause of the Korean War and the danger to Formosa. They were not always sure, however, just who should be assigned the primary responsibility for the situation. Nevertheless, between the Department of State and the IPR, and between Acheson and Lattimore, they could find ample common ground for agreement. Most of the earlier efforts to assign responsibility pointed more or less directly to the Department of State and to the man who was its chief during the last crucial years, Secretary Acheson. Johnson asserted:

We have shown that it is the Secretary himself and his associates, who have manipulated American support of China's cause so as to bring President Chiang and the Chinese Government to defeat and the Soviet Union's puppets to power. It is the "shrewd and cunning" American Communists, their fellow travelers and dupes within and without the State Department who have persuaded the Secretary to the beliefs he holds relative to the "facts" he presents. That is—unless he himself is a Communist or a fellow-traveler and believes it "shrewd and cunning" to so present China's catastrophy [sic] that he with the Communist Party may "ride this thing to victory and to power," . . . in the final dejure recognition by the U.S. and the U.N. of the Soviet Union's Peiping puppet regime.

. . . The pro-Russian groups of the State and War Departments won out over those backing American interests in the Pacific and peace in that region; for which a free and independent China was the first essential.[40]

Dresser's attitude on the question of responsibility was clearly revealed in his choice of quotations from Joseph Kamp. According to Kamp, Acheson was a "restlessly-ambitious man who wielded the real power in the State Department" under Hull, Stettinius and "the pliable James F. Byrnes. . . . The clutch which Acheson had gained on the State Department by the time the war ended was revealed startlingly in the events which followed the *Amerasia* Espionage Case in 1945."[41] Kamp did not explain the nature of Acheson's role in this case but left his readers to draw their own conclusions from this hint. In a later passage he enlarged the suggestion:

. . . The key to this sad story of the ruination of Free China, and the betrayal of American security in the Far East, is to be found in the character of Dean Acheson. With his back-stage control of the Department under four successive Secretaries, Acheson was the continuing link which bound together each sordid chapter in this running conspiracy. The other actors in the plot have come and gone on the Department stage. Acheson has remained the constant stage manager.[42]

Flynn was equally certain that traitors in the Department of State were responsible for Chiang's loss of power. Nevertheless, his approach is indicative of the manner in which later attacks from pro-Chiang sources were to be directed at lower-level personnel whose functions had been more directly concerned with China:

China, also, has fallen. The dark curtain that, with our consent, was rung down over our luckless allies in Europe . . . has now fallen on China. And this was made possible *wholly because of Russia's allies*—conscious and unconscious—*in America, in our government and even in our State Department.*
There were traitors in the State Department and in posts of power in many departments of the government.[43]

By the middle of 1951, these attacks on the Department of State had reached such intensity that they could apparently no longer be ignored. Consequently, on July 12, 1951, the Department suspended a number of employees pending new security clearances. Among them were three of its most highly trained China specialists, O. Edmund Clubb, John P. Davies, Jr. and John C. Vincent. All three had previously been "cleared" several times. In addition, John S. Service, an equally valuable specialist on China, was undergoing his eighth loyalty hearing.

Three of these Foreign Service officers, Davies, Service, and Vincent, had long been targets of the China lobby. Davies and Service were among those accused by Hurley in 1945 of having sabotaged his efforts.[44] Excerpts from their reports from the field in the days when they had served as Foreign Service officers in China had been reproduced in the White Paper and had been used extensively by China lobby spokesmen in efforts to prove State Department bias against Chiang.

In addition, all three men had been involved in at least one incident which increased their vulnerability. Service had been involved in the Amerasia Affair. Davies had once recommended six people —all of whom had either been accused of Communist affiliations or of having close connections with the IPR, or both—for use by the Central Intelligence Agency. Vincent had been closely associated with the Wallace mission and the dispatch of the Marshall mission to China. Also, he had served as head of both the China desk and the Far Eastern Division after 1944. This service made him a prime target. Clubb had not previously been involved in any of the incidents exploited by the China lobby, but he had served in diplomatic posts in China for many years and had been elevated to the position of Director of the Office of Chinese Affairs on July 6, 1950, one year before his suspension.[45]

Of the four persons under discussion, therefore, only Vincent occupied a position during the period 1944–1949 in which he could formulate policy, or aid in the formulation of policy, for China. The reports which Service and Davies had written while in China had, however, inspired the animosity of the Nationalist Government by warning repeatedly that Chiang could not possibly win a military struggle with the Communists. They correctly forecast a constantly closer relationship between Yenan and Moscow if the United States continued to give exclusive support to the Kuomintang Government. Service and Davies quite obviously based their suggestions on the belief that the United States *could not determine the outcome* of the internal struggle in China. They proposed, therefore, that American policy be designed to secure the maximum influence for the United States regardless of which side should win.

That proposal had not been adopted by the United States. The very fact that it had been seriously offered, however, was sufficient to cause grave concern to the supporters of Chiang Kai-shek. Thus, when the acceptance of China lobby attitudes had progressed sufficiently and the climate of opinion had become more favorable after the fall of China and the outbreak of war in Korea, efforts to remove these officials from positions where they might again influence American China policy were renewed.

As a result of the situation thus created, five congressional committees produced an almost unbroken series of headlines for three years following the victory of the Communists in 1949. Each one was concerned with investigating the policies which the United States had followed in China. Although each series of hearings produced unique features, all covered much the same ground, called many of the same witnesses, and considered the same charges. The House Committee on Un-American Activities, which had long concerned itself with the China question, held hearings at intervals throughout the entire period. Ultimately, it was this committee which apparently induced the Department of State to suspend Clubb.

Certain aspects of the investigations of four of these five congressional bodies have already been reviewed. For example, the review of the Amerasia Affair by the Tydings Subcommittee, the general conclusions of the MacArthur inquiry on China policy, the role of the House Un-American Activities Committee in the Hiss case, and the investigation of the IPR by the McCarran Subcommittee have been covered in some detail. In each of these cases, however, the effects of the investigation carried beyond the immediate object which has been considered here and influenced directly the careers of certain of the State Department China specialists.

The McCarran Subcommittee ultimately had the greatest impact so far as the China experts were concerned. Only after that committee began its deliberations did the position of the specialists on China who had for so long been the targets of the China lobby become critical. The direct relationship between their China service and the attack by the McCarran Subcommittee was noted by one commentator as follows:

So successful was the House Committee on Un-American Activities in its techniques of dismissal [of government employees] by "exposure" that in 1950 it won the accolade of imitation. The late Senator Pat McCarran of Nevada, chairman of the powerful Judiciary Committee, established a subcommittee on internal security and naturally established himself as its chairman. The new group took the headlines away from its House counterpart with a systematic and successful effort to purge from the State Department all the career Foreign Service officers who, in the 1940s, had warned that the Chinese Nationalist government of Chiang Kai-shek was a weak reed to rely on and that, as a condition of continued American aid, it should be required to broaden and democratize the base of its representation—the view taken, incidentally, by General George C. Marshall. Loyalty to Chiang was made the test of suitability for service in the Division of Far Eastern Affairs.[46]

Whether the test of suitability for continued service in the Department of State was loyalty to Chiang, or whether the test was a particular conception of the activities and attitudes proper to a Foreign Service officer, may well be a matter of judgment. A review of the records of the four officials named above should reveal, however, the extent to which the charges which resulted in their departure from government service reflected an acceptance of the China lobby viewpoint.

The first of the lower-ranking China specialists to be dismissed was John Stewart Service. Service was eminently suited by both training and experience for the Foreign Service in China. He had been born in China, spent his entire youth there, then returned to China in 1933, following completion of his education in the United States. He had served as a United States Foreign Service officer since 1935, spoke fluent Chinese, and had an unusually intimate familiarity with Chinese culture. He had repeatedly shown a rather remarkable ability to make contacts with and secure information from Chinese officials and acquaintances. From 1941 until late in 1944, Service was frequently assigned duties which required him to associate with the Chinese Communists, who were then maintaining a headquarters in Chungking for purposes of liaison with the Nationalist Government. During most of this period, he was detached from the Foreign Service of the Department of State and was assigned to General Stilwell's headquarters. He was responsible to Stilwell and the Department of the Army rather than to the Department of State. Nevertheless, his reports to Stilwell were sent to the embassy from which they were forwarded to Washington.[47]

In July of 1944, Service was assigned to accompany an American military mission to Yenan, the Communist capital of China. The mission—and Service's assignment to it—had been accomplished only after prolonged negotiations with the Chungking regime and as a result of the urgent and repeated insistence of General Stilwell. The motivation for the mission was twofold. First, Stilwell wanted information concerning the military capabilities of the Chinese Communists. Second, American groups in China—both military and civilian—greatly desired a firsthand report on the economic and political success which the Communists had achieved.

When arrangements for the mission were finally completed, Service was chosen—on the basis of these qualifications—to accompany it as a political reporter. He remained there from July 22 until October 23, 1944. When, at that time, Stilwell was recalled from China, Service was also returned to Washington. In January, 1945, however, Service returned to China at the specific request of General Wedemeyer who had taken over Stilwell's military duties. Almost immediately upon his return to Chungking, Service found himself in conflict with Ambassador Hurley over certain recommendations which Service had made to Stilwell in a memorandum from Yenan, dated October 10, 1944. Service, however, was on Wedemeyer's staff—not Hurley's. He was therefore not subject to Hurley's control.[48]

Under these circumstances, Service remained in China and, on March 9, 1945, returned to Yenan. Hurley, however, had returned to Washington for consultations and eventually succeeded in persuading Secretary of War Stimson to recall Service to the United States.[49] Service left Yenan on April 4th and arrived in Washington on April 12, 1945. Against this background, his role in the Amerasia Affair, and the later charges against him must be judged.

Upon his arrival in the United States, Service was eagerly sought by governmental officials and private individuals and groups interested in the Far East. At one of his many conferences, he met Andrew Roth, a naval intelligence officer who, in turn, introduced him to Philip Jaffe, the editor of *Amerasia*. According to his own testimony, apparently accepted as true by the loyalty boards, Service had never met Jaffe before April 19, 1945.[50] At the time of this meeting, Jaffe, Roth, and other participants in the Amerasia venture were under the surveillance of the FBI. Service had no knowledge—and was not informed—of this fact, nor was he aware that Jaffe was suspected of having close associations with American Communists. He considered Jaffe to be the reputable publisher of a reputable magazine dealing with Far Eastern matters.

Under these circumstances, Service appeared in Jaffe's company on several occasions between April 19th and May 29th. Service also gave Jaffe several (apparently eight or ten, although this was a point never entirely cleared up in the record) of his memoranda concerning economic and political conditions in China which he had prepared in Yenan. They were given as background material, and Service has indicated that he had some misgivings at the time:

". . . Jaffe . . . wished to take the memoranda with him for several days. I hesitated, but after considerable discussion and in view of the nonpolicy and purely factual nature of the papers, allowed Jaffe to keep them. It was arranged that I would pick them up when I visited New York.

"It was not usual [This appears to be a typographical error which should read "unusual"] to allow writers to have access to this type of factual material for background purposes, since reading the material or taking notes on it was always more satisfactory from the viewpoint of accuracy than merely relying on one's memory and oral recital. It was not, however, customary to loan such material and I have always regretted having turned it over to Jaffe, although at that time I had no reason to doubt his responsibility. . . ." [51]

Service was arrested on June 6, 1945, along with the other individuals involved in the affair. He had previously retrieved his reports, but copies of them were found in Jaffe's possession. As noted earlier, Service was cleared by unanimous vote of the grand jury and, after a hearing before the personnel board of the Foreign Service, he was restored to duty. During the succeeding four years, he served in various positions in Japan, Australia, and India. He successfully withstood at least four additional, apparently routine, loyalty investigations.

During the entire four years, however, Service's loyalty was questioned repeatedly in attacks stemming from China lobby sources. Hurley's accusations and Representative Dondero's attack, based on information attributed to Bishop Paul Yupin, represent two of the earliest examples. The *Plain Talk* article on the Amerasia case placed the major responsibility for the leak of government documents to Amerasia on Service and accused him of having supported the Chinese Communists.*

These attacks on Service increased sharply after publication of the White Paper, which contained excerpts from his China reports. Finally, Senator McCarthy's accusations in early 1950 set in motion a new series of investigations. McCarthy's charges can be traced primarily to three sources; namely, Hurley's charges, the articles

---

* In February, 1970, the Internal Security Subcommittee of the Senate Committee on the Judiciary released *The Amerasia Papers: A Clue to the Catastrophe of China*, 2 vols., 1,961 pages, in an attempt to reopen the case. John S. Service meticulously answers the charges in his *The Amerasia Papers: Some Problems in the History of U.S.-China Relations*, Center for Chinese Studies, China Research Monographs, no. 7 (University of California, Berkeley, 1971). For a review of these books, see Harrison E. Salisbury's "How America and Russia Lost China, A Country Neither Ever Had," *New York Times Book Review*, 19 September 1971.

based on Bishop Paul Yupin's statements, and the *Plain Talk* article.[52] The reaction of the Executive branch of the Government to McCarthy's attack on Service led to the filing of formal charges and a full-scale hearing before the State Department Loyalty Security Board. The Tydings Subcommittee also called Service for interrogation. The result in both cases was complete clearance for Service and a sharp denunciation—implicit in the one case and explicit in the other—of his accusers.

In concluding the report on its investigation of Service, the Loyalty Security Board declared:

> The Loyalty Security Board . . . concludes . . . that reasonable grounds do not exist for belief that John Service is disloyal to the Government of the United States. The Board further concludes that . . . he does not constitute a security risk to the Department of State.[53]

Similarly, the Tydings Subcommittee repudiated every accusation made against Service:

> We . . . conclude that John Stewart Service is neither a disloyal person, a pro-Communist, nor a security risk.[54]

These clearances did not end the repetition of the accusations from China lobby sources. Both Johnson and Dresser included Service among those whom they accused of aiding the Chinese Communists.[55] Flynn repeated Hurley's accusations and indicated his refusal to accept the decisions of the grand jury, the Tydings Subcommittee, and seven Department of State loyalty boards in clearing Service of any wrongdoing in the Amerasia Affair.[56] Senator McCarthy continued to repeat his accusations against Service, and quoted Hurley, Flynn, and Miss Utley as the sources of his information.[57]

Two techniques were employed in these continuing accusations. One was to quote Hurley and Bishop Paul Yupin and mention that Service had been arrested in the Amerasia case. The fact that Service had not been indicted was often not mentioned. A sentence from the report of the McCarran Subcommittee is typical of this technique:

> In 1945, hundreds of classified official United States documents were discovered in the Amerasia offices. In connection with that discovery, members of the editorial board and Mr. John S. Service of the State Department were indicted and two of them convicted.[58]

The second technique is illustrated by the following quotation from Dresser, which was, in turn, quoted from Joseph Kamp. The purpose was to imply improper influence from the Department of State:

"It would be expected that such a sensational exposure would have shaken the State Department from stem to stern, and would have critically weakened the Russia-appeasement faction. No such thing happened. Some mysterious influence promptly went to work to hush up the whole shameful scandal. . . .

"When an attempt was made by outraged Congressmen to institute a House investigation of this unsavory case, mysterious influences again intervened, and Administration leaders succeeded in smothering it. . . ."[59]

The criteria applied in the initial hearing of the Loyalty Security Board in the Service case were those provided by Executive Order 9835, issued by President Truman to guide the Executive departments in determining whether employees were loyalty or security risks.[60] Executive Order 9835 was subsequently amended, on April 28, 1951, by Executive Order 10241, creating new criteria for judging the fitness of governmental employees.[61] As a result, the Loyalty Review Board requested the Loyalty Security Board to reexamine its findings in the Service case. After conducting the requested reexamination, the Loyalty Security Board stated:

On July 31, 1951, the Loyalty Security Board reconsidered the case of John Stewart Service under the provisions of the loyalty standard as amended by Executive Order 10241 of April 28, 1951, and determined that no reasonable doubt exists as to his loyalty to the United States Government.[62]

On December 12, 1951, the Loyalty Review Board again took up the case. In the report subsequently issued, the review panel found:

We are satisfied that during the employee's service in China . . . the reports which he made from Yenan raise no reasonable doubt concerning his loyalty. . . .

Concerning the employee's conduct in other respects while on assignment in China, we have in the file no sufficient evidence to support a doubt on the question of loyalty. . . .

There is no evidence in the file that the employee was ever a member of the Communist Party or of any other organization on the Attorney General's list. . . .

There is no evidence that the employee stole or abstracted from the official files and transmitted to Jaffe or any other person any official files. Such files found in Jaffe's possession appear to have come from Emmanuel S. Larsen, Andrew Roth, or some other source. . . .

There is information [sic—an accusation?] in the file indicating that Service had met Jaffe in China some years previously, and had transmitted information to Jaffe from China. We find no corroboration of this.[63]

After stating these negative findings in the Service case, the Loyalty Review Board turned its attention to Service's associations with Jaffe between April 19th and May 29th 1945. During this period, Service saw Jaffe on seven separate occasions. Three of the meetings occurred at parties at which both were guests. Concerning the reports which Service loaned to Jaffe during the course of these meetings, the report stated:

> We have examined the 18 reports copies of which Service concedes were or may have been lent by him to Jaffe. Some of these are not classified; others are classified "secret" or "confidential." Service testified, and the evidence indicates, that these were his own classifications and that, in many cases at least, before he showed them to Jaffe by reason of lapse of time or otherwise they were no longer secret or confidential.
>
> From our examination of these reports, it appears to us that they were for the most part such as a newspaper reporter on the spot might transmit to his newspaper. Some of them, however, appear to us to be of a nature which no discreet person would disseminate without express authority, and some of them were dated within four to six weeks of the time they were lent to Jaffe, and the originals had not been in the hands of the State Department for more than a week. These recent reports therefore might be considered as "hot news."[64]

Because of his loan of these reports to Jaffe and continued association with him until May 29th, even though "he knew very early in his association with Jaffe that Jaffe was a very doubtful character, extremely left-wing," the board found "reasonable doubt" as to Service's loyalty:

> We are not required to find Service guilty of disloyalty, and we do not do so, but for an experienced and trusted representative of our State Department to so far forget his duty to his trust as his conduct with Jaffe so clearly indicates, forces us with great regret to conclude that there is reasonable doubt as to his loyalty. The favorable finding of the Loyalty Security Board of the Department of State is accordingly reversed.[65]

Following this decision by the Civil Service Loyalty Review Board, Service was dismissed from his position.[66] President Truman declined to review the decision[67] and thenceforth Service's accusers could point to the fact of his dismissal as proof of their charges against both him and the Department of State.[68]

The removal of Service from the Department of State was a significant victory for the pro-Chiang forces. It was not, however, to be the last such victory. The three China specialists who were suspended on July 12, 1951, soon found that doubts concerning their loyalty were not easily allayed. O. Edmund Clubb was the next to be called before a congressional committee.

The events which led Clubb into direct conflict with Congress were, in many ways, the strangest of all those encountered by the China experts. Prior to his suspension in 1951, he had not been an outstanding target of the pro-Chiang groups. He had remained in China after the Communist victory until the closing of the last American consular office in Peking, returned to the United States in 1950, and had become Director of the Office of Chinese Affairs on July 6, 1950. He was apparently cleared on a routine security check at that time.[69]

Clubb's difficulties with Congress and the loyalty boards apparently began with accusations which originated with Whittaker Chambers. Whether the information was first given to the Un-American Activities Committee, the FBI, or the McCarran Subcommittee is not clear.[70] In any case, Clubb was called before the House Committee on Un-American Activities on March 14, 1951, and questioned extensively concerning, among other things, a visit to the office of *New Masses* in 1932; certain messages which he was alleged to have delivered to various individuals in the United States from Agnes Smedley (a journalist and author of several books on the Chinese Communists); his connections with IPR; and an affidavit which he was alleged to have executed for Owen Lattimore in 1935 in connection with a lost passport.[71] He was also questioned concerning his acquaintance with a long list of individuals, including John Service, Philip Jaffe, Frederick V. Field, and Emmanuel Larsen.[72]

Clubb could remember few of the details concerning the events about which he was questioned in the March hearing. He was suspended from his position in the Department of State in July, and on August 20, 1951, was again called before the Un-American Activities Committee. In the meantime, he had secured two volumes of his diary from the British Consulate in Peking where he had left them at the time of his leaving China in 1950. The diary, which Clubb turned over to the committee, confirmed the fact that he had visited the office of *New Masses* in 1932, armed with a letter of introduction from Agnes Smedley to one Walt Carmon, who had been an editor of the magazine. The diary showed that upon his failure to find Carmon at the office, Clubb talked briefly with Whittaker Chambers. The conversation itself was apparently of little consequence.[73]

At a subsequent hearing before the same committee, on August 23, 1951, evidence was adduced to show that Clubb had called on Field at the IPR office in New York on two occasions. One of these visits had occurred in 1932, the other in 1937. Clubb had been unable to recall the circumstances of the visits until letters found in the IPR files provided the details. The above two incidents and an acknowledged acquaintance with Agnes Smedley and Owen Lattimore plus a brief meeting with Lawrence Todd of *Tass* in 1932 constituted the only accusations against Clubb which have ever been made public. No other charges were included in Senator McCarthy's brief resumé on Clubb in 1952.[74]

Following these appearances before the Un-American Activities Committee, the investigation of Clubb by the Loyalty Security Board continued. On February 11, 1952, the Department of State announced that Clubb had been cleared on both loyalty and security and that he had been restored to duty. The same announcement stated, however, that Clubb had chosen to resign because his usefulness had been impaired by the "unfounded" charges made against him.[75] A few days later Senator Ferguson implied by questions during a hearing before the McCarran Subcommittee that the State Department Loyalty Board had actually ruled against Clubb but that Secretary Acheson had overruled the board and cleared him, thus allowing Clubb to resign with full pension privileges.[76] Acheson later confirmed Ferguson's implication.[77]

In contrast with the experience of Clubb, virtually all the accusations against John Carter Vincent can be traced back at least as early as 1947. In April of that year, only a few months after Vincent had aroused the ire of pro-Chiang groups with his speech before the American Foreign Trade Council,[78] Vincent's nomination for promotion to the rank of career minister was submitted to the Senate Foreign Relations Committee. Senator Styles Bridges thereupon submitted to Senator Vandenberg, Chairman of the Foreign Relations Committee, a memorandum, the source of which was not revealed, setting forth "a number of charges relative to the policies and record of . . . Vincent." Vandenberg sent the memorandum to Senator George who, in turn, forwarded it to Acheson for reply.[79] Acheson's summary of the allegations contained in the memorandum are worthy of note since they embodied, in one form or another, all the accusations ever made public against Vincent. Twelve specific allegations were enumerated in Acheson's reply.

I.   It is alleged that "the actions, advice, and recommendations of Mr. Vincent" have been coordinated with the steps outlined in two official Communist documents:

1.   "The Program of the Communist International and its Constitution." . . .

2.   "The Revolutionary Movement in the Colonies and Semi-Colonies," adopted as a resolution by the 6th World Congress of the Comintern, Sept. 1, 1928.

II. It is charged that while at the Embassy in Chungking in 1941 Mr. Vincent "expressed dislike for Ambassador Gauss," "a general dislike of the Chinese," and "an anti-Japanese viewpoint" (prior to adoption of the Russo-Jap nonaggression pact in mid-April 1941), and that he "expressed sympathy for Communist aims and ideology" and dislike for "alleged American exploitation of cheap Chinese labor."

III. It is charged that, in 1945 while Mr. Vincent was first Chief of the Division of Chinese Affairs and later Director of the Office of Far Eastern Affairs, personnel in the State Department engaged in private correspondence with personnel of the Embassy in Chungking, via diplomatic pouch, and that this private correspondence was "leaked" to the Communists. It is stated that General Hurley's resignation came two months later.

IV. It is stated that "a statement issued by President Truman on December 15, 1945, at the time of the appointment of General Marshall as Ambassador, presumably drafted by Vincent, entirely overlooked the principles of the Open Door, made no mention of the November 26, 1941, note to Japan, and in brief invited the Republic of China to 'agree to the Communistic terms for a coalition government or get no more aid from us.' This constituted a repetition in China of the policy so disastrously followed in Yugoslavia and Poland previously."

V.   It is stated that "in September 1946, six members of the Military Affairs Committee of the House, visited General MacArthur in Tokyo. They issued (PM, N.Y., Sept. 10, 1946) 'an alarming statement about Soviet intentions in the Far East.' The next day General MacArthur issued a warning about the danger of communism in Japan. This 'was deeply resented by John Carter Vincent.'"

VI. It is charged that:

     (a) Mr. Vincent presented a draft statement to Secretary Byrnes "in the fall of 1946" which "recommended withdrawal of all aid to the National government." Senator Bridges' document then indicates that this alleged draft by Mr. Vincent could be compared to the act of the Soviet Union in continuing aid to the Communists in China despite its undertaking to support the Central government in the Sino-Soviet pacts of August 14, 1945.

     (b) Mr. Vincent on November 11, 1946, while Director of the Office of Far Eastern Affairs, delivered an address in which he said that it was "unsound to invest private or public capital in countries where there is widespread corruption in business and official circles; where a government is wasting its substance on excessive armament, where the fact or trend of Civil War exists."

The memorandum in reference characterizes this speech as an "indirect expression of American foreign policy in China" and points to the editorial disapproval of the speech as expressed in the New York *World Telegram* and approval given it by the *Daily Worker*, the Chicago *Star* and Communist party dailies.

VII. It is stated that Mr. Vincent accompanied "Owen Lattimore, member of the Editorial Board of *Amerasia*, pro-Communist magazine on Asia," and Henry Wallace on his trip to China in 1944. Mr. Wallace's report of his journey is said to have been "prepared with the direct assistance of Mr. Vincent" and it is alleged that it "should be examined for further indications of Mr. Vincent's approval of the Communist program in China, opposition to the support of the Nationalist Government and furtherance of extension of the influence of Russia in China."

VIII. It is alleged that "examination of the top secret and secret documents required by General Hurley, and passing between the State Department (Mr. Vincent) and General Hurley at the time of his incumbency, would prove revealing of the policy and aims of Mr. Vincent, contrary to the best interests of this country and contrary to its avowed Foreign Policy in China."

IX. It is charged that "at the Potsdam Conference in July 1945, Vincent, aware of the secret Yalta agreement with respect to agreement that Russia was to have certain rights in Manchuria, failed to properly advise Mr. Byrnes of this text, made a great show of opposing Russian demands with respect to China, and furthered a final agreement (which still remains secret) which gave Russia even more than agreed at Yalta. Under date of Oct. 31, 1946, Mr. John M. Patterson, Acting Assistant Chief, Division of Public Liaison, Department of State, replied to the request of the American China Policy Association, Inc., for release that 'No secret agreements concerning China were concluded at the Potsdam Conference.' [*sic*] It is thought that Mr. Vincent instructed Mr. Patterson in the writing of this letter (Why did Mr. Vincent conceal (if he did) from President Truman and Secretary Byrnes at Potsdam, the precise nature and extent of the previous secret Yalta commitments? It would seem that only the Russians could have been benefited by the concealment, as they were thus able to squeeze more concessions from our negotiators who were ignorant of the exact terms which had been squeezed from President Roosevelt)."

X. It is stated that "in late July or early August 1945, Ambassador Hurley finally secured clearance to show the Yalta text to the Chinese. He then exerted every effort to force T. V. Soong and Foreign Minister Wang Shi-hsueh to go to Moscow. When they got there, the Russians made additional demands and the Chinese Government appealed to Hurley to mediate. 'Somehow or other Washington learned of this' and Hurley received a cable believed to have read somewhat as follows: 'You will not advise, you will not mediate, you will not assist in Chinese Russian negotiations.' It was signed 'Grew,' but it is believed that Under Secretary Grew, who was then being forced out, did not compose it.''

XI. It is charged that apparently in the summer of 1945 ''Henry Luce of Time-Life-Fortune, who was represented in China by Theodore White, a strong pro-Communist, became uneasy about 'angled' dispatches and applied for a passport to fly out and see for himself. The State Department refused it. He appealed to General Hurley who cabled recommending the issuance. In reply Hurley received a reprimand advising him not to interfere. Mr. Luce finally obtained an official invitation from Chiang Kai-shek which brought the passport, investigated, and fired White for pro-Communist propaganda. White is a great admirer of Vincent and, like him, has been connected with the Institute of Pacific Relations.''

XII. It is charged that ''during the past two years, the Far Eastern Division of the State Department has been denuded of its former heads who were not pro-Soviet. Hornbeck, former Far Eastern Division head, who has been advanced to Political Adviser to the Secretary, was packed off as Ambassador to the Netherlands; Grew was forced to retire, as was Dooman, Drumright, and the Chief of China Section was sent to London. Now in control of the Far East Division, Lattimore and Vincent (Lattimore having no official connection although he lectures to Department personnel, and to the War College, and is known to advise Dean Acheson and President Truman as well as Vincent) have sent to General MacArthur, as well as to China, men and women of Red sympathies. A few names sent MacArthur are John S. Service (ardent pro-Communist, arrested in 1945 for turning State Department papers over to Communist Philip Jaffe of *Amerasia*), Theodore Cohen (Labor Adviser), Miriam Farley, and T. A. Bisson of the Institute of Pacific Relations, listed as a Communist front by the Dies committee of 1944, of which Vincent and Lattimore are both trustees). Lattimore, close friend and associate of Vincent, is reported to have loaded the OWI with Reds (both Chinese and American) and helped to secure the appointment of a man without qualifications (also without a Communist record) as head of UNRRA for China and helped him staff this division of UNRRA with Pro-Communists.''[80]

All the allegations contained in Bridges's memorandum were denied by Acheson. In each case, he declared that the accusation was either a figment of an overworked imagination, a distortion of an actual event, or a partial statement of an actual event for which Vincent's superiors—rather than Vincent himself—were responsible. Acheson's statement was apparently accepted by a Republican majority. Vincent's promotion, as well as his appointment to the post of Minister to Switzerland, was approved.

The removal of Vincent from any direct connection with Far Eastern affairs and Acheson's certainty of his loyalty did not, however, end the attacks. In 1950 Senator McCarthy placed Vincent second on his list of "eighty-one cases," and characterized him "as (1) a big Communist tremendously important to Russia, as (2) a part of an espionage ring in the State Department, and (3) as one who should 'not only be discharged but should be immediately prosecuted.' "[81] After reviewing Vincent's loyalty file, the Tydings Subcommittee concluded that "the McCarthy charges are absurd. The file does not show him to be disloyal or a security risk."[82] Budenz refused, during the hearings, to identify Vincent as a Communist.[83]

Following the United Nations intervention in Korea, the attacks on Vincent increased in frequency and intensity. His name was repeatedly injected into the investigation of the IPR by the McCarran Subcommittee. The bases for including Vincent in an investigation of the IPR were numerous. He had been a "complimentary" member of the board of trustees of the American Council in 1945.[84] He was well acquainted with a number of IPR officials over a period of several years and corresponded with them on occasion. The correspondence, of course, turned up in the files of the organization. In 1945 Vincent was invited to attend the IPR Conference at Hot Springs, Virginia, and, with the approval of Grew, accepted.[85] In addition, Vincent was naturally acquainted with many, if not most, of the Far Eastern specialists who were also associated in one way or another with the IPR.

During this investigation, Budenz identified Vincent, for the first time, as a member of the Communist party. In his usual style, Budenz repeatedly asserted that according to "official reports" Vincent was a member of the party and that, "The Communists were eager that Mr. Vincent advance and that he obtain a place in the State Department where he could get rid of Hurley and in addition to that could also influence policy."[86] Vincent emphatically denied these allegations and bluntly called Budenz a liar in sworn testimony before the subcommittee.[87] He was never prosecuted for perjury.

Vincent's denial of membership in the Communist party brought from the chairman, McCarran, a clear indication of the line of attack which was to be pursued by the subcommittee toward him. Immediately following Vincent's emphatic and absolute denial of party membership, McCarran stated:

Let me say to you, Mr. Vincent, that it is not alone membership in the Communist Party that constitutes a threat to the internal security of this country; it is sympathy with the Communist movement that raises one of the gravest threats that we have.[88]

Vincent also denied any sympathy with "the aims of the Communist Party," but the subcommittee set out to prove otherwise. The method employed was to attempt to show that the Communists—primarily writers for the *Daily Worker*—had, on occasion, shown approval of Vincent personally and had sometimes advocated policies for the Far East which paralleled to some extent those supposedly approved by Vincent.[89] Very early in the hearing it became quite clear that Vincent was almost totally unfamiliar with Communist purposes, methods, and programs. This revelation did not help to support his contention that his ideas and policies had not paralleled those of the Communists. Subcommittee members quite logically pointed out that if Vincent did not know what the policies of the Communists were he could hardly argue that he had not followed them.[90] On the other hand, Vincent's obvious lack of familiarity with Communist literature and doctrine weakened the subcommittee's original contention that Vincent had *consciously* followed Communist policies. The result was that the subcommittee concluded that Vincent had been influenced by Lattimore and the IPR.[91] The fact that he had been identified by Budenz as a member of the party was, however, not overlooked.[92]

In questioning Vincent, the McCarran Subcommittee concentrated its attention primarily on the allegations contained in the Bridges memorandum of 1947 which had been answered in detail by Acheson. Three weeks prior to Vincent's first appearance before the subcommittee, Senator McCarran submitted to the State Department a request for thirty-two categories of documents—or alleged documents—with which Vincent supposedly had some connection. Only three of the thirty-two categories concerned matters which had not been covered in the 1947 memorandum from Bridges. The three exceptions concerned events which occurred after 1947.[93] Thus the Senate subcommittee confined itself almost exclusively in Vincent's case to matters which had long before been raised by China lobby spokesmen.

The accusations before the McCarran Subcommittee resulted in the filing of formal charges against Vincent and a hearing before the Department of State Loyalty Security Board. Vincent has testified that the board dealt with three major charges; namely, (1) that he was "pro-Communist," (2) that he was a member of the Communist party, and (3) that he had associated "with people about whom the Department had derogatory information."[94] The detailed specifications to the charges were not revealed. On February 19, 1952, the Loyalty Security Board cleared Vincent of all charges and he was restored to duty.[95]

As in the case of Service, the Civil Service Loyalty Review Board took Vincent's case on review later the same year. On December 15th the review board announced that it had found that there was a "reasonable doubt" of Vincent's loyalty and he was again recalled by the Department of State.[96] Secretary Acheson, who was shortly to be replaced by Dulles, announced at this point that he had appointed a committee of legal and diplomatic experts, headed by Judge Learned B. Hand, to review Vincent's case.[97] What the committee may have decided—or whether it ever made a decision—has never been revealed. Three months later Dulles announced that he had personally cleared Vincent of all disloyalty charges yet forced him to retire against his will. Vincent, who had at first wanted to stay in the foreign service, was threatened with being fired on technical grounds of the McCarran Act and thus would have been severed without pension benefits. He worked out a compromise whereby he returned to his Ambassadorship to Morocco for one month and then "retired."[98]

The fourth of the State Department China specialists whose cases are being reviewed was, like Service, born and educated in China. He too was attached to General Stilwell's staff during World War II and ran afoul of Ambassador Hurley's ire. Furthermore, he had joined with Service in warning the Department of State that Chiang Kai-shek's future in China was doubtful and that the Kuomintang was likely to lose to the Communists. Like the other Foreign Service officers accused by Hurley, however, Davies was absolved of any wrongdoing by Secretary of State Byrnes and continued to advance in the Foreign Service. Nevertheless, his promotions were effected in the face of almost continuous attacks from China lobby sources. These attacks were substantially increased after publication of the White Paper, which contained a number of excerpts of his 1944 reports from China.[99]

In 1951 ex-Communists Freda Utley and Elizabeth Bentley renewed the charges that Davies had been sympathetic with the

Communists.[100] Miss Bentley's allegations were made before the
McCarran Subcommittee and thus aroused that body's interest in
Davies. She contended that reports made to the Department of State
by Davies had been transmitted to the Communist apparatus
through the Silvermaster group and that the reports showed that
Davies was sympathetic to the Communist cause.[101] In spite of these
allegations, however, Davies was cleared by the Loyalty Security
Board and restored to duty.[102] In September, he was promoted to
the post of Deputy Director of the Office of Political Affairs.[103]

During 1952 the McCarran Subcommittee made a strenuous
effort to persuade the Department of Justice to prosecute Davies for
perjury.[104] The basis of the request was an alleged discrepancy
between testimony given to the subcommittee by Davies and that
given by a former agent of the Central Intelligence Agency.[105] The
Department of Justice was unable to find sufficient evidence of perjury to sustain an indictment. Furthermore, after the conclusion of
these events between the McCarran Subcommittee and the Department of Justice, Davies was cleared of any "reasonable doubt of
loyalty" after new hearings before the Civil Service Loyalty Review
Board.[106]

The review board's clearance of Davies stood for just over a year.
On May 27, 1953, a new Executive Order—Number 10450—creating new loyalty and security criteria, was issued from the White
House.[107] The new criteria "related not only to loyalty, but also to
reliability and trustworthiness," and required that the head of the
Department determine in the case of each employee against whom
charges were made "whether continued employment 'is clearly consistent with the interests of the national security.' "[108] Executive
Order Number 10450 required that "the cases of all departmental
and Foreign Service employees who had been investigated under
the provisions of the old loyalty program should be readjudicated
under the new security standards."[109] On December 29, 1953, the
Department of State Office of Security concluded, as a result of this
requirement, that Davies should be suspended and processed under
the new security program.

Dulles exercised his prerogative and waived suspension, but directed that a special hearing board be convened to conduct a hearing. The hearings were held during the latter part of June and the
first half of July in 1954.

So far as can be ascertained from available information, there appear to have been eight broad accusations against Davies in the letter of charges issued by the hearing board.* The first was that Davies "actively opposed and sought to circumvent United States policy toward China," particularly during the period October, 1944, to January 9, 1945. The second accusation was apparently to the effect that Davies "was the leading proponent in the department (presumably 1947–51) of the separability of the Chinese Communists from Moscow." This charge is, of course, directly related to the question of whether the United States should attempt to bring about a situation in which it would be advisable to recognize the Chinese Communist regime. Davies recognized this in his comment to the board:

It touches upon one of the most important, if not the crucial problem confronting American diplomacy. If in our struggle with the Soviet world we are to win out without resort to war, a split in the Soviet-Chinese bloc would seem to be an essential prerequisite. . . .

Ten years ago, I believed that it was essential to our national interests to prevent the creation of a Soviet-Chinese bloc. After the bloc was formed, I believed—and continue to believe—that one of the major objectives of American grand strategy should be the fission of the Soviet-Chinese structure. . . .

The answer to the original question is that I was not the leading proponent in the Department of State of the separability of the Chinese Communist [sic]. I knew no proponents of such a dogma. I did believe, however, that certain factors suggested such a possibility and that the question should be examined. I am not surprised that I have been denounced for this.[110]

The third charge against Davies was apparently to the effect that some of his estimates concerning the strength and orientation of the Chinese Communists "were based on insufficient evidence." The fourth charge was that Davies had submitted from China "unevaluated reports, what is now termed raw intelligence, without labeling them as such or otherwise warning the department that I was not underwriting all that was reported." The fifth accusation referred to the relationship which Davies established with members of the press during his service in China. As Dulles expressed it, "the board

---

* The complete hearing record in the Davies case was never made public. The following enumeration of the charges is based on a letter, dated November 2, 1954, from Davies to the chairman of the hearing board and printed as part of the documentation referred to in Note 107, Chapter VII. The enumeration and wording are this author's except where otherwise indicated. There may have been charges in addition to these eight, but it seems unlikely.

. . . found that he made known his dissents from established policy outside of privileged boundaries."[111] The sixth charge concerned the relationship which Davies maintained with the Chinese Communists. As he expressed it: "I cultivated them. I did so for a purpose —to obtain information. I did so with the knowledge of my superiors and my American colleagues." The seventh charge was that Davies had associated with a list of individuals regarded by the government security officers as pro-Communist. The list would include, of course, a very large number of the private China specialists and some government officials. The eighth charge was closely related to the seventh but seemed to constitute—at least in Davies's mind—a distinct accusation. It concerned the relationship between Davies and General Stilwell and what Davies described as "recriminatory" testimony concerning this "deeply patriotic and selfless soldier." The exact nature of the charge is not clear.

On August 30th the board reached a unanimous decision that "the continued employment of Mr. Davies is not clearly consistent with the interests of the national security," and concluded that "his employment in the Foreign Service of the United States ought to be terminated."[112]

Following this decision, Dulles reviewed the case and, on November 5, 1954, announced his concurrence with the findings of the board. The Secretary remarked in his statement:

The security hearing board did not find, nor do I find, that Mr. Davies was disloyal in the sense of having any communistic affinity or consciously aiding or abetting any alien elements hostile to the United States, or performing his duties or otherwise acting so as intentionally to serve the interests of another government in preference to the interests of the United States.

Under the present Executive Order on security, it is not enough that an employee be of complete and unswerving loyalty. He must be reliable, trustworthy, of good conduct and character.

The members of the security board unanimously found that Mr. Davies' lack of judgment, discretion, and reliability raises a reasonable doubt that his continued employment in the Foreign Service of the United States is clearly consistent with the interests of national security.

This is a conclusion which I am also compelled to reach as a result of my review of the case.[113]

This review of the termination of the careers of four of the State Department's outstanding China specialists reveals several significant facts. First, it shows that, with the exception of Clubb, each of the victims had long been under heavy and continuous attack from China lobby sources. Second, it reveals that despite the lapse of time between their service in China and their separation from the service —again with the exception of Clubb—and in spite of many previous clearances on the same charges, the final hearings concentrated primarily on their China service. Third, it reveals that in all four cases one of the principal accusations was the fact that they had associated with other China specialists—mostly members of IPR— who had also been skeptical of Chiang's ability to retain his position in China and who had also, as a result, been accused of pro-communism by the China lobby. Fourth, in none of the four cases was actual membership in the Communist party the basis for an adverse finding. Fifth, only the two specialists who were actually connected with the American Embassy in China and served on General Stilwell's staff in the critical period of 1944 and 1945, and who were accused by Hurley, were dismissed from their positions. The other two were permitted to resign. Finally, in none of the four cases was there a positive finding of disloyalty. One is constrained to suggest that, as was once remarked of Harold Laski:

He was not of those—a large and influential band—who regard the omission from the beatitudes of the maxim "Blessed are the discreet" as a regrettable oversight. . . . But if impetuosity is a fault it is a more pardonable one than a self-regarding prudence.[114]

IV THE RESULTS
OF ACCEPTANCE
IN TERMS OF POLICY

8 THE ULTIMATE EFFECTS OF ACCEPTANCE ON AMERICAN POLICY

In an extensive analysis of the Kuomintang regime written in June of 1944, John Stewart Service warned the Department of State as follows:

The appeal [of the Chinese Government for help] will be made to us on many grounds besides the obvious, well-worn, but still effective one of pure sentiment. They have said in the past and will say in the future that they could long ago have made peace with Japan—on what are falsely stated would have been favorable terms. They have claimed and will claim again that their resistance and refusal to compromise with Japan saved Russia, Great Britain and ourselves—ignoring the truth that our own refusal to compromise with Japan to China's disadvantage brought on Pearl Harbor and our involvement before we were ready. They have complained and will continue to complain that they have received less support in the form of materials than any other major ally—forgetting that they have done less fighting, have not used the materials given, and would not have had the ability to use what they asked for. Finally, they have tried and will continue to try to lay the blame on us for their difficulties—distorting the effect of American Army expenditures in China and ignoring the fact that these expenditures are only a minor factor in the whole sorry picture of the mismanagement of the Chinese economy.

But however farfetched these appeals, our flat refusal of them might have several embarrassing effects. . . .

We would be blamed by large sections of both Chinese and American public opinion for "abandoning" China after having been responsible for its collapse. (In a measure we would have brought such blame upon ourselves because we have tended to allow ourselves to become identified not merely with China but also with the Kuomintang and its policies. Henceforth, it may be the better part of valor to avoid too close identification with the Kuomintang.)

. . . . On the other hand, if we come to the rescue of the Kuomintang on its own terms we would be buttressing—but only temporarily—a decadent regime which by its existing composition and program is incapable of solving China's problems. Both China and ourselves would be gaining only a brief respite from the ultimate day of reckoning. It is clear, therefore, that it is to our advantage to avoid a situation arising in which we would be presented with a Hobson's choice between two such unpalatable alternatives.[1]

A more accurate and detailed forecast of events than that made by Service would be difficult to conceive. It can now be seen that the

Chinese did make precisely the claims which Service predicted they would make. Those claims were further augmented and buttressed by reference to certain incidents and events which occurred in the United States and which could be made to appear directly related to American China policy. The Chinese planned and executed the exploitation of their claims and grievances through the skillful use of Americans who, motivated by fear, ambition, missionary zeal, and the desire for profitable markets, were disgruntled and upset at what they considered the loss of China. To some extent, the success of the Chinese—especially with the United States Congress—in gaining acceptance for their point of view was the result of fortuitous events over which they had neither control nor foreknowledge. The important point, however, is that as each opportune moment arrived, the Chinese and their American spokesmen were on hand with an explanation—an explanation which was emotionally satisfying whether or not it fitted the facts or contributed to an effective American policy.

The acceptance of that explanation had important repercussions in the United States. It can now be seen that it seriously affected the ability of the vast majority of China specialists in the United States to continue to provide the American people with objective reports and interpretations of events in China. The acceptance of China lobby views virtually destroyed the major organization in the United States which had financed and organized research and publication on the Far East. Those effects eventually extended far beyond the Institute of Pacific Relations and seriously impaired the effectiveness of most of the foundations and organizations in the United States which were concerned with questions of foreign policy. Thus, any competition with the views toward the Far East which prevailed in Congress were very largely stifled at the source.

The Department of State also was purged of personnel who had publicly disagreed with the attitudes toward China which had come to be accepted in Congress. This action was accomplished in the name of security. The permanent suppression of any opposing point of view was largely assured by the continued efforts to remove such officials as Vincent and Davies, long after they had ceased to be employed in the Far Eastern field and long after the major battles over China policy had ended in a stalemate.

Inevitably, these effects were reflected in American policy. Looking back, it is apparent that the acceptance of China lobby views began to affect policy as early as 1947. When Marshall returned from China early in that year, the attitude of the American Government was clearly that the United States should refrain from intervening in China's civil war.[2] President Truman apparently felt that the United States should not encourage or sanction Chinese Communist actions, but that their enmity should not be deliberately courted by continuing to aid Chiang, thereby further identifying the United States with the latter's cause. The Administration was clearly convinced that there was no reason to believe that Chiang could win the Chinese Civil War with any amount of support which the United States would be able to extend. It also felt that the chances of a Communist victory were sufficiently great to warrant caution. Action which would inevitably destroy any possibility of effecting a *rapprochement* with that regime if it should prove the stronger was not thought to be in the American interest.

In spite of this clearly expressed attitude, however, the policy of noninvolvement was not pursued in the strictest sense even in 1947. The attack, through Congress, on John Carter Vincent, the insistence of the House Foreign Affairs Committee and the Senate Appropriations Committee on giving economic aid to Chiang in return for giving aid to Greece and Turkey, and the pressure from Judd and others to make another survey of prospects in China (the Wedemeyer mission) all combined to force a modification in the Administration's opposition to aiding Chiang.

By 1948 the Administration was forced by the growing acceptance of China lobby views in Congress to make still further concessions. The result was the inclusion of military as well as economic aid in the China Aid Act of 1948.[3] The Administration generally, and the Department of State in particular, had not changed its view that the United States should refrain from becoming any more closely involved with the Kuomintang than absolutely necessary. The truth of this observation is clearly reavealed by the lack of urgency with which the military provisions of the China Aid Act were implemented.[4] The Administration was still following the principle that Europe was the decisive area of the world in the power struggle and if concessions had to be made to Congress on China policy in order to carry through the European program, then the Administration was willing to make them. Each such sacrifice, however, made it more difficult to maintain the appearance of impartiality to the contending forces in China.

By early 1949 two important facts were becoming clear. First, the likelihood of a Communist victory was steadily increasing. Second, it was becoming more apparent that the Chinese Communists were fully aware that the United States was not, in fact, remaining neutral in the struggle inside China. Nevertheless, the strength of the pro-Chiang forces in the United States was growing rapidly.[5] The Administration continued to make concessions on aid to China as the price of acceptance of NATO and additional aid to Europe. By the late spring of 1949, the Department of State was faced with a real dilemma; namely, how to satisfy the pro-Chiang forces in Congress and still cut loose from Chiang in time to avoid a permanent estrangement from the Chinese Communists when they established a new government. The answer to that dilemma was the White Paper on China. Here was an action which the State Department could take without congressional sanction—even without congressional knowledge until almost time for its release.

Assuming, as the Administration unquestionably did, that the Communists would very shortly establish a government and there would no longer be a Nationalist regime, this seemed to be a relatively safe course to pursue. If the White Paper helped to avoid a complete alienation of the Communists, it would serve its purpose in China. And if there were no Chiang regime, the China lobby forces in the United States would no longer have a rallying point.

The failure of the Communists to prevent the transfer of the Kuomintang Government to Formosa following the establishment of the new regime on October 1, 1949, however, prevented the consummation of the Administration's plans. Thus, there was still a Nationalist Government which might well hold out for some time even though it could not again become the Government of China. What it could do was to provide a rallying point for pro-Chiang Americans, a source of funds for Chinese in the United States, and an officially recognized embassy through which the Chinese could continue to bring pressure on the American Government. Thus, the White Paper, which the Department of State had hoped would provide a bridge for a *rapprochement* with the Chinese Communists and an explanation to the American people of Chiang's loss of power, actually provided neither.

The new dilemma which faced the Administration two months after the issuance of the White Paper was more difficult than that which had faced it in the spring. An intensive review of American policy toward China which was undertaken in a State Department conference in October of 1949 was a direct response to that dilemma. The result of the conference for the Administration was twofold. First, the conviction that Chiang was permanently out of China was substantially strengthened. Second, the Administration was further convinced that Formosa would soon be taken by the Communists and, thus, the problem of American relations with a Chiang Kai-shek regime would be ended. No other conclusion can explain the guidance paper on Formosa which was dispatched in December.[6]

Having reached the conclusion that Chiang would soon cease to be a problem, President Truman announced in January, 1950, that no further aid would be extended to him. There is no question that the Administration was expecting Formosa to fall and that it was seriously considering the recognition of the Communist Government in China. From the standpoint of the Department of State, recognition at this time was highly desirable. First, it would be a convincing demonstration to the Communists that the United States was not permanently hostile. Second, it would put an end to the State Department's problem with Congress over Chiang Kai-shek. A prerequisite to this action by the United States, however, was that the Communists themselves eliminate Chiang's governmental position.

Two developments, in addition to the failure of the Communists to take Formosa, account for the hesitation of the United States Government to extend recognition to the Communist regime in early 1950. First was the fact that the Chinese Communists were acting in such a manner as to increase the animosity toward them in the United States. Their failure to adhere to the accepted principles of diplomatic practice in their treatment of American personnel in China made the American problem exceedingly difficult.

The second factor, probably even more significant in view of the fact that plans for recognition were pushed ahead long after the Angus Ward incident, was that Congress was becoming increasingly insistent on the defense of Formosa. The addition of Taft and Hoover—ordinarily noninterventionist—to the front ranks of the China bloc demanding extreme military measures in early 1950 is indicative of the power which had accrued to this group.[7] The friends of Nationalist China had clearly demonstrated their capacity to upset other plans of the Administration if Chiang Kai-shek were completely abandoned. Under these circumstances, until Mao actually attacked Formosa the United States would have to remain to some extent identified with the Nationalists. The Department of State would have to delay a complete break with Chiang even though waiting increased the danger of a permanent rupture of American relations with mainland China.

Ultimately, of course, the outbreak of war in Korea—with Chiang still on Formosa—and the subsequent entry of the Chinese into that conflict, settled the policy issue for several years. The Department of State and the Administration had relied on what appeared in the late winter of 1949–1950 to be a sure course of events. When those events failed to materialize as expected, they lost the initiative in the formulation of policy. But certainly, in this case, the earlier inability of the Executive branch to make a firm policy decision in the face of congressional opposition may well have conditioned events in China as well as in the United States.

The Administration's loss of the initiative in formulating policy for China placed Congress in a vastly superior power position. After the outbreak of war in Korea, the pro-Chiang bloc, greatly strengthened both by events and by the rapidly increasing acceptance of China lobby views, could block any program requested by the Administration unless Congress were allowed to dictate policy toward China. Capitulation was therefore the only course open to the Executive branch.

The thoroughgoing nature of the demoralization of the Department of State after 1950 was made clearly evident by four specific developments which took place after that date. These developments were (1) the Administration's failure to secure Senate confirmation for the nomination of Philip Jessup to be the United States Representative to the United Nations in 1951, (2) the changes made in the loyalty clearance criteria and the gradual dismissal of the career State Department China specialists, (3) the all-out attacks from congressional sources on Marshall and Acheson, and (4) the nature of certain appointments made in the Department of State by the Eisenhower Administration.

In connection with these developments, it should be pointed out that Jessup had served the United States Government in various capacities for several years. In 1949 and 1950, he had served as President Truman's Ambassador at Large and, in that capacity, had undertaken several missions in the Far East. In addition, he had represented the United States in the Security Council of the United

Nations, in the Interim Committee of the General Assembly, and in one special and two regular sessions of the General Assembly.[8] His appointment to each of these positions had been ratified by the Senate.

Late in 1951, Jessup's name was again submitted to the Senate as a representative to the sixth session of the General Assembly which was scheduled to meet in Paris. His appointment was routine—one in a list of ten. Except for the fact that he had long been a target of the China lobby and Senator McCarthy, the Administration apparently had no reason to believe that Jessup's appointment would be particularly controversial. Nevertheless, it was singled out for special attention and sent to a subcommittee headed by Senator Sparkman. Democrats on the Foreign Relations Committee offered no resistance to this move by the Republican minority.[9] A long series of hearings followed in which all the old charges against Jessup were again given public airing. Senator McCarthy was one of the chief accusers.[10]

On October 18, 1951, the subcommittee voted three to two against confirmation of Jessup's appointment. The vote recorded Sparkman and Fulbright for confirmation, Smith (Alexander), Brewster, and Gillette against. Senator Gillette crossed party lines to cast the decisive vote.[11] The following day the Senate pointedly bypassed the Jessup nomination while confirming the other nine appointees.[12]

Neither the Administration nor the Democratic members of the Senate made any real effort to secure confirmation for Jessup's appointment. Following the failure of the Senate to ratify the nomination, President Truman gave Jessup a recess appointment under which he continued to serve until his resignation on December 2, 1952, without further action by the Senate.[13] Thus were Jessup's services terminated under a cloud of doubt and public confusion.

What the Jessup experience revealed concerning the weakness of the Executive branch in the case of individuals who had been the targets of the China lobby was even more startlingly portrayed by changes made in the national government's loyalty and security program. The manner in which certain China specialists were dismissed from the State Department under this program has already been surveyed. It should merely be noted here that these dismissals occurred after 1950 and after the changes in loyalty criteria had been put into effect.

Tightening of the loyalty and security program in response to congressional pressures began in earnest in 1951. The previously existing program was based on Executive Order 9835, issued by President Truman on March 21, 1947. The primary criterion for removing an employee on grounds of disloyalty was that, "on all the evidence, reasonable grounds exist for belief that the person involved is disloyal to the Government of the United States."[14] The new order (Executive Order 10241), issued on April 28, 1951, modified the old standard and substituted the criterion that discharge was justified if, "on all the evidence, there is a reasonable doubt as to the loyalty of the person involved."[15] This subtle, but nevertheless significant, change provided the standard under which Service and Clubb were removed from their government positions.

Application of the new standard of loyalty during the last two years of the Truman Administration failed to end congressional dissatisfaction with the program. The McCarran Subcommittee, for example, made five specific recommendations for further action on the subject in its report issued on July 2, 1952.[16] Also, it is not without significance that of all the "witnesses" called before that body, and accused of disloyalty, during its year-long investigation of the IPR, only two—Davies and Vincent—were then still in active government service.[17]

The McCarthy charges and investigations continued throughout these two years. By 1953 it had become standard practice for the appropriations committees in Congress to question representatives of Executive agencies as to their diligence in enforcing loyalty standards.[18] One student of loyalty board activities during this period has concluded that the very act of clearing an accused official itself became evidence of disloyalty on the part of members of the loyalty board.[19] In other words, only by finding accused officials guilty of disloyalty could the members of a loyalty board themselves escape being charged with disloyalty.

The cumulative result of these pressures was a further capitulation by the Eisenhower Administration. On May 27, 1953, a new Executive Order, Number 10450, was issued. This order extended to the head of every agency in the Executive branch of government the power to dismiss, "in his absolute discretion and when deemed necessary in the interest of national security," any employee in the federal service under his supervision.[20] It further provided that, "any position in a department or agency whose occupant 'could bring about . . . a material adverse effect on the national security' should be designated a 'sensitive position,' and that all occupants of such positions should be subjected to a full field investigation."[21]

In addition to these extensions of existing regulations, the new order once again established new criteria for determining the fitness of an individual for government employment. It substituted for the old standard of no reasonable doubt as to loyalty, the radically new provision that the head of an agency must find the employment of an individual "clearly consistent with the interests of the national security."[22] All employees who had already been subjected to full field investigations under Executive Order 9835 were to have their files reviewed in light of the criteria set forth in the new directive.

As a result of these changes, every position in the Department of State was classified as sensitive.[23] Every member of the Department was thus subjected to a new investigation or review. Vincent had been removed just prior to the effective date of the new order, but Davies was required to undergo a new hearing under its provisions and was ultimately dismissed. Congressional demands relating to the security program had at last been met. As one writer has commented:

> Indeed, the gradual subsidence of spectacular Congressional investigations in the loyalty-security field is due mainly to the fact that, since Eisenhower's inauguration, the executive branch has taken precisely the position on these questions that the extremists in Congress had previously advocated, thereby stealing their thunder.[24]

Unquestionably, the adoption of more rigid security policies and the dismissal from the Department of State of some of the outstanding targets of congressional critics eventually resulted in an abatement of the attacks on the Administration from the Legislative branch. This result was not achieved, however, until after the chief policy-making officials, Secretaries Marshall and Acheson, had also been subjected to bitter personal attack. The fact that such attacks —especially those on Marshall—could be made with impunity provides further evidence of the demoralization of the State Department and of the low esteem in which it had come to be held as a result of the acceptance of China lobby attitudes.

The nature of the attacks on Acheson has already been indicated. Those attacks had begun at a time when Marshall was largely immune as a result of a deliberate policy of restraint which had been adopted by the Chinese.[25] This restraint was undoubtedly due in part to a desire to avoid alienating Senator Vandenberg. After 1950, however, no such moderation was exercised. The attack was launched from a number of sources and concerned virtually every phase of Marshall's career.[26] The most elaborate and thorough version was contributed, however, by Senator McCarthy in a bitter sixty-thousand word speech delivered on the Senate floor on June 14, 1951.[27] McCarthy included every known accusation from both Chinese and American sources, and added a good many of his own. Space does not permit a detailed account of McCarthy's charges. His conclusions, however, reveal the nature of the accusations and the techniques employed:

How can we account for our present situation unless we believe that men high in this Government are concerting to deliver us to disaster? This must be the product of a great conspiracy, a conspiracy on a scale so immense as to dwarf any previous such venture in the history of man.

Who constitutes the highest circles of this conspiracy? About that we cannot be sure. We are convinced that Dean Acheson . . . must be high on the roster. The President? He is their captive. . . .

It is when we return to an examination of General Marshall's record since the spring of 1942 that we approach an explanation of the carefully planned retreat from victory. Let us again review the Marshall record. . . .

It was Marshall who . . . sought to compel the British to invade across the Channel in the fall of 1942 upon penalty of our quitting the war in Europe.

[It was Marshall who] . . . took the strategic direction of the war out of Roosevelt's hands and fought the British desire . . . to advance from Italy into the eastern plains of Europe ahead of the Russians.

[It was Marshall who] . . . sponsored [a] memorandum, advising appeasement of Russia in Europe and the enticement of Russia into the Far Eastern war . . . which foreshadowed our whole course at Teheran, at Yalta, and until now in the Far East.

[It was Marshall who] . . . made common cause with Stalin on the strategy of the war in Europe. . . .

[It was Marshall who] . . . enjoined his chief of military mission in Moscow under no circumstances to "irritate" the Russians by asking them questions about their forces, their weapons, and their plans, while . . . opening our training schools, factories, and gradually our secrets to them.

[It was Marshall who] . . . prevented us having a corridor to Berlin . . . [and prevented] the capture and occupation of Berlin and Prague ahead of the Russians.

[It was Marshall who] . . . sent Deane to Moscow to collaborate with Harriman in drafting the terms of the wholly unnecessary bribe paid to Stalin at Yalta . . . manipulated intelligence reports, brushed aside the potentials of the A-bomb, and finally induced Roosevelt to reinstate Russia in its pre-1904, imperialistic position in Manchuria; an act which, in effect, signed the death warrant of the Republic of China.

[It was Marshall who] . . . created the China policy which, destroying China, robbed us of a great and friendly ally. . . .

[It was Marshall who] . . . went to China to execute the criminal folly of the disastrous Marshall mission.

[It was Marshall who] . . . upon returning from a diplomatic defeat for the United States at Moscow, besought the reinstatement of forty millions in lend-lease for Russia.

[It was Marshall who] . . . for two years suppressed General Wedemeyer's report, which is a direct and comprehensive repudiation of the Marshall policy.

[It was Marshall who] . . . disregarding Wedemeyer's advices on the urgent need for military supplies [for China] . . . proposed instead a relief bill bare of support.

[It was Marshall who] . . . sabotaged the $125,000,000 military-aid bill to China in 1948.

[It was Marshall who] . . . fixed the dividing line for Korea along the thirty eighth parallel. . . .

It was Marshall's strategy for Korea which turned that war into a pointless slaughter, reversing the dictum of Von Clausewitz and every military theorist after him that the object of a war is not merely to kill but to impose your will on the enemy.

It is Marshall-Acheson strategy for Europe to build the defense of Europe around the Atlantic Pact nations, excluding the two great wells of anti-Communist manpower in Western Germany and Spain . . . another case of following the Lattimore advice. . . .

It was Marshall who . . . put a brake on the preparations to fight. . . .

If Marshall were merely stupid, the laws of probability would have dictated that at least some of his decisions would have served this country's interest. Even if Marshall had been innocent of guilty intention, how could he have been trusted to guide the defense of this country further?

What is the objective of the conspiracy? . . . to diminish the United States in world affairs, to weaken us militarily, to confuse our spirit with talk of surrender in the Far East and to impair our will to resist evil. To what end? To the end that we shall be contained and frustrated and finally fall victim to Soviet intrigue from within and Russian military might from without. Is that far-fetched?[28]

Acheson, it will be noted, also played a role in McCarthy's story of a "great conspiracy." Early in 1953, however, the period which one writer of the McCarthy school of thought has called the "Acheson-Hiss-Marshall-Jessup era" came to an end.[29] Control of the Department of State was taken over by a Republican Administration determined to remove all cause for congressional attacks on American foreign-policy makers. The Secretary of State was a staunch

Republican whose reported "intention was to rid himself of the administrative problems of the Secretaryship and devote his attention to high policy."[30]

Into the Department to handle the administrative problems of security, Secretary Dulles brought R. W. Scott McLeod. A man better calculated to stop congressional attacks on the State Department would have been difficult to find. McLeod was a former FBI agent who had served as administrative assistant to Senator Styles Bridges from 1949 to 1953. In that position, he had helped to write the minority (Republican) report on the hearings concerning the recall of General MacArthur. Some idea of the attitude which McLeod brought to his job may be gleaned from a remark to the American Legion convention at Topeka, that sometimes

". . . it is extremely difficult because of the Civil Service Act, the Veterans' Preference Act, and the Foreign Service Act to replace an individual whose viewpoint does not coincide with that of the Republican Party. . . . Until such time as we can re-educate those employees or replace them with proper personnel the progress which we make is sometimes very slow."[31]

To the Rock Creek Republican Women's Club in Washington, McLeod declared that his object was not to establish "if a man is loyal or disloyal, but if he is a good security risk." He then added, "Not *all* New Dealers are necessarily security risks."[32]

McLeod's original position had given him control over both the Bureau of Security and Consular Affairs and the Personnel Office. Traditionally, personnel and security matters had been administered separately on the theory that the same individual should not act as both policeman and judge. In the spring of 1954, the two offices were again severed, but not before McLeod had succeeded in placing at its head a former administrative aide to Senator Knowland, George F. Wilson. Thus, within a few months after taking office, McLeod was reported to have claimed:

For the first time in twenty years . . . the House Un-American Activities Committee under Chairman Velde, the Senate Internal Security Subcommittee under Senator Jenner, and the Special Investigating Subcommittee under McCarthy have received the complete and unequivocal support of the State Department.[33]

These developments show clearly the extent to which the Administration had attempted to appease its pro-Chiang critics. The concessions had been made by both Democrats and Republicans.

The Democratic Administration under Truman had allowed the appointment of Jessup to fail of confirmation without a fight. It had made important changes in loyalty criteria in response to congressional demands and had dismissed two of its most experienced remaining China specialists. In addition, it had proved totally incapable of preventing or refuting the highly partisan attacks against its highest officials.

The Republicans had been forced to continue all the concessions made by their predecessors and add new ones of their own. The Eisenhower Administration made new and far-reaching changes in security criteria, dismissed the remaining China specialists who had incurred the displeasure of the China lobby, and, in effect, turned over the administration of the Department of State to its congressional critics. Concessions on matters of procedure and organization were not sufficient, however, to satisfy the demands of Chiang's followers. Their program required—in the words of one of their spokesmen in 1950—"the pledge of the United States of full cooperation with the Chinese Republic in military and training operations for the recovery of China's freedom."[34] The Democrats had never been willing to give that pledge. At most, they had held out the hope of weening Mao away from his close ties with Moscow. The Republicans were willing to go much further. The "unleashing of Chiang" from the restraint imposed by the Seventh Fleet was a first step.

Just what the action of the Eisenhower Administration in withdrawing the Seventh Fleet as a bar to attacks from Formosa on the Communist-held mainland was expected to accomplish has never been made clear. It did, however, foreshadow a firmer policy of refusing to seek a *rapprochement* with the Chinese Communist regime. Such a policy was clearly in accord with congressional sentiment.

On numerous occasions after 1950, both houses of Congress passed resolutions, without recorded dissent, opposing the seating of the Chinese Communist delegation in the United Nations. These resolutions, together with individual and group expressions of opposition to United States recognition of the Government of the Chinese People's Republic, indicated with increasing clarity that Congress was opposed to any policy which would seek to bring about a closer relationship between the United States and China.[35] The frequency with which the resolutions were passed served as constant reminders to the Administration that Congress had not changed its mind. The Eisenhower Administration capitulated completely to the congressional viewpoint.

That it was a capitulation—at least on the part of Dulles—may be seen from the fact that in 1950 Dulles believed that the United States should not attempt "to appraise closely those [states] which are 'good' and those which are 'bad.' " On the contrary, he believed that "if in fact they are 'governments'—that is, if they 'govern'—then they have a power which should be represented in any organization that purports to mirror world reality." More specifically, he believed:

> If the Communist government of China in fact proves its ability to govern China without serious domestic resistance, then it, too, should be admitted to the United Nations.[36]

The policy of the Department of State in 1954 was just the opposite of that indicated above. Dulles had clearly established "the ability to govern" as the major—if not the only—criterion upon which he thought a decision to recognize a new government should be based. By 1954, however, three new criteria for the recognition of governments—by either the United States or the United Nations—had been added by the Division of Chinese Affairs.[37] The new criteria meant that the United States had, in fact, decided that the Chinese Communist Government was "bad" and that it would therefore not be recognized.

Refusal of American recognition was specifically extended to encompass opposition to recognition by the United Nations. In a speech before a group of American scholars on April 2, 1954, the State Department's officer in charge of Chinese political affairs indicated clearly the extent to which that opposition had become fixed American policy:

> We cannot recognize this regime, and we shall continue vigorously to oppose attempts to accept it in any United Nations organization as representing the Chinese people. We earnestly solicit the support of the entire free world in these policies. We would view with deep concern a "creeping acceptance" of the Peiping regime by the world community of nations.[38]

Even as these statements were being formulated, the paradox between American policy and the requirements of diplomacy were becoming more obvious. The great-power conference on Indochina to be held in Geneva in April, 1954, was then being planned. Reality demanded that the United States agree to the inclusion of representatives of the Mao regime among the conferees. Dulles thus found himself in the position of having to insist that it be "understood that neither the invitation to, nor the holding of, the . . . conference shall be deemed to imply diplomatic recognition in any case where it has not already been accorded."[39] The realities of Chinese Communist power required the United States to negotiate with its representatives. Official policy, however, precluded the conducting of those negotiations through the normal channels of either bilateral diplomacy or the international organization.

A year later the necessity of a Chinese-American *rapprochement* was made even clearer when direct bilateral conferences at the ambassadorial level were begun at Geneva. The purpose of the conferences was to discuss the repatriation of civilians held prisoner in China and other "practical matters at issue." From a practical standpoint, the discussions achieved very little. They could hardly have been expected to produce results so long as the general framework of American policy remained unchanged. They do serve, however, to point up the inconsistency of the American position.

Increasingly, the Department of State has been forced by circumstances and the unreality of its position to fall back on subjectivity and a reliance on faith to support, explain, and justify its policy. Thus, by 1954, the Deputy Director of the Office of Chinese Affairs assured an audience to which he was explaining American policy toward China that Americans must give "profound attention to our own spiritual foundations," and build their house upon "the rock of faith," for, "This is the consideration which transcends in importance all other elements in the formulation of our China policy."[40]

The faith to which this speaker referred was abstract and general; another speaker for the State Department was more specific. He felt that Americans could "take comfort . . . in the belief that a divinely implanted inner voice inclines all humanity to our side."[41] The question which persistently arises, however, is whether the Chinese people can hear the "inner voice" or feel the "spiritual richness" through the wall of silence and suspicion which the acceptance of China lobby attitudes has helped to erect and maintain between the United States and China.

SUMMARY
AND CONCLUSIONS

The story of the China lobby, and the acceptance of the views espoused by it, must ultimately be seen against the broad mosaic of the American experience. The most significant point about the entire development is that the China lobby view of events was widely accepted. It was accepted because of the climate of feeling in the United States. And, once accepted, it helped to choke off debate over alternatives—both outside and within the government. Those who argued a less black-and-white view were in real danger of being tarred with the charge of subversion. For this drying up of foreign policy debate, the American people have continued to pay a fearful price.

In restrospect, it is clear that American ignorance concerning China, the increasing degree to which the assumptions underlying their foreign policy aims became untenable, and their tendency to believe naïve charges of conspiracy when their expectations were unfulfilled, rendered them vulnerable to a well-organized and well-financed pro-Chiang lobby. That such a lobby functioned from the beginning of World War II and was staffed by the paid agents of Chiang Kai-shek, and directed at crucial periods by Madame Chiang herself, is quite clear. It is equally clear that this inner core of Chinese agents was joined by a host of Kuomintang fellow travelers whose efforts were skillfully coordinated by Chiang's Washington staff.

The Americans who aided and supported the China lobby ranged from missionaries expelled from China by the Communists, to businessmen who had large financial stakes in China's future, military leaders disappointed by the inability of the United States to control events in China after World War II, and members of Congress who found in the China problem a lucrative source of "issues" with which to challenge the Administration. No question concerning the "loyalty" or "patriotism" of these Americans need be raised. By and large, they were as "patriotic," as "loyal" to the United States, as concerned with what they conceived to be American interests, as were any other public-spirited citizens. To raise doubts as to their loyalty, in fact, would be to adopt the tactics of the China lobby and would serve only to becloud the real issues.

These issues, of course, far transcend the problems of American policy toward China. In the first place, China lobby writers and spokesmen, from the beginning of their efforts, utterly failed to observe commonly accepted standards of objectivity in the presentation of information concerning China or American policy toward China. Furthermore, they consistently impugned the loyalty and the motives of those scholars and specialists on the Far East who did attempt to present factual information and objective analyses. Any criticism of the Chinese Nationalist regime which was not accompanied by absolute and unqualified support for Chiang Kai-shek was equated with disloyalty to the United States. This tendency was revealed most clearly in the China lobby's long-sustained attacks on General Marshall, Secretary Acheson, and the State Department and private China specialists. The inexcusable lack of objectivity, the willingness to suppress and distort evidence, and the propensity to present accusation and innuendo as fact were particularly apparent in China lobby treatment of the Yalta agreements, the Amerasia Affair, and so on. Ultimately, as the supporters of the Kuomintang gained greater access to the channels of congressional power, they proceeded, with the most cynical disregard for other requirements of American security, to bludgeon the Administration into accepting their demands for support of Chiang Kai-shek. They made a farce of congressional investigations and turned that most essential device —with its almost unlimited potential for properly focusing public attention on important issues—into a weapon of slander, intimidation, and deception. Tactics less likely to clarify issues and create the conditions necessary for a rational decision on important questions of foreign policy would be difficult to conceive.

The arguments, the attitudes, and the proposals of the China lobby gained increasing public acceptance in the United States from late in 1947, through the crucial years of 1951 and 1952. That acceptance was reflected in virtually all media of communication, in congressional action, and in Executive decisions. The results have been serious and continuing. The ability of the Administration to secure the information necessary to perceive and evaluate all possible policy alternatives has been sharply curtailed. The Department of State, and especially the Foreign Service, has been purged so frequently and under such adverse circumstances as seriously to undermine its ability to recruit competent personnel. Of even greater consequence is the overwhelming evidence that American officials in foreign posts consistently fail to seek out, to recognize, or to report the activities of, political groups which are not acceptable in Washington. This situation is a direct result of the treatment of the China specialists.

The tragic results of the acceptance of China lobby views, however, do not end here. As noted in detail earlier, the destruction of the reputations of the private China specialists and all they stood for in the way of objectivity, intellectual honesty, and emotional detachment was a necessary prerequisite to securing the complete emotional attachment of the American people to Chiang Kai-shek. This objective was achieved, partly through direct and purposeful action on the part of the China lobby, and partly as a result of the fear and emotionalism with which Americans responded to postwar events. The actions of the China lobby, on the one hand, and American fears on the other, were interacting causal processes which are probably not subject to separate analysis. Nevertheless, the constant attacks on the loyalty, the patriotism, and even the honesty, of the private China specialists in the United States was undoubtedly an important factor in ultimately undermining public confidence in their reports and in their judgments. The coupling of these attacks with a massive assault on the IPR, as well as other organizations engaged in research and study on China, served further to undermine the ability of the American public to give serious attention to any but a positively pro-Chiang view of American China policy. When these developments were followed by the adoption of an official policy which prohibited all direct contact by Americans—either private or governmental—with mainland China, the gulf between American attitudes and realities in China became virtually complete.

The myths created and propagated by the China lobby were supported and reinforced by congressional action and adopted as the official views of the Republican party. Many Democrats also accepted these myths as realities. And even those who did not accept them, supinely succumbed to the pressures to act as though they were true. In doing so, the policy makers in both the Legislative and Executive branches of government have effectively severed all direct communications with China; have forced the United States to depend on the distortions, the falsehoods, and the self-serving propaganda of the Formosa regime; and have destroyed any possibility of influencing Chinese policy in directions more compatible with American aims. They have placed the United States in a position of total, unyielding hostility to China which under no conceivable circumstances can lead to the furthering of peaceful relations.

Finally, the major issue which confronts the American people today as a result of their acceptance of China lobby attitudes concerns the basic premise which underlies United States policy toward China. The China lobby approach is based on the assumption that no negotiation or agreement with the Communists is possible except on terms which will lead inevitably to their aggrandizement and to the defeat of the West. This assumption is not peculiar to the China lobby. It has long been held by Russophobes and extreme anti-Communist groups. Such a premise cannot readily be disproved. On the other hand, neither can it be confirmed on the basis of past experience. And even if it should prove to be true where Russia is concerned, it does not follow that it is true for China. The United States cannot know what the Chinese want or will agree to, and is not likely to find out, so long as Americans persist in viewing the Peking regime as something that exists in the abstract, independently of the outside world and of what the United States might or might not be prepared to do under certain given contingencies.

That the Chinese Communists will not accept a settlement at the price of their own defeat is axiomatic. But the United States has not, so far, attempted a settlement on any other terms. Nor is any other approach possible so long as American policy is bound fast to the Chiang regime on Formosa—so long as it demands the preservation of that regime and expects Chiang to reconquer the mainland or to play any significant role in the freeing of the mainland from Communist control. Nevertheless, it is totally unrealistic to expect the Peking Government to attempt seriously a *rapprochement* with the United States if that *rapprochement* requires the Chinese to acquiesce in American protection and active connivance with a regime which is sworn to destroy their government, which persistently attacks its territory and kills its citizens and soldiers, which constantly harasses its shipping, which carries on a perpetual campaign of propaganda and vilification against it. These are the only terms, however, on which the United States has ever offered to negotiate with Peking.

Certainly, it should not be assumed that negotiation on any basis will be easy to conduct, free of suspicion, or lacking in tension, or that it will result in a relationship completely satisfactory to the United States. On the other hand, neither should it be assumed that any agreements which the Chinese are willing to make will necessarily be disadvantageous to the West. The present American policy of total opposition, if persisted in long enough, and if the present government remains in power in China, can lead ultimately only to war. This is neither the time nor the place to discuss in detail the alternatives which are now open to the United States. What is important is that, so long as the viewpoint of the China lobby is accepted as final and conclusive, no exploration of the alternatives is possible. It is the climate of opinion in the United States concerning China, rather than the climate of opinion in China, which must change, before any real negotiations can be carried on between the two governments.

The current Chinese action in Tibet in no way alters this proposition. The attempt of American officials and the American press to act as though there is a moral difference between Chinese action in Tibet and French action in Algeria, for example, only serves to underscore the bankruptcy of American thinking on foreign policy. It is no accident that those who are loudest in their denunciation of China's activities in Tibet are also loudest in urging that the United States give greater heed to French advice, all the while ignoring France's activities in Algeria. There are differences in the two situations, but none of the differences is moral, in spite of the fact that official and press reaction in the United States constantly implies that it is. This statement does not suggest that Americans must approve the Chinese actions in order to negotiate with Peking any more than continued negotiation with Paris requires approval of French action. Even so, no change in attitude can be expected so long as Americans are blinded by the moralistic fulminations of the Kuomintang fellow travelers.

The initiative for a change in American policy toward China can hardly come from the present Administration or from any Republican executive. President Eisenhower has, and the late Secretary Dulles had, entirely too deep a vested interest in the present policy to be able to reexamine it in the light of Asian realities. It was the present Administration, after all, which "unleashed Chiang" immediately upon taking office; which insisted on a formal, binding alliance with Chiang; which has allowed the CIA to cooperate with the Formosa Army in making constant raids on the Chinese mainland; and which has maintained the ridiculous fiction that Quemoy is essential to the defense of Formosa and that Formosa is essential to the defense of the United States. A party and an Administration which has continued such policies for more than six years can hardly be expected to admit the ficitious basis upon which they were adopted.

More serious, however, is the fact that *no* President or Secretary of State can afford to make a serious effort to change American policy until Congress repudiates its past actions and clears the way for a major reexamination of the American position. The logical deduction, therefore, is that the Democrats in Congress, the Democratic party, and the next Democratic presidential candidate must provide the leadership for such a move. Any change in American policy—or even any real examination of available alternatives—will require, in short, that foreign policy be returned to the arena of partisan politics where it belongs. A decision to do so will demand courage, perseverance, and determined and intelligent leadership. It will necessitate long (perhaps acrimonious at times) congressional hearings, *held in public*. It will require the calling of the leading China specialists—including those who have been discredited in the past—to air their views and present information, in a setting free of intimidation or the fear of reprisals. It will require that the motives and interests of those—including some members of Congress—who have foisted the China lobby myths on the American public be exposed to the light of day.

The decision to undertake such a campaign would be difficult—perhaps even dangerous. But it is unlikely that a clean break with the past can be made in any other way. If the American people are as intelligent and aware as their form of government assumes, a campaign fought in this manner and on this issue can result in a proudly won victory. In any case, a conscientious effort to establish peaceful relations with China, to restore a measure of American influence over Chinese policies, is a cause worth risking defeat to further. It is a cause, however, not to be undertaken by any party which is dominated by the kind of fear and suspicion typified by the dragon whose shadow continues to haunt the corridors on Capital Hill.

APPENDIX A

DEPARTMENT OF STATE
PUBLIC AFFAIRS AREA—POLICY ADVISORY STAFF
(Special guidance No. 28, December 23, 1949)
Policy Information Paper—Formosa*

I. *Problem*

To formulate information policy which will minimize damage to United States prestige and others' morale by the possible fall of Formosa to the Chinese Communist forces.

II. *Background*

A. Comment on Formosa is on the increase as the Communist advances on the Chinese mainland leave the island as the last substantial part of China under Nationalist control. Attention is focused by three principal elements.

  1. Communists, world-wide, who charge the United States with conspiring to build the island into a fortress to be taken over by the United States (if it does not already control it), thereby trying to brand the United States with the mark of aggressive imperialism, and also hoping to get us involved in a risky and unpromising venture;

  2. Pro-Nationalists (principally in the United States) who consider Formosa a redoubt in which the Government could survive, and who tend to create an impression the United States is delinquent if it fails to "save Formosa";

  3. Groups in the United States who are inclined to be critical of the United States for failure to act to prevent loss of the island to the Communists, largely because of mistaken popular conception of its strategic importance to United States defense in the Pacific.

B. Loss of the island is widely anticipated, and the matter [*sic*] in which civil and military conditions there have deteriorated under the Nationalists adds weight to the expectation. Its fall would threaten:

  1. Loss of United States prestige at home and abroad to the extent we have become committed in the public mind to hold it;

  2. Damage to the morale of other nations, particularly in the Far East, which are disturbed by the Communist gains and fear its possible further advances.

C. Formosa, politically, geographically, and strategically, is part of China in no way especially distinguished or important. Although ruled by

---

* This document was declassified and reprinted—over the strenuous objections of Secretary of State Acheson—in *Military Situation in the Far East*, Pt. 3, pp. 1667–1669.

the Japanese (as "Taiwan") for 50 years, historically it has been Chinese. Politically and militarily it is a strictly Chinese responsibility.

It is true that the technical status of the island remains to be determined by the Japanese peace settlement, but the Cairo agreement and Potsdam declaration and the surrender terms of September 2, 1945, looked to its return to China and the United States facilitated its take over by Chinese troops shortly after VJ-day.

Even the small United States military advisory group sent there at Chinese Government request was completely withdrawn a year ago. Merely a handful of military attaché personnel with diplomatic status remains. The United States never has had military bases there, and never has sought any special concessions there.

ECA work done on the island, particularly through the Joint Commission on Rural Reconstruction, has been of purely economic and technical nature for assistance in improvement of conditions, and no quid pro quo has been sought.

D. United States public opinion has concerned itself primarily with the question of the island's strategic importance; there has been insistent demand from a few sources for military action by the United States, but it has not assumed significant proportions. Rather public opinion obviously is divided and uncertain, and there is no apparent consensus for a particular course of active intervention.

III. *Treatment*

A. If rising public interest warrants it, gradually increasing attention may be paid Formosa, to establish, publicly, the facts indicated below. Overseas use should be made of unofficial materials in public analysis and comment appearing both at home and abroad, as well as official statements as they may appear. Label conflicting public statements properly as "individual expressions of opinion," as "unofficial," etc.

B. All material should be used best to counter the false impressions that:
   1. Formosa's retention would save the Chinese Government;
   2. The United States has a special interest in or "designs on" the island or any military bases on Formosa;
   3. Its loss would seriously damage the interests of either the United States or of other countries opposing communism;
   4. The United States is responsible for or committed in any way to act to save Formosa.

C. Without evidencing undue preoccupation with the subject, emphasize as appropriate any of the following main points:
   1. Formosa is exclusively the responsibility of the Chinese Government:
      (*a*) Historically and geographically a part of China;
      (*b*) The national government has run the island's affairs since the take-over and is responsible for present conditions there;
      (*c*) The United States has assumed no responsibilities or obligations, actual or moral.
   2. Formosa has no special military significance:

(*a*) It is only approximately 100 miles off the China coast;

(*b*) Other potential objects of Communist aggression are closer to points on the Chinese mainland than to Formosa;

(*c*) China has never been a sea power and the island is of no special strategic advantage to the Chinese Communist armed forces.

3. Economic assistance in Formosa has been for economic and social purposes, has been consistent with demonstrated United States concern for the welfare of the Chinese generally, and has involved no thought of special concessions for the United States.

4. In areas of insistent demand for United States action, particularly in the United States itself, we should occasionally make clear that seeking United States bases on Formosa, sending in troops, supplying arms, dispatching naval units, or taking any similar action would:

(*a*) Accomplish no material good for China or its Nationalist regime;

(*b*) Involve the United States in a long-term venture producing at best a new area of bristling stalemate, and at worst possible involvement in open warfare;

(*c*) Subject the United States to a violent propaganda barrage and to reaction against our "militarism, imperialism, and interference" even from friendly peoples, and particularly from Chinese, who would be turned against us anew;

(*d*) Eminently suit purposes of the U.S.S.R., which would like to see us "substantiate" its propaganda, dissipate our energies and weaken effectiveness of our policies generally by such action.

5. In reflecting United States unofficial demands for action of various kinds in Formosa, avoid giving them prominence unwarranted by their limited (usually individual) source, and make clear that the total of such demands evidences concern and frustration in some quarters but does not add up to a consensus on any particular position different from that officially taken.

D. Avoid:

1. Speculation which would show undue concern with whether Nationalists can hold the island or when Communists may take it;

2. References which would indicate important strategic significance, or that the island is a political entity;

3. In output to China, any emphasis on bad conditions in Formosa under the Nationalists, although to other areas reference can be made among reasons why Nationalists are vulnerable there as elsewhere;

4. Statements that Formosa's final status still is to be determined by the Japanese peace treaty;

5. Name "Taiwan"; use "Formosa."

APPENDIX B

COMPARISON OF MCCARTHY AND KOHLBERG CHARGES
Against Institute of Pacific Relations
and Associated Personnel*

EXHIBIT NO. 71
COMPARISON OF MCCARTHY AND KOHLBERG

Kohlberg	*McCarthy*
Appointed Editor *Pacific Affairs*, 1934. Accompanied E. C. Carter to Moscow. "This trip apparently completed his conversion to an admiration of the Soviet Union's system of government" (*China Monthly*, Oct. 1945).	McCarthy notes somewhere on page 231–35 in a hearing that Lattimore was editor of *Pacific Affairs* from 1934–1941.
"Lattimore told a friend (Freda Utley) in London in 1936 that he almost lost his job for publishing an article by Harold Isaacs, a Trotskyite" (*China Monthly*, Oct. 1945).	McCarthy, in a hearing (p. 194) quotes from Freda Utley's book *Lost Illusion* "he [Lattimore] told me a few months later in London how he almost lost his position as Editor of *Pacific Affairs* because he had published an article by the Trotskyist, Harold Isaacs."
"Lattimore continued with other duties including service on the editorial board of *Amerasia* and the editorship of *Pacific Affairs* until 1941" (*China Monthly*, Oct. 1945).	P. 226 (*Hearing Record*) introduced Exhibit L-2 which connected Lattimore with *Amerasia* editorial board.

---

* *State Department Employee Loyalty Investigation*, Pt. 2, pp. 1641–1646. This comparison was prepared and submitted, as Exhibit 71, to the Tydings Subcommittee by Owen Lattimore. It appears here exactly as it was reproduced in the hearing record.

Kohlberg (continued)

Kohlberg's version of the Communist line as allegedly followed by IPR and IPR publications in reference to Chinese government.

(Letter from Alfred Kohlberg dated March 18, 1947, to members of AIPR:)

(1) "Beginning 1937 and up to the end of 1939, the IPR articles uniformly praised the government of Chiang Kai-shek."

(2) "After the Hitler-Stalin alliance of Aug. 23, 1939, the IPR soured on Chiang Kai-shek and by 1941 were stating that in the government of China 'uncertain quarters were "pro-Nazi" and were "willing to make peace with Japan." ' 'Fascist ideas were popularized among and praised by Kuomintang members' " (Compare Lattimore's secret letter to E. C. Carter in the enclosed article from *Plain Talk*).

(3) "Then came the day that shook the pro-Communist world when Hitler invaded Russia, June 22, 1941. That day was a Sunday if I remember correctly and it caught Frederick V. Field, formerly Secretary and now member of the Executive Committee of the IPR leading the picket line in front of the White House with placards proclaiming 'FDR is a War-Monger.***' This same day caught the IPR and the Communist press equally flatfooted. So the IPR and Communist line switched again to the most fulsome praise of Chiang Kai-shek and the Kuomintang.*** No longer did they charge Chiang Kai-shek with 'Negotiating to join the Axis.' This praise of Chiang Kai-shek's government continued until the summer of 1943."

McCarthy (continued)

(Page 4440, *Cong. Record,* March 30, 1950:) "In 1935 at the World Communist meeting in Moscow*** the so-called United Front or Trojan horse policy was adopted—a policy calling for the Communists to combine with the governments in power and to get into strategic positions so that Moscow could control or at least exert influence on governments in question. At this time in 1935*** Chiang Kai-shek made an agreement with the Chinese Communists.

"From 1935 to 1939 the Communist line was pro-Chiang Kai-shek.

"In 1939 after the signing of the Hitler-Stalin Pact and the Stalin-Matsouka Pact, the Communist Party line again became anti-Chiang Kai-shek.

"As the Senate will recall, this continued until June 22, 1941, the day Hitler invaded Russia, at which time the Communist Party line again switched and was pro-Chiang Kai-shek.

"This continued until 1943. The Senate will recall the Russian victory at Stalingrad in the early spring of 1943 and the reversal in the course of the war at that point. *** The Communist Party line again definitely became anti-Chiang Kai-shek."

Kohlberg (continued)

(4) "Beginning in the summer of 1943, both IPR and the Communist press changed to abuse of China."

Lattimore Defended Purge Trials (*China Monthly,* Oct. 1945): The real point, of course, for those who live in democratic countries, is whether the discovery of the conspiracies was a triumph for democracy or not. I think that can be easily determined. The accounts of the most widely read Moscow correspondents all emphasize that since the close scrutiny of every person in a responsible position, following the trials, a great many abuses have been discovered and rectified. A lot depends on whether you emphasize the discovery of the abuse or the rectification of it; but habitual rectification can hardly do anything but give the ordinary citizen more courage to protest, loudly, whenever in the future he finds himself being victimized by "someone in the party" or "someone in the Government." That sounds to me like democracy. *Pacific Affairs,* Sept. 1938, p. 371.

Book jacket *Solution In Asia* quoted by Kohlberg (*China Monthly,* Oct. 1945): He shows that all the Asiatic peoples are more interested in actual democratic practices, such as they see in action across the Russian border, than they are in the fine theories of Anglo-Saxon democracies which come coupled with ruthless imperialism. He inclines to support American newspapermen who report that the only real democracy in China is found in Communist areas. *Solution in Asia.* The jacket.

McCarthy (continued)

On page 237 of the *Hearing Record* McCarthy says: "Mr. Lattimore praised the net result of the Moscow trials and the blood purge by which Stalin secured his dictatorship in 1936–1939 'as a triumph for democracy.' "

(Page 4447, *Cong. Record,* March 30, 1950): "This is what the editor says about the book: 'He shows that all Asiatic people are more interested in actual democratic practices such as the ones they can see in action across the Russian border than they are in the fine theories of Anglo-Saxon democracies which come coupled with ruthless imperialism. ***' He inclines to support American newspapermen who report that the only real democracy in China is found in Communist areas."

Kohlberg (continued)

Article, "I.P.R.—Tokyo Axis" by Sheppard Marley in *Plain Talk*, Dec. 19, 1946 (attached). In which was discussed IPR as action and pressure group.

Letter to *Watertown Daily Times,* Watertown, N.Y., Dec. 6, 1946: Attacked Lattimore for his alleged shift in attitude toward Chiang between 1943 and 1946.

Letter to members of IPR, March 18, 1947: "Members of our Board of Trustees and our Staff managed to get control of the Far Eastern Division of the State Dept., UNRRA, and OWI where they loaded all three with pro-Communists. Two of them, Owen Lattimore and John Carter Vincent, accompanied Henry Wallace to China in 1944 and talked that adolescent into reporting to Roosevelt that 'we were backing the wrong horse in China. *** ' "

"Owen Lattimore, Director, School of International Relations, Johns Hopkins University. Advisor to Pres. Roosevelt, Pres. Truman, Henry Wallace, was connected with pro-Communist Nat'l Emergency conference for Protection of Human Rights; Washington Committee to Aid China, Writers Congress. Defense of Moscow Purge Trials, Associate editor of *Amerasia.* Maintains liaison with heads of Communist Party. Reportedly operative for Soviet Military Intelligence in Far East."

McCarthy (continued)

Article read into record by McCarthy (Pages 4461 to 4463, *Cong. Record*).

(*Cong. Record*, p. 4441:) "The Senate will recall the date of this letter, June 15, 1943, the time when Chiang Kai-shek was our very badly needed ally in the Pacific. *** It was at this time that Lattimore sends this highly secret letter in which he twice urges the strictest secrecy be followed in getting rid of any Chinese who are loyal to our ally, Chiang Kai-shek. ***"

(*Cong. Record*, p. 4447:) "In 1944 he [Lattimore] and John Carter Vincent accompanied Henry Wallace on a tour of China after which Wallace made his report to the State Dept., recommending the torpedoing on Chiang Kai-shek." [*sic*]

(*Hearing Record*, pp. 259–62:) Associates Lattimore with Maryland Asso. for Democratic Rights which he alleges to be an affiliate of the Nat'l Emergency Conference for Democratic Rights.

Principal speaker at meeting of Wash. Committee for Aid to China.

On Oct. 1, 2, 3, of 1943 meeting of Writers Congress and Hollywood Writers of Mobilization at the Univ. of Calif., L. A., campus in Westwood "appearing as the representative of the Office of War Information was Mr. Owen Lattimore."

Kohlberg (continued)

McCarthy (continued)

"In the magazine *Pacific Affairs* of Sept. 1938, Owen Lattimore described the Moscow Purge Trials as a 'triumph for Democracy.'"

(Pages 333–334, Hearing Record:) "It perhaps should be mentioned here that Owen Lattimore was formerly an editor of *Amerasia.*

See previous statement by Kohlberg.

(*Cong. Record,* p. 4445:) "The testimony will be that the head of the Russian Intelligence told this witness [the Russian General] *** that they were having excellent success through the Institute of Pacific Relations which the Soviet Intelligence through Communists in the U. S. had taken over. In connection with this he particularly mentioned Owen Lattimore. ***"

(*China Monthly,* Oct. 1948:) "Lattimore, head of OWI Far East Division, San Francisco, sent orders to his superior in New York (Joseph F. Barnes, later Foreign Editor N. Y. Herald Tribune ***) to fire all Chinese staff members who sympathized with their own government and replace them with Communist from the newly launched New China Daily News, [*sic*] New York Chinese language daily."

(Cong. Record, p. 4440:) "This is a letter *** dated 6–15–1943 which is when the line had again swung to anti-Chiang Kai-shek. This is a letter from Owen Lattimore, Director of Pacific Operations, OWI. The odd thing is that he is writing to his boss in the government service, telling the story to him, not writing to someone who is working for him. ***

"In it he directs the recipient of the letter to get rid of the Chinese in OWI who were loyal to either the Nationalist gov't or Wang Ching-wei. ***

"He then issues instructions that the personnel be recruited from the shareholders of the *New China Daily News,* a Chinese Communist paper in New York."

(*Cong. Record,* p. 4460:) "In 1947 one of the members of the Board [of IPR], one of the good American

Kohlberg (continued)

McCarthy (continued)

members insisted that there be an investigation to determine the extent to which the Communists had taken over control of the American Council of IPR."

(*China Monthly*, Dec. 1949, p. 243:) "The White Paper and the State Dept. categorically deny that Vice President Wallace made any written report to Pres. Roosevelt on his return from China. In spite of this denial, Amb. Hurley states that he read Mr. Wallace's report which was shown to him by John Carter Vincent who accompanied Wallace."

(*Cong. Record*, p. 4447:) "Incidentally in this connection the State Dept. issued a press release *** denying the existence of such a report and stating as follows:"

(*China Monthly*, Sept. 1946, p. 325:) "Editorial suggestions (according to the introduction) were made by John Hazard, Owen Lattimore, Joseph Barnes, Albert Rhys Taylor, and Dr. Treadwell Smith. ***"

(*Cong. Record*, p. 4447:) Upon his return from this trip, Henry Wallace wrote a book entitled *Soviet Asia Mission* in which he pay [*sic*] tribute to Owen Lattimore for his invaluable assistance.

Kohlberg's article "China via Stilwell Road," *China Monthly*, Oct. 1948, has the central idea that Stilwell was a sucker for Owen Lattimore and others such as Theodore White, John Fairbank, and Joseph Barnes.

(*Cong. Record*, p. 4445:) "I think Lattimore was as much responsible if not more so for Stilwell's activities in China than any other one individual."

(*Cong. Record*, p. 4446:) "He [a mystery witness] points out that: the Lattimore crowd was responsible for the indoctrination of Stilwell against Chiang Kai-shek."

(Article entitled "Who Is Responsible for Chinese Tragedy" *China Monthly*, Dec. 1949:) Main thesis is that a pro-Soviet clique headed by

(*Cong. Record*, p. 4445:) "*** I am sure that if the Senator will sit here and will listen to the material which I am presenting he will be

Kohlberg (continued)

Dean Acheson was responsible for yielding China to Communists.

McCarthy (continued)

convinced that the clique of Lattimore, Jessup, and Service has been responsible, almost completely—under Acheson of course—for what went on in the Far East. ***"

(Letter to members of IPR. March 18, 1947:) "Our Board of Trustees (47) scattered all over the country never meets. The Executive Committee (10) is chairmaned by a Californian who never attends. The connections of the others are as per attached sheet. Most of our Trustees are of course not Communists. ***

(*Cong. Record,* p. 4463:) "Since its creation it has had on both Board of Trustees and Executive Committee a very sizable number of outstanding and loyal Americans. Membership on the Board of Trustees or on the Executive Committee in no way in and of itself indicates any Communist sympathies or learnings. *** However, as far as I know, the Board actually never meets but does its business by having the various members send in their proxies. [*sic*]

(*China Monthly,* Dec. 1949:) "The White Paper reveals in reports of Embassy attachés Ludden, Davies, Service, and George Atcheson a determination to discredit the National Government and to build up a picture of the Chinese Communists as ardent fighters for democracy."

(*Cong. Record,* p. 4447:) "*** the reports from its foreign service officials in China during the war as given in the White Paper read like extracts from Lattimore's books. *** These Chinese Communists are represented by Lattimore and his friends in the State Dept., as 'democrats,' 'liberal agrarian reformers,' 'progressives not under Moscow's direction' or more recently as 'detachable from' Soviet Russia."

(*China Monthly,* Aug. 1949:) "Under Philip Jessup's direction the Far Eastern Survey of July 14, 1943, the first blast in the campaign against the Nationalist government of China was published." "Referring to what is called the two Chinas, it said in an article signed by T. A. Bisson. ***"

(*Cong. Record,* p. 4463:) "The first blast in this campaign was fired in Jessup's publication on July 14, 1943, in an article signed by T. A. Bisson."

Kohlberg (continued)

(*China Monthly*, Aug. 1949:) "One is now generally called Kuomintang China, the other is called Communist China. However, these are only Party labels. To be more descriptive, the one might be called feudal China, the other democratic China." (Bisson's statement).

"This theme song of Democratic Communist China and 'feudal fascist reactionary' Nationalist China was taken up the following month by the *Daily Worker*, the *New Masses*, and others."

(*China Monthly*, Aug. 1949:) "When charges of Communist-line activities were made against the IPR in 1947 he signed a letter denying the charges and questioning motives behind such charges. When the question of appointing a committee to investigate came before a membership meeting, he voted against any investigation."

(*China Monthly*, Aug. 1949, p. 168:) "Professor Jessup must therefore be honored by our State Dept.,

McCarthy (continued)

"Under him [Dr. Jessup] the Council bi-weekly publication, *Far Eastern Survey*, pioneered the smear campaign against Chiang Kai-shek, and the idea the Communists in China were merely agrarian reformers and not Communists at all."

(Page 4464:) "Prof. Jessup must, therefore, be credited by the American people with having pioneered the smear campaign against Nationalist China and Chiang Kai-shek, and with being the originator of the myth of the "Democratic" Chinese Communists. From that time onward we witness the spectacle of this 3-horse team of smears and untruths thundering down the stretch—Jessup's publications, *Far Eastern Survey*, the *Daily Worker*, and *Isvestzia*."

(Jessup) (*Cong. Record*, p. 4460:) "In 1947 one of the members of the board, one of the good American members, insisted that there be an investigation to determine extent to which the Communists had taken over control of the American Council of IRP [*sic*]. That was very vigorously opposed. Keep in mind that at that time Frederick V. Field was a member of the Board. Hiss was then a member or was shortly thereafter. One of the men who vigorously protested, and sent a letter over his name, which I have, objecting strenuously to any such investigation, was our Ambassador at Large, Phillip Jessup."

(*Cong. Record*, p. 4464:) "Prof. Jessup must, therefore, be credited by the American people with having

Kohlberg (continued)	*McCarthy (continued)*

as the initiator of the smear campaign against Nationalist China and Chiang Kai-shek, and the originator of the myth of the democratic Chinese Communists."

pioneered the smear campaign against Nationalist China and Chiang Kai-shek, and with being the originator of the myth of the 'democratic' Chinese Communists."

(*China Monthly,* August 1949, p. 168:) Communist fronts sponsored by Jessup according to Kohlberg:
The American-Russian Institute
National Emergency Conference
American Law Students Asso.
Nat'l Emergency Conference for Democratic Rights
Coordinating Committee to Lift the Embargo

(*Cong. Record,* p. 4465:) McCarthy's list:
American Law Students Asso.
United Students Peace Conference
Nat'l Emergency Conference for Democratic Rights
National Emergency Conference

(*China Monthly,* August, 1949, p. 168:) "[Jessup was] signer of letter in the *N.Y. Times,* Feb. 16, 1946, urging 'the cessation of atomic bomb production.' "

(*Cong. Record,* p. 4465:) "I have in my hand a photostat of the N.Y. Times dated Feb. 16, 1946. *** In this letter the brilliant Dr. Jessup urges not only that we quit producing atomic bombs but that we eliminate the necessary ingredients which were produced for the atomic bomb by 'means such as dumping them in the ocean.' "

(Letter to Mr. E. C. Carter Dec. 26, 1946:) "In my opinion this organization (Committee for a Democratic Far Eastern Policy) was set up by the IPR. *** just as much as *Amerasia* was (which was also not officially connected although it made its office with you in the early years)."

(*Cong. Record,* p. 4464–65:) "The magazine *Amerasia* about whose Communist line there can be no question for a period of time had its offices right next to the offices of the Jessup publication for IPR."

NOTES

1. THE AMERICAN PERSPECTIVE ON THE FAR EAST

1. McGeorge Bundy (ed.), *The Pattern of Responsibility* (Boston: Houghton Mifflin Co., 1952), p. 149.
2. Kenneth Scott Latourette, *The American Record in the Far East, 1945–1951* (issued under the auspices of the American Institute of Pacific Relations) (New York: The Macmillan Co., 1952), p. 11.
3. *Ibid.*, pp. 12–15.
4. Statement of John Hay, to whom American historians usually attribute the Open Door policy, quoted from a letter from Secretary of State Stimson to Senator Borah in James W. Christopher's *Conflict in the Far East: American Diplomacy in China from 1928–1933* (Leiden: E. J. Brill, 1950), p. 318. Christopher presents an interesting argument in which he says, "The Chinese themselves introduced the Open Door policy and have always insisted on it," *ibid.*, p. 30.
5. George F. Kennan, *American Diplomacy, 1900–1950* (Charles R. Walgreen Foundation Lectures) (Chicago: The University of Chicago Press, copyright 1951 by the University of Chicago), p. 37.
6. *Ibid.*, p. 35.
7. Harold M. Vinacke, *The United States and the Far East, 1945–1951* (published under the auspices of the American Institute of Pacific Relations, Inc.) (Stanford: Stanford University Press, 1952), p. 13.
8. *Ibid.*, pp. 13–14.
9. The fourth and fifth examples are the subject of Christopher, *op. cit.* It is the most thorough available treatment of the attitude of the United States toward the Soviet-Chinese conflict of 1929.
10. Vinacke, *op. cit.*, p. 12.
11. These different policy alternatives will be considered in some detail at the end of this chapter.
12. Herbert Feis, "Europe Versus Asia in American Strategy," *The Yale Review*, XLIII (March 1954), 351–363.
13. Herbert Feis, *The China Tangle: The American Effort in China from Pearl Harbor to the Marshall Mission* (Princeton: Princeton University Press, 1953), Chap. 10, "To Make China a Great Power."
14. Henry L. Stimson and McGeorge Bundy, *On Active Service in Peace and War* (New York: Harper, 1948), p. 415. For the reasoning behind this decision see Feis, "Europe Versus Asia," *Yale Review*, XLIII (March, 1954), 355–356.
15. For a detailed account of the "Rainbow" plans, see Mark Skinner Watson, *Chief of Staff: Prewar Plans and Preparations*, Vol. I of *The War Department*, Ser. IV, *The United States Army in World War II* (Washington: U.S. Government Printing Office, 1950), pp. 103–104.
16. Charles F. Romanus and Riley Sunderland, *Stilwell's Mission to China*, Vol. I of *China-Burma-India Theater*, Series IX, *The United States Army in World War II*, gen. ed. Kent Roberts Greenfield, under the Office of the Chief of Military History, Department of the Army (Washington: U.S. Government Printing Office, 1952), p. 63 (hereinafter cited as *Stilwell's Mission*).
17. Reported by H. Bradford Westerfield, in *Foreign Policy and Party Politics: Pearl Harbor to Korea* (New Haven: Yale University Press, 1955), p. 242 (hereinafter cited as *Foreign Policy and Party Politics*).
18. *Ibid.*, p. 243.

19. Walter Millis (ed.), *The Forrestal Diaries* (New York: The Viking Press, 1951), pp. 17–18.

20. Cordell Hull, *The Memoirs of Cordell Hull,* II (New York: The Macmillan Co., 1948), 1583. For an account of the difficulties connected with the Moscow Declaration, see Feis, *The China Tangle,* pp. 98–100.

21. *Stilwell's Mission* provides such ample documentation for this statement that it would seem to be beyond reasonable dispute. It is also the contention made by Herbert Feis, less clearly in *The China Tangle,* but unequivocally in his article "Europe Versus Asia," *The Yale Review,* XLIII (March, 1954), 351–363.

22. For an example of this point of view, see the speech by Representative Walter H. Judd in the *Congressional Record,* 79th Cong., 1st Sess., Vol. 91, Pt. 2 (March 15, 1945), pp. 2294–2302.

23. See, for example, Pearl Buck, "A Warning About China," *Life* (May 10, 1943), pp. 53–56; Edgar Snow, "Sixty Million Lost Allies," *Saturday Evening Post* (June 10, 1944), pp. 12–13; Darrell Berrigan, "Uncle Joe Pays Off," *ibid.* (June 17, 1944), pp. 20–21, and E. O. Hauser, "China Needs a Friendly Nudge," *ibid.* (August 26, 1944), pp. 28–29. This interpretation of events in China received vastly increased attention in the American press after the recall of General Stilwell in October, 1944. See, for example, the New York *Times,* October 31, 1944, pp. 1, 4; Mark Gayn, Edgar Snow, "Must China Go Red?" *Saturday Evening Post* (May 12, 1945), pp. 9–10; Samuel Lubell, "Vinegar Joe and the Reluctant Dragon," *ibid.* (February 24, 1945), pp. 9–11, and "Is China Washed Up?" *ibid.* (March 31, 1945), pp. 20, 93–94.

24. Theodore White and Annalee Jacoby, *Thunder Out of China* (New York: William Sloane Associates, 1946); Harrison Forman, *Report from Red China* (New York: Henry Holt and Co., 1945); Edgar Snow, *Red Star Over China* (New York: Random House, 1938).

25. In addition to the books noted above, these views were presented in such works as, Claire and William Band, *Two Years with the Chinese Communists* (New Haven: Yale Univ. Press, 1948); Israel Epstein, *Unfinished Revolution in China* (Boston: Little, Brown and Co., 1947); Lawrence K. Rosinger, *China's Crisis* (New York: Alfred A. Knopf, 1945); Agnes Smedley, *Battle Hymn of China* (New York: Alfred A. Knopf, 1943); Guenther Stein, *The Challenge of Red China* (New York: McGraw-Hill, 1945); Anna Louise Strong, *The Chinese Conquer China* (Garden City, New York: Doubleday and Co., 1949).

26. William R. Johnson, "The United States Sells China Down the Amur," *The China Monthly,* VIII (December, 1947), 412–415, 425–427; reprinted in "condensed and revised" form in the *Congressional Record,* 80th Cong., 2nd Sess., Vol. 94, Pt. 10, Appendix (March 25, 1948), pp. 1909–1910. For confirmation of the extent to which this view had come to be accepted, see Sumner Welles, *Seven Decisions That Shaped History* (New York: Harper, 1950), Chap. VI; Dean G. Acheson, "Crisis in Asia—An Examination of United States Policy," *The Department of State Bulletin,* XXII (1950), 112–115; Vinacke, *op. cit.,* p. v.

27. United States Department of State, *United States Relations with China, with Special Reference to the Period 1944–1949* (hereinafter cited as DOS, *United States Relations with China,* 1949), Department of State Publication 3573 (Washington: U.S. Government Printing Office, 1949).

28. McGeorge Bundy confirms this view in *The Pattern of Responsibility,* pp. 181–182. He quotes from Acheson's testimony in *Military Situation in the Far East,* pp. 1769–1770, as proof of his point.

29. United States Department of Defense, "Increase in battle casualties for week ending May 11, 1951," reprinted in U.S. Congress, Senate, Committee on Armed Services and Committee on Foreign Relations, *Hearings, Military Situation in the Far East,* 82nd Cong., 1st Sess. (Washington: Government Printing

Office, 1951), p. 3296 (hereinafter cited as *Military Situation in the Far East*).

30. Many of the "revisionists" after World War II have shown a peculiar dichotomy in their treatment of this question of "winning the war" in relation to Korea and World War II. As a typical example, William Henry Chamberlin, in his book *Beyond Containment* (Chicago: Henry Regenery Co., 1953), is extremely critical of the Roosevelt Administration for its insistence on total victory in World War II (Chap. III, "Can We Escape from Victory?"). His complaint is that the political goals of the war were given insufficient attention. He is equally critical of the Truman Administration, however, for giving greater attention to the political goals in Korea than to winning the military struggle (Chap. V, "The Struggle for East Asia"). In both cases, Chamberlin's criticism stems primarily from the fact that he disliked the methods applied to the political problems.

31. DOS, *United States Relations with China, 1949*, p. x.

32. *Ibid.*

33. Latourette, *op. cit.*, p. 102.

34. DOS, *United States Relations with China, 1949*, p. x. A recent American writer on this subject has suggested that even if the Department of State correctly assessed the mood of the American people in this respect, they should have been forced, through their representatives, to make their sentiments known beyond the shadow of any future doubt. He suggests that this could have been accomplished by placing the decision squarely in the hands of Congress. He does not, however, consider the effects such a public decision might have had inside China and on America's allies. See Westerfield, *Foreign Policy and Party Politics*, pp. 256–259.

35. Latourette, *op. cit.*, pp. 102–103.

36. DOS, *United States Relations with China, 1949*, p. x.

37. Latourette, *op. cit.*, p. 104.

38. Many of the critics of American policy who fall into this group will protest that they were not anti-Chiang. In all fairness, many of them were probably not anti-Chiang in a personal sense. Nevertheless, the term is a proper one in the sense that those who criticized United States policy from this point of view were extremely skeptical of Chiang's ability to solve China's internal problems or exercise sufficient control over the Kuomintang to create a truly united, democratic government. Many of them were equally doubtful that any other non-Communist group in China could win and hold power.

39. DOS, *United States Relations with China, 1949*, p. xvi.

40. Owen Lattimore, "The Roots of Conflict in the Modern Orient," Mayling Soong Foundation Address at Wellesley College, October 23, 1950; reproduced in Norman J. Padelford (ed.), *Contemporary International Relations Readings, 1950–1951* (Cambridge: Harvard University Press, 1951), p. 169.

41. William R. Johnson, "The United States Sells China Down the Amur," *The China Monthly*, VIII (December, 1947), 412–415, 425–427.

42. Alfred Kohlberg, "Stupidity and/or Treason," *ibid.*, Vol. IX (June 1948).

43. Walter Lippmann, *Public Opinion* (New York: Harcourt, Brace and Co., 1922). Lippmann, in fact, goes considerably further and argues that a truly successful propaganda campaign must prepare the soil by artificial means. "Without some form of censorship, propaganda in the strict sense of the word is impossible. In order to conduct a propaganda campaign there must be some barrier between the public and the event." See p. 43.

44. Leonard W. Doob, *Propaganda: Its Psychology and Technique* (New York: Henry Holt and Company, 1935), p. 54 (italics omitted).

45. Norman J. Powell, *Anatomy of Public Opinion* (New York: Prentice-Hall, Inc., 1951), p., 414.

46. *Ibid.*, pp. 414–415.

47. Edward L. Bernays, *Propaganda* (New York: Liveright Publishing Corporation, 1928), p. 109.
48. Powell, *op. cit.*, p. 440.

2. THE CHINA LOBBY IDENTIFIED

1. Romanus and Sunderland, *Stilwell's Mission*, p. 23.
2. *Ibid.*, pp. 82–83.
3. See for example, *ibid.*, pp. 277–283; Stimson and Bundy, *On Active Service*, pp. 528–541; Robert E. Sherwood, *Roosevelt and Hopkins—An Intimate History* (New York: Harper, 1948), p. 405.
4. *Congressional Record*, 80th Cong., 1st Sess., Vol. 93, Pt. 4 (May 7, 1947), pp. 4694, 4722.
5. Communist party of New York State, "Information Release, To All Sections and Counties," March 1, 1949.
6. See *U.S. News & World Report*, "Insiders Got Rich on China Aid" (August 26, 1949), pp. 15–17. Representative Mansfield's suggestions on the subject appeared in the *Congressional Record*, 81st Cong., 1st Sess., Vol. 95, Pt. 9 (August 25, 1949), pp. 12290–12292.
7. *Military Situation in the Far East*, Pt. 3, pp. 2070ff., 2183ff., and 2264ff.
8. *Congressional Quarterly, Weekly Report* (Special Supplement), "The China Lobby: A Case Study," IX (June 29, 1951). Quotation is from p. 939.
9. Max Ascoli, "Starting the Job," *The Reporter*, VI (April 15, 1952), 2. Reprinted in the *Congressional Record*, 82nd Congress, 2nd Sess., Vol. 98, Pt. 5 (June 6, 1952), pp. 6770–6787 (inserted by Senator Cain, R., Wash.).
10. *Congressional Quarterly* (Special Supplement), IX (June 29, 1951), 939.
11. A broad range of definitions for the term "lobby" emerges from the literature on the subject. In most cases, however, it is applied to groups which attempt to influence legislative bodies. For a rather extensive examination of the subject, see United States Congress, House of Representatives, House Select Committee on Lobbying Activities, *Hearings*, Pt. I, "The Role of Lobbying in Representative Self-Government" (Washington: U.S. Government Printing Office, 1950), pp. 5–25.
12. For a discussion of the relationship between support of Chiang and the requirements of American security, see pp. 20–21.
13. DOS, *United States Relations with China, 1949*, pp. 1043–1044.
14. The initial draft of the United States-China Financial Aid Agreement covering this loan appears at *ibid.*, pp. 479–481.
15. Numerous documents concerning American efforts to secure control over or information concerning the disposition of these funds appear at *ibid.*, pp. 470–509. Pages 506–509 contain a list of information requested of the Chinese Government in connection with the uses to which the credits were put. A footnote states: "To date, the information requested has not been received."
16. Wertenbaker, "The China Lobby," *The Reporter*, VI (April 15, 1952), 5. For further confirmation of the nature and extent of Soong's contacts, see Feis, *The China Tangle*, pp. 19ff.; DOS, *United States Relations with China, 1949*, pp. 470–509; Sherwood, *Roosevelt and Hopkins* (rev. ed.), II, 88ff.
17. Wertenbaker, *op. cit.*, p. 6.
18. Feis, *The China Tangle*, p. 79.
19. *Ibid.*, p. 221, n. 25.
20. *Ibid.*
21. Wertenbaker, *op. cit.*, p. 8.
22. New York *Times*, September 11, 1947.
23. Wertenbaker, *op. cit.*, p. 17.

24. This information is from *Congressional Quarterly* (Special Supplement), IX (June 20, 1951), 944–945.
25. Quoted at *ibid.*
26. Quoted at *ibid.*, p. 945.
27. Quoted at *ibid.*
28. *Ibid.*
29. *Ibid.*, pp. 945–946.
30. *Ibid.*, p. 946.
31. See Joseph Alsop's testimony concerning the CC Clique in U.S. Congress, Senate, Committee on the Judiciary, Internal Security Subcommittee, *Institute of Pacific Relations: Hearings,* July 25, 1951–June 20, 1952, Pt. 5, 82nd Cong., 2nd Sess. (Washington: Government Printing Office, 1952), p. 1417 (hereinafter cited as *IPR Hearings).*
32. Wertenbaker, *op. cit.,* p. 18.
33. *Congressional Quarterly* (Special Supplement), IX (June 20, 1951), 947.
34. Alsop testimony, *IPR Hearings,* Pt. 5, p. 1417.
35. Quoted in Wertenbaker, *op. cit.,* p. 18.
36. *Ibid.*
37. Quoted in *ibid.,* pp. 18–19.
38. See above, p. 30.
39. DOS, *United States Relations with China, 1949,* p. 489.
40. See, for example, Wertenbaker, "The China Lobby," *The Reporter,* VI (April 15, 1952), 8–9, and *U.S. News & World Report* (August 26, 1949), pp. 15–17.
41. See, in addition to the above, Drew Pearson, "Washington Merry-Go-Round," Washington *Post* (March 1, 1949; June 18, 1951); Marquis Childs, Washington *Post* (May 5, 1950); Doris Fleeson, (Washington) *Evening Star* (January 16, 1950).
42. For confirmation of this statement, see Arthur H. Vandenberg, Jr. (ed.) *The Private Papers of Senator Vandenberg* (Boston: Houghton Mifflin Co., 1952), pp. 526–532 (hereinafter cited as Vandenberg, *Papers).*
43. See the New York *Times,* December 1, 1948, p. 2, for an account of Madame Chiang's arrival and the purposes behind it.
44. For confirmation of this view and further substantiation, see Philip Horton, "The China Lobby—Part II," *The Reporter,* VI (April 26, 1952), 5–8.
45. *Ibid.,* p. 5.
46. *Ibid.,* p. 5.
47. *Ibid.,* p. 6. See also Senator Cain's (R., Washington) "list of participants" in what he called those who "collaborated in sending a sort of weekly newsletter to the authorities in Formosa," in the *Congressional Record,* 82nd Cong., 2nd Sess., Vol. 98, Pt. 5 (June 6, 1952) (p. 6871 in Daily Record).
48. DOS, *United States Relations with China, 1949,* pp. 293–294.
49. *Ibid.,* p. 295.
50. *Ibid.,* p. 303.
51. Cable, Chinese agents to Chiang, June 22, 1949.
52. *Ibid.,* November 28, 1949.
53. The act referred to is the "Foreign Agents Registration Act of 1938 as Amended," *United States Code* (1952 edition), Title 22 (Washington: U.S. Government Printing Office, 1953), Vol. II, pp. 2942–2949.
54. K. E. Ettinger, "Foreign Propaganda in America," *Public Opinion Quarterly,* 10 (Fall, 1946), pp. 329–330.
55. Wertenbaker, "The China Lobby," *The Reporter,* VI (April 15, 1952), 22. The Yangtze Trading Corporation was barred in June, 1951, from licensing for foreign trade after having been charged with illegally shipping tin to Communist China.

56. For a colorful and interesting account of some of the activities of "Major" Kung, see *ibid.*, pp. 20–24.

57. *Congressional Quarterly* (Special Supplement), IX (June 20, 1951), 944.

58. The activities of the American public-relations firm as an agent of the Bank of China will be dealt with later.

59. *Congressional Quarterly* (Special Supplement), IX (June 20, 1951), 941.

60. *Ibid.*, p. 955.

61. *Ibid.*

62. Quoted at *ibid.*

63. Quoted at *ibid.*

64. *Congressional Quarterly* (Special Supplement), IX (June 20, 1951), 941, 944.

65. Quoted in *Congressional Quarterly* (Special Supplement), IX (June 20, 1951), 943.

66. Quoted at *ibid.*

67. *Ibid.*

68. *Ibid.*, p. 944. For an interesting account of certain of the activities engaged in by Allied Syndicates, Inc., see, Wertenbaker, "The China Lobby," *The Reporter*, VI (April 15, 1952), 20–22.

69. Wertenbaker, "The China Lobby," p. 21.

70. *Ibid.*

71. Only a formal legal test could finally answer the question of the status of CIC under the Registration Act. No such test was ever instituted.

72. The available information on Commerce International (China), Inc., was pieced together from the sources given on the following pages.

73. New York *Times*, August 22, 1951, p. 1.

74. *Ibid.*, August 31, 1951, p. 2.

75. *Ibid.*, August 22, 1951, p. 1.

76. *Ibid.*

77. *Ibid.*, March 4, 1952, pp. 1, 3.

78. *Congressional Record*, 82nd Cong., 1st Sess., Vol. 97, Pts. 8–9, 15 (Sept. 10, 11, 13, and 18, 1951), pp. 11066–11068, 11120–11121, 11252–11254, and (Appendix) 5664–5665.

79. *Ibid.* (Sept. 10, 1951), p. 11066.

80. Parts of this story also appeared in the New York *Times*, August 31, September 6, 10, 1951.

81. *Ibid.*, August 31, 1951, p. 2.

82. *Congressional Record*, 82nd Cong., 1st Sess., Vol. 97, Pt. 8 (Sept. 10, 1951), p. 11066—a reprint of the first article in the series by Alfred Friendly.

83. These documents were filed in the offices of the law firm of Roberts and McInnis in Washington, D.C.

84. All information on CIC and the American Advisory Group is taken from *Congressional Record*, 82nd Cong., 1st Sess., Vol. 97, Pt. 8 (Sept. 10, 1951), pp. 11066–11068; the New York *Times*, September 10, 1951, p. 2; and Philip Horton, "The China Lobby—Part II," *The Reporter*, VI (April 29, 1952), 10–11. *The Reporter* Series is reprinted in, *Congressional Record*, 82nd Cong., 2nd Sess., Vol. 98, Pt. 5 (June 6, 1952), pp. 6770–6787.

85. See *IPR Hearings*, Pt. 5, pp. 1491–1550.

86. See above, p. 39.

87. Reported by Charles Wertenbaker in *The Reporter*, VI (April 15, 1952), 18.

88. From the report of an interview with Goodwin in the *Congressional Quarterly* (Special Supplement), IX (June 29, 1951), 955.

89. Cable, Chinese agents to Chiang, August 8, 1949. (Bracketed interlineations in original translation from Chinese Embassy.)

90. *Ibid.*, January 12, 1950.

91. *Ibid.,* August 15, 1949. (Italics added; brackets in original.)
92. This statement usually appeared in the December and June issues.
93. *The China Monthly,* V (February, 1944), p. 3.
94. Letter from Father Tsai, March 11, 1954.
95. Mark Tsai, "Now It Can Be Told," *The China Monthly,* IX (September, 1948), 255.
96. See, for example, the following in the *Congressional Record:* 79th Cong., 1st Sess., Vol. 91, Pt. 12 (Appendix), p. 3444, Cormac Shanahan, "China's Communist Puzzle," inserted by Rep. Judd; *ibid.,* p. 3490, Pan Chao-ying (former editor of *The China Monthly* and secretary to Archbishop Paul Yu-pin), "China's Contribution to the United Nations," inserted by Rep. John W. McCormack; 80th Cong., 1st Sess., Vol. 93, Pt. 13 (Appendix), p. 3962, Geraldine Fitch, "Blunder Out of China," inserted by Rep. Judd; *ibid.,* p. 4599, Archbishop Paul Yu-pin, "Report submitted to the trustees of the Institute of Chinese Culture," inserted by Rep. Judd; 80th Cong., 2nd Sess., Vol. 94, Pt. 10 (Appendix), p. 1909, William R. Johnson, "The United States Sells China Down the Amur," inserted by Sen. Elbert Thomas; 81st Cong., 1st Sess., Vol. 95, Pt. 13 (Appendix), p. 2185, Anthony T. Bouscaren, "The China Tragedy," inserted by Rep. Clemente; 81st Cong., 2nd Sess., Vol. 96, Pt. 14 (Appendix), p. 2577, Alfred Kohlberg, "A Red Dream," inserted by Rep. Lawrence Smith.
97. Lattimore testimony in *State Department Employee Loyalty Investigation,* Pt. 1, p. 455. (Lattimore incorrectly named the publication "Chinese Monthly.") The reference, however, is to Kohlberg's article, "Owen Lattimore: 'Expert's Expert,'" *The China Monthly,* VI (October, 1945), 10–13, 26. See also the testimony of John S. Service before the Loyalty Security Board of the Department of State as incorporated into the record of the *State Department Employee Loyalty Investigation* at Pt. 2, p. 2025.
98. Charles Wertenbaker, "The World of Alfred Kohlberg," *The Reporter,* VI (April 29, 1952), 20.
99. Affidavit of Alfred Kohlberg to a subcommittee of the Committee on the Judiciary of the United States Senate, *IPR Hearings,* Pt. 14, p. 4937 (hereinafter referred to as "Kohlberg Affidavit").
100. *Ibid.,* p. 4940. For a full account of Kohlberg's attack on the IPR and its relation to the larger effort of the China lobby, see below, pp. 134ff.
101. The following is a selected list of these articles: "Owen Lattimore: 'Expert's Expert,'" VI (October, 1945), 10–13. "The Soviet-Chinese Pact," VI (November, 1945), 14–17."Reply to a Reply," VII (March, 1946), 104. "A Red Dream," VIII (January, 1947), 20–22. "Ten Years After Marco Polo Bridge," VIII (July, 1947), 227–230. "Stupidity and/or Treason," IX (June, 1948). "China Via Stilwell Road," IX (October, 1948), 283–287. "Who Is Responsible for China's Tragedy?" X (December, 1949), 242–245. "United States Military Aid to China," XI (March, 1950), 44–47.
102. See "Kohlberg Affidavit," *IPR Hearings,* Pt. 14, esp. pp. 4942–4943. The author has a substantial collection of Kohlberg's letters, speeches, and articles, collected from various sources, including Kohlberg himself. The magazines which he subsidized were one called *Plain Talk,* published from 1946–1950, and the *Freeman* after that date. The *Freeman* has since been taken over by the Foundation for Economic Education.
103. An extremely critical and revealing discussion of one event in the publishing history of *Plain Talk* appears in United States Congress, Senate, *State Department Employee Loyalty Investigation: Report,* of the Committee on Foreign Relations pursuant to S. Res. 231, "A Resolution to Investigate Whether There Are Employees in the State Department Disloyal to the United States," 81st

Congress, 2nd Session (Washington: United States Government Printing Office, 1950), pp. 146–148 (hereinafter cited as *State Department Employee Loyalty Investigation: Report*). The event concerned the publication in *Plain Talk* of an article concerning the Amerasia Affair. (See below, pp. 64–65.) Evidence before the committee showed clearly that the editors had rewritten the author's version of the article so that false and misleading conclusions were drawn. The committee concluded that the action of the editors was "one of the most despicable instances of a deliberate effort to deceive and hoodwink the American people in our history."

104. A 1955 advertisement for *Human Events* carried the following endorsement by Alfred Kohlberg:
  "In spite of the fact that I live in New York and seldom visit Washington, I have become known widely as the 'China Lobby.' . . . Don't look now, but nearly all I know about the Washington scene is derived from assiduous reading of *Human Events,* to which I have subscribed since 1944."

105. Indicative of the character of the attacks of the *Union Leader* against the American Government for its policy in Asia is a telegram which the owner, William Loeb, sent to President Eisenhower on July 4, 1953, and then had reprinted as a front-page editorial in his paper. The telegram read: "Suggest that if you want peace at any price in Korea, you and the Joint Chiefs of Staff celebrate this fourth of July by crawling on your collective bellies before the Communists . . . No president in this nation's history has so dishonored the United States as you have. . . ."

106. For example, Regnery published *The China Story,* by Freda Utley, while Devin-Adair published John T. Flynn's *While You Slept: Our Tragedy in Asia and Who Made It,* and *The Lattimore Story: The Full Story of the Most Incredible Conspiracy of Our Time.*

107. Kohlberg Affidavit, *IPR Hearings,* Pt. 14, p. 4942.

108. *Ibid.*

109. *Ibid.*

110. American China Policy Association, Inc., "Press Release," July 27, 1947.

111. Many of the books, pamphlets, articles, and speeches of this group are cited throughout this study. Many others may be found in *The China Monthly, Plain Talk,* and in the periodicals listed on p. 52.

112. This information concerning directors and the Executive Committee is from a letterhead of the organization.

113. *Congressional Quarterly* (Special Supplement), IX (June 29, 1951), 949.

114. *Ibid.,* p. 954.

115. *Ibid.* Names of the officeholders were confirmed by the organization's letterheads. A letter to the author from Marguerite Atterbury, dated September 12, 1953, states that the Committee to Defend America was disbanded in December, 1952, in the belief that the Eisenhower Administration would not need such pressuring. Marguerite Atterbury was also on the Board of Directors of ACPA.

116. In 1955 the Free Trade Union Committee distributed throughout Latin America a pamphlet entitled *Por qué no debe Admitirse a la China Communista en las Naciones Unidas.* The pamphlet contained a list of five additional titles concerning China printed in Spanish for distribution by the Free Trade Union Committee.

117. *Congressional Quarterly* (Special Supplement), IX (June 29, 1951), 951.

118. American China Policy Association, "News Release," June 10, 1951.

119. *State Department Employee Loyalty Investigation,* Pt. 1, pp. 619–625.

120. See, for example, Lattimore's testimony in *State Department Employee Loyalty Investigation,* Pt. 1, p. 820. See also Appendix B which is a comparison of the

McCarthy and Kohlberg charges against the Institue of Pacific Relations. The original may be found in *State Department Employee Loyalty Investigation*, Pt.2. pp. 1641–1646.

121. *Congressional Quarterly* (Special Supplement), IX (June 29, 1951), 956.

3. Major Issues Exploited by the China Lobby

1. Felix Wittmer, *The Yalta Betrayal—Data on the Decline and Fall of Franklin Delano Roosevelt* (Caldwell, Idaho: The Caxton Printers, Ltd., 1953; used by special permission of the copyright owners), p. 82.
2. Editorial, "Russian Security, or a Just and Acceptable Peace?" *The China Monthly*, VI (April, 1945), 4.
3. The New York *Times*, May 15, 1946, p. 12. Excerpts from the statement were reprinted in *The China Monthly*, VII (June, 1946), 183. It was also published as a "news release" by the American China Policy Association.
4. Editorial, "The Sins of Yalta," *The China Monthly*, VII (February, 1947), 44.
5. Alfred Kohlberg, "Ten Years After Marco Polo Bridge," *The China Monthly*, VIII (July, 1947), 227 (italics added by the author).
     It should be noted that there are two falsifications in this statement. First, President Roosevelt did not demand that the Government of China be put under Stilwell or any other American. The full text of the message to which Kohlberg refers is reprinted in *Military Situation in the Far East*, pp. 2867–2868. The copy of the cable is incorrectly dated February instead of September. Kohlberg has repeated this falsehood in other media and it appears twice in William R. Johnson's *China, Key to the Orient—and to Asia* (Polo, Ill.: 1950), pp. 9 and 21. Second, the fact that Stalin had *demanded* everything he was given at Yalta and more, as a prerequisite to Russian participation in the Pacific war, has been attested by many reputable officials. See especially, Harriman statement, *Military Situation in the Far East*, Pt. 5, pp. 3328–3342. The most objective and comprehensive (although generally favorable) treatment of the Yalta Conference which has appeared to date is John L. Snell (ed.), *The Meaning of Yalta* (Baton Rouge, La.: Louisiana State Univeristy Press, 1956).
6. William C. Bullitt, "Report on China," *Life* (October 13, 1947), pp. 35–37.
7. Editorial, "The Bullitt's Report on China," *The China Monthly*, VIII (November, 1947), 368–369.
8. *Ibid.*
9. William R. Johnson, "The United States Sells China Down the Amur," *The China Monthly*, (Decemger, 1947), 425–427 (italics in original).
10. *Ibid.*, p. 426.
11. Alfred Kohlberg, "Stupidity and/or Treason," *The China Monthly*, IX (June, 1948).
12. The two pamphlets were: Robert B. Dresser, *How We Blundered Into Korean War and Tragic Future Consequences* (New York: Committee for Constitutional Government, 1950); and William R. Johnson, *China, Key to the Orient—and to Asia* (Polo, Ill., 1950).
13. Dresser, *How We Blundered Into Korean War*, p. 15.
14. Johnson, *China, Key to the Orient*, p. 28.
15. Werner Levi, *Modern China's Foreign Policy* (Minneapolis: University of Minnesota Press, 1953), p. 244.
16. *State Department Employee Loyalty Investigation, Hearings* (testimony of Robert M. Hitchcock, who in 1945 was special assistant to the Attorney General assigned to the Criminal Division of the Department of Justice), p. 1003.
17. *Ibid.*, "Memorandum for the Files" (an interview by members of the staff

of the subcommittee with Archbold van Beuren, who was "Chief of the Branch of Security for the Office of Strategic Services" at the time the case broke), p. 1207.

18. This information and that which follows, except where otherwise indicated, is taken from *ibid.,* pp. 923–1211. It is further supplemented and corroborated by extensive testimony and documentation in the "Transcript of Proceedings" of the Loyalty Security Board hearings in the Case of John S. Service in *ibid.,* Pt. II, pp. 1958–2509, *passim,* and in *ibid., Report,* pp. 96–144, and 229–240.

19. *State Department Employee Loyalty Investigation, Report,* p. 229.

20. *IPR Hearings,* Pt. 1, p. 114.

21. *State Department Employee Loyalty Investigation, Report,* p. 229

22. *IPR Hearings,* Pt. 1, pp. 79–80.

23. Testimony of Frederick V. Field, *IPR Hearings,* Pt. 1, p. 115.

24. *State Department Employee Loyalty Investigation, Report,* p. 230; *IPR Hearings, Report,* p. 148.

25. *Ibid.,* p. 149.

26. *State Department Employee Loyalty Investigation, Hearings,* pp. 1213–1227.

27. *Ibid.,* p. 974.

28. The following note from David J. Dallin, *Soviet Espionage* (New Haven: Yale University Press, 1955), pp. 448–450n., bears on Jaffe's case:

"Now independent in every respect, Jaffe denies ever having served a Soviet intelligence venture. In a statement made in June 1955 to this author Jaffe said:

" 'More than ten years after the Amerasia case first made headlines, it is still regarded by many people as an "unsolved" cause célèbre. In part, this is my fault, because I have not written my side of the story, with the result that many distortions of fact, as well as out and out fabrication, have gone unchallenged. My chief reasons for not having written my story were: (1) the enormous publicity given to the charges against me, which made it seem very unlikely that I would be believed if I attempted to correct the errors and distortions in the Amerasia story; (2) the difficulty of proving that I did *not* do something of which I was accused. For example, it has often been charged that I was a "frequent visitor" to the Soviet Consulate and that therefore I was in "constant touch" with Soviet officials. The truth is that I was never at the Soviet Embassy in Washington and that only once did I visit the Soviet Consulate in New York. That one visit occurred in the spring of 1945 when I attended a large banquet in honor of a number of high-ranking American Army and Navy officers to celebrate the continued victories of the Allied forces. I sat next to an American Colonel's wife, with whom I exchanged the usual small talk. I met no Russians, and of course talked to none. But how can I prove that I had not been at the Consulate a dozen other times? Proof of the negation of a fact is always impossible. Similar difficulties arose in connection with a number of other accusations.

" 'Another example will help to illustrate my point. I was accused of operating a photostat machine "day and night." I did have a duplicating machine that cost fifty-eight dollars. I attempted to use it just twice with very poor results. And because it was too inferior a product or I was too incompetent an operator, I ceased using it thereafter and ultimately discarded it. But there it stood in the center of my office for all to see and "discover." Is this the way an intelligence operative would function? Wouldn't such an operative rather possess a high-grade microfilm camera hidden in some obscure cellar? And yet how can I prove my duplicating machine was not working "day and night"?' "

29. The Hobbs committee was Subcommittee IV of the Committee on the Judiciary of the House of Representatives, 79th Cong., 2nd Sess., authorized pursuant to

H. Res. 430 "to investigate the circumstances with respect to the disposition of the charges of espionage and the possession of documents stolen from secret Government files." The full proceedings of the committee may be found in the *Congressional Record*, 81st Cong., 2nd Sess., Vol. 96, Pt. 6 (May 22, 1950).

30. Quoted in *State Department Employee Loyalty Investigation, Hearings*, p. 1025.
31. Quoted at *ibid.*, p. 975.
32. *Ibid.*, p. 980 (testimony of James M. McInerney, Assistant Attorney General in charge of the Criminal Division, Department of Justice).
33. *Ibid., Report*, pp. 137, 144. It should be noted that Senator Henry Cabot Lodge, Jr., was not in full agreement with the majority on all these points. His views, however, can be properly evaluated only in light of a careful reading of the transcript of the hearings and the *Report* of the majority. His "Individual Views" are reprinted as Part 2, of *ibid.*, pp. 1–34.
34. Editorial, " 'The Six' Arrested," *The China Monthly*, VI (July–August, 1945), 7–10.
35. McInerney testified (*State Department Employees Loyalty Investigation*, pp. 997–998) that the articles were "more or less factual, except for the conclusions and overtones contained in them; and, immediately after the three people in this case were nobilled, the author of these articles came to Washington, Mr. Woltman, and he was very exasperated and took the view that as a result of the nobills, someone could be sued for libel. . . ."
36. Editorial, " 'The Six' Arrested," *The China Monthly*, VI (July–August 1945), 7–10.
37. *Ibid.*, p.10.
38. Emmanuel S. Larsen, "The State Department Espionage Case," *Plain Talk*, I (October, 1946), reprinted in *State Department Employee Loyalty Investigation*, Pt. 2, pp. 2492–2501.
39. The quotation is the conclusion of the majority in *ibid., Report*, p. 147.
40. Larsen's testimony appears at *ibid., Hearings*, Pt. 1, pp. 1116–1128, and Pt. 2, pp. 2202–2225. The original draft of the article appears in Pt. 2, pp. 1739–1753.
41. The difference in titles alone is instructive. The draft submitted by Larsen was entitled "They Called Me a Spy." In the magazine the article became "The State Department Espionage Case." Larsen wrote the article in an attempt to vindicate himself. Economic necessity apparently led him to approve publication of the edited version, which he testified was false and misleading.
42. *Ibid., Report*, p. 145. The subcommittee's conclusions concerning the entire article appear at pp. 146–148. For Isaac Don Levine's criticism of Larsen's character and comments, see his "communication" in the *Congressional Record*, 81st Cong., 2nd sess., 31 August 1950, pp. 1–2.
43. The substance of McCarthy's attacks on the State Department is contained in two speeches made on the Senate floor and found in the *Congressional Record*, 81st Cong., 2nd. Sess., Vol. 96, Pt. 2 (February 20, 1950), and Pt. 4 (March 30, 1950). Additional allegations, made against specific individuals in his testimony before the Tydings Subcommittee, may be found in *State Department Employee Loyalty Investigation, Hearings*, pp. 1–292.
44. For a list of these charges, source citations, and a partial comparison of the charges with statements in the *Plain Talk* aricle, see *ibid., Report*, p. 76.
45. Cable, Chinese agents to Chiang, May 24, 1950.
46. Dresser, *How We Blundered Into Korean War*, pp. 23–24, quoting from Joseph P. Kamp, *America Betrayed, The Tragic Consequences of Reds on the Government Payroll*, a pamphlet issued by the New York Constitutional Educational League in 1950. Similar accounts of the Amerasia case, but with additional details, may

be found in John T. Flynn, *The Lattimore Story*, pp. 45–50; *While You Slept*, pp. 134–144; Freda Utley, *The China Story*, pp. 158–163. An example of the lingering suspicion which the rumors concerning the Amerasia case have left is shown in the remarks of David J. Dallin in *Soviet Espionage*, p. 448: "During the decade that has passed since these developments [in the Amerasia case] a large number of Soviet espionage cases have come to light in this country, many names of foreign agents have been recorded, and many secret ties have been exposed. Although no traces have led to *Amerasia* or its chiefs, there is no doubt that the amazing collection of secret documents in the hands of the magazine and its ability to procure confidential material from government agencies must have been alluring for the zealous and ubiquitous Soviet intelligence operators."

47. DOS, *United States Relations with China*, 1949, Annex 45, p. 562.
48. *Ibid.*, p. 71.
49. *Ibid.*, p. 73.
50 Feis, *The China Tangle*, p. 308. The text of Stimson's letter may be found in Joseph C. Grew, *Turbulent Era*, II (Boston: Houghton Mifflin Co., 1952), pp. 1457–1459.
51. The text of Hurley's letter of resignation may be found in DOS, *United States Relations with China*, 1949, pp. 581–584.
52 Hurley testimony, *Military Situation in the Far East*, pp. 2936–2937.
53. Feis, *op. cit.*, p. 409.
54. *Ibid.*
55. Feis, *The China Tangle*, pp. 404–405, 407–408. The account which Feis gives of the Hurley resignation was written with the benefit of some important information which is not available to the public; e.g., most of the testimony given by Secretary Byrnes and Ambassador Hurley before the Senate Foreign Relations Committee on December 5, 6, 7, and 10, 1945; the Hurley Papers, and "several private memos."
56. Hurley's reference was to Congressman Hugh De Lacy of California whose speech attacking Hurley appears in the *Congressional Record*, 79th Cong., 1st Sess., Vol. 91, Pt. 8 (November 26, 1945), pp. 10993–10995.
57. Hurley testimony, *Military Situation in the Far East*, p. 2937 (Italics added by the author). It is scarcely possible that Congressman De Lacy's speech had any effect on Hurley's actions except perhaps the final decision to release the text of his resignation. All the evidence indicates that the latter was written by the morning of the same day the speech was delivered. In fact, Hurley brought the letter to Secretary Byrnes during the morning, but the Secretary refused to pass it on to the President.
58. *Congressional Record*, 79th Cong., 1st Sess., Vol. 91, Pt. 8 (November 28, 1945), pp. 11109ff.
59. S. Res. 197, the text of which appears in *ibid.*, p. 11114.
60. Feis, *op. cit.*, p. 411.
61. Reprinted in *State Department Employee Loyalty Investigation, Hearings*, Pt. 2, p. 2501 (italics in original).
62. DOS, *United States Relations with China*, 1949, p. 73.
63. *Ibid.*, pp, 105–110.
64. *State Department Employee Loyalty Investigation*, Pt. 2, p. 1911.
65. The single exception, and it can hardly be classed as an attack or accusation, occurs in an article by Anthony Bouscaren in *The China Monthly*, X (March, 1949), 59–63, 74–76. In that article, Bouscaren asserts: "On the basis of the Wallace report, successive American representatives, Patrick Hurley and George Marshall, sought, as part of their efforts to achieve peace and 'broaden' the Government, to force Chiang into a coalition with the Communists."

66. Some examples of the manner in which this technique was employed may be found in the following: Raymond K. Wu, "United States' China Policy," *The China Monthly*, IX (March, 1949), 59–63; Alfred Kohlberg, "Who Is Responsible for China's Tragedy?", *ibid.*, X (December, 1949), 242–245; Robert B. Dresser, *How We Blundered Into Korean War*, p. 10; Dresser, *What Caused the Nation's Crisis*, pp. 13–14; Flynn, *While You Slept*, pp. 171–172; *The Lattimore Story*, pp. 106–107; Utley, *The China Story*, pp. 110–113.

67. The individuals accused by Hurley and the results of the attacks made on them by the China lobby will be dealt with in detail in Chapter VII.

68. Flynn, *The Lattimore Story*, pp. 106–107. The quotation is from Hurley's letter of resignation to President Truman, November 26, 1945, reproduced in DOC, *United States Relations with China*, 1949, pp. 581–584. There are errors in the subquote from Hurley where noted. Flynn's substitution of "Nationalist" for Hurley's "National" does convey a difference in meaning.

69. See Exhibit 801, *IPR Hearings*, Pt. 14, pp. 4987–4996, which is a compilation of all staff members of IPR from 1936–1951.

70. See Exhibit 1403, *IPR Hearings*, Pt. 14, pp. 5506–5633, which is a list of contributors to the *Far Eastern Survey* and *Pacific Affairs* for 1931–1951 compiled by the staff of the Library of Congress.

71. Dresser, *How We Blundered Into Korean War*, p. 25.

72. Early expressions of this attitude toward Marshall may be found in Johnson, "Falsehoods and Some Truths About China," *The China Monthly*, X (April, 1949), 92–96 (the source of the quotation); Bouscaren, "The China Tragedy," *ibid.* (March, 1949), 59–63, and Johnson, "The United States Sells China Down the Amur," *ibid.*, VIII (December, 1947), 412–415. Later changes in the methods used will be discussed in Chapter VII.

73. DOS, *United States Relations with Cina*, 1949, p. 132.

74. See *ibid.*, p. 608.

75. See Acheson testimony, *Military Situation in the Far East*, p. 1842.

76. *Ibid.*, p. 1843, quoting a speech made by Chiang on September 14, 1943.

77. An excellent brief summary of these military maneuvers appears in Acheson's testimony, pp. 1855–1856. A longer account is interspersed with the story of the political negotiations in DOS, *United States Relations with China*, 1949, pp. 145–216.

78. This point is covered in detail in Feis, *op. cit.*, p. 419. Curiously, Marshall was never questioned about it during his testimony in the MacArthur hearings.

79. Marshall testimony, *Military Situation in the Far East*, p. 549.

80. *Ibid.* The Political Consultative Conference was a joint body composed of Kuomintang, Communist, third-party, and nonpartisan members created to make recommendations for the establishment of a government in which all parties would participate. See DOS, *United States Relations with China*, 1949, pp. 108, 111; for a complete account of the resolutions adopted by the PCC and initial reaction to them, see *ibid.*, pp. 138–144, and 610–621.

81. The text of the "Press Release on Order for Cessation of Hostilities, January 10, 1946," is reprinted in DOS, *United States Relations with China*, 1949, Annex 63, pp. 609–610. The nature of the truce violations is discussed in *ibid.*, pp. 145–172 *passim*.

82. *Ibid.*, p. 181.

83. Marshall testimony, *Military Situation in the Far East*, p. 659.

84. Several of these items are discussed in *Military Situation in the Far East*, pp. 1900–1909, 2060ff., 2092–2099, and 2237–2239.

85. *Ibid.*, pp. 1900–1909.

86. Most of the evidence and arguments for the pro-Chiang position are summed

up in excellent fashion in Freda Utley, *The China Story* (Chicago: Henry Regnery Company, 1951), pp 30–54. The opposing arguments are placed in startling juxtaposition by the testimony of Major General David G. Barr and Vice Admiral Oscar C. Badger in *Military Situation in the Far East,* pp. 2948–3053 and 2727–2807 respectively. Documents bearing directly on this controversy will be found in *ibid.,* pp. 2807–2823. and DOS, *United States Relations with China,* 1949, pp. 890–919, 940–942, and 945–980.

It should be noted that there are numerous direct contradictions between the figures cited by Miss Utley and those provided in the documents indicated.

87. Michael Lindsay (Lord Lindsay of Birker), a British citizen and teacher, who spent several years in China, has given the following estimate of the chances of averting a Kuomintang defeat. Lindsay had lived in Kuomintang China, Japanese-occupied China, and Communist areas of China.

"All the arguments that the outcome of the civil war could have been changed by a limited extension of military aid to the Kuomintang depend on completely unrealistic estimates of the relative military strength and general competence of the Kuomintang and the Communists. My estimates of the military prospects in 1946 and 1947 proved to be much more nearly correct than those which were generally accepted at the time. In an analysis written at the end of 1946, based on the experience of the Communist-Japanese fighting, I argued that, even with full-scale American assistance and the use of American troops, it would take the Kuomintang a minimum of four or five years to win the war; that with only limited American assistance the Kuomintang might win positional battles to begin with but would probably end by being completely defeated by the Communists, also in four or five years (*Virginia Quarterly Review,* Vol. 23, No. 2). By the middle of 1947 I was pointing out that the Kuomintang seemed to have weakened to the point where it could not even win positional battles and suggested that while this might be altered by increased American intervention there was the possibility that fullscale American intervention on one side might produce Russian intervention on the other (*Fabian Quarterly,* June 1947)."— Sworn statement of Michael Lindsay, *IPR Hearings,* Pt. 14, p. 5377.

88. China lobby spokesmen invariably stated that the coalition policy was forced on China by the United States.

89. Johnson, "The United States Sells China Down the Amur," *The China Monthly,* VIII (December, 1947), 412–415.

90. Alfred Kohlberg, "Stupidity and/or Treason," *The China Monthly,* Vol. IX (June, 1948).

91. Vincent P. Torossian, "China in Crisis," *ibid.* (July, 1948), pp. 191–192 (italics in original).

92. Colonel W. Bruce Pirnie, "Who Hamstrings U.S. Military Aid to China?" *The China Monthly,* IX (October, 1948), 288–291.

93. The series of four articles is as follows: Anthony T. Bouscaren, "The China Tragedy," *ibid.,* X (March, 1949), 59–63, 74–76; William R. Johnson, "Falsehoods and Some Truths About China," *ibid.* (April, 1949), pp. 92–96; Alfred Kohlberg, "Who Is Responsible for China's Tragedy?" *ibid.* (December, 1949), pp. 242–245, 250–251, and "United States Military Aid to China," *ibid.,* XI (March, 1950), 44–47.

94. Utley, *The China Story,* pp. 30–54.

95. *Ibid.,* p. 30.

96. Flynn, *While You Slept,* p. 175; Utley, *The China Story,* pp. 34–35. Flynn's use of the quotation is instructive in regard to his own tactics in addition to any "proof" it may offer. According to him, the quotation was produced by Senator Owen Brewster of Maine during the MacArthur hearings from "the report of

Colonel L. B. Moody, U.S. Army Ordnance Corps officer, who had made a study of China's military needs and supplies with one of our missions" (*While You Slept*, p. 175).

The real source for Senator Brewster, however, was Freda Utley's book (see *Military Situation in the Far East*, Pt. 3, p. 1954). The quotation was from a speech made by Moody in Washington in 1950—not from a "report" (see *The China Story*, p. 34). Finally, the "mission" which Moody had accompanied to China was the Nelson mission in 1944, and had no bearing on China's postwar needs. There is no indication that he had ever been to China except for that one brief visit.

97. Dresser, *How We Blundered Into Korean War*, pp. 3, 13, 17, and 21–22.

98. Dresser, *What Caused the Nation's Crisis*, pp. 12–13.

99. United States Congress, House of Representatives, 80th Cong., 2nd Sess., Committee on Un-American Activities, *Hearings Regarding Communist Espionage in the United States Government* (Washington: U.S. Government Printing Office, 1948).

100. Testimony, of Louis Budenz, *IPR Hearings*, Pt. 2, pp. 625, 679; Pt. 4, pp.1079ff.

101. Testimony of Louis Budenz, *ibid.*, pp. 632, 678–679; Pt. 4, pp. 1078–1079.

102. Testimony of Elizabeth Bentley, *ibid.*, Pt. 2, p. 439. A clearer understanding of the importance of the second factor to the China lobby will emerge in Chapters VI, VII, and VIII where the later accusations of the ex-Communists are examined.

103. United States Department of State, *Foreign Relations of the United States—Diplomatic Papers, The Conferences at Malta and Yalta 1945* (Washington: U.S. Government Printing Office, 1955), pp. 766–800, 895–897, 980ff. (hereinafter referred to as *Conferences at Malta and Yalta 1945*). See also, on this point, Snell, *et. al., The Meaning of Yalta*, pp. 143–150, and sources cited there.

104. New York *Times*, March 17, 1955, p. 79.

105. Kohlberg, "Who Is Responsible for China's Tragedy?" *The China Monthly*, X (December, 1949), 242–245ff.

106. *Ibid.*

107. Quoted by Robert B. Dresser, in *How We Blundered Into Korean War and Tragic Future Consequences*, p. 23.

108. Flynn, *The Lattimore Story*, pp. 32–33.

109. See below, pp. 99–101ff.

110. Cable, Chinese agents to Chiang, June 27, 1950.

111. *Ibid.*, June 29, and September 13, 1950.

112. *Ibid.*, September 30, 1950.

113. *Ibid.*, August 16, 1950. See also cable of August 4, 1950.

114. For further information regarding McCarthy's attack on Marshall, see below, Chapter VIII.

4. The Pattern of Acceptance

1. See Westerfield, *Foreign Policy and Party Politics*, p. 254, and Don Lohbeck, *Patrick J. Hurley* (Chicago: Henry Regnery Company, 1956), pp. 440–446.

2. One student of the subject has written: "During the seventeen month period from August, 1945 to January, 1947, Republicans in the Senate seemed to be wholly acquiescent to the Administration's policy—with perhaps a single exception, Senator Wherry. Within the limits of their knowledge of the facts and the policies being attempted (and that seemed fairly good), Republican Senators

followed a non-partisan line in foreign policy in quite a non-questioning manner. At least, judging from the lack of any expression of disapproval, it must be assumed that Republican Senators were sympathetic with the China policy as expressed by the President. . . . Republicans made no effort to adopt an alternative policy such as all-out open support for China." John R. Skretting, *Republican Attitudes Toward the Administration's China Policy, 1945–1949.* Publication 4105 (Ann Arbor: University Microfilms, 1952), pp. 33–34.

3. New York *Journal-American,* August 20, 1944. The headline for this dispatch by Ray Richards read, "China's Peril Laid to Reds in Russia, U.S."

4. *Ibid.*

5. For examples of each type of insertion by Judd, see the *Congressional Record,* 79th Cong., 1st Sess., Vol. 91 (Appendix), Pt. 11, p. 2283; Pt. 12, p. 3287 and pp. 3388–3390. Similar efforts were made in behalf of the Chinese throughout 1946.

6. Reprinted in *The China Monthly,* VI (January, 1945), 11.

7. *Congressional Record,* 79th Cong., 1st Sess., Vol. 91 (Appendix), Pt. 13, p. 5394.

8. See *ibid.,* 2nd Sess., Vol. 92 (Appendix), Pt. 12 (July 26, 1946), pp. 4494–4497. This "Extension of Remarks" by Mrs. Luce was reprinted by the American China Policy Association and distributed to its members in a form closely resembling official Congressional Committee reprints.

9. See on this point, Westerfield, *op. cit.,* pp. 254–259.

10. Vandenberg, *Papers,* p. 522.

11. *Ibid.,* p. 523.

12. Twice in the early months of 1947, Vandenberg expressed the opinion that bipartisanship had not applied to China. See the *Congressional Record,* 80th Cong., 1st Sess., Vol. 93, Pt. 2 (March 18, 1947), p. 2167, and *ibid.,* Pt. 3 (April 16, 1947), p. 3474.

13. Westerfield attributes all these "concessions" to pressure from the China bloc in Congress. See his *Foreign Policy and Party Politics,* pp. 259–260. For further discussion of Vincent's transfer to Switzerland, see below, pp. 212–216.

14. *Military Situation in the Far East,* Pt. 3, pp. 2296, 2312.

15. Reported in Westerfield, *op. cit.,* p. 260.

16. William C. Bullitt, "A Report to the American People on China," *Life* (October 13, 1947), pp. 35–37.

17. Westerfield, *op.cit.,* p. 261.

18. Bullitt, *op. cit.,* pp. 35–37.

19. See his testimony, *IPR Hearings,* Pt. 13, pp. 4521–4539.

20. Westerfield, *op. cit.,* pp. 261–262.

21. United States Congress, House, 80th Cong., 1st Sess., House Committee on Foreign Affairs, *Emergency Foreign Aid to China, Hearings* (Washington: U.S. Government Printing Office, 1947).

22. United States Congress, Senate, 80th Cong., 1st Sess., Committee on Appropriations, *Third Supplemental Appropriations Bill for 1948, Hearings, on H.R. 4784* (Washington: U.S. Government Printing Office, 1948), pp. 119–187.

23. *Ibid.,* p. 129.

24. *Ibid.*

25. Undated release from the American China Policy Association.

26. American China Policy Association news release, December 28, 1947.

27. *Congressional Record,* 80th Cong., 1st Sess., Vol. 93 (December 19, 1947), pp. 11679–11680.

28. New York *Times,* November 25, 1947, p. 18.

29. *Ibid.* The text of Dewey's speech was reprinted and distributed by the American China Policy Association.

30. Acheson testimony, *Military Situation in the Far East*, p. 1854.
31. *Ibid.*, p. 1855. This entire discussion follows rather closely the summary given by Secretary Acheson in *ibid.*, pp. 1854–1855.
32. See New York *Times*, March 28, 1948.
33. The revised report was reprinted and distributed by the American China Policy Association in a news release dated July, 1948.
34. *Military Situation in the Far East*, Pt. 3, p. 1903.
35. Reported in "A Realistic China Recovery Plan," *The China Monthly*, IX (April–May 1948), 114.
36. Reported in an editorial, "Too Late for Dollars," *ibid.*, p.113.
37. Reported in *ibid.*
38. United States Congress, House, 80th Cong., 2nd Sess., Committee on Un-American Activities, "Report on the Communist Party of the United States as an Advocate of Overthrow of Government by Force and Violence," *Investigation of Un-American Activities in the United States*, House Report No. 1920 (Washington: U.S. Government Printing Office, 1948), pp. 88–95.
39. American China Policy Association news release dated May 12, 1948 (for release May 23, 1948).
40. United States Congress, Senate, Committee on Appropriations, 80th Cong., 2nd Sess., *Hearings on Economic Cooperation Administration* (Washington: U.S. Government Printing Office, 1948), pp. 533–534. Note that this is a somewhat different version of this question from that presented by Kohlberg in his article "Stupidity and/or Treason," *The China Monthly*, IX (June 1948), quoted above at p. 20.
41. U.S. Senate, Committee on Appropriations, 80th Cong., 2nd Sess., *Hearings on Economic Cooperation Administration*, 1948, p. 535.
42. Wertenbaker, "The China Lobby," *Reporter*, VI (April 15, 1952), 19.
43. Reported at *ibid.*
44. *Ibid.*
45. Westerfield, *op. cit.*, p. 347.
46. *Congressional Record*, 81st Cong., 1st Sess., Vol. 95 (February 25, 1949), pp. 1566–1567 (daily edition).
47. New York *Times*, March 11, 1949, p. 13.
48. Acheson's letter explaining his reasons for opposing the McCarran proposal appears in DOS, *United States Relations with China, 1949*, pp. 1053–1054.
49. *Congressional Record*, 81st Cong., 1st Sess., Vol. 95 (April 4, 1949), p. 3864 (daily edition).
50. The debates appear at *ibid.* (April 2, 1949, April 4, 1949).
51. See *ibid.* (April 15, 1949, April 21, 1949).
52. Butterworth had been filling much the same job since September, 1947, when he replaced John Carter Vincent. The reorganization of the State Department under the provisions of the Hoover Commission recommendations now required that the Senate confirm him in his new rank if he were to continue to hold the position.
53. *Congressional Record*, 81st Cong., 1st Sess., Vol. 95 (June 24, 1949), 8292–8293.
54. *Ibid.*
55. *Ibid.* (September 27, 1949). The same partisan cleavage is apparent in the paired votes of eight of the twenty absent members. The vote on confirmation was forty-nine yeas to twenty-seven nays.
56. New York *Times*, June 25, 1949, p. 1.
57. Vandenberg, *Papers*, p. 534 (italics in original).
58. *Ibid.*, p. 535.
59. New York *Times*, August 22, 1949, p. 1. This statement characterized the

White Paper as "a 1,054–page whitewash of a wishful, do-nothing policy which has succeeded only in placing Asia in danger of Soviet conquest."

60. Many examples of this failure could be cited, but the climax was reached on October 24 when the Communists jailed the American consular staff in Mukden (Manchuria) after having held them in house arrest for almost a year.

61. See the testimony of Secretary of State Acheson and Secretary of Defense Louis Johnson in *Military Situation in the Far East*, Pt. 3, pp. 1667–1682, and Pt. 4, pp. 2576–2579. Johnson testified that on December 22, 1949, he "found out that I had lost my fight on Formosa. . . . I was told . . . that [President Truman] wasn't going to argue with me about the military considerations but that on political grounds he would decide with the State Department." Neither Acheson nor Johnson seemed to be very clear in 1951 (the time of their testimony) just what the "political grounds" on which the decision was based were. My analysis is therefore to some extent deductive, but I believe it is the only proper interpretation to be made. Acheson did say at one point that the policy was decided on the basis of a lack of sufficient armed strength to defend Formosa (p. 1672). He later implied that it was not quite that simple (pp. 1674–1675). More important, however, such an explanation fails to accord with the fact that when the policy was reversed a far greater commitment of force was necessary.

62. According to both Acheson and Johnson, the December, 1949, decision not to defend Formosa was formally reversed in meetings with the President on June 25, 26, and 27, 1950. See *ibid.*, pp. 1681, 2579–2582. The position of various individuals in the Executive branch on the question of whether the United States should defend Fomosa remains somewhat ambiguous. Prior to October, 1949, there seemed to be general agreement that Formosa should not be defended. Between October aand December, however, the Defense Department seems to have shifted ground, thereby precipitating the rift between State and Defense which resulted in the necessity for a presidential decision to resolve the conflict in December. (See Johnson testimony cited above.)

63. The text of the guidance paper appears at *ibid.*, pp. 1667–1669. It is reproduced below as Appendix A.

64. The text of the United Press wire concerning the guidance paper, and letters written by Knowland after reading it, appear at *ibid.*, pp. 1675–1676.

65. The text of Smith's letters to Acheson and his report to the Senate Foreign Relations Committee on his trip to the Far East appear at *ibid.*, Pt. 5, pp. 3315–3326.

66. *State Department Employee Loyalty Investigation, Report*, p. 2.

67. *Ibid.*, pp. 144–145.

68. *Ibid.*, p. 167.

69. For more detailed evidence on this point, see below, Chapters V and VII.

70. Utley, *The China Story*, p. 177. Miss Utley appeared before the Tydings Committee, apparently at her own request, but was given somewhat hostile treatment when it was discovered she had no "evidence" other than her own interpretation of Lattimore's writing. See also Flynn, *The Lattimore Story*, pp. 4–5; Dresser, *How We Blundered into Korean War*, pp. 30–31.

71. *Military Situation in the Far East*, Pt. 5, p. 3575.

72. *Congressional Record*, 81st Cong., 2nd Sess., Vol 96 (June 28, 30 1950).

73. *Military Situation in the Far East*, Pt. 5, p.3575.

74. *Ibid.*, p. 3576.

75. See his testimony in *ibid.*, Pt. 4, pp. 2727–2807.

76. *Ibid.*, Pt. 5, pp. 3593–3594.

77. *Ibid.*, p. 3539.

78. *Ibid.*, p. 3575.

79. *Ibid.*, p. 3591. This statement was a major theme of the American China Policy Association from the time it was organized.

80. *Ibid.*, pp. 3591–3600.

81. *Ibid.*, p. 3600.

82. *Ibid.*, pp. 3603–3604.

83. Harold M. Vinacke, *The United States and the Far East, 1945–1951* (Stanford: Stanford University Press, 1952), pp. 92–93.

84. New York *Times,* June 10, 1944, p. 14.

85. *Ibid.*, October 31, 1944, p. 4.

86. *Ibid.*, August 28, 1945.

87. New York *Times,* December 27, 1952, p. 8.

88. *Ibid.*, August 26, 1952, p. 8.

89. *Ibid.*, September 24, 1952, p. 32.

90. Henry L. Stimson, in Stimson and Bundy, *On Active Service,* p. xi.

5. EFFECTS OF ACCEPTANCE ON PRIVATE FAR EASTERN SPECIALISTS

1. For an excellent discussion of the relation between the anti-communist point of view and the problem of American policy toward China, see Frederick H. Hartmann, *The Relations of Nations* (New York: The Macmillan Co., 1957), pp. 438–442.

2. Chennault's views were set forth in detail in Claire Lee Chennault, *Way of a Fighter; The Memoirs of Claire Lee Chennault* (New York: G. P. Putnam's Sons, 1949).

3. Walter Lippmann has written, for example: "On the prospects of Chiang and his government, the judgment of all the generals was the same. None thought that Chiang would win, all were convinced that Chiang was losing, the civil war. Marshall's estimate supported Stilwell's and Wedemeyer's supported Marshall's and Barr's report confirmed the estimate. The generals differed, however, on what to do about Chiang. Stilwell's conclusion was that we should abandon him. . . . Wedemeyer's conclusion . . . was that we should take charge of the Chinese government and of the civil war. Marshall's decision . . . was that we could not abandon Chiang but that neither could we take over his powers, his responsibilities and his liabilities" ("Today and Tomorrow," New York *Herald Tribune,* September 8, 1949).

4. See below, Chapter VII.

5. For a moderate and carefully phrased statement of this position, without polemics or the implication that pro-communism was necessarily involved, see Paul M. A. Linebarger, "Outside Pressures on China, 1945–1950," in H. Arthur Steiner (ed.), *Report on China, The Annals of the American Academy of Political and Social Science,* Vol 277 (September, 1951), pp. 177–181.

6. The views of these specialists can most easily be determined from their testimony before the McCarran Subcommittee and may be found in the *IPR Hearings* as follows: Rowe—Pt. 11, pp. 3967–4031; McGovern—Pt. 4, pp. 1007–1034; Wittfogel—Pt. 1, pp. 273–342; Colegrove—Pt. 3, pp. 905–935, and Pt. 5, pp. 1277–1296; and Taylor—Pt. 1, pp. 342–352. It is interesting to note that of this group, Wittfogel was a former Communist according to his own testimony (see *IPR Hearings,* Pt. 1, p. 274), Colegrove was primarily a Japan specialist, and McGovern had previously been employed by the House Committee on Un-American Activities. Taylor had been employed by OWI during the war.

7. G. Barry O'Toole, "Debunking an 'Imperial' Debunker," *The China Monthly,* V (February, 1944), 12–13.

8. *Ibid.*, Peffer's article, "Our Distorted View of China," appeared in the *New York Times Magazine* (November 7, 1943), p. 7.

9. Editorial, "Criticisms on China," *The China Monthly*, V (June 1944), pp. 3–5.

10. See *The China Monthly*, V (September, 1944), esp. 3–5.

11. Chen Chih-mai to the Overseas Press Club in New York. The address was inserted into the *Congressional Record*, 79th Cong., 1st Sess., Vol. 91, Pt. 10 (Appendix, February 14, 1945), pp. 946–947, by Congresswoman Clare Booth Luce.

12. See, editorial, "China Refuses," *The China Monthly*, VI (September, 1945), 5–7, and *Amerasia*, X (January, 1946), 38.

13. See, for example, the following reviews in *The China Monthly:* Wilfred A. Marsh, "Lawrence K. Rosinger, *China's Crisis,*" VI (September, 1945), 29–30; Cormac Shanahan, "False Solution in Asia," VI (December, 1945), 22–24; William R. Johnson, "The Moscow Line on China," VIII (January, 1947), 32–33; editorial, "Russian Spies in Your Own House," VIII (November, 1947), 370–371; "China Through Red Eyes," IX (July, 1948), 76; Alfred Kohlberg, "China Via Stilwell Road," IX (October, 1948), 283–287; book review, "The United States and China," IX (July, 1948), 207–208; "Books Through Red Eyes," X (April, 1949), 91. An extensive effort to discredit the White-Jacoby book *Thunder Out of China* was made by the American China Policy Association by publishing and distributing, on June 4, 1947, a thirty-two-page pamphlet entitled *Blunder Out of China*, by Geraldine Fitch.

14. Lin Yutang, *The Vigil of a Nation* (New York: John Day, 1945); Hollington K. Tong, *Dateline: China* (New York: Rockport Press, Inc., 1950).

15. Johnson, *China, Key to the Orient*, p. 17.

16. Dresser, *How We Blundered Into Korean War, and What Caused the Nation's Crisis?*

17. Judd, *Autopsy on Our Blunders in Asia.*

18. Chennault, *A Reprint of the Foreword to Way of a Fighter*, published and distributed by the American China Policy Association.

19. Flynn, *Why Korea?*

20. Chennault, *Way of a Fighter.*

21. Tong, *Dateline: China.*

22. Utley, *The China Story.*

23. Flynn, *While You Slept.*

24. Utley, *The China Story*, p. 139.

25. Flynn, *While You Slept*, pp. 95 and 96.

26. *Ibid.*, pp. 66–94 *passim.*

27. Utley, *The China Story*, pp. 139–163.

28. *Ibid.*, p. 143.

29. *Ibid.*, pp. 143–144.

30. *Ibid.*, p. 140.

31. *Congressional Record*, 82nd Cong., 1st Sess., Vol 97 (June 5, 1951), pp. 6297–6302.

32. *Military Situation in the Far East*, Pt. 5, pp. 3217–3228.

33. Lattimore had served in various governmental capacities between 1941 and 1945, including a period as special adviser to Generalissimo Chiang Kai-shek (1941–1942), Deputy Director of Pacific Operations, and, later, consultant for the OWI (1942–1945), and for a short time as member of the Pauley reparations mission to Japan (1945). See his statement in *State Department Employee Loyalty Investigation*, Pt. 1, pp. 421–422. Lattimore is essentially, regardless of his wartime governmental service, a private specialist and scholar. Most of the time since 1945, he has been on the faculty of the Johns Hopkins University.

34. Alan Barth, *Government by Investigation* (New York: The Viking Press, 1955), p. 96.

35. Kohlberg, "Owen Lattimore; 'Expert's Expert' The Monocle, the Commissar, the Old Homestead, and Snafu," *The China Monthly,* VI (October, 1945), 10–13.

36. *Ibid.,* Lattimore attempted to answer some of Kohlberg's charges in a "Reply to Mr. Kohlberg," in *The China Monthly,* VI (December, 1945), 15–17. A rejoinder by Kohlberg appeared in *ibid.,* VII (March, 1946), 104.

37. Kohlberg's relations with the IPR will be treated in detail in Chapter VI.

38. *Congressional Record,* 79th Cong., 1st Sess., Vol. 91, Pt. 8 (November 28, 1945), p. 11110. Lattimore had no connection with the Department of State at the time of Wherry's reference. Rather, he was serving as a special adviser to Chiang Kai-shek, appointed by President Roosevelt after Chiang had requested that a specialist on Asian affairs be sent to advise him.

39. Chia-you Chen, "The Confusion and Ignorance of the Self-Proclaimed China Expert," *The China Monthly,* X (February, 1949), 35–38.

40. *Congressional Record,* 81st Cong., 2nd Sess., Vol. 98, Pt. 3 (March 30, 1950), pp. 4436ff. McCarthy had previously given the same information to the Tydings Subcommittee on March 13, and repeated it, along with the allegation that Lattimore was the top Soviet espionage agent in the United States, in an executive session on March 21 (see *State Department Employee Loyalty Investigation,* Pt. 1, 92–104, and 277–292). For a detailed comparison of McCarthy's charges with similar charges previously made by Kohlberg, see Appendix B.

41. *State Department Employee Loyalty Investigation,* Pt. 1, p. 491.

42. *Ibid.,* p. 526. In response to questions as to when he had first mentioned Lattimore to the FBI, Budenz's answers showed that he had never done so until after McCarthy's public accusations.

43. *Ibid.,* p. 491.

44. *Ibid.,* p. 492.

45. *Ibid.,* pp. 492, 495.

46. *Ibid.,* pp. 491–505, 516–529.

47. *Ibid.,* pp. 590–596.

48. *Ibid.,* p. 770.

49. *Ibid.,* p. 738.

50. *Ibid.,* p. 741

51. *Ibid.,* p. 768.

52. *Ibid.,* p. 780.

53. *Ibid.*

54. *Ibid., Report,* pp. 72–73.

55. *Ibid.,* Pt. 2, pp. 16–17.

56. Barth, *op.cit.,* pp. 97–98.

57. *IPR Hearings,* Pt. 9, pp. 2897–2898.

58. The basis for this method, or approach may be found in the remarks of Professor George E. Taylor of the University of Washington in which he offered the subcommittee "a method of identification for those who . . . were never party members:

"You have to build up a frame of references as to what the Soviet Union is after in general, what its relationships are to parties in the rest of the world, how they operate in general and how they operate in particular. Then you have to study your own field. You have to find out—and there are ways of doing this, of course—you have to find out what the general party line is on a given subject at a given time.

"Then in the areas you know best you examine a man's writings and by what he leaves out sometimes as well as by what he puts in you decide whether he is dealing with all the facts that he should know if he knows anything about it at all or whether he is angling them in any particular manner.

"Obviously with that type of interpretation it is extremely difficult to say exactly where a man would be in the hierarchy, how far away from the sun he would be, but you can, I think, with reasonable assurance over a given length of time decide whether certain people are following a consistent line or whether they are not" *(ibid., Report,* p. 11).

A recent study concerning what the author calls "The Art of Political Dynamiting," offers an observation which is pertinent to this method. Walter E. Quigley, a veteran of fifty years' practice in this "art" is quoted as having remarked, "I certainly like to campaign against a man who has written a book. . . . No matter how sincere he may be, one can take a couple of dozen of these . . . paragraphs from the book and crucify him" (Frank H. Jonas, "The Art of Political Dynamiting," *The Western Political Quarterly,* X [June 1957], p. 378, n. 11).

59. *IPR Hearings, Report,* p. 216.
60. The report did, however, cite a number of references in the record of the hearings which supposedly show that Lattimore "did not tell the truth." These citations can be used by the reader of the report to locate a part of Lattimore's testimony concerning the events in question.
61. See esp. *ibid.,* pp. 214–218.
62. *Ibid.,* p. 218.
63. *Ibid.,* pp. 224–225.
64. *Ibid.,* p. 226.
65. New York *Times,* July 1, 1955, p. 43.
66. Drew Pearson reported that "the Lattimore case . . . was brought . . . in the final month of the Truman Administration by retiring Attorney General James McGranery as the result of a pledge he gave the late Sen. Pat McCarran of Nevada, that if confirmed by the Senate he would prosecute Lattimore"; "Merry-Go-Round" (Jacksonville, Florida), *Times Union,* July 1, 1955, p. 5.
67. *IPR Hearings, Report,* p. 147.
68. *Ibid.,* pp. 147–148.
69. *Ibid.,* pp. 151–159.
70. *Ibid.,* p. 147.
71. The tabulation of reviews and reviewers for the period 1945–1950 is from two tables, "Nonfiction books on China published and reviewed in the United States, 1945–1950, inclusive," *Military Situation in the Far East,* Pt. 5, p. 3225. The tables were inserted in the record of the hearing at the request of Senator Brewster. An independent spot check of the sources indicates that the information is reasonably accurate. The conclusions concerning the later five-year period are based on the fact that the *Book Review Digest,* which digests the reviews in both mewspapers shows that, with the exceptions noted, none of the books on China which appeared during the period 1951–1956, inclusive, were reviewed by any of the persons named for the earlier period.

6. EFFECTS OF ACCEPTANCE ON SCHOLARLY ORGANIZATIONS AND FOUNDATIONS

1. Testimony of Edward C. Carter, *IPR Hearings,* Pt. 2, p. 462.
2. An excerpt from the publication, *IPR in Wartime,* which is a report of the American Coucil of the Institute of Pacific Relations for the years 1941 to 1943, illustrates the kind of relationship which developed between the private scholars, government, educational institutions, and scholarly organizations during this period. This excerpt is from a reprint of a portion of the report in *IPR Hearings,* Pt. 4, p. 972:
    "The first months of the war, therefore, placed exceptionally heavy demands

on the Institute of Pacific Relations for direct services to Government agencies as staffs and libraries were hastily assembled to handle far-eastern questions first with the demand for Institute of Pacific Relations publications and bibliographical aids [sic]. Happily, a large number of Institute of Pacific Relations' studies begun as far back as 1936 were nearing completion in 1941. Together they provided a mine of up-to-date information on the resources, government economy, and problems of Japan, China, Burma, Thailand, Formosa, the Dutch East Indies, Malaya, et cetera. They were rushed into publication, or in some cases made available in proof or manuscript.

"Institute of Pacific Relations libraries were exclusively used by officials from a dozen departments. Staff members gave freely of their time in consulting on research materials and programs; second, with requests for aid in recruiting far eastern experts for Government service. Here the IPR's extensive knowledge of scholars, journalists, and businessmen in the far eastern field was put at the disposal of Government agencies. This mobilization of key scholars, so few in number, has had its distressing aspects for it has stripped the universities and educational institutions of virtually all their trained far eastern personnel, but it was necessary and it will have its compensations in the enormous impetus to far eastern studies which the war will give. Hundreds of men are being trained in the far eastern languages through cooperative arrangements among the universities, the Government, and the American Council of Learned Societies which has taken the lead in this field."

3. William L. Holland, *Truth and Fancy About the Institute of Pacific Relations,* two statements made before the Subcommittee on Internal Security of the Senate Committee on the Judiciary (the McCarran Subcommittee), October 10, 1951, and March 19, 1952 (New York: American Institute of Pacific Relations, 1953), pp. 4–5.

4. W.L. Holland, as quoted in *IPR Hearings, Report,* pp. 3–4.

5. Kohlberg Affidavit to the McCarran Subcommittee, *IPR Hearings,* Pt. 14, p. 4936. Hereinafter cited as "Kohlberg Affidavit."

6. *Ibid.*

7. *Ibid.*

8. Sworn statement of Edward C. Carter to the McCarran Subcommittee, *IPR Hearings,* Pt. 14, p. 5344. Hereinafter cited as "Carter Affidavit."

9. "Kohlberg Affidavit," *ibid.,* p. 4937.

10. *Ibid.,* p. 4938.

11. *Ibid.*

12. *Ibid.*

13. *Ibid.* According to Carter, this reply was the result of a careful study and analysis of Kohlberg's charges by two committees of the Executive Committee and Board of Trustees of the IPR. See "Carter Affidavit," *ibid.,* p. 5343.

14. *Ibid.,* p. 5343.

15. See above, pp. 51–53. The parallels between Kohlberg's actions in this instance and his actions after his failure to secure control of United China Relief are interesting. After his charges against Carter and Edwards were dismissed in 1944, Kohlberg resigned from ABMAC and turned his attention to the IPR and Lattimore. After his failure with the IPR in 1947, he resigned and shifted his attention to the Department of State and John Carter Vincent, the head of the Far Eastern Division. This development will be discussed in Chap. VII, below.

16. "Kohlberg Affidavit," *IPR Hearings,* Pt. 14, p. 4941. Item 8 is factually incorrect. Only two of the six arrested in the Amerasia case had any connection with IPR other than membership. But if membership is a "connection," then the statement should read "five of the six," for five of those arrested had at some time been members of the IPR.

17. *Ibid.*
18. For an item-by-item comparison of McCarthy's and Kohlberg's accusations, see Appendix B.
19. The files of the IPR had been seized the previous February, apparently as the direct result of the efforts of Senator McCarthy. See the quotation from the New York *Post* of September 18, 1951, in "Carter Affidavit," *IPR Hearings*, Pt. 14, p. 5353.
20. *IPR Hearings, Report*, p. 2. Capitalization and punctuation follow that used in the text of the *Report*.
21. A list of witnesses before the subcommittee appears in *IPR Hearings*, Pt. 15, pp. 5713–5714.
22. For examples of the tactics used, see particularly the testimony of John K. Fairbank, *ibid.*, Pt. 11, pp. 3720–3822; John Carter Vincent, *ibid.*, Pts. 6 and 7, and Joseph Alsop, *ibid.*, Pt. 5, pp. 1403–1489. The same tactics were used in the questioning of Lattimore, Carter, and Holland.
23. For examples of this, see particularly the testimony of Louis Budenz, *ibid.*, Pt. 2, pp. 513–701, and Pt. 4, pp. 1077–1110; General Wedemeyer, Pt. 3, pp. 775–841; David N. Rowe, Pt. 11, pp. 3967–4031; Kenneth Colegrove, Pt. 3, pp. 905–935 and Pt. 5, pp. 1277–1296, and Karl A. Wittfogel, Pt. 1, pp. 273–342.
24. *IPR Hearings, Report*, p. 5.
25. *Ibid.*, p. 6.
26. *Ibid., Report*, p. 189.
27. *Ibid.*, pp. 190–191.
28. *IPR Hearings, Report*, pp. 3–62, presents the arguments of the subcommittee to sustain this accusation. It should be noted, however, that there is considerable repetition, both of arguments and evidence, throughout the report.
29. See Exhibit No. 37, *IPR Hearings*, Pt. 1, pp. 189–190, which is a translation of an article from the Soviet quarterly *Tikhii Okean*, proclaiming the creation of the Soviet Council.
30. Testimony of Alexander Barmine, *ibid.*, pp. 202–206.
31. Testimony of Igor Bogolepov, *ibid.*, Pt. 13, p. 4491.
32. *Ibid., Report*, pp. 63–119. It cannot be argued here that the subcommittee was merely presenting the evidence on the basis of which the reader should draw his own conclusions. Rather, the evidence was designed to lead the reader to the conclusions which the subcommittee wanted him to reach. In fact, as previously noted, the evidence in the report specifically excluded anything which might lead to a conclusion contrary to that stated above.
33. *Ibid.*, pp. 65–66.
34. *Ibid.*, p. 70.
35. *Ibid.*, pp. 70–73.
36. The most important citations are to (1) a table "which shows that a significant number of IPR individuals were connected with one or more of these Communist-controlled organizations," at *ibid.*, pp. 145–146; (2) Exhibit No. 1334, showing "Interlocking between the Institute of Pacific Relations and the Committee for a Democratic Far Eastern Policy," in *Hearings*, Pt. 13, pp. 4610–4611; and (3) Exhibits 98 and 99, showing the officers, directors, and Executive Committee members of the China Aid Council.
37. *IPR Hearings, Report*, pp. 93–94.
38. *Ibid.*, p. 99.
39. *Ibid.*, p. 95.
40. *Ibid.*, p. 105.
41. *Ibid.*, p. 74.
42. *Ibid.*, p. 79.

43. *Ibid.*

44. *Ibid.*, p. 76.

45. See, for example, Freda Utley's characterization of Lattimore quoted above at p. 126.

46. *IPR Hearings, Report,* pp. 122–123.

47. *Ibid.*, p. 11. The list may be found on pp. 147–148.

48. *Ibid.*, pp. 11, n. 1.

49. *Ibid.*, pp. 151–159.

50. *Ibid.*, pp. 149–150.

51. No exact figure on the number of individuals considered by the subcommittee to have been "connected" with the IPR during the period covered by the investigation is available. According to the report, however, a total of 1,390 separate contributors to the two publications *Pacific Affairs* and *Far Eastern Survey* can be distinguished (*Report,* p. 100). Exhibit No. 801 (*Hearings,* Pt. 14, pp. 4987–4996) consists of two lists of the paid employees of IPR. One list, covering the years 1936–1951, the source of which is not given, contains 431 entries. With allowances for duplications, it contains about 410 different names. The second list, covering the period 1944–1951, submitted by Holland, contains 256 different names. IPR thus employed a minumum of 400 individuals between 1936 and 1951.

52. Saionji, p. 157.

53. Barnes, p. 151.

54. See Exhibit No. 1403, *Hearings,* Pt. 14, pp. 5506–5633, which is a bibliography of contributors to *Pacific Affairs* and *Far Eastern Survey.*

55. This individual, Harriet L. Moore, was employed as a research associate from 1934 to 1944 and for a few months as acting executive secretary.

56. According to the report (p. 149), Mrs. Schneider's testimony was taken in an executive hearing on March 21, 1952. It was not included in the record of the hearings. This was the only case in which the testimony of a witness who refused to answer questions concerning alleged Communist affiliations was not made a part of the printed hearings.

57. *IPR Hearings, Report,* p. 178.

58. *Ibid.*, p. 186.

59. *Ibid.*, p. 179.

60. *Ibid.*, pp. 179–181.

61. *Ibid.*, pp. 181–183.

62. *Ibid.*, pp. 187–189.

63. *Ibid.*, pp. 189–192.

64. *Ibid.*, pp. 195–196.

65. *Ibid.*, p. 197.

66. *Ibid.*, p. 198.

67. *Ibid.*, p. 203.

68. A footnote to this subtitle (p. 204) reads, "General Marshall is listed as a member of the board of trustees of the Institute of Pacific Relations in 1951 (p. 568) even though he was not in 1946."

69. These subtitles in the report may be found at *ibid.*, pp. 203–207.

70. *Ibid.*, pp. 211–214.

71. John T. Flynn, broadcasts of March 17 to 21, 1952, issued in pamphlet form and distributed by America's Future, Inc., 210 East 43rd Street, New York City. Hereinafter cited as, Flynn, "Why Korea?"

72. *Ibid.*, pp. 3–4.

73. John T. Flynn, *The Lattimore Story* (New York: The Devin-Adair Co., 1953).

74. Flynn, *While You Slept,* 1951.

75. Westerfield, *Foreign Policy and Party Politics*, p. 246, n. 7. It is impossible to determine just what standards the author of these remarks considered applicable to congressional probes. His comment that "this one was conscientious," while unquestionably true, tells nothing about the *objectivity* of the hearings or report. It is apparent, however, that he had read little more than the *Report* from the sixteen-volume *Hearings* of the McCarran Subcommittee. Otherwise he could not have been unaware of the fact that there is an almost incredible *lack* of order in the documentation and that much very important documentation, which the subcommittee had at its disposal, is missing.

76. The following information is from the "American IPR Annual Report," for 1951, 1952, 1955–56, and 1956–57. Dollar figures are indicated to the nearest thousand.

77. The membership figure of 1951 had remained relatively constant since 1941. A slight increase—to 371—was noted in the 1956–57 report, and by February, 1959, membership in the American Council had risen slowly to about 430.

78. The initial statement concerning "The Tax Problem" appeared in "IPR Annual Report," 1955–56, pp. 9–11. The quotation comes from a supplementary notice to the Annual Report which the author has subsequently misplaced.

79. *Ibid.*, 1956–57, p. 9.

80. *Ibid.*, p. 2.

81. *Ibid.*

82. United States Congress, House, 83rd Cong., 2nd Sess., *Report of the Special Committee to Investigate Tax-Exempt Foundations and Comparable Organizations* (Washington: U.S. Government Printing Office, 1955), hereinafter cited as *Tax Exempt Foundations: Report.*

83. H. Res. 217, 83rd Cong., 1st Sess., as quoted at *ibid.*, p. 1.

84. *Ibid.*, p. 4.

85. *Ibid.*, p. 20.

86. Kohlberg's testimony was given before the so-called Cox Committee which investigated the foundations in 1952.

87. *Tax Exempt Foundations: Report*, p. 19.

88. *Ibid.*, p. 54.

89. *Ibid.*, pp. 168–169.

90. *Ibid.*, p. 169.

91. *Ibid.*, p. 29.

92. *Ibid.*, p. 54.

93. Criticism of the Ford Foundation is scattered throughout the report, but see especially pp. 110–117, and 161–167. On p. 186 is a criticism specifically related to China.

94. *Ibid.*, pp. 53–168, *passim.*

95. *Ibid.*, pp. 170–188.

96. *Ibid.*, p. 430. The minority report was submitted by Representatives Wayne L. Hays and Gracie Pfost.

7. EFFECTS OF ACCEPTANCE ON STATE DEPARTMENT FAR EASTERN SPECIALISTS

1. *Congressionl Record*, 79th Cong., 1st Sess., Vol. 91, Appendix (December 10, 1945), pp. 5403–5404. For an account of the Amerasia Affair, see above, pp. 61–66.

2. For a detailed account of the sources of Dondero's speech and the bishop's various connections, see *State Department Employee Loyalty Investigation*, Pt. 2, pp. 2024–2026.

3. See above, pp. 50, 64. The text of the *Plain Talk* article is reprinted in *State Department Employee Loyalty Investigation*, Pt. 2, pp. 2492–2501.
4. *Ibid.*, p. 2501.
5. Flynn, *The Lattimore Story*, pp. 76–77.
6. Dooman's testimony appears in *IPR Hearings*, Pt. 3, pp. 703–754.
7. *IPR Hearings*, Pt. 13, p. 4546.
8. *State Department Employee Loyalty Investigation*, Pt. 1, p. 1277.
9. Judd, *Autopsy on Our Blunders in Asia*, p. 16 (italics added). During the period mentioned, Hiss was an assistant to Hornbeck. At no time did he hold a policy-making position such as Head of the China desk or Director of the Far Eastern Division.
10. Quoted in American China Policy Association, "News Release," December 4, 1946. The text of this speech appears in *IPR Hearings*, Pt. 7. pp. 2256–2260.
11. *World-Telegram*, November 20, 1946, and December 10, 1946.
12. American China Policy Association, "News Release," December 4, 1946.
13. Editorial, "Two-Faced State Department Action," *The China Monthly*. VII (December, 1946); "Our Retreat in China," *ibid.*, VIII (January, 1947).
14. Quoted at *ibid.*, p. 11.
15. Theodore H. White, *The Stilwell Papers* (New York: Sloane and Co., 1948).
16. Alfred Kohlberg, "China Via Stilwell Road," *The China Monthly*, IX (October, 1948), 283–287.
17. *Ibid.*
18. Cable, Chinese agents to Chiang, August 24, 1949. The cable stated: "In the past year I have been extremely patient with Marshall, but he hasn't changed his attitude in the slightest. But I feel it is advisable to continue to refrain from attacking him as an individual in order to avoid a direct break with the administration authorities."
19. William R. Johnson, *China, Key to the Orient*, p. 7.
20. See Wallace's testimony in *IPR Hearings*, Pt. 5, pp. 1297–1402; Vincent's testimony in *ibid.*, Pt. 6, pp. 1819–1823, Pt. 7, pp. 2036–2039; Lattimore's testimony in *ibid.*, Pt. 10, pp. 3658–3659.
21. The complete text of Wallace's report was printed in the New York *Times*, January 19, 1950. It was thus available to Johnson at the time the above statements were made. Wallace's comments on the report appear in the *IPR Hearings*, Pt. 5, pp. 1357–1390. Strangely enough, the report itself was not printed in the *IPR Hearings*.
22. See Wallace and Vincent testimony referred to above.
23. See above, pp. 35ff.
24. Cable, Chinese agents to Chiang, July 6, 1949.
25. Kohlberg, "Who Is Responsible for China's Tragedy?" *The China Monthly*, X (December, 1949), 242–245, 250–251.
26. *Ibid.*
27. *Ibid.*
28. Chia-you Chen, "Democratic Ideals and the American China Policy," *The China Monthly*, XI (February, 1950), 25–28, 35.
29. Judd, *op. cit.*, pp. 15–16.
30. This leakage of information to the Kuomintang and its agents is difficult to document in detail. The evidence throughout the period under discussion, however, is unmistakable. Ambassador Gauss gave some specific information on the subject during his testimony in the Service loyalty hearing which may be found in *State Department Employee Loyalty Investigation*, Pt. 2, p. 2071. Although apparently no inquiries were ever made on the subject, evidence that FBI agents, former FBI agents, members of the Justice Department, and members

of Congress gave out unauthorized information and secret documents connected with the Amerasia Affair is overwhelming. Certainly, there can be no doubt that Kohlberg frequently had access to information not generally available to the public. Finally, the series of cablegrams sent from the Chinese Embassy in the United States to Chiang Kai-shek, during the period of 1949 when Li Tsung-jen was Acting President of China, shows unmistakable evidence of access to information which would normally be considered classified.

31. *Johnson, op. cit.,* p. 32.
32. *Ibid.,* pp. 7–8.
33. *Ibid.,* p. 17.
34. Dresser, *How We Blundered Into Korean War.*
35. See Senator Joe McCarthy, *McCarthyism—The Fight for America: Documented Answers to Questions Asked by Friend and Foe* (New York: The Devin-Adair Co., 1952).
36. Johnson, *op. cit.,* p. 27.
37. Dresser, *What Caused the Nation's Crisis?*
38. Johnson, *op. cit.,* p. 32.
39. Dresser, *What Caused the Nation's Crisis?* p. 23.
40. Johnson, *op. cit.,* p. 16.
41. Dresser, *How We Blundered Into Korean War,* p. 23.
42. *Ibid.,* p. 25. There is a striking similarity between the language used by Kamp and quoted by Dresser in this passage and that used in the report of the Republican minority in the MacArthur Hearings. (See the last two paragraphs of the quotation from that report on pp. 105–106.)
43. Flynn, *While You Slept,* p. 185 [italics added].
44. Other Foreign Service officers were also among those accused by Hurley. None of them, however, were available as victims by 1949 when Chiang had lost his position. George Atcheson was killed in a plane crash, John Emmerson was primarily a Japan officer, Raymond Ludden and Arthur Ringwalt were transferred from the China service early in the postwar period.
45. Clubb testimony, House Un-American Activities Committee, *Hearings,* August 20, 1951, p. 1986.
46. Alan Barth, *Government by Investigation* (New York: The Viking Press, 1955), p. 64.
47. Most of these details were covered in Part One of Service's "personal statement" to the State Department Loyalty Security Board, reprinted in *State Department Employee Loyalty Investigation,* Pt. 2, pp. 1961–1974. Cross-examination and corroborating testimony before the board further clarified and supported the initial statement. The statement itself is an exceptionally well-written, lucid, and objective account of certain aspects of the political situation in wartime China. Its factual accuracy on the points covered is supported by virtually every source cited in this work, including testimony of Wedemeyer, Hurley, and Alsop.
48. See, on this point, the documents in the Service loyalty hearing, reprinted in *ibid.,* at pp. 1993–2000.
49. Service's sworn statement on this point reads, "I found that Hurley had forced my recall by going to Secretary of War Stimson, the Department of State having told him that it had no authority to give me orders while I was under assignment to the Army" (*State Department Employee Loyalty Investigation,* Pt. 2, p. 1974).
50. "Personal Statement of John S. Service—Part 2," reprinted in *ibid.,* at p. 2234. The documents setting forth the conclusions of the State Department Loyalty Security Board and the Civil Service Loyalty Review Board in the Service case were reprinted in *IPR Hearings,* Pt. 13, pp. 4837–4849. Only a careful reading of the entire transcript of Service's hearing before the Loyalty Security Board

and the testimony bearing on the case before the Tydings Subcommittee, however, will provide an adequate basis for judging the issues.

51. Reprinted in *State Department Employee Loyalty Investigation*, Pt. 2, p. 2235. Service may have been unjust to himself in this testimony. John P. Davies Jr., who
was also in China during this period, has testified that it was general practice
in the China theater, under specific orders of General Stilwell, to keep the press
informed in quite intimate detail concerning political conditions in China. Stilwell maintained this policy, in part, because, "He felt that the American people
were being misled about many of the realities in China" (*ibid.,* p. 2095). Davies
gave many examples—in China, Manchukuo, Moscow, and Washington—to
indicate the widespread nature of this practice. Specifically, Davies testified:
   "Q. I am going to ask whether in your personal practice you had ever
permitted a correspondent to read classified material for background information? A. Yes. Q. Was that considered normal procedure? A. Yes, throughout
the theater. . . . Q. Did this course you followed with General Stilwell deviate
from the procedure you followed on your various Foreign Service posts, Mr.
Davies? A. No. Would you like two examples? . . . Q. . . . Would you have
loaned a copy of Mr. Service's report . . . to a correspondent to have taken out
overnight, or 2 or 3 hours? A. I don't recall having done that, but depending
on my judgment of the correspondent and the material at that time, I would not
exclude the possibility of doing that. Mr. Stevens [Q]. That would not have
been anything which would have been so unusual for you as to remember it;
in other words, it may have been a practice that was followed? A. Yes. (*ibid.,*
pp. 2097–2100).

52. McCarthy's accusations against Service were made in three speeches to the
Senate. See the *Congressional Record,* 81st Cong., 2nd Sess., Vol. 96 (January 5,
1950), p. 90; *ibid.* (February 20, 1950), p. 2046, and *ibid.* (March 30, 1950),
p. 4440. He repeated the charges before the Tydings Subcommittee on March
14, 1950. See *State Department Employee Loyalty Investigation*, Pt. 1, pp. 130–131.
A summary of McCarthy's charges, the sources of these charges, and the Tydings Subcommittee's conclusions concerning them, appears at *ibid., Report,* pp.
74–79.

53. *IPR Hearings*, Pt. 13, p. 4844.

54. *State Department Employee Loyalty Investigation, Report,* p. 92.

55. Johnson, *op. cit.,* p. 17; Dresser, *How We Blundered Into Korean War,* pp. 23–45.

56. Flynn, *While You Slept,* pp. 36–37, and 134–135.

57. McCarthy, *McCarthyism,* pp. 32–35.

58. *IPR Hearings, Report,* p. 71.

59. Quoted in Dresser, *How We Blundered Into Korean War,* p. 24.

60. See the documents in the Service case in *IPR Hearings,* Pt. 13, p. 4837–4839.

61. For a review of the changes in criteria for judging loyalty, see below, pp.
203–205.

62. *IPR Hearings*, Pt. 13 pp. 4844–4845.

63. *Ibid.,* pp. 4845–4846. It is apparent from this report that the board made no
clear distinction between evidence, information, and accusations. The point
covered in the last paragraph quoted is quite obviously the same accusation as
that which had appeared in the *Plain Talk* article, which, in turn, was based on
information from Kohlberg's files and appears to have originated with Bishop
Paul Yupin.

64. *Ibid.,* p. 4847. Whether the question of classification at the time of dissemination
was one on which anyone other than State Department personnel could com-
pentently pass would seem to be a pertinent question which the board did not
raise.

65. *Ibid.,* p. 4849.

66. New York *Times,* December 14, 1951, p. 1.

67. *Ibid.,* April 4, 1952, p. 10.

68. See, for example, McCarthy, *op. cit.,* pp. 13, 33, and *IPR Hearings, Report,* pp. 71, 157. Six years later the United States Supreme Court ruled that the Loyalty Review Board had no legal authority to review Service's case after clearance by the Loyalty Security Board and that under the State Department's own regulations Service had been illegally dismissed. The Court ordered the finding of doubt as to Service's loyalty expunged from the record and that he be reinstated in his position and paid all back salary and allowances. See the New York *Times,* June 18, 1957, pp. 1, 23; July 4, 1957, p. 14.

69. House of Representatives, Committee on Un-American Activities, *Hearings, Testimony of Oliver Edmund Clubb,* 82nd Cong., 1st Sess., March 14, August 20, August 23, 1951 (Washington: U.S. Government Printing Office, 1952), pp. 1967, 1986 (hereinafter cited as *Clubb Hearings*).

70. Chambers gave his testimony concerning Clubb in an open session of the McCarran Subcommittee on August 16, 1951. He had previously testified, however, in closed session and, of course, had long been used as a source of information by the FBI. See his testimony in *IPR Hearings,* Pt. 2, pp. 495–497.

71. See *Clubb Hearings,* pp. 1968–1981.

72. *Ibid.*

73. *Ibid.,* pp. 1983–2042.

74. McCarthy, *op. cit.,* pp. 29–30.

75. New York *Times,* February 12, 1952, p. 10.

76. *Ibid.,* February 28, 1952, p. 1 and *IPR Hearings,* pp. 2943–2944.

77. Department of State Press Release (No. 171), March 5, 1952, p. 3.

78. See above, pp. 163–164.

79. Secretary Acheson's reply to Senator George, and his analysis of the allegations contained in the memorandum, may be found in *IPR Hearings,* Pt. 13, pp. 4540–4547. No reference to Acheson's reply to these allegations appeared in the report of the McCarran Subcommittee, although all the accusations made against Vincent in the memorandum were repeated and accepted as true.

80. *Ibid.,* pp. 4541–4546.

81. *State Department Employee Loyalty Investigation, Report,* p. 95.

82. *Ibid.*

83. *State Department Employee Loyalty Investigation,* Pt. 1, p. 613.

84. *IPR Hearings,* Pt. 3, p. 713, and Pt. 6, pp. 1831–1832.

85. *Ibid.,* Pt. 2, p. 628, and Pt. 6, p. 1833.

86. *Ibid.,* Pt. 2, pp. 626–627, Pt. 4, pp. 1079ff.

87. *Ibid.,* Pt. 6, pp. 1687–1689.

88. *Ibid.,* p. 1689.

89. The attempt to show that Vincent was held in high personal esteem by the Communists is perhaps best illustrated by the repeated references in the *Hearings* and *Report* to an incident related by Henry Wallace in his book *Soviet Asia Mission.* In that book, Wallace told how a Soviet official had proposed a toast, during a dinner given for Wallace, Vincent, and Lattimore, to "Owen Lattimore and John Carter Vincent, American experts on China, on whom rests great responsibility for China's future." The excerpt from Wallace's book was reprinted at *ibid.,* Pt. 2, p. 627.

The alleged parallel between Vincent's policies and those of the Communists is well illustrated by the opposition of the *Daily Worker* to Ambassador Hurley. Articles from the *Daily Worker* showing this opposition were placed in the record at *ibid.,* pp. 632–640.

90. Vincent's original testimony concerning his familiarity with Communist litera-

ture appears at *ibid.*, Pt. 6, pp. 1689–1690. See also the discussion on this point at pp. 1961–1965.

91. *Ibid., Report*, pp. 198–214.
92. *Ibid.*, pp. 147, 159.
93. The correspondence between McCarran and the Department of State, including the list of thirty-two categories of documents, appears in *IPR Hearings*, Pt. 6, pp. 1915–1917. The State Department—and later the President—refused to release many of the categories; in several other cases it was reported that no such documents existed.
94. *Ibid.*, p. 1778.
95. New York *Times*, February 20, 1952, p. 1.
96. *Ibid.*, December 16, 1952, p. 1.
97. *Ibid.*, January 4, 1953, p. 1. The text of Acheson's announcement appeared on p. 49.
98. *Ibid.*, March 4, 1953, p. 1. And from a conversation by Kagan with Vincent on September 18, 1971.
99. See *United States Relations with China, 1949*, pp. 572–578, for excerpts of reports made by Davies.
100. See Utley, *The China Story*, pp. 110–113.
101. *IPR Hearings*, Pt. 2, p. 439.
102. New York *Times*, July 31, 1951, p. 1.
103. *Ibid.*, September 23, 1951, p. 30.
104. The exchange of correspondence between McCarran and the Department of Justice appears in *IPR Hearings*, Pt. 14, pp. 5437–5443.
105. The testimony appears at *ibid.*, pp. 5443–5483, and *ibid., Report*, pp. 220–222.
106. New York *Times*, November 15, 1952, p. 6, and December 16, 1952, p. 1.
107. This and the following information is taken from "Texts of Statements by Davies and Dulles on the Former's Ouster," published in *ibid.*, November 6, 1954, p. 8. Quotations will be designated either as "Dulles Statement" or "Davies Statement."
108. Dulles Statement.
109. *Ibid.*
110. Davies Statement.
111. Dulles Statement.
112. *Ibid.*
113. *Ibid.* In 1969, the State Department, which still refused to make a public announcement, "leaked" to a New York *Times* reporter the information that Davies had received security clearance again. For an up-to-date discussion of Davies' struggles, see John W. Finney, "The Long Trial of John Paton Davies," New York *Times Magazine Section*, 31 August 1961, pp. 7–8, 23–28, 35. The New York *Times* finally changed its sympathies when C. L. Sulzberger nominated Davies for the post of U.S. Ambassador to the People's Republic of China. New York *Times*, 27 June 1971, editorial page.
114. "Harold Laski, An Appreciation," *Manchester Guardian Weekly*, March 20, 1950.

8. The Ultimate Effects of Acceptance on American Policy

1. Reprinted in *State Department Employee Loyalty Investigation*, Pt. 2, p. 2042.
2. *United States Relations with China, 1949*, Annex 114, "Statement by President Truman on United States Policy Toward China, December 18, 1946," p. 694.
3. The extent to which the provisions of the China Aid Act of 1948 were a direct response to pro-Chiang forces and were included as a *quid pro quo* for the

European aid is shown by Westerfield, *Foreign Policy and Party Politics,* pp. 262–266.

4. See *ibid.,* pp. 266–268.
5. See above, pp. 95–98.
6. Appendix A.
7. See above, p. 99.
8. A brief but fairly complete summary of Jessup's service with the United States Government up to March 20, 1950, may be found in *State Department Employee Loyalty Investigation,* Pt. 1, pp. 228–230.
9. See the New York *Times,* September 18, 1951, p. 18.
10. United States Senate, Committee on Foreign Relations, *Hearings on the Nomination of Philip Jessup,* 81st Cong., 1st Sess., September–October, 1951 (Washington: U.S. Government Printing Office, 1952).
11. See the New York *Times,* October 19, 1951, p. 1.
12. *Ibid.,* October 23, 1951, p. 1.
13. *Ibid.,* December 3, 1952, p. 12.
14. As quoted in Robert N. Johnson, "The Eisenhower Personnel Security Program," *The Journal of Politics,* 18 (November, 1956), p. 628.
15. Quoted at *ibid.,* p. 629.
16. *IPR Hearings, Report,* p. 226.
17. See the "Table of Witnesses and Testimony," in *IPR Hearings,* Pt. 15, pp. 5713–5714.
18. See the citations in Eleanor Bontecou, *The Federal Loyalty-Security Program* (Ithaca: Cornell University Press, 1953), p. 104, n. 9.
19. *Ibid.,* pp. 103–104.
20. Quoted in Johnson, "The Eisenhower Personnel Security Program," p. 630.
21. *Ibid.*
22. Quoted at *ibid.*
23. William Harlan Hale, " 'Big Brother' in Foggy Bottom," *The Reporter,* 11 (August 17, 1954), p. 11.
24. Johnson, "The Eisenhower Personnel Security Program," p. 625.
25. See above, p. 256, n. 18.
26. See, for example, Dresser, *How We Blundered Into Korean War,* pp. 10–12 and sources cited there, and Flynn, *While You Slept,* pp. 108–109, 157–170.
27. *Congressional Record,* 82nd Cong., 1st Sess., Vol 97 (June 14, 1951).
28. *Ibid.,* as reprinted in Senator Joseph R. McCarthy, *America's Retreat from Victory: The Story of George Catlett Marshall* (New York: The Devin-Adair Co., 1952), pp. 168–172.
29. Wittmer, *The Yalta Betrayal,* p. 98.
30. Hale, " 'Big Brother' in Foggy Bottom," p. 15.
31. Quoted at *ibid.,* p. 13.
32. Quoted at *ibid.,* p. 13.
33. Quoted at *ibid.,* p. 16.
34. Johnson, *China, Key to the Orient,* p. 29.
35. The first resolutions expressing opposition to the seating of the Chinese Communist delegation in the United Nations were introduced in Congress in 1950, but were never acted on by the full body. See H. Con. Res. 223, H. Res. 841 and 852, and S. Res. 345, in *Congressional Record,* Vol. 96, Pt. 7 (June 19, 1950), p. 8857; Pt. 11 (Sept. 11, 1950), p. 14569—(Sept. 14, 1950), p. 14873, and (Sept. 7, 1950), p. 14267. The increasing support in the Senate for this point of view was shown, however, by letters to the President from members of that body urging that the United States use all means in its power to prevent seating of the Chinese Communist delegation. The first letter, dated June 24, 1949, was signed by twenty-one senators; the second, dated May 2, 1950, was

signed by thirty-five members; the third, in September of 1951, was signed by
fifty-six members. All three letters were inserted into the *Congressional Record*,
Vol. 97, Pt. 9 (Sept. 14, 1951), pp. 11370–11371, by Senator Knowland.

Both the House and Senate passed resolutions—without recorded dissent—
expressing the same point of view early in 1951. See H. Res 77 and 96 and S.
Res. 36, in *ibid.*, Vol. 97, Pt. 1 (Jan. 19, 1951), Pt. 4 (May 15, 1951), pp.
5376–5379, and Pt. 1 (Jan. 23, 1951), pp. 560–561. In 1953, similar expressions were attached as a rider to the State, Justice, Commerce Appropriations
Act. The amendment was the subject of separate recorded votes in both houses
of Congress, receiving 76 votes in the Senate and 379 votes in the House. See
ibid., Vol. 99, Pt. 5 (June 3, 1953), p. 5973, and Pt. 7 (July 21, 1953), pp.
9406–9407. Bridges reported to the Senate that the amendment had the "full
endorsement" of the President (*ibid.*, Pt. 5 [June 3, 1953], p. 5972). In 1954,
a similar resolution (H. Res. 627) passed the House 381 to 0 (*ibid.*, Vol. 100,
Pt. 8 [July 15, 1954], p. 10649). The recorded views of Eisenhower and Dulles
were introduced to support the resolution (pp. 10636–10638). A few days later
the Senate adopted an amendment to the Mutual Security Act of 1954, introduced by Senator Knowland, which contained the same wording as that of the
previous year. The amendment was adopted by a vote of 91 to 0 (*ibid.*, Pt. 9
[July 29, 1954], p. 12520).

36. All quotations are from John Foster Dulles, *War or Peace* (New York: The
Macmillan Co., 1950), p. 190.

37. Walter P. McConaughy, "China in the Shadow of Communism," Department
of State Publication 5383, 1954, p. 5, as reprinted from the *Department of State
Bulletin*, January 11, 1954. The four criteria listed by McConaughy as the basis
for the recognition of a "new regime . . . as a legitimate government and its
acceptance into the sisterhood of nations," were "(1) effective control over the
territory of the country; (2) sovereign independence; (3) truly representative
character—something in the nature of a mandate from the people governed, or
at least their consent without coercion; and (4) acceptance of its inherited and
generally recognized treaty and other international obligations and adherence
to a pretty well established minimum standard of decency in its treatment of
foreign nationals and interests within its borders."

38. Alfred le Sesne Jenkins, "Present United States Policy Toward China," an
address made before the American Academy of Political and Social Science,
Philadelphia, Pa., April 2, 1954, Department of State Publication 5460, 1954,
pp. 16–17, as reprinted from the *Department of State Bulletin*, April 26, 1954.

39. Quoted in Jenkins, "Present United States Policy Toward China," p. 18.

40. Edwin W. Martin, "Considerations Underlying U.S. China Policy," an address
made before the China Committee of the National Council of the Churches of
Christ in the U.S.A., March 24, 1954, Department of State Publications 5460,
1954, p. 11, as reprinted from the *Department of State Bulletin*, April 12, 1954.

41. McConaughy, "China in the Shadow of Communism," p. 9.

BIBLIOGRAPHY OF CITED SOURCES

Newspapers—General

Newspapers—General

Christian Science Monitor
Jacksonville (Fla.) *Times-Union*
Los Angeles *Examiner*
Manchester (N.H.) *Union Leader*
New York *Journal-American*
New York *Times*
Oakland *Tribune*
St. Louis *Post-Dispatch*
San Francisco *Examiner*
Washington *Post*
Washington *Times-Herald*

Periodicals—General

American China Policy Association, Publications of
American Mercury
The China Monthly
Collier's
Economic Council Letter, published by the National Economic Council, Inc.
Far Eastern Survey
Human Events
Life
The New Leader
Pacific Affairs
Reader's Digest
The Reporter
Spotlight for the Nation, published by the Committee for Constitutional Government
Time
United Nations World
U.S. News & World Report

Articles

Acheson, Dean G., "Crisis in Asia—An Examination of United States Policy," *Department of State Bulletin*, Vol. XXII (1950).

Ascoli, Max, Charles Wertenbaker, and Philip Horton, "The China Lobby," *The Reporter*, Vol. VI (April 15 and April 29, 1952).

Berrigan, Darrell, "Uncle Joe Pays Off," *Saturday Evening Post* (June 17, 1944).

Bouscaren, Anthony, "The China Tragedy," *The China Monthly*, Vol. X (March, 1949).

Buck, Pearl, "A Warning About China," *Life* (May 10, 1943).

Bullitt, William C., "Report on China," *Life* (October 13, 1947).

"The Bullitt's Report on China," *The China Monthly*, Vol. VII (November, 1947).

Chen Chia-you, "The Confusion and Ignorances of the Self-Proclaimed China Expert," *The China Monthly*, Vol. X (February, 1949).

263

————, "The Democratic Ideals and the American China Policy," *The China Monthly*, Vol. XI (February, 1950).

"The China Lobby: A Case Study," *Congressional Quarterly, Weekly Report* (Special Supplement), Vol. IX (June 29, 1951).

Collins, Frederic W., "Washington Impasse: Red China," *United Nations World*, Vol. VII (September–October, 1953).

"Critcisms on China," *The China Monthly*, Vol. V (September, 1944).

Ettinger, K. E. "Foreign Propaganda in America," *Public Opinion Quarterly*, Vol. 10 (Fall, 1946).

Feis, Herbert, "Europe Versus Asia in American Strategy," *The Yale Review*, Vol. XLIII (March, 1954).

Gayn, Mark, "The Causes of China's Tragedy," *Collier's* (January 13, 1945).

Hale, William Harlan, " 'Big Brother' in Foggy Bottom," *The Reporter*, Vol. 11 (August 17, 1954).

Hauser, E. O., "China Needs a Friendly Nudge," *Saturday Evening Post* (August 26, 1944).

"Insiders Got Rich on China Aid," *U.S. News & World Report* (August 26, 1949).

Johnson, Robert E. "The Eisenhower Personnel Security Program," *Journal of Politics*, Vol. 18 (November, 1956).

Johnson, William R., "Falsehoods and Some Truths About China," *The China Monthly*, Vol. X (April, 1949).

————, "The United States Sells China Down the Amur," *The China Monthly*, Vol. VII (December, 1947).

Jonas, Frank H., "The Art of Political Dynamiting," *The Western Political Quarterly*, Vol. X (June, 1957).

Judd, Walter H., "Power Politics in the Far East," address before the Chamber of Commerce of the State of New York, Chamber of Commerce of the State of New York *Monthly Bulletin*, Vol. 43 (November, 1951).

Kohlberg, Alfred, "China Via Stilwell Road," *The China Monthly*, Vol. IX (October, 1948).

————, "Owen Lattimore: 'Expert's Expert,' " *The China Monthly*, Vol. VI (October, 1945).

————, "A Red Dream," *The China Monthly*, Vol. VII (January, 1947).

————, "Reply to a Reply," *The China Monthly*, Vol. VII (March, 1946).

————, "the Soviet-Chinese Pact," *The China Monthly*, Vol. VI (November, 1945).

————, "Stupidity and/or Treason," *The China Monthly*, Vol. IX (June, 1948).

————, "Ten Years After Marco Polo Bridge," *The China Monthly*, Vol. VIII (July, 1947).

———— "United States Military Aid to China," *The China Monthly*, Vol. XI (March, 1950).

————, "Who Is Responsible for China's Tragedy?" *The China Monthly*, Vol. X (December, 1949).

Larsen, Emmanuel S., "The State Department Espionage Case," *Plain Talk*, Vol. I (October, 1946).

Lattimore, Owen, "Reply to Mr. Kohlberg," *The China Monthly*, Vol. VI (December, 1945).

————, "The Roots of Conflict in the Modern Orient," Mayling Soong Foundation Addresss at Wellesley College, October 23, 1950. *Contemporary International Relations Readings, 1950–1951.* Edited by Norman J. Padelford. Cambridge: Harvard Univ. Press, 1951.

Linebarger, Paul M. A., "Outside Pressures on China, 1945–1950," *Report on China.* Edited by H. Arthur Steiner. *The Annals of the American Academy of Political and Social Science*, Vol. 277 (September, 1951).

Lubell, Samuel, "Is China washed Up?" *Saturday Evening Post* (March 31, 1945).

——, "Vinegar Joe and the Reluctant Dragon," *Saturday Evening Post* (February 24, 1945).

O'Toole, G. Barry, "Debunking an 'Imperial' Debunker," *The China Monthly*, Vol. V (February, 1944).

"Our Retreat in China," *The China Monthly*, Vol. VIII (January, 1946).

Peffer, Nathaniel, "Our Distorted View of China," *New York Times Magazine* (November 7, 1943).

Pirnie, Colonel W. Bruce, "Who Hamstrings U.S. Military Aid to China?" *The China Monthly*, Vol. IX (October, 1948).

"A Realistic China Recovery Plan," *The China Monthly*, Vol. IX (April–May, 1948).

Reinhardt, H. R. "What Chance Chiang?" *United Nations World*, Vol. 6 (April 1952).

"Russian Security, or a Just and Acceptable Peace?" *The China Monthly*, Vol. VI (April, 1945).

"The Sins of Yalta," *The China Monthly*, Vol. VIII (February, 1947).

" 'The Six' Arrested," *The China Monthly*, Vol. VI (July–August, 1945).

Snow, Edgar, "Must China Go. Red?" *Saturday Evening Post* (May 12, 1945).

——, "Sixty Million Lost Allies," *Saturday Evening Post* (June 10, 1944).

Torossian, Vincent P., "China in Crisis," *The China Monthly*, Vol. IX (July, 1948).

Tsai, Mark, "Now It Can Be Told," *The China Monthly*, Vol. IX (September, 1948).

"Two-Faced State Department Action," *The China Monthly*, Vol. VII (December, 1946).

Wu, Raymond K., "United States' China Policy," *The China Monthly*, Vol. IX (March, 1949).

Books, Monographs, and Pamphlets

American Institute of Pacific Relations. *Commentary on the McCarran Report on the IPR* (mimeographed). New York: American Institute of Pacific Relations, 1953.

Anderson, Jackson, and Ronald W. May. *McCarthy: The Man, The Senator, The Ism.* Boston: The Beacon Press, 1952.

Baker, Roscow. *The American Legion and American Foreign Policy.* New York: Bookman Associates, 1954.

Band, Claire and William. *Two Years with the Chinese Communists.* New Haven: Yale Univ. Press, 1948.

Barth, Alan. *Government by Investigation.* New York: Viking, 1955.

——. *The Loyalty of Free Men.* New York: Viking, 1951.

Belden, Jack. *China Shakes the World.* New York: Harper, 1949.

Beloff, Max. *The Foreign Policy of Soviet Russia, 1929–1941.* 2 vols. New York: Oxford Univ. Press, 1947, 1948.

——. *Soviet Policy in the Far East, 1944–1951.* London: Oxford Univ. Press, 1953.

Bernays, Edward L. *Propaganda.* New York: Liveright Publishing Corp., 1928.

Bisson, Thomas A. *American Policy in the Far East, 1931–1941.* Rev. ed. New York: International Secretariat, I.P.R., 1941.

Bontecou, Eleanor. *The Federal Loyalty-Security Program.* Ithaca: Cornell Univ. Press, 1953.

Budenz, Louis. *Men Without Faces.* New York: Harper, 1950.

Bundy, McGeorge (ed.,) *The Pattern of Responsibility.* Boston: Houghton Mifflin Co., 1952.

Carleton, William G. *The Revolution in American Foreign Policy, 1945–1954.* Doubleday Short Studies in Political Science. Garden City, New York: Doubleday and Co., 1954.

Chamberlin, William H. *Beyond Containment.* Chicago: Henry Regnery Co., 1953.

Chennault, Claire L. *Way of a Fighter: The Memoirs of Claire Lee Chennault.* New York: G. P. Putnam's Sons, 1949.

Chiang Kai-shek. *China's Destiny.* Authorized translation by Wang Chung-hui. New York: The Macmillan Co., 1947.

———. *China's Destiny and Chinese Economic Theory.* With notes and commentary by Philip Jaffe. New York: Roy Publishers, 1947.

China Ministry of Information. *China Handbook, 1937–1945.* Compiled by the China Handbook Editorial Board. New York: The Macmillan Co., 1947.

———. *China Handbook, 1950.* Compiled by the China Handbook Editorial Board. New York: Rockport Press, 1950.

Christopher, James W. *Conflict in the Far East: American Diplomacy in China from 1928–1933.* Leiden: E. J. Brill, 1950.

Churchill, Winston S. *The Hinge of Fate.* Boston: Houghton Mifflin Co., 1950.

Dallin, David. *The Rise of Russia in Asia.* New Haven: Yale Univ. Press, 1949.

———. *Soviet Espionage.* New Haven: Yale Univ. Press, London: Oxford Univ. Press, 1955.

———. *Soviet Russia and the Far East.* New Haven: Yale Univ. Press, 1948.

Deane, John R. *The Strange Alliance.* New York: Viking Press, 1947.

Dedijer, Vladimir. *Tito.* New York: Simon and Schuster, 1953.

Deutscher, Isaac. *Russia: What Next?* New York: Oxford Univ. Press, 1953.

———. *Stalin: A Political Biography.* New York: Oxford Univ. Press, 1949.

Doob, Leonard W. *Propaganda: Its Psychology and Technique.* New York: Henry Holt and Co., 1935.

Dresser, Robert B. *How We Blundered Into Korean War and Tragic Future Consequences.* New York: Committee for Constitutional Government, 1950.

———. *What Caused the Nation's Crisis—Incompetency or Treachery?* New York: Committee for Constitutional Government, 1951.

Dulles, John Foster. *War or Peace.* New York: The Macmillan Co., 1950.

Epstein, Israel. *Unfinished Revolution in China.* Boston: Little, Brown and Co., 1947.

Fairbank, J. K. *The United States and China.* Cambridge: Harvard Univ. Press, 1948.

Feis, Herbert. *The China Tangle: The American Effort in China from Pearl Harbor to the Marshall Mission.* Princeton: Princeton Univ. Press, 1953.

Fitch, Geraldine. *Blunder Out of China: A Commentary on the White-Jacoby Book.* New York: American China Policy Association [1947].

Fitzgerald, Charles P. *China; A Short Cultural History.* 3rd ed. New York: Praeger, 1950.

———. *Revolution in China.* New York: Praeger, 1952.

Flynn, John T. *The Lattimore Story.* New York: The Devin-Adair Co., 1953.

———. *While You Slept: Our Tragedy in Asia and Who Made It.* New York: The Devin-Adair Co., 1951.

———. *Why Korea? Story of Blackest Intrigue and Betrayal in America's History.* Broadcasts of March 17 to 21, 1952. New York: America's Future, Inc., 1952.

Forman, Harrison, *Blunder in Asia.* New York: Didier, 1950.

———. *Report from Red China.* New York: Henry Holt and Co., 1945.

Grew, Joseph C. *Turbulent Era.* Vol. II. Boston: Houghton Mifflin Co., 1952.

Hartmann, Frederick H. *The Relations of Nations.* New York: The Macmillan Co., 1957.

Holland, William L. *Truth and Fancy About the Institute of Pacific Relations.* Two Statements Made Before the Senate Judiciary Subcommittee on Internal Security, October 10, 1951, and March 19, 1952. New York: American Institute of Pacific Relations, 1953.

Hull, Cordell. *The Memoirs of Cordell Hull.* Vol. II. New York: The Macmillan Co., 1948.

Johnson, William R. *China, Key to the Orient—and to Asia.* Polo, Ill., 1950.

Judd, Walter H. *Autopsy on Our Blunders in Asia.* A supplement to the Autumn, 1950, number of *American Affairs.* New York: National Industrial Conference Board, Inc., 1950.

Kennan, George F. *American Diplomacy, 1900–1950.* Charles R. Walgreen Foundation Lectures. Chicago: The University of Chicago Press, 1951.

Lasky, Victor. *The Case Against Dean Acheson.* New York: Committee for Constitutional Government, 1951.

Latourette, Kenneth S. *The American Record in the Far East, 1945–1951.* Issued under the auspices of the American Institute of Pacific Relations. New York: The Macmillan Co., 1952.

Leahy, William D. *I Was There: The Personal Story of the Chief of Staff to Presidents Roosevelt and Truman Based on His Notes and Diaries Made at the Time.* New York: McGraw-Hill, 1950.

Levi, Werner. *Modern China's Foreign Policy.* Minneapolis: Univ. of Minnesota Press, 1953.

Lippmann, Walter. *Public Opinion.* New York: Harcourt, Brace and Co., 1922.

Lohbeck, Don. *Patrick J. Hurley.* Chicago: Henry Regnery Co., 1956.

Low, Sir Francis. *Struggle for Asia.* New York: Praeger, 1955.

McCarthy, Joseph R. *America's Retreat from Victory: The Story of George Catlett Marshall.* New York: The Devin-Adair Co., 1952.

McCarthy, Senator Joe. *McCarthyism—The Fight for America: Documented Answers to Questions Asked by Friend and Foe.* New York: The Devin-Adair Co., 1952.

Mandel, William (Compiler). *Soviet Source Materials on USSR Relations with East Asia, 1945–1950.* New York: International Secretariat, Institute of Pacific Relations [1950].

Millis, Walter (ed.). *The Forrestal Diaries.* New York: Viking Press, 1951.

Moorad, George. *Lost Peace in China.* New York: E. P. Dutton, 1949.

Mowrer, Edgar A. *The Nightmare of American Foreign Policy.* New York: Alfred A. Knopf, 1948.

North, Robert C., with the collaboration of Ithiel de Sola Pool. *Kuomintang and Chinese Communist Elites,* Hoover Institute Studies, Series B: Elite Studies No. 8. Stanford University Press, 1952.

Por qué no debe Admitirse a la China Communista en las Naciones Unidas. New York: Free Trade Union Committee, 1955.

Powell, Norman J. *Anatomy of Public Opinion.* New York: Prentice-Hall, Inc., 1951.

Rosinger, Lawrence K. *China's Crisis.* New York: Alfred A. Knopf, 1945.

Sherwood, Robert E. *Roosevelt and Hopkins—An Intimate History.* New York: Harper, 1948.

Skretting, John R. *Republican Attitudes Toward the Administration's China Policy, 1945–1949.* Unpublished dissertation, Publication 4105. Ann Arbor: University Microfilms, 1952.

Smedley, Agnes. *Battle Hymn of China.* New York: Alfred A. Knopf, 1943.

Snell, John L. (ed.), and others. *The Meaning of Yalta: Big Three Diplomacy and the New Balance of Power.* Baton Rouge: Louisiana State Univ. Press, 1956.

Snow, Edgar. *Red Star Over China.* New York: Random House, 1938.

Spolansky, Jacob. *The Communist Trail in America.* New York: The Macmillan Co., 1951.

Stein, Guenther. *The Challenge of Red China.* New York: McGraw-Hill, 1945.

Stimson, Henry L., and McGeorge Bundy. *On Active Service in Peace and War.* New York: Harper, 1948.

Stripling, Robert. *The Red Plot Against America.* New York: Bell Publishers, 1949.

Strong, Anna Louise. *The Chinese Conquer China.* Garden City, N.Y.: Doubleday and Co., 1949.

Utley, Freda. *The China Story.* Chicago: Henry Regnery Co., 1951.

————. *Last Chance in China.* Indianapolis: Bobbs-Merrill Co., 1947.

Vandenberg, Arthur H., Jr. (ed.), Joe Alex Morris. *The Private Papers of Senator Vandenberg.* Boston: Houghton Mifflin Co., 1952.

Van der Sprenkel, Otto B., Robert Guillain, and Michael Lindsay. *New China: Three Views.* London: Turnstile Press, 1950.

Vinacke, Harold M. *Far Eastern Politics in the Postwar Period.* New York: Appleton-Century-Crofts, Inc., 1956.

————. *The United States and the Far East: 1945–1951.* Published under the auspices of the American Institute of Pacific Relations, Inc. Stanford: Stanford Univ. Press, 1952.

Welch, Robert R. W. *May God Forgive Us.* Chicago: Henry Regnery Co., 1952.

Welles, Sumner. *Seven Decisions That Shaped History.* New York: Harper, 1950.

Westerfield, H. Bradford. *Foreign Policy and Party Politics: Pearl Harbor to Korea.* New Haven: Yale Univ. Press, 1955.

White, Theodore H. *The Stilwell Papers.* New York: Sloane, 1948.

————, and Annalee Jacoby. *Thunder Out of China.* New York: Sloane, 1946.

Winfield, Gerald F. *China, the Land and the People.* American Institute of Pacific Relations. New York: Sloane, 1948.

Wittmer, Felix. *The Yalta Betrayal: Data on the Decline and Fall of Franklin Delano Roosevelt.* Caldwell, Idaho: Caxton Printers, 1953.

Woltman, Frederick. *The Amerasia Case.* New York: *World-Telegram,* 1950.

United States Government Documents and Publications

The Congressional Record, 1943–1954.

"Foreign Agents Registration Act of 1938 as Amended," *United States Code* (1952 edition). Title 22, Vol. II. Washington: Government Printing Office, 1953.

Romanus, Charles F., and Riley Sunderland. *Stilwell's Mission to China. Vol. I of China-Burma-India Theater.* Series IX of *The United States Army in World War II.* Edited by Kent Roberts Greenfield under the Office of the Chief of Military History, Department of the Army. Washington: Government Printing Office, 1950.

U.S. Congress, House of Representatives, Committee on Foreign Affairs. *Emergency Foreign Aid to China, Hearings.* 80th Cong., 1st Sess. Washington: Government Printing Office, 1947.

U.S. Congress, House of Representatives, Committee on Un-American Activities. *Hearings Regarding Communist Espionage in the United States Government.* 80th Cong., 2nd Sess. Washington: Government Printing Office, 1948.

U.S. Congress, House of Representatives, Committee on Un-American Activities. "Report on the Communist Party of the United States as an Advocate of Overthrow of Government by Force and Violence," *Investigation of Un-American Activities in the United States.* House Report No. 1920. 80th Cong., 2nd Sess. Washington: Government Printing Office, 1948.

U.S. Congress, House of Representatives, Committee on Un-American Activities. *Testimony of Oliver Edmund Clubb: Hearings.* Hearings held on March 14, August 20, August 23, 1951. 82nd Cong., 1st Sess. Washington: Government Printing Office, 1952.

U.S. Congress, House of Representatives, House Select Committee on Lobbying Activities. *Lobbying, Direct and Indirect, Hearings, June 27–August 25, 1950.* Pt. 5. "Committee for Constitutional Government." 81st Cong., 2nd Sess. Washington: Government Printing Office, 1950.

U.S. Congress, House of Representatives, House Select Committee on Lobbying Activities. *The Role of Lobbying in Representative Self-Government: Hearings.* Part 1. 82nd Cong., 2nd Sess. Washington: Government Printing Office, 1950.

U.S. Congress, House of Representatives, Special Committee to Investigate Tax-Exempt Foundations and Comparable Organizations. *Tax-Exempt Foundations: Report*. House Report No. 2681. 83rd Cong., 2nd Sess. Washington: Government Printing Office, 1955.

U.S. Congress, Senate, Committee on Appropriations. *Hearings on Economic Cooperation Administration*. 80th Cong., 2nd Sess. Washington: Government Printing Office, 1948.

U.S. Congress, Senate, Committee on Appropriations. *Third Supplemental Appropriations Bill for 1948, Hearings on H.R. 4784*. 80th Cong., 1st Sess. Washington: Government Printing Office, 1948.

U.S. Congress, Senate, Committee on Armed Services and Committee on Foreign Relations. *Hearings, Military Situation in the Far East*. 5 parts. 82nd Cong., 1st Sess. Washington: Government Printing Office, 1951.

U.S. Congress, Senate, Committee on Foreign Relations. *Hearings on the Nomination of Philip C. Jessup To Be United States Representative to the Sixth General Assembly of the United Nations*. 82nd Cong., 1st Sess. Washington: Government Printing Office, 1951.

U.S. Congress, Senate, Committee on Foreign Relations. *State Department Employee Loyalty Investigation: Report*. 81st Cong., 2nd Sess. Senate Report No. 2108. Washington: Government Printing Office, 1950.

U.S. Congress, Senate, Committee on the Judiciary, Internal Security Subcommittee. *Institute of Pacific Relations: Hearings*. 15 parts. 82nd Cong., 2nd Sess. Washington: Government Printing Office, 1951, 1952.

U.S. Congress, Senate, Committee on the Judiciary, Internal Security Subcommittee. *Institute of Pacific Relations: Report*. 82nd Cong., 2nd Sess. Washington: Government Printing Office, 1952.

U.S. Congress, Senate, Subcommittee of the Committee on Foreign Relations. *State Department Employee Loyalty Investigation: Hearings*. 2 parts, 81st Cong., 2nd Sess. Washington: Government Printing Office, 1950.

U.S. Department of State. *Foreign Relations of the United States—Diplomatic Papers. The Conferences at Malta and Yalta, 1945*. Washington: Government Printing Office, 1955.

U.S. Department of State. *Transcript of Proceedings, Meeting; Conference on Problems of United States Policy in China, October 6, 7, and 8, 1949* (mimeographed). Washington: Division of Central Services, 1949.

U.S. Department of State. *United States Relations with China, with Special Reference to the Period 1944–1949*. Department of State Publication 3573, 1949, Far Eastern Series 30. Washington: Government Printing Office, 1949.

Watson, Mark S. *Chief of Staff: Prewar Plans and Preparations*. Vol. I of *The War Department*. Series IV of *The United States Army in World War II*. Edited by Kent Roberts Greenfield under the Office of the Chief of Military History, Department of the Army. Washington: Government Printing Office, 1950.

INDEX

Revised January, 1970

hARpER ✦ τoRchbooks

American Studies: General

HENRY ADAMS Degradation of the Democratic Dogma. ‡ Introduction by Charles Hirschfeld. TB/1450

LOUIS D. BRANDEIS: Other People's Money, and How the Bankers Use It. Ed. with Intro. by Richard M. Abrams TB/3081

HENRY STEELE COMMAGER, Ed.: The Struggle for Racial Equality TB/1300

CARL N. DEGLER: Out of Our Past: The Forces that Shaped Modern America CN/2

CARL N. DEGLER, Ed.: Pivotal Interpretations of American History
Vol. I TB/1240; Vol. II TB/1241

A. S. EISENSTADT, Ed.: The Craft of American History: Selected Essays
Vol. I TB/1255; Vol. II TB/1256

LAWRENCE H. FUCHS, Ed.: American Ethnic Politics TB/1368

MARCUS LEE HANSEN: The Atlantic Migration: 1607-1860. Edited by Arthur M. Schlesinger. Introduction by Oscar Handlin TB/1052

MARCUS LEE HANSEN: The Immigrant in American History. Edited with a Foreword by Arthur M. Schlesinger TB/1120

ROBERT L. HEILBRONER: The Limits of American Capitalism TB/1305

JOHN HIGHAM, Ed.: The Reconstruction of American History TB/1068

ROBERT H. JACKSON: The Supreme Court in the American System of Government TB/1106

JOHN F. KENNEDY: A Nation of Immigrants. Illus. Revised and Enlarged. Introduction by Robert F. Kennedy TB/1118

LEONARD W. LEVY, Ed.: American Constitutional Law: Historical Essays TB/1285

LEONARD W. LEVY, Ed.: Judicial Review and the Supreme Court TB/1296

LEONARD W. LEVY: The Law of the Commonwealth and Chief Justice Shaw: The Evolution of American Law, 1830-1860 TB/1309

GORDON K. LEWIS: Puerto Rico: Freedom and Power in the Caribbean. Abridged edition TB/1371

RICHARD B. MORRIS: Fair Trial: Fourteen Who Stood Accused, from Anne Hutchinson to Alger Hiss TB/1335

GUNNAR MYRDAL: An American Dilemma: The Negro Problem and Modern Democracy. Introduction by the Author.
Vol. I TB/1443; Vol. II TB/1444

GILBERT OSOFSKY, Ed.: The Burden of Race: A Documentary History of Negro-White Relations in America TB/1405

CONYERS READ, Ed.: The Constitution Reconsidered. Revised Edition. Preface by Richrd B. Morris TB/1384

ARNOLD ROSE: The Negro in America: The Condensed Version of Gunnar Myrdal's An American Dilemma. Second Edition TB/3048

JOHN E. SMITH: Themes in American Philosophy: Purpose, Experience and Community TB/1466

WILLIAM R. TAYLOR: Cavalier and Yankee: The Old South and American National Character TB/1474

American Studies: Colonial

BERNARD BAILYN: The New England Merchants in the Seventeenth Century TB/1149

ROBERT E. BROWN: Middle-Class Democracy and Revolution in Massachusetts, 1691-1780. New Introduction by Author TB/1413

JOSEPH CHARLES: The Origins of the American Party System TB/1049

HENRY STEELE COMMAGER & ELMO GIORDANETTI, Eds.: Was America a Mistake? An Eighteenth Century Controversy TB/1329

WESLEY FRANK CRAVEN: The Colonies in Transition: 1660-1712† TB/3084

CHARLES GIBSON: Spain in America † TB/3077

CHARLES GIBSON, Ed.: The Spanish Tradition in America + HR/1351

LAWRENCE HENRY GIPSON: The Coming of the Revolution: 1763-1775. † Illus. TB/3007

JACK P. GREENE, Ed.: Great Britain and the American Colonies: 1606-1763. + Introduction by the Author . HR/1477

AUBREY C. LAND, Ed.: Bases of the Plantation Society + HR/1429

JOHN LANKFORD, Ed.: Captain John Smith's America: Selections from his Writings ‡ TB/3078

LEONARD W. LEVY: Freedom of Speech and Press in Early American History: Legacy of Suppression TB/1109

PERRY MILLER: Errand Into the Wilderness TB/1139

PERRY MILLER T. H. JOHNSON, Eds.: The Puritans: A Sourcebook of Their Writings
Vol. I TB/1093; Vol. II TB/1094

---

† The New American Nation Series, edited by Henry Steele Commager and Richard B. Morris.
‡ American Perspectives series, edited by Bernard Wishy and William ·E. Leuchtenburg.
a History of Europe series, edited by J. H. Plumb.
§ The Library of Religion and Culture, edited by Benjamin Nelson.
‖ Researches in the Social, Cultural, and Behavioral Sciences, edited by Benjamin Nelson.
Σ Harper Modern Science Series, edited by James A. Newman.
° Not for sale in Canada.
+ Documentary History of the United States series, edited by Richard B. Morris.
# Documentary History of Western Civilization series, edited by Eugene C. Black and Leonard W. Levy.
Λ The Economic History of the United States series, edited by Henry David et al.
¶ European Perspectives series, edited by Eugene C. Black.
** Contemporary Essays series, edited by Leonard W. Levy.
* The Stratum Series, edited by John Hale.

EDMUND S. MORGAN: The Puritan Family: *Religion and Domestic Relations in Seventeenth Century New England* TB/1227

RICHARD B. MORRIS: Government and Labor in Early America TB/1244

WALLACE NOTESTEIN: The English People on the Eve of Colonization: 1603-1630. † *Illus.* TB/3006

FRANCIS PARKMAN: The Seven Years War: *A Narrative Taken from Montcalm and Wolfe, The Conspiracy of Pontiac, and A Half-Century of Conflict. Edited by John H. McCallum* TB/3083

LOUIS B. WRIGHT: The Cultural Life of the American Colonies: 1607-1763. † *Illus.* TB/3005

YVES F. ZOLTVANY, Ed.: The French Tradition in America + HR/1425

American Studies: The Revolution to 1860

JOHN R. ALDEN: The American Revolution: 1775-1783. † *Illus.* TB/3011

MAX BELOFF, Ed.: The Debate on the American Revolution, 1761-1783: *A Sourcebook* TB/1225

RAY A. BILLINGTON: The Far Western Frontier: 1830-1860. † *Illus.* TB/3012

STUART BRUCHEY: The Roots of American Economic Growth, 1607-1861: *An Essay in Social Causation. New Introduction by the Author.* TB/1350

WHITNEY R. CROSS: The Burned-over District: *The Social and Intellectual History of Enthusiastic Religion in Western New York, 1800-1850* TB/1242

NOBLE E. CUNNINGHAM, JR., Ed.: The Early Republic, 1789-1828 + HR/1394

GEORGE DANGERFIELD: The Awakening of American Nationalism, 1815-1828. † *Illus.* TB/3061

CLEMENT EATON: The Freedom-of-Thought Struggle in the Old South. *Revised and Enlarged. Illus.* TB/1150

CLEMENT EATON: The Growth of Southern Civilization, 1790-1860. † *Illus.* TB/3040

ROBERT H. FERRELL, Ed.: Foundations of American Diplomacy, 1775-1872 HR/1393

LOUIS FILLER: The Crusade against Slavery: 1830-1860. † *Illus.* TB/3029

DAVID H. FISCHER: The Revolution of American Conservatism: *The Federalist Party in the Era of Jeffersonian Democracy* TB/1449

WILLIAM W. FREEHLING, Ed.: The Nullification Era: *A Documentary Record* ‡ TB/3079

WILLIM W. FREEHLING: Prelude to Civil War: *The Nullification Controversy in South Carolina, 1816-1836* TB/1359

PAUL W. GATES: The Farmer's Age: *Agriculture, 1815-1860* △ TB/1398

FELIX GILBERT: The Beginnings of American Foreign Policy: *To the Farewell Address* TB/1200

ALEXANDER HAMILTON: The Reports of Alexander Hamilton. ‡ *Edited by Jacob E. Cooke* TB/3060

THOMAS JEFFERSON: Notes on the State of Virginia. ‡ *Edited by Thomas P. Abernethy* TB/3052

FORREST MCDONALD, Ed.: Confederation and Constitution, 1781-1789 + HR/1396

BERNARD MAYO: Myths and Men: *Patrick Henry, George Washington, Thomas Jefferson* TB/1108

JOHN C. MILLER: Alexander Hamilton and the Growth of the New Nation TB/3057

JOHN C. MILLER: The Federalist Era: 1789-1801. † *Illus.* TB/3027

RICHARD B. MORRIS, Ed.: Alexander Hamilton and the Founding of the Nation. *New Introduction by the Editor* TB/1448

RICHARD B. MORRIS: The American Revolution Reconsidered TB/1363

CURTIS P. NETTELS: The Emergence of a National Economy, 1775-1815 △ TB/1438

DOUGLASS C. NORTH & ROBERT PAUL THOMAS, Eds.: *The Growth of the American Economy to 1860* + HR/1352

R. B. NYE: The Cultural Life of the New Nation: 1776-1830. † *Illus.* TB/3026

GILBERT OSOFSKY, Ed.: Puttin' On Ole Massa: *The Slave Narratives of Henry Bibb, William Wells Brown, and Solomon Northup* ‡ TB/1432

JAMES PARTON: The Presidency of Andrew Jackson. *From Volume III of the Life of Andrew Jackson. Ed. with Intro. by Robert V. Remini* TB/3080

FRANCIS S. PHILBRICK: The Rise of the West, 1754-1830. † *Illus.* TB/3067

MARSHALL SMELSER: The Democratic Republic, 1801-1815 † TB/1406

TIMOTHY L. SMITH: Revivalism and Social Reform: *American Protestantism on the Eve of the Civil War* TB/1229

JACK M. SOSIN, Ed.: The Opening of the West + HR/1424

GEORGE ROGERS TAYLOR: The Transportation Revolution, 1815-1860 △ TB/1347

A. F. TYLER: Freedom's Ferment: *Phases of American Social History from the Revolution to the Outbreak of the Civil War. Illus.* TB/1074

GLYNDON G. VAN DEUSEN: The Jacksonian Era: 1828-1848. † *Illus.* TB/3028

LOUIS B. WRIGHT: Culture on the Moving Frontier TB/1053

American Studies: The Civil War to 1900

W. R. BROCK: An American Crisis: *Congress and Reconstruction, 1865-67* ° TB/1283

T. C. COCHRAN & WILLIAM MILLER: The Age of Enterprise: *A Social History of Industrial America* TB/1054

W. A. DUNNING: Reconstruction, Political and Economic: 1865-1877 TB/1073

HAROLD U. FAULKNER: Politics, Reform and Expansion: 1890-1900. † *Illus.* TB/3020

GEORGE M. FREDRICKSON: The Inner Civil War: *Northern Intellectuals and the Crisis of the Union* TB/1358

JOHN A. GARRATY: The New Commonwealth, 1877-1890 + TB/1410

JOHN A. GARRATY, Ed.: The Transformation of American Society, 1870-1890 + HR/1395

HELEN HUNT JACKSON: A Century of Dishonor: *The Early Crusade for Indian Reform.* ‡ *Edited by Andrew F. Rolle* TB/3063

ALBERT D. KIRWAN: Revolt of the Rednecks: *Mississippi Politics, 1876-1925* TB/1199

ARTHUR MANN: Yankee Reforms in the Urban Age: *Social Reform in Boston, 1800-1900* TB/1247

ARNOLD M. PAUL: Conservative Crisis and the Rule of Law: *Attitudes of Bar and Bench, 1887-1895. New Introduction by Author* TB/1415

JAMES S. PIKE: The Prostrate State: *South Carolina under Negro Government.* ‡ *Intro. by Robert F. Durden* TB/3085

WHITELAW REID: After the War: *A Tour of the Southern States, 1865-1866.* ‡ *Edited by C. Vann Woodward* TB/3066

FRED A. SHANNON: The Farmer's Last Frontier: *Agriculture, 1860-1897* TB/1348

VERNON LANE WHARTON: The Negro in Mississippi, 1865-1890   TB/1178

American Studies: The Twentieth Century

RICHARD M. ABRAMS, Ed.: The Issues of the Populist and Progressive Eras, 1892-1912 + HR/1428
RAY STANNARD BAKER: Following the Color Line: American Negro Citizenship in Progressive Era. ‡ Edited by Dewey W. Grantham, Jr. Illus.   TB/3053
RANDOLPH S. BOURNE: War and the Intellectuals: Collected Essays, 1915-1919. ‡ Edited by Carl Resek   TB/3043
A. RUSSELL BUCHANAN: The United States and World War II. † Illus.
    Vol. I TB/3044;   Vol. II TB/3045
THOMAS C. COCHRAN: The American Business System: A Historical Perspective, 1900-1955   TB/1080
FOSTER RHEA DULLES: America's Rise to World Power: 1898-1954. † Illus.   TB/3021
JEAN-BAPTISTE DUROSELLE: From Wilson to Roosevelt: Foreign Policy of the United States, 1913-1945. Trans. by Nancy Lyman Roelker   TB/1370
HAROLD U. FAULKNER: The Decline of Laissez Faire, 1897-1917   TB/1397
JOHN D. HICKS: Republican Ascendancy: 1921-1933. † Illus.   TB/3041
ROBERT HUNTER: Poverty: Social Conscience in the Progressive Era. ‡ Edited by Peter d'A. Jones   TB/3065
WILLIAM E. LEUCHTENBURG: Franklin D. Roosevelt and the New Deal: 1932-1940. † Illus.   TB/3025
WILLIAM E. LEUCHTENBURG, Ed.: The New Deal: A Documentary History +   HR/1354
ARTHUR S. LINK: Woodrow Wilson and the Progressive Era: 1910-1917. † Illus. TB/3023
BROADUS MITCHELL: Depression Decade: From New Era through New Deal, 1929-1941 ∆   TB/1439
GEORGE E. MOWRY: The Era of Theodore Roosevelt and the Birth of Modern America: 1900-1912. † Illus.   TB/3022
WILLIAM PRESTON, JR.: Aliens and Dissenters: Federal Suppression of Radicals, 1903-1933   TB/1287
WALTER RAUSCHENBUSCH: Christianity and the Social Crisis. ‡ Edited by Robert D. Cross   TB/3059
GEORGE SOULE: Prosperity Decade: From War to Depression, 1917-1929 ∆   TB/1349
GEORGE B. TINDALL, Ed.: A Populist Reader: Selections from the Works of American Populist Leaders   TB/3069
TWELVE SOUTHERNERS: I'll Take My Stand: The South and the Agrarian Tradition. Intro. by Louis D. Rubin, Jr.; Biographical Essays by Virginia Rock   TB/1072

Art, Art History, Aesthetics

CREIGHTON GILBERT, Ed.: Renaissance Art ** Illus.   TB/1465
EMILE MALE: The Gothic Image: Religious Art in France of the Thirteenth Century. § 190 illus.   TB/344
MILLARD MEISS: Painting in Florence and Siena After the Black Death: The Arts, Religion and Society in the Mid-Fourteenth Century. 169 illus.   TB/1148
ERWIN PANOFSKY: Renaissance and Renascences in Western Art. Illus.   TB/1447
ERWIN PANOFSKY: Studies in Iconology: Humanistic Themes in the Art of the Renaissance. 180 illus.   TB/1077

JEAN SEZNEC: The Survival of the Pagan Gods: The Mythological Tradition and Its Place in Renaissance Humanism and Art. 108 illus.   TB/2004
OTTO VON SIMSON: The Gothic Cathedral: Origins of Gothic Architecture and the Medieval Concept of Order. 58 illus.   TB/2018
HEINRICH ZIMMER: Myths and Symbols in Indian Art and Civilization. 70 illus.   TB/2005

Asian Studies

WOLFGANG FRANKE: China and the West: The Cultural Encounter, 13th to 20th Centuries. Trans. by R. A. Wilson   TB/1326
L. CARRINGTON GOODRICH: A Short History of the Chinese People. Illus.   TB/3015
DAN N. JACOBS, Ed.: The New Communist Manifesto and Related Documents. 3rd revised edn.   TB/1078
DAN N. JACOBS & HANS H. BAERWALD, Eds.: Chinese Communism: Selected Documents   TB/3031
BENJAMIN I. SCHWARTZ: Chinese Communism and the Rise of Mao   TB/1308
BENJAMIN I. SCHWARTZ: In Search of Wealth and Power: Yen Fu and the West   TB/1422

Economics & Economic History

C. E. BLACK: The Dynamics of Modernization: A Study in Comparative History   TB/1321
STUART BRUCHEY: The Roots of American Economic Growth, 1607-1861: An Essay in Social Causation. New Introduction by the Author.   TB/1350
GILBERT BURCK & EDITORS OF Fortune: The Computer Age: And its Potential for Management   TB/1179
JOHN ELLIOTT CAIRNES: The Slave Power. ‡ Edited with Introduction by Harold D. Woodman   TB/1433
SHEPARD B. CLOUGH, THOMAS MOODIE & CAROL MOODIE, Eds.: Economic History of Europe: Twentieth Century #   HR/1388
THOMAS C. COCHRAN: The American Business System: A Historical Perspective, 1900-1955   TB/1180
ROBERT A. DAHL & CHARLES E. LINDBLOM: Politics, Economics, and Welfare: Planning and Politico-Economic Systems Resolved into Basic Social Processes   TB/3037
PETER F. DRUCKER: The New Society: The Anatomy of Industrial Order   TB/1082
HAROLD U. FAULKNER: The Decline of Laissez Faire, 1897-1917 ∆   TB/1397
PAUL W. GATES: The Farmer's Age: Agriculture, 1815-1860 ∆   TB/1398
WILLIAM GREENLEAF, Ed.: American Economic Development Since 1860 +   HR/1353
J. L. & BARBARA HAMMOND: The Rise of Modern Industry. || Introduction by R. M. Hartwell   TB/1417
ROBERT L. HEILBRONER: The Future as History: The Historic Currents of Our Time and the Direction in Which They Are Taking America   TB/1386
ROBERT L. HEILBRONER: The Great Ascent: The Struggle for Economic Development in Our Time   TB/3030
FRANK H. KNIGHT: The Economic Organization   TB/1214
DAVID S. LANDES: Bankers and Pashas: International Finance and Economic Imperialism in Egypt. New Preface by the Author TB/1412
ROBERT LATOUCHE: The Birth of Western Economy: Economic Aspects of the Dark Ages   TB/1290

3

W. ARTHUR LEWIS: Economic Survey, 1919-1939
TB/1446
W. ARTHUR LEWIS: The Principles of Economic Planning. *New Introduction by the Author*°
TB/1436
ROBERT GREEN MC CLOSKEY: American Conservatism in the Age of Enterprise   TB/1137
PAUL MANTOUX: The Industrial Revolution in the Eighteenth Century: *An Outline of the Beginnings of the Modern Factory System in England*°   TB/1079
WILLIAM MILLER, Ed.: Men in Business: *Essays on the Historical Role of the Entrepreneur*
TB/1081
GUNNAR MYRDAL: An International Economy. *New Introduction by the Author*   TB/1445
RICHARD S. WECKSTEIN, Ed.: Expansion of World Trade and the Growth of National Economies **   TB/1373

Historiography and History of Ideas

HERSCHEL BAKER: The Image of Man: *A Study of the Idea of Human Dignity in Classical Antiquity, the Middle Ages, and the Renaissance*   TB/1047
J. BRONOWSKI & BRUCE MAZLISH: The Western Intellectual Tradition: *From Leonardo to Hegel*   TB/3001
EDMUND BURKE: On Revolution. Ed. by Robert A. Smith   TB/1401
WILHELM DILTHEY: Pattern and Meaning in History: *Thoughts on History and Society.*° *Edited with an Intro. by H. P. Rickman*
TB/1075
ALEXANDER GRAY: The Socialist Tradition: *Moses to Lenin*°   TB/1375
J. H. HEXTER: More's Utopia: *The Biography of an Idea. Epilogue by the Author*   TB/1195
H. STUART HUGHES: History as Art and as Science: *Twin Vistas on the Past*   TB/1207
ARTHUR O. LOVEJOY: The Great Chain of Being: *A Study of the History of an Idea* TB/1009
JOSE ORTEGA Y GASSET: The Modern Theme. *Introduction by Jose Ferrater Mora* TB/1038
RICHARD H. POPKIN: The History of Scepticism from Erasmus to Descartes. *Revised Edition*
TB/1391
G. J. RENIER: History: *Its Purpose and Method*
TB/1209
MASSIMO SALVADORI, Ed.: Modern Socialism #
HR/1374
BRUNO SNELL: The Discovery of the Mind: *The Greek Origins of European Thought* TB/1018
W. WARREN WAGER, ed.: European Intellectual History Since Darwin and Marx   TB/1297
W. H. WALSH: Philosophy of History: In Introduction   TB/1020

History: General

HANS KOHN: The Age of Nationalism: *The First Era of Global History*   TB/1380
BERNARD LEWIS: The Arabs in History TB/1029
BERNARD LEWIS: The Middle East and the West °   TB/1274

History: Ancient

A. ANDREWS: The Greek Tyrants   TB/1103
ERNST LUDWIG EHRLICH: A Concise History of Israel: *From the Earliest Times to the Destruction of the Temple in A.D. 70*°   TB/128

THEODOR H. GASTER: Thespis: *Ritual Myth and Drama in the Ancient Near East*   TB/1281
MICHAEL GRANT: Ancient History °   TB/1190
A. H. M. JONES, Ed.: A History of Rome through the Fifgth Century # *Vol. I: The Republic*   HR/1364
Vol. II The Empire: HR/1460
SAMUEL NOAH KRAMER: Sumerian Mythology
TB/1055
NAPHTALI LEWIS & MEYER REINHOLD, Eds.: Roman Civilization *Vol. I: The Republic*
TB/1231
Vol. II: The Empire   TB/1232

History: Medieval

MARSHALL W. BALDWIN, Ed.: Christianity Through the 13th Century #   HR/1468
MARC BLOCH: Land and Work in Medieval Europe. *Translated by J. E. Anderson*
TB/1452
HELEN CAM: England Before Elizabeth TB/1026
NORMAN COHN: The Pursuit of the Millennium: *Revolutionary Messianism in Medieval and Reformation Europe*   TB/1037
G. G. COULTON: Medieval Village, Manor, and Monastery   HR/1022
HEINRICH FICHTENAU: The Carolingian Empire: *The Age of Charlemagne. Translated with an Introduction by Peter Munz*   TB/1142
GALBERT OF BRUGES: The Murder of Charles the Good: *A Contemporary Record of Revolutionary Change in 12th Century Flanders. Translated with an Introduction by James Bruce Ross*   TB/1311
F. L. GANSHOF: Feudalism   TB/1058
F. L. GANSHOF: The Middle Ages: *A History of International Relations. Translated by Rémy Hall*   TB/1411
DENYS HAY: The Medieval Centuries °   TB/1192
DAVID HERLIHY, Ed.: Medieval Culture and Socitey #   HR/1340
J. M. HUSSEY: The Byzantine World   TB/1057
ROBERT LATOUCHE: The Birth of Western Economy: *Economic Aspects of the Dark Ages* °
TB/1290
HENRY CHARLES LEA: The Inquisition of the Middle Ages. || *Introduction by Walter Ullmann*   TB/1456
FERDINARD LOT: The End of the Ancient World and the Beginnings of the Middle Ages. *Introduction by Glanville Downey*   TB/1044
H. R. LOYN: The Norman Conquest   TB/1457
GUIBERT DE NOGENT: Self and Society in Medieval France: *The Memoirs of Guilbert de Nogent*. || *Edited by John F. Benton* TB/1471
MARSILIUS OF PADUA: The Defender of Peace. *The Defensor Pacis. Translated with an Introduction by Alan Gewirth*   TB/1310
CHARLES PETET-DUTAILLIS: The Feudal Monarchy in France and England: *From the Tenth to the Thirteenth Century* °   TB/1165
STEVEN RUNCIMAN: A History of the Crusades *Vol. I: The First Crusade and the Foundation of the Kingdom of Jerusalem. Illus.*
TB/1143
Vol. II: The Kingdom of Jerusalem and the Frankish East 1100-1187. Illus.   TB/1243
Vol. III: The Kingdom of Acre and the Later Crusades. Illus.   TB/1298
J. M. WALLACE-HADRILL: The Barbarian West: *The Early Middle Ages, A.D. 400-1000*
TB/1061

ALBERT GOODWIN, Ed.: The European Nobility in the Enghteenth Century TB/1313
ALBERT GOODWIN: The French Revolution TB/1064
ALBERT GUERARD: France in the Classical Age: *The Life and Death of an Ideal* TB/1183
JOHN B. HALSTED, Ed.: Romanticism # HR/1387
J. H. HEXTER: Reappraisals in History: *New Views on History and Society in Early Modern Europe* ° TB/1100
STANLEY HOFFMANN et al.: In Search of France: *The Economy, Society and Political System In the Twentieth Century* TB/1219
H. STUART HUGHES: The Obstructed Path: *French Social Thought in the Years of Desperation* TB/1451
JOHAN HUIZINGA: Dutch Civilisation in the 17th Century and Other Essays TB/1453
LIONAL KOCHAN: The Struggle for Germany: *1914-45* TB/1304
HANS KOHN: The Mind of Germany: *The Education of a Nation* TB/1204
HANS KOHN, Ed.: The Mind of Modern Russia: *Historical and Political Thought of Russia's Great Age* TB/1065
WALTER LAQUEUR & GEORGE L. MOSSE, Eds.: Education and Social Structure in the 20th Century. ° *Volume 6 of the* Journal of Contemporary History TB/1339
WALTER LAQUEUR & GEORGE L. MOSSE, Ed.: International Fascism, 1920-1945. ° *Volume 1 of the* Journal of Contemporary History TB/1276
WALTER LAQUEUR & GEORGE L. MOSSE, Eds.: Literature and Politics in the 20th Century. ° *Volume 5 of the* Journal of Contemporary History. TB/1328
WALTER LAQUEUR & GEORGE L. MOSSE, Eds.: The New History: *Trends in Historical Research and Writing Since World War II.* ° *Volume 4 of the* Journal of Contemporary History TB/1327
WALTER LAQUEUR & GEORGE L. MOSSE, Eds.: 1914: *The Coming of the First World War.* ° *Volume3 of the* Journal of Contemporary History TB/1306
C. A. MACARTNEY, Ed.: The Habsburg and Hohenzollern Dynasties in the Seventeenth and Eighteenth Centuries # HR/1400
JOHN MCMANNERS: European History, 1789-1914: *Men, Machines and Freedom* TB/1419
PAUL MANTOUX: The Industrial Revolution in the Eighteenth Century: *An Outline of the Beginnings of the Modern Factory System in England* TB/1079
FRANK E. MANUEL: The Prophets of Paris: *Turgot, Condorcet, Saint-Simon, Fourier, and Comte* TB/1218
KINGSLEY MARTIN: French Liberal Thought in the Eighteenth Century: *A Study of Political Ideas from Bayle to Condorcet* TB/1114
NAPOLEON III: Napoleonic Ideas: *Des Idées Napoléoniennes, par le Prince Napoléon-Louis Bonaparte. Ed. by Brison D. Gooch* ¶ TB/1336
FRANZ NEUMANN: Behemoth: *The Structure and Practice of National Socialism, 1933-1944* TB/1289
DAVID OGG: Europe of the Ancien Régime, 1715-1783 ° α TB/1271
GEORGE RUDE: Revolutionary Europe, 1783-1815 ° α TB/1272
MASSIMO SALVADORI, Ed.: Modern Socialism # TB/1374
HUGH SETON-WATSON: Eastern Europe Between the Wars, 1918-1941 TB/1330

DENIS MACK SMITH, Ed.: The Making of Italy, 1796-1870 # HR/1356
ALBERT SOREL: Europe Under the Old Regime. *Translated by Francis H. Herrick* TB/1121
ROLAND N. STROMBERG, Ed.: Realism, Naturalism, and Symbolism: *Modes of Thought and Expression in Europe, 1848-1914* # HR/1355
A. J. P. TAYLOR: From Napoleon to Lenin: *Historical Essays* ° TB/1268
A. J. P. TAYLOR: The Habsburg Monarchy, 1809-1918: *A History of the Austrian Empire and Austria-Hungary* ° TB/1187
J. M. THOMPSON: European History, 1494-1789 TB/1431
DAVID THOMSON, Ed.: France: Empire and Republic, 1850-1940 # HR/1387
ALEXIS DE TOCQUEVILLE & GUSTAVE DE BEAUMONT: Tocqueville and Beaumont on Social Reform. *Ed. and trans. with Intro. by Seymour Drescher* TB/1343
G. M. TREVELYAN: British History in the Nineteenth Century and After: 1792-1919 ° TB/1251
H. R. TREVOR-ROPER: Historical Essays TB/1269
W. WARREN WAGAR, Ed.: Science, Faith, and MAN: *European Thought Since 1914* # HR/1362
MACK WALKER, Ed.: Metternich's Europe, 1813-1848 # HR/1361
ELIZABETH WISKEMANN: Europe of the Dictators, 1919-1945 ° α TB/1273
JOHN B. WOLF: France: 1814-1919: *The Rise of a Liberal-Democratic Society* TB/3019

Literature & Literary Criticism

JACQUES BARZUN: The House of Intellect TB/1051
W. J. BATE: From Classic to Romantic: *Premises of Taste in Eighteenth Century England* TB/1036
VAN WYCK BROOKS: Van Wyck Brooks: The Early Years: *A Selection from his Works, 1908-1921 Ed. with Intro. by Claire Sprague* TB/3082
ERNST R. CURTIUS: European Literature and the Latin Middle Ages. *Trans. by Willard Trask* TB/2015
RICHMOND LATTIMORE, Translator: The Odyssey of Homer TB/1389
SAMUEL PEPYS: The Diary of Samual Pepys. ° *Edited by O. F. Morshead. 60 illus. by Ernest Shepard* TB/1007
ROBERT PREYER, Ed.: Victorian Literature ** TB/1302
ALBION W. TOURGEE: A Fool's Errand: *A Novel of the South during Reconstruction. Intro. by George Fredrickson* TB/3074
BASIL WILEY: Nineteenth Century Studies: *Coleridge to Matthew Arnold* ° TB/1261

Philosophy

HENRI BERGSON: Time and Free Will: *An Essay on the Immediate Data of Consciousness* ° TB/1021
LUDWIG BINSWANGER: Being-in-the-World: *Selected Papers. Trans. with Intro. by Jacob Needleman* TB/1365
H. J. BLACKHAM: Six Existentialist Thinkers: *Kierkegaard, Nietzsche, Jaspers, Marcel, Heidegger, Sartre* ° TB/1002
J. M. BOCHENSKI: The Methods of Contemporary Thought. *Trans. by Peter Caws* TB/1377
CRANE BRINTON: Nietzsche. *Preface, Bibliography, and Epilogue by the Author* TB/1197

ERNST CASSIRER: Rousseau, Kant and Goethe.
Intro. by Peter Gay   TB/1092
FREDERICK COPLESTON, S. J.: Medieval Philos-
ophy   TB/376
F. M. CORNFORD: From Religion to Philosophy:
*A Study in the Origins of Western Specula-
tion* §   TB/20
WILFRID DESAN: The Tragic Finale: *An Essay on
the Philosophy of Jean-Paul Sartre* TB/1030
MARVIN FARBER: The Aims of Phenomenology:
*The Motives, Methods, and Impact of Hus-
serl's Thought*   TB/1291
MARVIN FARBER: Basic Issues of Philosophy: *Ex-
perience, Reality, and Human Values*
                                          TB/1344
MARVIN FARBERS: Phenomenology and Existence:
Towards a Philosophy within Nature TB/1295
PAUL FRIEDLANDER: 'Plato: *An Introduction*
                                          TB/2017
MICHAEL GELVEN: A Commentary on Heidegger's
"Being and Time"   TB/1464
J. GLENN GRAY: Hegel and Greek Thought
                                          TB/1409
W. K. C. GUTHRIE: The Greek Philosophers:
From Thales to Aristotle °   TB/1008
G. W. F. HEGEL: On Art, Religion Philosophy:
*Introductory Lectures to the Realm of Ab-
solute Spirit.* || *Edited with an Introduction
by J. Glenn Gray*   TB/1463
G. W. F. HEGEL: Phenomenology of Mind. ° ||
Introduction by George Lichtheim   TB/1303
MARTIN HEIDEGGER: Discourse on Thinking.
*Translated with a Preface by John M. An-
derson and E. Hans Freund. Introduction by
John M. Anderson*   TB/1459
F. H. HEINEMANN: Existentialism and the Mod-
ern Predicament   TB/28
WERER HEISENBERG: Physics and Philosophy:
*The Revolution in Modern Science. Intro. by
F. S. C. Northrop*   TB/549
EDMUND HUSSERL: Phenomenology and the
Crisis of Philosophy. § *Translated with an
Introduction by Quentin Lauer*   TB/1170
IMMANUEL KANT: Groundwork of the Meta-
physic of Morals. *Translated and Analyzed by
H. J. Paton*   TB/1159
IMMANUEL KANT: Lectures on Ethics. § *Intro-
duction by Lewis White Beck*   TB/105
WALTER KAUFMANN, Ed.: Religion From Tolstoy
to Camus: *Basic Writings on Religious Truth
and Morals*   TB/123
QUENTIN LAUER: Phenomenology: *Its Genesis
and Prospect. Preface by Aron Gurwitsch*
                                          TB/1169
MAURICE MANDELBAUM: The Problem of Histori-
cal Knowledge: *An Answer to Relativism*
                                          TB/1198
H. J. PATON: The Categorical Imperative: *A
Study in Kant's Moral Philosophy*   TB/1325
MICHAEL POLANYI: Personal Knowledge: *To-
wards a Post-Critical Philosophy*   TB/1158
KARL R. POPPER: Conjectures and Refutations:
The Growth of Scientific Knowledge TB/1376
WILLARD VAN ORMAN QUINE: Elementary Logic
Revised Edition   TB/577
WILLARD VAN ORMAN QUINE: From a Logical
Point of View: *Logico-Philosophical Essays*
                                          TB/566
JOHN E. SMITH: Themes in American Philos-
ophy: *Purpose, Experience and Communi.y*
                                          TB/1466
MORTON WHITE: Foundations of Historical
Knowledge   TB/1440
WILHELM WINDELBAND: A History of Philosophy
Vol. I: Greek, Roman, Medieval   TB/38
Vol. II: Renaissance, Enlightenment, Modern
                                          TB/39

LUDWIG WITTGENSTEIN: The Blue and Brown
Books °   TB/1211
LUDWIG WITTGENSTEIN: Notebooks, 1914-1916
                                          TB/1441

Political Science & Government

C. E. BLACK: The Dynamics of Modernization:
A Study in Comparative History   TB/1321
DENIS W. BROGAN: Politics in America. *New
Introduction by the Author*   TB/1469
CRANE BRINTON: English Political Thought in the
Nineteenth Century   TB/1071
ROBERT CONQUEST: Power and Policy in the
USSR: *The Study of Soviet Dynastics* °
                                          TB/1307
ROBERT A. DAHL & CHARLES E. LINDBLOM: Politics,
Economics, and Welfare: *Planning and Po-
litico-Economic Systems Resolved into Basic
Social Processes*   TB/1277
HANS KOHN: Political Ideologies of the 20th
Century   TB/1277
ROY C. MACRIDIS, Ed.: Political Parties: *Con-
temporary Trends and Ideas* **   TB/1322
ROBERT GREEN MC CLOSKEY: American Conserva-
tism in the Age of Enterprise, 1865-1910
                                          TB/1137
MARSILIUS OF PADUA: The Defender of Peace.
*The Defensor Pacis. Translated with an In-
troduction by Alan Gewirth*   TB/1310
KINGSLEY MARTIN: French Liberal Thought in
the Eighteenth Century: *A Study of Political
Ideas from Bayle to Condorcet*   TB/1114
BARRINGTON MOORE, JR.: Political Power and
Social Theory: *Seven Studies* || TB/1221
BARRINGTON MOORE, JR.: Soviet Politics—The
Dilemma of Power: *The Role of Ideas in
Social Change* || TB/1222
BARRINGTON MOORE, JR.: Terror and Progress—
USSR: *Some Sources of Change and Stability*
JOHN B. MORRALL: Political Thought in Medieval
Times   TB/1076
KARL R. POPPER: The Open Society and Its
Enemies *Vol. I: The Spell of Plato* TB/1101
*Vol. II: The High Tide of Prophecy: Hegel,
Marx, and the Aftermath*   TB/1102
CONYERS READ, Ed.: The Constitution Recon-
sidered. *Revised Edition, Preface by Richard
B. Morris*   TB/1384
JOHN P. ROCHE, Ed.: Origins of American Po-
litical Thought: *Selected Readings* TB/1301
JOHN P. ROCHE, Ed.: American Political
Thought: *From Jefferson to Progressivism*
                                          TB/1332
HENRI DE SAINT-SIMON: Social Organization, The
Science of Man, and Other Writings. ||
*Edited and Translated with an Introduction
by Felix Markham*   TB/1152
CHARLES SCHOTTLAND, Ed.: The Welfare State **
                                          TB/1323
JOSEPH A. SCHUMPETER: Capitalism, Socialism
and Democracy   TB/3008

Psychology

ALFRED ADLER: The Individual Psychology of
Alfred Adler: *A Systematic Presentation in
Selections from His Writings. Edited by
Heinz L. & Rowena R. Ansbacher*   TB/1154
LUDWIG BINSWANGER: Being-in-the-World: *Se-
lected Papers.* || *Trans. with Intro. by Jacob
Needleman*   TB/1365
HADLEY CANTRIL: The Invasion from Mars: *A
Study in the Psychology of Panic* || TB/1282
MIRCEA ELIADE: Cosmos and History: *The Myth
of the Eternal Return* §   TB/2050
MIRCEA ELIADE: Myth and Reality   TB/1369

MIRCEA ELIADE: Myths, Dreams and Mysteries: *The Encounter Between Contemporary Faiths and Archaic Realities* §   TB/1320
MIRCEA ELIADE: Rites and Symbols of Initiation: *The Mysteries of Birth and Rebirth* §   TB/1236
HERBERT FINGARETTE: The Self in Transformation: *Psychoanalysis, Philosophy and the Life of the Spirit* || TB/1177
SIGMUND FREUD: On Creativity and the Unconscious: *Papers on the Psychology of Art, Literature, Love, Religion.* § *Intro. by Benjamin Nelson*   TB/45
J. GLENN GRAY: The Warriors: *Reflections on Men in Battle. Introduction by Hannah Arendt*   TB/1294
WILLIAM JAMES: Psychology: *The Briefer Course. Edited with an Intro. by Gordon Allport*   TB/1034
C. G. JUNG: Psychological Reflections. *Ed. by J. Jacobi*   TB/2001
KARL MENNINGER, M.D.: Theory of Psychoanalytic Technique   TB/1144
JOHN H. SCHAAR: Escape from Authority: *The Perspectives of Erich Fromm*   TB/1155
MUZAFER SHERIF: The Psychology of Social Norms. *Introduction by Gardner Murphy*   TB/3072
HELLMUT WILHELM: Change: *Eight Lectures on the I Ching*   TB/2019

Religion: Ancient and Classical, Biblical and Judaic Traditions

W. F. ALBRIGHT: The Biblical Period from Abraham to Ezra   TB/102
SALO W. BARON: Modern Nationalism and Religion   TB/818
C. K. BARRETT, Ed.: The New Testament Background: *Selected Documents*   TB/86
MARTIN BUBER: Eclipse of God: *Studies in the Relation Between Religion and Philosophy*   TB/12
MARTIN BUBER: Hasidism and Modern Man. *Edited and Translated by Maurice Friedman*   TB/839
MARTIN BUBER: The Knowledge of Man. *Edited with an Introduction by Maurice Friedman. Translated by Maurice Friedman and Ronald Gregor Smith*   TB/135
MARTIN BUBER: Moses. *The Revelation and the Covenant*   TB/837
MARTIN BUBER: The Origin and Meaning of Hasidism. *Edited and Translated by Maurice Friedman*   TB/835
MARTIN BUBER: The Prophetic Faith   TB/73
MARTIN BUBER: Two Types of Faith: *Interpenetration of Judaism and Christianity* °   TB/75
MALCOLM L. DIAMOND: Martin Buber: *Jewish Existentialist*   TB/840
M. S. ENSLIN: Christian Beginnings   TB/5
M. S. ENSLIN: The Literature of the Christian Movement   TB/6
ERNST LUDWIG EHRLICH: A Concise History of Israel: *From the Earliest Times to the Destruction of the Temple in A.D. 70* °   TB/128
HENRI FRANKFORT: Ancient Egyptian Religion: *An Interpretation*   TB/77
ABRAHAM HESCHEL: The Earth Is the Lord's & The Sabbath. *Two Essays*   TB/828
ABRAHAM HESCHEL: God in Search of Man: *A Philosophy of Judaism*   TB/807
ABRAHAM HESCHEL: Man Is not Alone: *A Philosophy of Religion*   TB/838
ABRAHAM HESCHEL: The Prophets: *An Introduction*   TB/1421

T. J. MEEK: Hebrew Origins   TB/69
JAMES MUILENBURG: The Way of Israel: *Biblical Faith and Ethics*   TB/133
H. J. ROSE: Religion in Greece and Rome   TB/55
H. H. ROWLEY: The Growth of the Old Testament   TB/107
D. WINTON THOMAS, Ed.: Documents from Old Testament Times   TB/85

Religion: General Christianity

ROLAND H. BAINTON: Christendom: *A Short History of Christianity and Its Impact on Western Civilization. Illus.*   Vol. I TB/131; Vol. II TB/132
JOHN T. MCNEILL: Modern Christian Movements. *Revised Edition*   TB/1402
ERNST TROELTSCH: The Social Teaching of the Christian Churches. *Intro. by H. Richard Niebuhr*   Vol. TB/71; Vol. II TB/72

Religion: Early Christianity Through Reformation

ANSELM OF CANTERBURY: Truth, Freedom, and Evil: *Three Philosophical Dialogues. Edited and Translated by Jasper Hopkins and Herbert Richardson*   TB/317
MARSHALL W. BALDWIN, Ed.: Christianity through the 13th Century #   HR/1468
W. D. DAVIES: Paul and Rabbinic Judaism: *Some Rabbinic Elements in Pauline Theology. Revised Edition* °   TB/146
ADOLF DEISSMAN: Paul: *A Study in Social and Religious History*   TB/15
JOHANNES ECKHART: Meister Eckhart: *A Modern Translation by R. Blakney*   TB/8
EDGAR J. GOODSPEED: A Life of Jesus   TB/1
ROBERT M. GRANT: Gnosticism and Early Christianity   TB/136
WILLIAM HALLER: The Rise of Puritanism   TB/22
GERHART B. LADNER: The Idea of Reform: *Its Impact on the Christian Thought and Action in the Age of the Fathers*   TB/149
ARTHUR DARBY NOCK: Early Gentile Christianity and Its Hellenistic Background   TB/111
ARTHUR DARBY NOCK: St. Paul °   TR/104
GORDON RUPP: Luther's Progress to the Diet of Worms °   TB/120

Religion: The Protestant Tradition

KARL BARTH: Church Dogmatics: *A Selection. Intro. by H. Gollwitzer. Ed. by G. W. Bromiley*   TB/95
KARL BARTH: Dogmatics in Outline   TB/56
KARL BARTH: The Word of God and the Word of Man   TB/13
HERBERT BRAUN, et al.: God and Christ: *Existence and Province. Volume 5 of Journal for Theology and the Church, edited by Robert W. Funk and Gerhard Ebeling*   TB/255
WHITNEY R. CROSS: The Burned-Over District: *The Social and Intellectual History of Enthusiastic Religion in Western New York, 1800-1850*   TB/1242
NELS F. S. FERRE: Swedish Contributions to Modern Theology. *New Chapter by William A. Johnson*   TB/147
WILLIAM R. HUTCHISON, Ed.: American Protestant Thought: *The Liberal Era* ‡   TB/1385
ERNST KASEMANN, et al.: Distinctive Protestant and Catholic Themes Reconsidered. *Volume 3 of Journal for Theology and the Church,*

edited by Robert W. Funk and Gerhard
Ebeling   TB/253
SOREN KIERKEGAARD: On Authority and Revela-
tion: *The Book on Adler, or a Cycle of
Ethico-Religious Essays. Introduction by F.
Sontag*   TB/139
SOREN KIERKEGAARD: Crisis in the Life of an
Actress, *and Other Essays on Drama. Trans-
lated with an Introduction by Stephen Crites*
                                            TB/145
SOREN KIERKEGAARD: Edifying Discourses. *Edited
with an Intro. by Paul Holmer*   TB/32
SOREN KIERKEGAARD: The Journals of Kierke-
gaard. ° *Edited with an Intro. by Alexander
Dru*   TB/52
SOREN KIERKEGAARD: The Point of View for My
Work as an Author: *A Report to History.* §
Preface by Benjamin Nelson   TB/88
SOREN KIERKEGAARD: The Present Age. § *Trans-
lated and edited by Alexander Dru. Intro-
duction by Walter Kaufmann*   TB/94
SOREN KIERKEGAARD: Purity of Heart. *Trans. by
Douglas Steere*   TB/4
SOREN KIERKEGAARD: Repetition: *An Essay in
Experimental Psychology* §   TB/117
SOREN KIERKEGAARD: Works of Love: *Some
Christian Reflections in the Form of Dis-
courses*   TB/122
WILLIAM G. MCLOUGHLIN, Ed.: The American
Evangelicals: 1800-1900: *An Anthology*
                                            TB/1382
WOLFHART PANNENBERG, et al.: History and Her-
meneutic. *Volume 4 of Journal for Theol-
ogy and the Church, edited by Robert W.
Funk and Gerhard Ebeling*   TB/254
JAMES M. ROBINSON, et al.: The Bultmann
School of Biblical Interpretation: New Direc-
tions? *Volume 1 of Journal for Theology
and the Church, edited by Robert W. Funk
and Gerhard Ebeling*   TB/251
F. SCHLEIERMACHER: The Christian Faith. *Intro-
duction by Richard R. Niebuhr.*
              Vol. I TB/108; Vol. II TB/109
F. SCHLEIERMACHER: On Religion: *Speeches to
Its Cultured Despisers. Intro. by Rudolf
Otto*   TB/36
TIMOTHY L. SMITH: Revivalism and Social Re-
form: *American Protestantism on the Eve
of the Civil War*   TB/1229
PAUL TILLICH: Dynamics of Faith   TB/42
PAUL TILLICH: Morality and Beyond TB/142
EVELYN UNDERHILL: Worship   TB/10

Religion: The Roman & Eastern Christian
Traditions

A. ROBERT CAPONIGRI, Ed.: Modern Catholic
Thinkers II: *The Church and the Political
Order*   TB/307
G. P. FEDOTOV: The Russian Religious Mind:
*Kievan Christianity, the tenth to the thir-
teenth Centuries*   TB/370
GABRIEL MARCEL: Being and Having: *An Ex-
istential Diary. Introduction by James Col-
lins*   TB/310
GABRIEL MARCEL: Homo Viator: *Introduction to
a Metaphysic of Hope*   TB/397

Religion: Oriental Religions

TOR ANDRAE: Mohammed: *The Man and His
Faith* §   TB/62

EDWARD CONZE: Buddhism: *Its Essence and De-
velopment.* ° *Foreword by Arthur Waley*
                                            TB/58
EDWARD CONZE: Buddhist Meditation   TB/1442
EDWARD CONZE et al, Editors: Buddhist Texts
through the Ages   TB/113
ANANDA COOMARASWAMY: Buddha and the Gos-
pel of Buddhism   TB/119
H. G. CREEL: Confucius and the Chinese Way
                                            TB/63
FRANKLIN EDGERTON, Trans. & Ed.: The Bhaga-
vad Gita   TB/115
SWAMI NIKHILANANDA, Trans. & Ed.: The
Upanishads   TB/114
D. T. SUZUKI: On Indian Mahayana Buddhism.
° *Ed. with Intro. by Edward Conze.* TB/1403

Religion: Philosophy, Culture, and Society

NICOLAS BERDYAEV: The Destiny of Man TB/61
RUDOLF BULTMANN: History and Eschatology:
The Presence of Eternity °   TB/91
RUDOLF BULTMANN AND FIVE CRITICS: Kerygma
and Myth: *A Theological Debate*   TB/80
RUDOLF BULTMANN and KARL KUNDSIN: Form
Criticism: *Two Essays on New Testament Re-
search. Trans. by F. C. Grant*   TB/96
WILLIAM A. CLEBSCH & CHARLES R. JAEKLE: Pas-
toral Care in Historical Perspective: *An
Essay with Exhibits*   TB/148
FREDERICK FERRE: Language, Logic and God.
New Preface by the Author   TB/1407
LUDWIG FEUERBACH: The Essence of Christianity.
·§ *Introduction by Karl Barth. Foreword by
H. Richard Niebuhr*   TB/11
ADOLF HARNACK: What Is Christianity? § *Intro-
duction by Rudolf Bultmann*   TB/17
KYLE HASELDEN: The Racial Problem in Chris-
tian Perspective   TB/116
MARTIN HEIDEGGER: Discourse on Thinking.
*Translated with a Preface by John M. Ander-
son and E. Hans Freund. Introduction by
John M. Anderson*   TB/1459
IMMANUEL KANT: Religion Within the Limits of
Reason Alone. § *Introduction by Theodore
M. Greene and John Silber*   TB/FG
WALTER KAUFMANN, Ed.: Religion from Tol-
stoy to Camus: *Basic Writings on Religious
Truth and Morals. Enlarged Edition* TB/123
H. RICHARD NIEBUHR: Christ and Culture TB/3
H. RICHARD NIEBUHR: The Kingdom of God in
America   TB/49
ANDERS NYGREN: Agape and Eros. *Translated by
Philip S. Watson* °   TB/1430
JOHN H. RANDALL, JR.: The Meaning of Reli-
gion for Man. *Revised with New Intro. by
the Author*   TB/1379
WALTER RAUSCHENBUSCHS Christianity and the
Social Crisis. ‡ *Edited by Robert D. Cross*
                                            TB/3059

Science and Mathematics

JOHN TYLER BONNER: The Ideas of Biology. Σ
Illus.   TB/570
W. E. LE GROS CLARK: The Antecedents of
Man: *An Introduction to the Evolution of
the Primates.* ° *Illus.*   TB/559
ROBERT E. COKER: Streams, Lakes, Ponds. *Illus.*
                                            TB/586
ROBERT E. COKER: This Great and Wide Sea: *An
Introduction to Oceanography and Marine
Biology. Illus.*   TB/551
W. H. DOWDESWELL: Animal Ecology. *61 illus.*
                                            TB/543

9

DATE DUE

DEC 2 2 1994			

DEMCO 38-297